Pillars of Prosperity

The Yrjö Jahnsson Lectures

Year	Lecturer and title	Publisher
1963	Kenneth J. Arrow: *Aspects of the Theory of Risk-Bearing*	Yrjö Jahnsson Foundation
1967	Assar Lindbeck: *Monetary-Fiscal Analysis and General Equilibrium*	Yrjö Jahnsson Foudation
1968	L. R. Klein: *An Essay on the Theory of Economic Prediction*	Yrjö Jahnsson Foundation
1970	Harry G. Johnson: *The Two-Sector Model of General Equilibrium*	George Allard Unwin
1973	John Hicks: *The Crises in Keynesian Economics*	Blackwell
1976	Edmund Malinvaud: *The Theory of Unemployment Reconsidered*	Blackwell
1978	James Tobin: *Asset Accumulation and Economic Activity*	Blackwell
1980	János Kornai: *Growth, Shortage and Efficiency*	Blackwell
1983	Jacques H. Drèze: *Labour Management, Contracts and Capital Markets*	Blackwell
1985	Robert E. Lucas: *Models of Business Cycles*	Blackwell
1987	Amartya Sen: *Rational Behavior*	Not yet published
1990	A. B. Atkinson: *Three Lectures on Poverty in Europe*	Blackwell
1992	Bengt Holmström: *Models of the Firm*	Not yet published
1996	Paul R. Krugman: *Economic Theory and the East Asia Miracle*	Not yet published
1999	Hans-Werner Sinn: *The New Systems Competition*	Blackwell
2002	Alvin Roth: *The Timing of Transactions*	Not yet published
2005	Ricardo Caballero: *Macroeconomics and Restructuring in the Global Economy*	MIT Press
2007	Peter Diamond: *Thinking about Taxes*	Not yet published
2010	Timothy Besley and Torsten Persson: *Pillars of Prosperity: The Political Economics of Development Clusters*	Princeton University Press

Pillars of Prosperity

The Political Economics of Development Clusters

TIMOTHY BESLEY *and* TORSTEN PERSSON

PRINCETON UNIVERSITY PRESS
Princeton and Oxford

Published by Princeton University Press, 41 William Street, Princeton, New Jersey 08540

In the United Kingdom: Princeton University Press, 6 Oxford Street, Woodstock, Oxfordshire OX20 1TW

press.princeton.edu

Library of Congress Cataloging-in-Publication Data

Besley, Timothy.

Pillars of prosperity : the political economics of development clusters / Timothy Besley and Torsten Persson.

p. cm. — (The Yrjö Jahnsson lectures)

Includes bibliographical references and index.

ISBN 978-0-691-15268-4 (hardcover : alk. paper)

1. Economic policy. 2. Economic development. 3. Business incubators. I. Persson, Torsten. II. Title.

HD87.B464 2011

338.8′7—dc22 2011016080

British Library Cataloging-in-Publication Data is available

This book has been composed in Sabon using ZzTEX by Princeton Editorial Associates, Inc., Scottsdale, Arizona.

Printed on acid-free paper. ∞

Printed in the United States of America

10 9 8 7 6 5 4 3 2 1

Contents

Series Foreword

The Yrjö Jahnsson Foundation was established in 1954 by Mrs. Hilma Jahnsson, in accordance with the wishes of her deceased husband, Professor Yrjö Jahnsson. Yrjö Jahnsson was not only an academic but also a versatile entrepreneur. The Jahnssons' wealth accumulated in the 1920s and 1930s through successful real estate investments.

The purpose of the Foundation is to develop and support Finnish research in economics and medical science. In the field of economics the Foundation is one of the most important sources of private research funding in Finland.

In 1963 the Foundation launched a special series of the Yrjö Jahnsson Lectures to be organized every two or three years in Helsinki. The aim of the Lectures is to offer an internationally renowned economist a forum to synthesize and develop novel research ideas, and to offer the Finnish economics community firsthand access to the latest scholarly developments. The lectures are published in a special series.

The Yrjö Jahnsson Lectures have been a great success. Since the first lecture, which was given on December 16, 1963, by Kenneth J. Arrow, all lecturers have been the leading researchers in the field of economic science.

The Foundation is proud to have Professor Timothy Besley and Professor Torsten Persson as the 19th Yrjö Jahnsson Lecturers. The lectures were given in 2010 in Helsinki. Professors Besley and Persson are among the most influential thinkers in contemporary political economics and beyond. Their scientific prizes include the Yrjö Jahnsson Award, which Proferssor Besley received in 2005 and Professor Persson received in 1997 at the Annual Congress of the European Economic Association.

The Yrjö Jahnsson Foundation

Elli Dahl, *Managing Director*
Ari Hyytinen, *Research Director*

Preface

This monograph was written for graduate students and researchers who would like to learn about what we hope will be a new and exciting area of research—the political economics of development clusters. By development clusters we mean the observed tendency for effective state institutions, the absence of political violence, and high income per capita to be positively correlated with one another. We see this if we look across countries at a given point in time, as well as if we look across time within a given country. Owing to the nature of this topic, our main story is macroeconomic and macropolitical, taking a bird's-eye view of aggregate patterns at a country level. But we also attempt to provide some microeconomic and micropolitical foundations for the reduced-form relations that tell the main story. Moreover, the prospective integration of micro and macro offers ample opportunities for future work. The topic requires a dynamic analysis, so that both the capabilities of the state and the presence of violence in our modeling reflect purposeful and forward-looking investments by different groups in society. The book is primarily an exploration of theory, but we always try to stay in close contact with the patterns in the data.

The proximate reason for writing this book was the Yrjö Jahnsson Lectures that we gave together in Helsinki in June 2010. We are immensely grateful to the Yrjö Jahnsson Foundation for the invitation in the first place and to Hannu Vartiainen and Pentti Vartia, the Foundation's Research Director and Chairman of the Board at the time, for their warm hospitality during our stay in Helsinki. Our preparations for the lectures and the valuable comments that we received when we gave them were very important milestones in our preparation of the material for this book. As it turned out, the topic grew and the book goes deeper and wider than the four lectures that we gave in Helsinki in several ways.

Naturally, the book would not have come about without our joint research in the last few years. This research has also produced a number of research papers, the first of which appeared in print in the summer of 2008. Our initial ideas were conceived in a brainstorming session about state capacity in Stockholm in the fall of 2006.

However, our interest in these ideas was kindled at meetings of the Canadian Institute for Advanced Research (CIFAR) program on Institutions, Organizations and Growth (IOG), to which we have both been lucky enough to belong. Directed by Elhanan Helpman, this program collects a remarkable group of economists, political scientists, and historians, who have met for three days three times a year since 2003. We have learned an enormous amount from this sustained interaction with the 26 other members of the program and its steering committee. It was a delight to present a crude version of the manuscript in October 2010. Membership of the IOG program is a real privilege and this book is a small token of repayment to CIFAR for the faith that it has shown in this area of research. Without our joint discussions of institutions and development in this setting, the book would simply not have been written. For its research underpinnings, our ongoing dialogues with Daron Acemoglu, Jim Fearon, Jim Robinson, and Guido Tabellini have been particularly important. Their patient and supportive criticism has helped to shape our thinking on almost every aspect of the book. Although they are not members of the CIFAR group, we have also learned a lot from frequent discussions with Paul Collier and from joint research with Ethan Ilzetzki, a coauthor of one of our underlying, as of yet, unpublished research papers.

During the last few years, we have had the opportunity to present our emerging ideas on these issues to a large number of seminar audiences and at several plenary lectures: the Richard T. Ely Lectures (Johns Hopkins, 2008), the Econometric Society Presidential Address (Pittsburgh, Wellington, Singapore, Milan, and Rio, 2008), the Conference on Economics and Democracy (Canberra, 2008), GSE Lecture (Barcelona, 2009), the Central Planning Bureau Lecture (Amsterdam, 2009), the Manchot Lecture (Bonn, 2009), the Agnar Sandmo Lecture (Bergen, 2010), the CEPR-CREI Conference on Political Economy of Economic Development (Barcelona, 2010), the Yan-fu Lecture (Beijing, 2010), the John von Neumann Lecture (Budapest, 2010), the ABCDE Conference (Stockholm, 2010), The Twenty-First School in Economic Theory (Jerusalem,

2010), EEA Presidential Address (Glasgow, 2010), and the First Annual Meeting of Swedish Economists (Lund, 2010). We are grateful to participants in these seminars and attendees at these lectures for many perceptive comments, which made us think even harder about both substance and presentation.

Many people have given us feedback on the papers that jointly form the stepping stone for the book, including Daron Acemoglu, Philippe Aghion, Alberto Alesina, Oriana Bandiera, Bob Bates, Marco Battaglini, Jeremy Bulow, Robin Burgess, Mauricio Cardenas, Anne Case, Paul Collier, Chris Coyne, Steve Coate, Angus Deaton, Avinash Dixit, Jim Fearon, Avner Grief, Elhanan Helpman, Anke Hoeffler, Henrik Kleven, Roger Myerson, Patrick O'Brien, Philippe Martin, Erik Melander, Eric Neumayer, Gerard Padro i Miquel, Rohini Pande, Raghu Rajan, Jim Robinson, Guido Tabellini, Ragnar Torvik, Andrei Shleifer, Jan van Ours, Barry Weingast, Ruixue Xie, and Magnus Öberg.

Jean-Paul Azam, Oriana Bandiera, Pete Boetkke, Mauricio Cardenas, Chris Coyne, Mark Dincecco, Joan Esteban, Mark Gradstein, Geoff Hodgson, Arye Hillman, Ethan Ilzetzki, Adnan Khan, Tim Leunig, Elena Paltseva, Louis Putterman, Simon Quinn, Marta Reynal-Querol, Andrei Shleifer, Guido Tabellini, Jon Temple, and John Wallis were kind enough to read and comment on a preliminary version of the manuscript that we circulated, despite an unreasonably tight deadline for responding. We are also very grateful for the detailed and very helpful comments from our Princeton University Press reviewers: Jim Fearon and Daniel Treisman.

The research has benefited a great deal from us being able to use parts of the material in our graduate courses in Development and Political Economics, in London and Stockholm. Some of our students helped us out by reading various chapters carefully in the last month of our work on the book, and we are grateful for the comments by Michael Best, Anne Brockmeyer, Konrad Burchardi, Timothée Demont, Laura Derksen, Erika Deserranno, Anders Jensen, Sam Marden, Prakarsh Singh, and Fredrik Naess Thomassen. Some of our students have also served as industrious research assistants throughout the research program: Anne Brockmeyer, Dario Caldara, Jason Garred, Alice Kuegler, David Seim, and Prakarsh Singh.

Our research over the last few years has received generous funding from a number of sources. We gratefully acknowledge financial support from the Tore Browaldh Research Foundation, CIFAR, the ESRC, the iiG program of DFID, the European Research Council, the Swedish Research Council, and the Torsten and Ragnar Söderberg Foundation.

The two of us have joint appointments at two institutions (LSE and IIES) with daunting and vibrant traditions in economics. It is striking how frequently in this work we have stood on the shoulders of current and former colleagues whose ideas are, in some cases, neglected in mainstream economics. These include Peter Bauer, Ronald Coase, Friedrich Hayek, Assar Lindbeck, and Gunnar Myrdal, all of whom have written perceptively about the topics in this book.

In the final hectic stages of the work, we were fortunate enough to be able to call on the cheerful and expert editorial assistance of Christina Lönnblad. We are also grateful to our editors Seth Ditchik, Terri O'Prey, and Peter Strupp for their professional handling of the manuscript.

With so much help, we can only blame each other for any remaining errors and infelicities.

Last, but not least, our families have suffered, off and on, from our preoccupation with the manuscript during the time of writing, from the middle of September to the end of December 2010. Without their love, support, and understanding, the project would not have been worthwhile. We dedicate this book to them.

London and Stockholm

Pillars of Prosperity

CHAPTER 1

Development Clusters

Little else is required to carry a state to the highest degree of opulence from the lowest barbarism, but peace, easy taxes, and a tolerable administration of justice, all the rest being brought about by the natural course of things.

Adam Smith, 1755

Almost all economic analyses presume the existence of an effective state. Specifically, economists invoke the existence of an authority that can tax, enforce contracts, and organize public spending for a wide range of activities. We then study concepts such as market failure and the state's response to it, the provision of public goods, and optimal taxation for the funding of state activities. But many of the major developments in world history have been about creating this starting point. Arguably, the situation presumed by economists is relevant only to the past 100 years of history for a fairly small group of rich countries.

The effective state is not only of historical interest. A tour of the developing world today rapidly confirms that the building of a state capable of taxing, spending effectively, and enforcing contracts remains a huge challenge. Weak and failing states are a fact of life and a source of human misery and global disorder.

These observations are especially poignant because income per head in the world's richest countries is about 200 times higher than in the poorest. This enormous income gap is certainly one of the most pressing issues facing humanity. Why some countries are rich and others poor is indeed a classic research question not only in economics, but in other social sciences such as economic history and political science as well. To better grasp the roots of wealth or poverty of nations is interesting in and of itself. But these roots are also of paramount importance for donors seeking to improve the lot of poor communities through various forms of development assistance.

It has long been understood that economic development is about much more than rising incomes. Indeed, state effectiveness is now given center stage in practical policymaking, with a greater focus on how to deal with countries hobbled by weak, fragile, or failed states. A number of national and international actors—such as the World Bank, the European Union, DFID in the United Kingdom, and SIDA in Sweden—have recently launched initiatives targeted toward such problem states.

Specific Indexes of State Weakness and Fragility Alternative attempts have been made to map the problem empirically, relying on a variety of measurable indicators.[1] Figures 1.1 and 1.2 illustrate two specific indexes of state fragility/weakness, namely the Brookings Institution's *Index of State Weakness* for all but the richest countries in 2008 and the Polity IV project's *State Fragility Index* for all countries in 2009. Both of these maps illustrate the underlying classification on a gray scale. Specifically, the countries in the decile with the weakest or most fragile countries are colored in black, whereas deciles higher up in the classification are marked on a sliding gray scale, with white denoting the decile with the strongest states (missing countries are marked by a hatch pattern).[2]

Although the precise classifications behind the indexes differ, both studies find that some 40–50 states suffer from serious weakness or fragility, with the strongest concentrations in Sub-Saharan Africa and South and Central Asia. Of course, there is no general agreement on exactly what defines a weak or fragile state. The *State Fragility Index*, e.g., is derived by aggregating indicators in eight dimensions, aimed at capturing the effectiveness and legitimacy of the state in the security, political, economic, and social spheres.[3]

A closer look at the underlying indicators raises a number of issues. Economic legitimacy is measured by the export share in manufacturing, but exactly

1. See Rice and Patrick (2008) for an overview of different attempts to empirically measure state weakness or fragility.

2. Since the Brookings index is not defined for 36 of the most developed countries (also marked by a hatch pattern), we do not use the white end of the scale in Figure 1.1.

3. Each country is scored in each of the eight dimensions on its situation from 1994 and onward. Specifically, security effectiveness is gauged by three measures of the frequency of outright conflict, 1994–2007; security legitimacy by a measure of state repression; political effectiveness by three measures of regime and leader durability and the frequency of coups; politcal legitimacy by three measures of factionalism, ethnicity, and fragmentation; economic effectiveness by GDP per capita; economic effectiveness by the share of exports in manufacturing production; social effectiveness by the Human Development Index; and social legitimacy by the infant mortality rate.

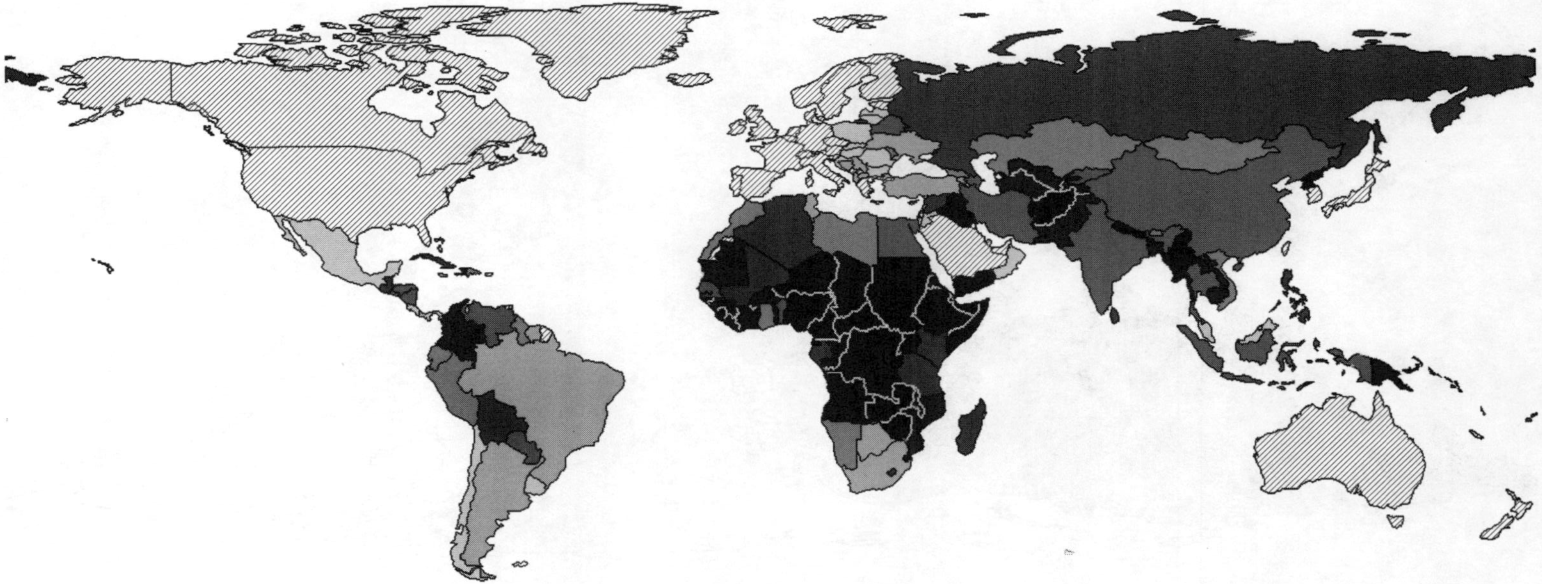

Figure 1.1 Brookings Index of State Weakness, 2008.

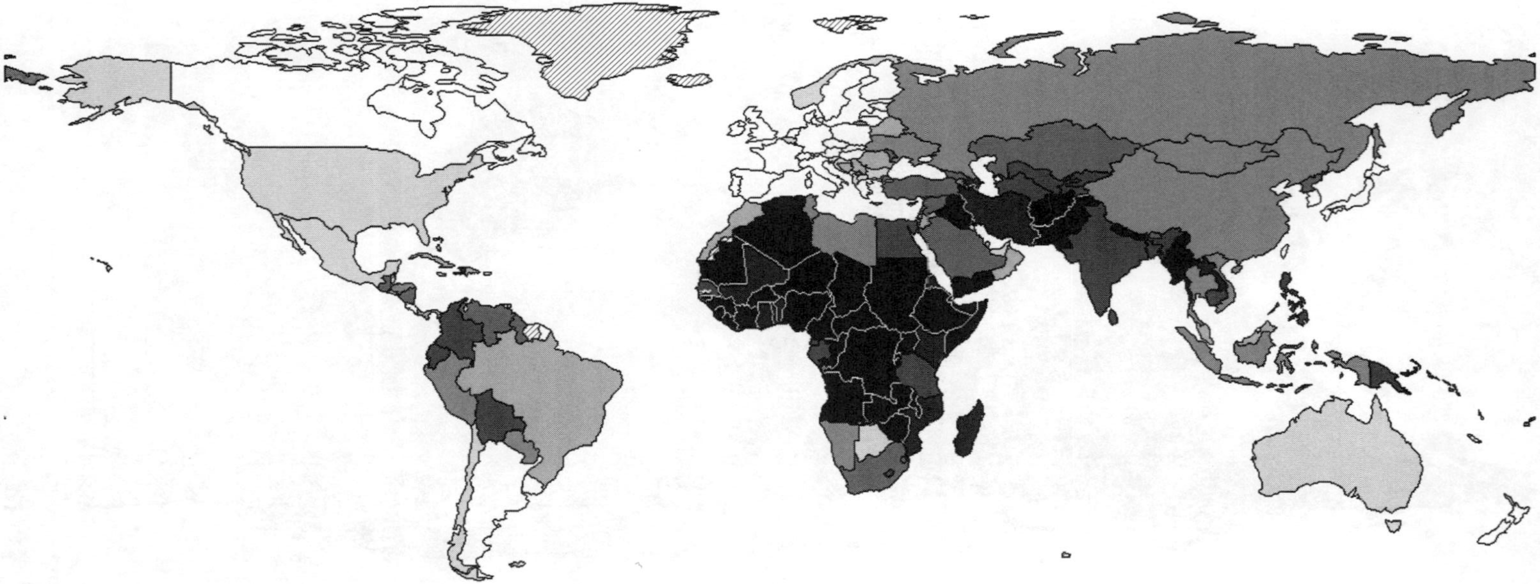

Figure 1.2 Polity IV State Fragility Index, 2009.

how to read this indicator is unclear. Leadership duration is the indicator for political effectiveness, where the direction of the relation is also opaque. Although these may seem like minor quibbles, they touch upon a deeper issue in understanding state fragility—the need to distinguish carefully between symptoms and causes. But this is next to impossible absent a properly developed conceptual framework. These questions notwithstanding, the indexes in Figures 1.1 and 1.2 clearly bring home one point on which we certainly can agree: state fragility (or state weakness) is inherently a multidimensional concept.

A Challenging Agenda This book offers an approach to studying weak or fragile states, taking a first step toward bringing them into mainstream economic analyses. It is the hallmark of mature science that existing ideas should be expanded into new domains. We proceed in this spirit by using more-or-less standard ideas and methods to study the basics of state building. A key issue is to understand what creates effective states.

Central to our approach is the idea of complementarities. As shown in what follows, almost all dimensions of state development and effectiveness are positively correlated. Moreover, historical accounts demonstrate vividly that state authority, tax systems, court systems, and democracy coevolve in a complex web of interdependent causality. Simplistic stories that try to paste in unidirectional pathways are thus bound to fail.

However, this complexity does not mean that a quantitative approach of theorizing and looking at data is hopeless. On the contrary, we argue throughout the book that building models as stripped-down representations of reality provides useful windows onto complex processes, which allow us to see particular features more clearly. Furthermore, looking at data and trying to codify empirical regularities does more than simply breathe life into the narrative. The data play a central role in developing our thinking about what is important and what can be observed. Indeed, the modeling we put forward is structured around variables and magnitudes that can be both theoretically defined and, in principle, empirically measured. This disciplines the theory and extends the domain of its applicability.

This introductory chapter lays out many of our main ideas in brief but accessible form. It is also an opportunity to review some of the historical evidence and discuss some narrative accounts of development that shape our thinking. But we do not intend our review to be exhaustive. Our primary aim is to demonstrate a strong link between our work, with its clear roots in mainstream economics, and research within other disciplines and less mainstream approaches.

1.1 *Salient Correlations*

Several characteristics beyond *income per capita* enter our intuitive perception of the defining qualities of a developed country. One is the institutional capability of the state to carry out various policies that deliver benefits and services to households and firms. We refer to this capability as *state capacity.* Another development characteristic is that conflicting interests can be resolved peacefully, rather than by alternative forms of violence. We refer to (the inverse of) this feature as *political violence.*

Policy failures owing to weak state institutions tend to be found in countries riddled with massive poverty and in societies plagued by violent internal conflicts. In most developed countries, by contrast, nearly everything works: we see strong policies supported by strong state institutions, high incomes, and conflicts of interest resolved peacefully. These correlations create *development clusters,* where the level of state capacity and the propensity for political violence vary systematically with the level of income. Thus, our notion of clusters does not describe a strong correlation for the *same* outcome variable in a set of neighboring countries (even though Figures 1.1 and 1.2 hint at such geographical clustering). Rather, we use the concept to describe strong correlations among *different* outcome variables in the same country. To better understand these clusters as manifestations of the general development problem is one of the major objectives of this book.

Fiscal and Legal Capacity To illustrate the clustering, we need some concrete empirical measures. For state capacity, we can distinguish two broad types of capabilities that allow the state to take action. One concerns the extractive role of the state. We call this capability *fiscal capacity.* Does a government have the necessary infrastructure—in terms of administration, monitoring, and enforcement—to raise revenue from broad tax bases such as income and consumption, revenue that can be spent on income support or services to its citizens? The other type of capacity concerns the productive role of the state. Is it capable of raising private-sector productivity via physical services such as road transport or the provision of power? Or does it have the necessary infrastructure—in terms of courts, educated judges, and registers—to raise private incomes by providing regulation and legal services such as the protection of property rights or the enforcement of contracts? We focus on the latter capability, which we refer to as *legal capacity.*

In later chapters, we consider different measures of both types of state capacity. For now, we illustrate them with two specific measures. The first is total tax revenue as a share of GDP, as measured by the IMF at the end of the 1990s (in 1999). We treat the overall tax take as an indicator of fiscal capacity. The second is an index of government antidiversion policies, as measured by the International Country Risk Guide, also at the end of the 1990s (in 1997), and normalized to lie between 0 and 1. This index is itself an aggregation of different perception indexes, but it has been commonly used in the macro development literature to gauge the protection of property rights.[4] We treat it as an indicator of legal capacity.

As we emphasize later, fiscal and legal capacity are concepts that have not been much studied by economists, so precise measurement is certainly an issue. For example, using the total tax take raises obvious questions about the capacity to tax versus the willingness to tax. The measures we use in this book are at best approximations of different aspects of state capacity. As we will see, however, the empirical patterns tend to be quite similar for a number of alternative proxies. Chapters 2 to 4 provide much more detail and discussion about our data and their sources.

Some Basic Facts Figure 1.3 shows that these indicators of fiscal and legal capacity are positively correlated. It plots the tax share on the vertical axis and the property-rights protection index on the horizontal axis. A clear picture emerges. Countries that have better fiscal capacity also tend to have better legal capacity. Both measures are also positively correlated with contemporaneous GDP per capita. When we divide the observations into low-, middle-, and high-income countries, according to their 2000 GDP per capita in the Penn World Tables, almost all of the high-income countries lie to the northeast in the chart, whereas the low-income countries lie to the southwest. Moreover, the positive relationship between fiscal and legal capacity is apparent within each of the three income groups.

The two uppermost observations in the northeast corner of the graph are Denmark and Sweden, both with high income, an overall tax take above 50%, and a level of property-rights protection on a par with other top performers such as Switzerland. The two leftmost observations in the southwest corner are Mali and Niger, both with low income, among the lowest tax takes, and the

4. See, e.g., Acemoglu, Johnson, and Robinson (2001) and Hall and Jones (1999).

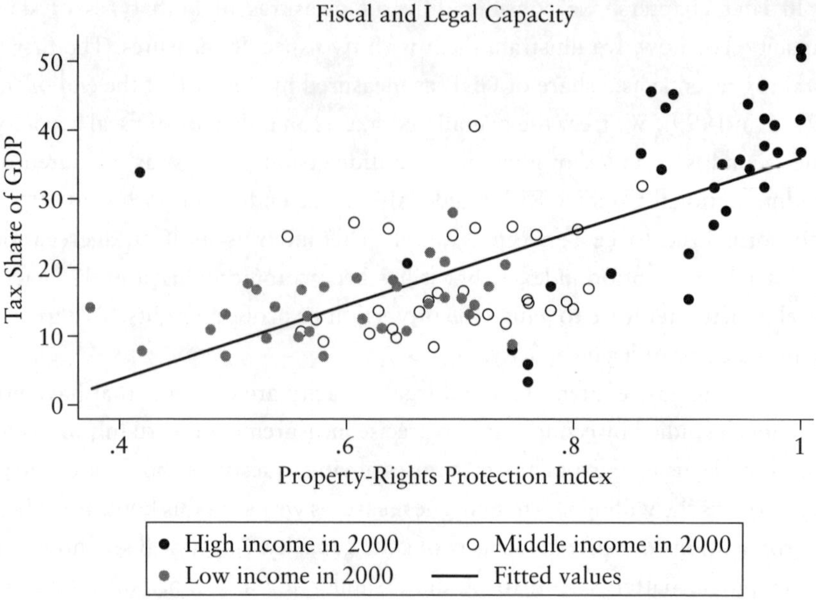

Figure 1.3 Legal and fiscal capacity conditional on income.

two worst scores in our sample on the property-rights protection index. A few outliers among the high-income countries stand out by deviating significantly from the regression line. The observation with a tax share above 30% of GDP and one of the lowest indexes of property-rights protection is the Seychelles. The group of three high-income countries charging less than 10% of GDP in taxes is made up of the oil states of Bahrein, Kuwait, and Oman.

Figure 1.4 illustrates that the two dimensions of state capacity are also systematically correlated with political violence. Specifically, we divide the countries into two groups: those that have experienced at least one year in civil war in the half-century between 1950 and 2000 and those that have not, according to the Armed Conflict Dataset (ACD). Clearly, past civil-war experience is much more common at low levels of state capacity. Two countries in the upper part of the graph stand out a bit. The high tax-take country with some civil-war experience is France and the peaceful country with taxes above 40% of GDP and midrange property-rights protection is Botswana.

Figure 1.5 revisits the fiscal-cum-legal capacity plot, once again, when the observations are subdivided by their scores on the 2009 *State Fragility Index*—i.e., the index underlying Figure 1.2. Here, the correlation is even starker. When we classify countries by having some fragility or not, the observations divide

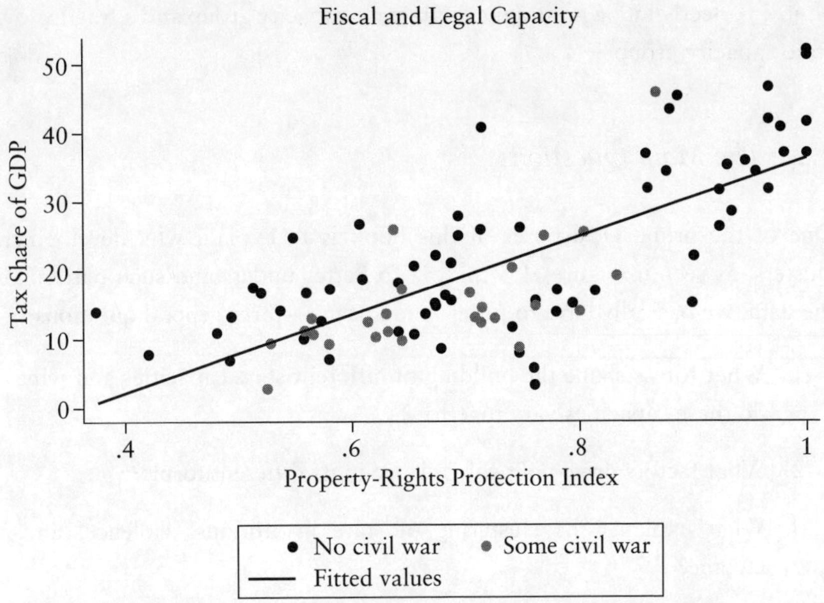

Figure 1.4 Legal and fiscal capacity conditional on civil war.

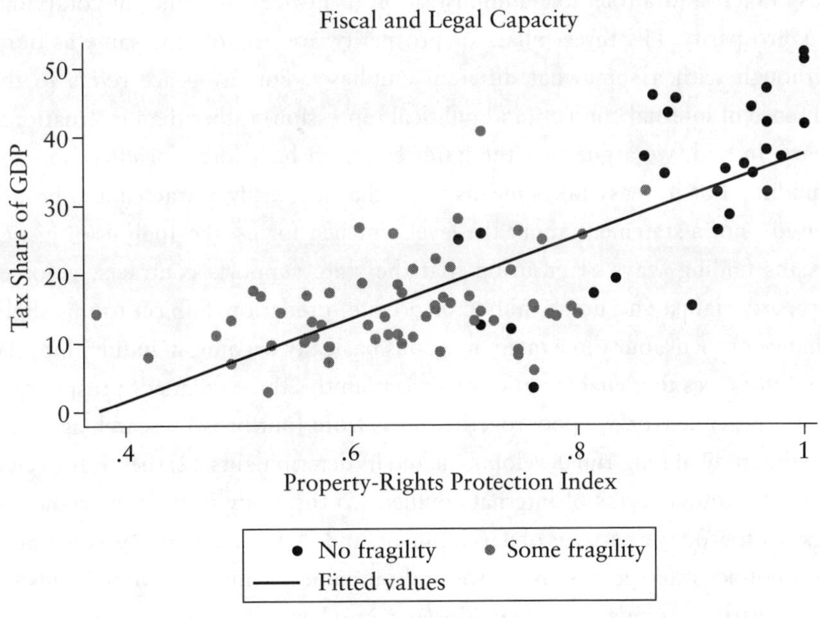

Figure 1.5 Legal and fiscal capacity conditional on fragility.

almost perfectly into a nonfragile, high-state-capacity group and a fragile, low-state-capacity group.

1.2 *The Main Questions*

One of the primary purposes of this book is to explain why development clusters, as seen in Figures 1.3 to 1.5. To better understand such patterns in the data, we basically have to pose—and answer—three general questions:

1. What forces shape the building of different state capacities and why do these capacities vary together?
2. What factors drive political violence in its different forms?
3. What explains the clustering of state institutions, violence, and income?

Adam Smith saw things very clearly more than 250 years ago when he wrote the passage quoted at the beginning of this chapter. Smith listed "peace, easy taxes, and a tolerable administration of justice" as sufficient conditions for prosperity. His three pillars of prosperity are broadly the same as ours, although with a somewhat different emphasis. For us, peace refers to the absence of internal conflict (and political repression) rather than international wars. Indeed, we argue that the latter can even be a force for effective state building. For us, easy taxes means taxes that are easily extracted and broad-based—not a statement about the level. Further, for us, the analysis of justice means finding ways of ensuring that the state supports contracts, enforces property rights, and limits (public or private) predation. Subject to this slight change of focus, our three main questions basically become an inquiry into the circumstances that enable nations to erect Smith's three pillars of prosperity.

In this endeavor, we pool together ideas from four broad research agendas: (1) the study of long-run development and its determinants, (2) the study of civil wars and other forms of internal conflict, (3) the study of the importance of history for today's patterns of development, and (4) the study of how economics and politics interact in shaping societal outcomes. Thus, our work builds on many earlier strands of scholarship, and in what follows we try to give due credit to our predecessors in the large and in the small.

When grappling with the three central questions, we draw extensively on our own research during the last few years on the economics and politics of state building and violence in the process of development [see, e.g., Besley and Persson (2009b, 2010a,b, 2011)]. Even though we rely heavily on this earlier research, the book goes far beyond our articles and papers in terms of synthesis and overall perspective. Like our research papers, it aims at presenting new theory as well as new evidence. In line with that goal, most of the chapters interweave theoretical and empirical material.

The theory appears as a sequence of formal models, designed to gradually shed more light on the development clusters that we observe in the data. In the grand scheme of development, of course, many economic and political outcomes are jointly determined in a web of two-way relations, but to untangle this web requires an approach that starts out simply and gradually adds new layers of more complex interactions. For example, political institutions are taken as given and as a determinant of other outcomes all the way up to Chapter 7, where we start analyzing how these institutions might themselves be determined.

Aside from providing motivation for the theory, the empirics largely take the form of raw or partial correlations in cross-sectional contemporary and historical data. These correlations are closely related to the predictions of the theory. But with only a few exceptions, we stop short of an empirical strategy that seriously tries to isolate the causal relations in the data. Taking that further step is not so easy, because the whole point of our analysis is that most of the variables of interest are determined jointly. Laying bare causal relations in the data thus requires that we credibly isolate an exogenous variation in some particular variable of interest. As usual with cross-country data, that is not a trivial task.

The rest of this introductory chapter provides an overview of the book and its main messages. We explain our theoretical approach, describe the most important ideas that arise from it, and take an initial look at some data. As we continue with the overview, we also outline the contents of the seven chapters to follow. At the end of the chapter, we highlight some of the main themes that recur in the gradual development of our argument.

1.3 *Fiscal Capacity*

Existing Research by Economists State capacity is not a concept that appears prominently in traditional approaches by economists. With a few exceptions, macroeconomic analyses of development view income per capita, rather than policy-supporting institutions of the state, as the main outcome to be explained. Consider the two measures of state capacity illustrated in Figures 1.3–1.5. When it comes to fiscal capacity, theories of taxation—be it in public finance or political economics—emphasize constraints on the government's ability to impose a certain tax rate on a certain tax base. But these are generally incentive constraints, tied to asymmetric information or political forces, rather than constraints owing to lack of an administrative infrastructure. As for legal capacity, the government's capability to enforce contracts or protect investors is almost universally assumed, rather than analyzed, in contract theory or finance. To abstract in this way from the hurdles for policymaking raised by the extractive and productive capacities of government seems unwarranted in view of the history of today's rich countries and the reality of today's poor countries.

Existing Research by Historians The lack of attention by economists stands in stark contrast to the view taken by many political and economic historians who see the state's capacity to raise revenue as an important phenomenon in itself. Moreover, historians link this capacity to a thirst for military success and regard it as a key factor behind the successful development of nation states [see, e.g., Brewer (1989), Hintze (1906), or Tilly (1975, 1985)]. As famously stated, "war made the state and the state made war" (Tilly, 1975, p. 42).

In line with the core thesis, tax systems in countries such as the United States, the United Kingdom, and Sweden have indeed been reformed and expanded in connection with actual or latent external conflicts. Political scientists such as Migdal (1988) have emphasized that one of the major problems of developing countries is that their states are often too weak and lack the capacity to raise revenue and govern effectively. However, historians have not really systematically explored the links between the fiscal (extractive) capacity and legal (productive) capacity of the state, although Strayer (1970) does stress the building of fiscal and judicial institutions in the early development of European states.

Basic Theoretical Approach One cornerstone of our framework is to distinguish between policymaking and institution building. In particular, the capacity of the state is built up over time, and current capacity constrains the policies pursued by the current incumbent government. For example, today's ability to levy an income tax is constrained by the existing fiscal capacity of the state, e.g., the administrative capacity to monitor and enforce tax payments and the

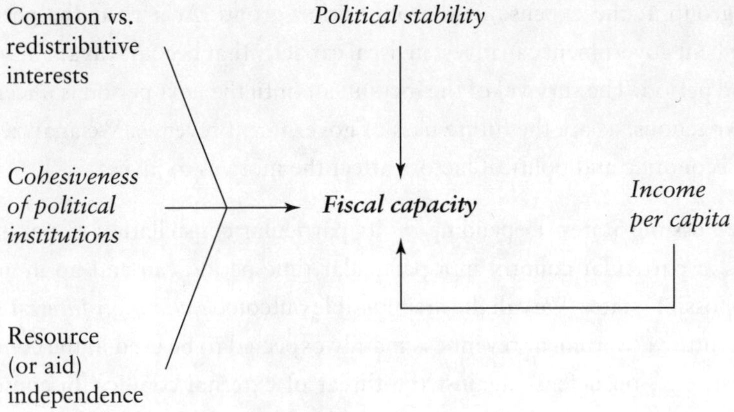

Figure 1.6 Scope of Chapter 2.

institutions necessary to implement income-tax withholding by firms. Another cornerstone of our framework is to consider state building as the outcome of purposeful and forward-looking decisions by successive incumbents. Specifically, we model decisions about future state capacity as an explicit investment problem. In this problem, incumbents weigh the present costs of investing against uncertain future expected benefits.

Investments in Fiscal Capacity Chapter 2 lays down the very first building block in our theoretical framework by formulating the simplest possible model by which to analyze state building. The flowchart in Figure 1.6 is a stylized illustration of the analysis in Chapter 2. The fonts in the chart as well as in the flowcharts to follow have specific meanings. Thus, we use bold italics for those outcomes that are endogenous in the analysis, italics for those that are temporarily taken as given but will eventually be made endogenous, and a regular font for those outcomes that are taken as given throughout the book. As Figure 1.6 illustrates, most political and economic factors are taken as given in Chapter 2, where they are represented by exogenous parameters; but when we generalize the analysis in later chapters, several of these parameters are turned into endogenous variables.

The simplest version of our core model has two symmetric groups, two time periods, and a single form of state capacity. In each period, a government representing one of the groups sets a tax rate on a given level of income. The revenue can be used for various forms of spending, although existing political institutions constrain how much money can be transferred to the incumbent's own group at the expense of the opposition group. At a cost, the period-1 incumbent government can invest in fiscal capacity that becomes available in the second period. The survival of the incumbent until the next period is uncertain, but exogenous, as are the future uses of government revenue. We analyze how given economic and political factors affect the motives to invest.

Three Possible States Depending on its particular constellation of parameter values, a particular country in a particular time period can end up in any of three possible states. We call the first possible outcome a *common-interest state.* Here, future government revenue is mainly expected to be used in the common interest, e.g., on defense against the threat of external conflict. In common-interest states, any incumbent makes considerable investments in fiscal capacity.

The second possibility is a *redistributive state.* In such states, government revenue is predominantly used for redistribution with the incumbent being more or less constrained by political institutions. Incumbents still invest in fiscal capacity, as there is enough political stability.

Finally, we may have a *weak state,* in which case government revenue is also used for redistribution, but political institutions are noncohesive and political instability is high. Under these circumstances, no incumbent invests in the fiscal powers of the state.

A simple regression analysis shows that cross-country correlations in the data are consistent with some of the basic theoretical predictions of the core model.

Extensions of the Basic Framework Chapter 2 also shows how our core model can be given microeconomic underpinnings. Moreover, it shows how one can relax a number of the stark assumptions underlying the basic framework: only two periods, no economic distortions by taxation, linear functional forms, only one good, no income inequality, equally sized groups, the absence of political polarization, and so on. In each of these extensions, we show how the core model is altered, what the alterations mean for the analysis of investments in fiscal capacity, and the principal additional insights obtained.

1.4 *Legal Capacity*

In Chapter 3, we begin our successive extension of the core model formulated in Chapter 2. In particular, we introduce a second dimension of policy and state capacity, namely market-supporting regulation and the constraints imposed by legal capacity. This extension serves two useful purposes. It allows us to study the relationship between the two aspects of state building. It also serves to endogenize income, as better market support helps raise private incomes. The chapter presents alternative microeconomic foundations for the reduced-form model that we use in later chapters. One of these microfoundations emphasizes imperfect contracting opportunities in the capital market and the other stresses imperfect protection of private property rights against predation by other private agents or government bureaucrats. Chapter 3 also demonstrates a way to introduce private capital accumulation into our model on top of government investments in the state.

Complementarities in State Capacity An immediate result in Chapter 3 is that fiscal and legal capacity tend to be *complements*. In other words, investments in one aspect of the state reinforce the motives to invest in the other. If future fiscal capacity is higher, additional fiscal benefits make it more advantageous to invest in legal capacity to expand market incomes and the prospective tax base. Analogously, if future legal capacity is higher, it makes market incomes and tax bases higher, which, in turn, raise the motive to invest in fiscal capacity.

This complementarity has important implications. On the one hand, it provides a clear hint as to why fiscal and legal capacity may be positively correlated with one another, as well as with income, as they are in Figure 1.3. On the other hand, it suggests that many determinants of state capacity should be *common,* i.e., factors that raise fiscal capacity should be expected to raise legal capacity as well and *vice versa.*

Which major determinants does the approach in Chapters 2 and 3 identify? A precise statement of the results must await our formal analysis. But it is useful to preview some of the main predictions of the theory, the intuition behind these predictions, and some of the correlations we find in the data. Figure 1.7 gives a hint of the different determinants we consider. Note that income is in bold italics rather than italics in this flowchart to illustrate the broader scope of the analysis compared to Chapter 2.

The Use of Public Revenue If additional tax revenue is expected to be spent in the common interest of both groups, say on classic public goods rather than on redistribution, then incumbents from any group are happy to build additional fiscal capacity. This prediction is clearly in tune with the argument put forward

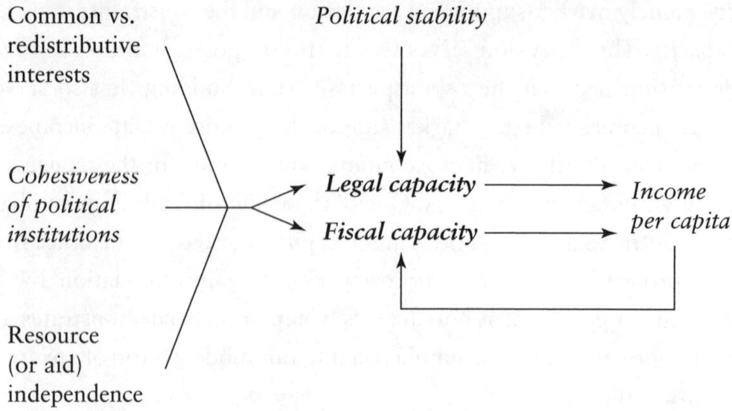

Figure 1.7 Scope of Chapter 3.

by the writers on economic and political history. By complementarity, however, we get an auxiliary prediction: incumbents would also have stronger incentives to build more market-supporting legal capacity, as higher tax rates can then be imposed on a higher tax base.

War as a Measure of Common Interests Are the data consistent with this basic idea? Consider defense, the classic example of a public good, as an instance of common-interest spending. Assume that a high incidence of actual external conflict in the past proxies well for a high perceived risk of conflict. Then, we can crudely gauge the past demand for public goods by the historical prevalence of war. The theory identifies the past demand for public goods as a positive determinant of past investments in legal and fiscal capacity and therefore as a positive determinant of the stock of state capacity we observe today. For each country where the data exist, we use the Correlates of War data set to compute the historical prevalence of war as the share of years in external war since 1816 or the year of independence, whichever occurs later, until the year 2000.

Of course, by taking past wars as given, this procedure does not address the fact that wars reflect the joint interactions between two (or among many) countries. Addressing this properly would require analyzing at least two countries and the joint determination of state capacities and the risk of war. Such an approach would certainly be natural and interesting, but is beyond the scope of the present book.

Let us correlate past wars with the two measures of fiscal and legal capacity in Figures 1.3 to 1.5. We show in Chapters 2 and 3 that alternative measures yield similar results. Specifically, we compute the partial correlations between state capacities and past prevalence of war, while holding constant other determinants of state capacity such as ethnic homogeneity, political institutions, and political stability, as well as legal origins (Chapters 2 and 3 give further details on the data and the computation of the partial correlations.)

Figure 1.8 shows that the partial correlations are consistent with the prediction of the theory: a larger incidence of war in the past is indeed associated

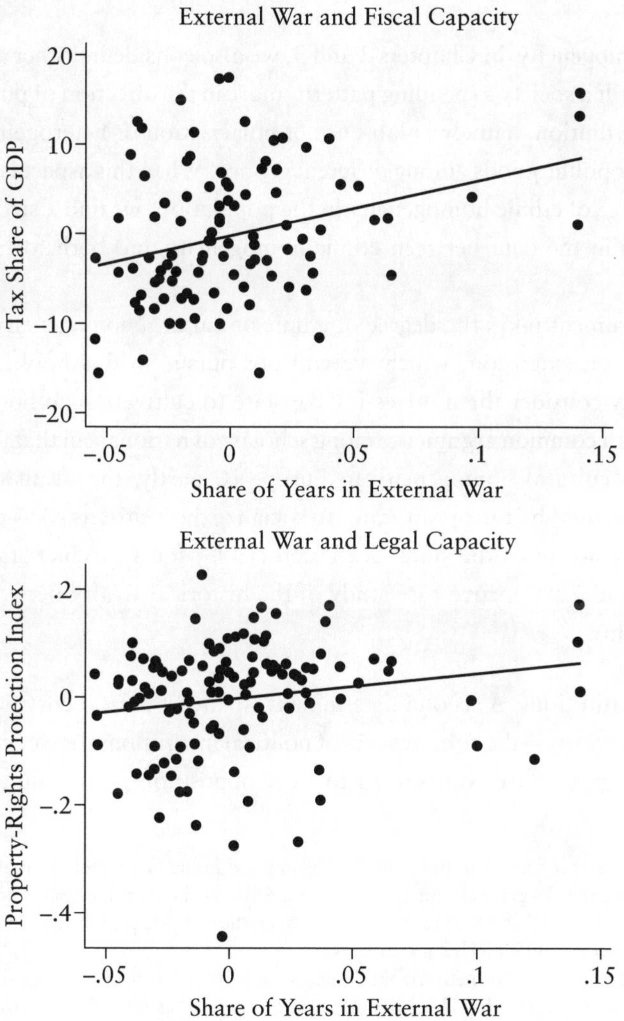

Figure 1.8 State capacity and external war.

with higher state capacity today.[5] The upper panel is for fiscal capacity, plotting the overall tax share against the share of years in war.[6] The slope is positive with a magnitude such that a state with 20% more of its history in wartime has a higher tax take in the present by 10% of GDP. The lower panel is for legal capacity, plotting the index of property-rights protection against time in war. Again, the slope is positive, and although the magnitude of this index is harder to interpret directly, we see that part of its variation is associated with variation in wartime experience. This preliminary evidence is thus consistent with the extended Hintze-Tilly hypothesis.

Ethnic Homogeneity In Chapters 2 and 3, we also consider another aspect that is likely to tilt a society's spending patterns more in the direction of public goods than redistribution, namely an absence of polarization or heterogeneity in the demand for public goods among different groups. When this aspect is measured by the degree of ethnic homogeneity in the population, we find a strong partial correlation in the data between ethnic homogeneity and both forms of state capacity.

This argument takes the degree of ethnic or cultural homogeneity as given. An interesting extension, which we will not pursue in this book, would be to explicitly consider the motives for the state to cultivate such homogeneity. Indeed, it is a common argument among scholars of nationalism that the relative ethnic and cultural homogeneity in Europe is, partly, the result of various mechanisms used by European states to socialize their citizens so as to increase the military power of the state. See Posen (1993) for a succinct statement of this view and a supportive case study of the historical rivalry between France and Germany.

Political Institutions A second determinant isolated by the theory is the structure or—as we say—the cohesiveness of political institutions. In some countries, incumbent groups are constrained to treat opposition groups quite well, by

5. There are two outliers in the sample: England and France with more than 40% of their history in wartime. To get nicer pictures, Figure 1.8 shows the partial correlations with state capacity when England and France are excluded from the sample, even though these countries have little effect on the underlying estimates.

6. Both the vertical and the horizontal axes include negative as well as positive numbers. This is because we hold other determinants of the tax share as well as the share of years in wartime constant. When partialing out the effects of these determinants, we obtain residuals of each variable, which are centered at zero.

institutions such as checks and balances on the executive or election systems that grant a relatively large representation for electoral losers. Such political institutions will tend to promote common-interest rather than redistributive spending, whichever group holds power. This, in turn, ensures current incumbents that the state will not be used against their own interests in the future, which promotes investment in the state. Suppose now that we take cohesiveness of political institutions as given, as we do until Chapter 7. Then, a high incidence of cohesive political institutions in the past should be correlated with high investments in both forms of state capacity in the past. As a result, we should observe high levels of legal and fiscal capacity today.

Once again, let us look at the broad patterns in the data. We measure the institutional constraints in the theory by the executive constraints variable in the Polity IV data set (alternative measures of political institutions give similar results in Chapters 2 and 3). Specifically, for each country, we compute its average score on this variable in between 1800 (or the year of independence) and 2000. The original variable is coded on a scale from 1 to 7, but we normalize the average score for each country to lie between 0 and 1. Figure 1.9 plots the partial correlations, computed in the same way as for Figure 1.8, between cohesive political institutions in the past and current fiscal capacity (upper graph) and legal capacity (lower graph), respectively.

Evidently, the correlations with both types of state capacity are strong and positive. The slope of the regression line in the upper graph indicates that a country with average executive constraints one standard deviation (about 0.31) higher than another has about 5% of GDP higher taxes today. Clearly, the partial correlation between legal capacity and executive constraints displayed in the lower panel is also positive and even stronger than the correlation with fiscal capacity.

Political Stability Another determinant of state capacity in Figure 1.7 is political stability. If common interests are weak and political institutions are noncohesive, each incumbent will tend to devote most of the state's revenue to redistribution in favor of her own group. If instability is high, so that a current incumbent faces a high probability of replacement, investments in fiscal capacity may stop altogether, as such investments may backfire in the future by enabling more redistribution away from the incumbent's own group. As we will see in Chapters 2 and 3, empirical measures of political stability do in fact covary positively with alternative representations of fiscal and legal capacity.

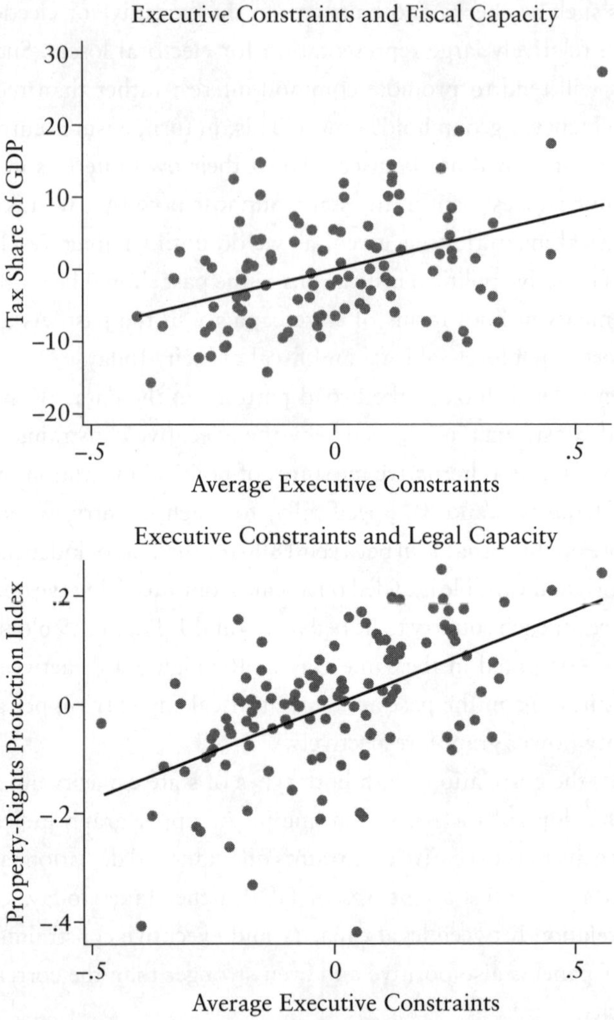

Figure 1.9 State capacity and executive constraints.

However, in many poor countries—especially those with weak or fragile states—instability is intimately associated with political violence, one of the topics to be considered later in the book. We thus return to political instability later.

Economic Structure In addition to these *political* determinants of state capacity, Figure 1.7 also highlights some *economic* determinants. One is economic structure. If we hold constant the level of income, the relative shares of resource rents, or (cash) aid, in income become important. To the extent that such resource flows accrue directly to the government, a higher dependence on resources or aid means that market incomes are smaller. The smaller tax base diminishes the motives to invest in market-supporting legal capacity. By complementarity, this also makes investments in fiscal capacity less attractive. Clearly, this simple argument may provide an important clue as to why resource-dependent or aid-dependent countries in Africa or parts of Asia may have weaker incentives to build their states. This observation is similar to a standard argument about obstacles to development in so-called rentier states [see, e.g., Mahdavy (1970) for an early contribution with an application to oil revenue in Iran].

Income per Capita If we hold economic structure constant, a higher level of income per capita means a higher level of market income, which raises the incentives to invest in both sides of the state. Low income can thus serve to diminish the investments in fiscal and legal capacity. That argument takes income as given, however, and it is very likely that we also have feedback effects in the other direction. In particular, low legal capacity to support markets will keep income low, ceteris paribus. We show how such an effect arises in the microfounded versions of the model.

In Chapter 3, we also discuss how low fiscal capacity may cause low income. The mechanism for this is more subtle: without the capability for redistribution via taxes and transfers, incumbents may try to redistribute by seeking rents for their groups. Rent seeking pursued via measures such as inefficient regulation creates production distortions that feed on to low incomes. We show that this is not only a logical possibility, but may well be a plausible political equilibrium when fiscal capacity is endogenously determined. The chapter explains how we can interpret this result as a positive analog to the Diamond-Mirrlees normative theory of production efficiency in the context of optimal taxation.

Correlations between state capacity and income such as those in Figure 1.3 may thus reflect causal links in both directions. Figure 1.7 illustrates such prospective two-way feedback effects. Moreover, the existence of positive feedback effects can create virtuous or vicious circles that may help produce clusters of strong state capacities in strong economies or weak state capacities in weak economies.

State-Capacity Traps We would expect states that lack sufficient state capacity to acquire it by investing in economic institutions to raise taxes and support markets. Our analysis gives insights into two main reasons why this may not be the case.

In a weak state, there is no incentive to invest in fiscal capacity because institutions are not cohesive. If a country ends up in such a fiscal-capacity trap, this trap will seriously limit the ability of the state to provide public goods.

We also study predatory states. These arise when poor governance allows a narrow elite to engage in predatory behavior that extracts transfers from private producers. Such predation is typically related to high levels of corruption, but may also include other forms of extralegal predation. Poor governance means that the state is sanctioning and reinforcing such behavior by not extending legal protection to producers. Such states end up in a legal-capacity trap with no incentive to create effective legal systems so as to establish the rule of law.

1.5 *Political Violence*

Our analysis in Chapters 2 and 3 suggests that the risk of external violence can promote state building by enhancing common interests relative to redistributive interests across different groups in society. The risk of internal political violence appears to be very different. Conditions that sow the seeds for internal violence are hardly a sign of common interests but rather of extreme redistributive struggles across groups. It is thus quite intuitive to suppose that the risks of internal violence might drive the motives for state building in a different direction compared to the risks of external violence. Consistent with that intuition, we have already seen that countries where civil wars are common tend to have low levels of state capacity (recall Figure 1.4). Chapters 4 and 5 take a closer look at this aspect of development clusters. We now preview some of that analysis.

Some Basic Facts Sadly, civil war—the armed struggle between the government and some insurgent group—has been quite a common phenomenon in the last 60 years. According to the ACD, more than 10% of all country-years in the world since 1950 have been associated with civil war. In addition to such two-sided violence, many governments try to enhance their probability of remaining in office by engaging in violent acts against the population without civil war breaking out; we refer to this kind of one-sided violence as repression. According to the Banks (2005) data set, 8% of all country-years since 1950 have been associated with repression in the stark form of purges (elimination of political opponents) in the absence of civil war (see Chapter 4 for more details on the data).

The upper and lower panels on the left of Figure 1.10 show the worldwide prevalence of civil war and repression over time, plotting the share of countries with civil war or repression by year. Clearly, civil war was on the rise until a turnaround at the end of the Cold War, whereas repression (without civil war) was on the decline during the same time period. The panels on the right of the figure plot the prevalence of violence by country against per capita income (measured in 1980). Civil war is mostly a poor-country feature, whereas repression has its main mass a bit higher up in the world income distribution. Interestingly, both sets of graphs give a clear sense of substitutability between these two forms of political violence.

Existing Research by Economists and Political Scientists Not surprisingly, many political scientists and some economists have studied the economic and political determinants of civil war. This research is quite fragmented, however, at least from our perspective of understanding the development clusters we observe in the data. Existing theoretical work on conflicts and civil war has little room for institutions, including state capacities, and is not particularly well connected to the data. Existing empirical work on civil war and repression, on the other hand, has weak connections to theory so some of its results are not easy to interpret. Virtually all empirical research takes income as given, even though violence and income may well have similar determinants; e.g., there are two separate literatures on the "resource curse," one claiming that resource dependence may cause low income and growth and the other arguing that resource dependence may cause civil war. Finally, there are separate literatures on civil war and repression, even though both phenomena seem to reflect the fact that political institutions fail to resolve conflicting interests in a peaceful way.

Our approach to analyzing political violence has two steps. First, we extend our core model to incorporate the possibility of both repression and civil war and make predictions about how these forms of violence are related to the major determinants of investments in state capacity. This extended core model effectively endogenizes one of the determinants of state building, namely political stability. As a second step, we jointly analyze political violence and state building in that richer framework.

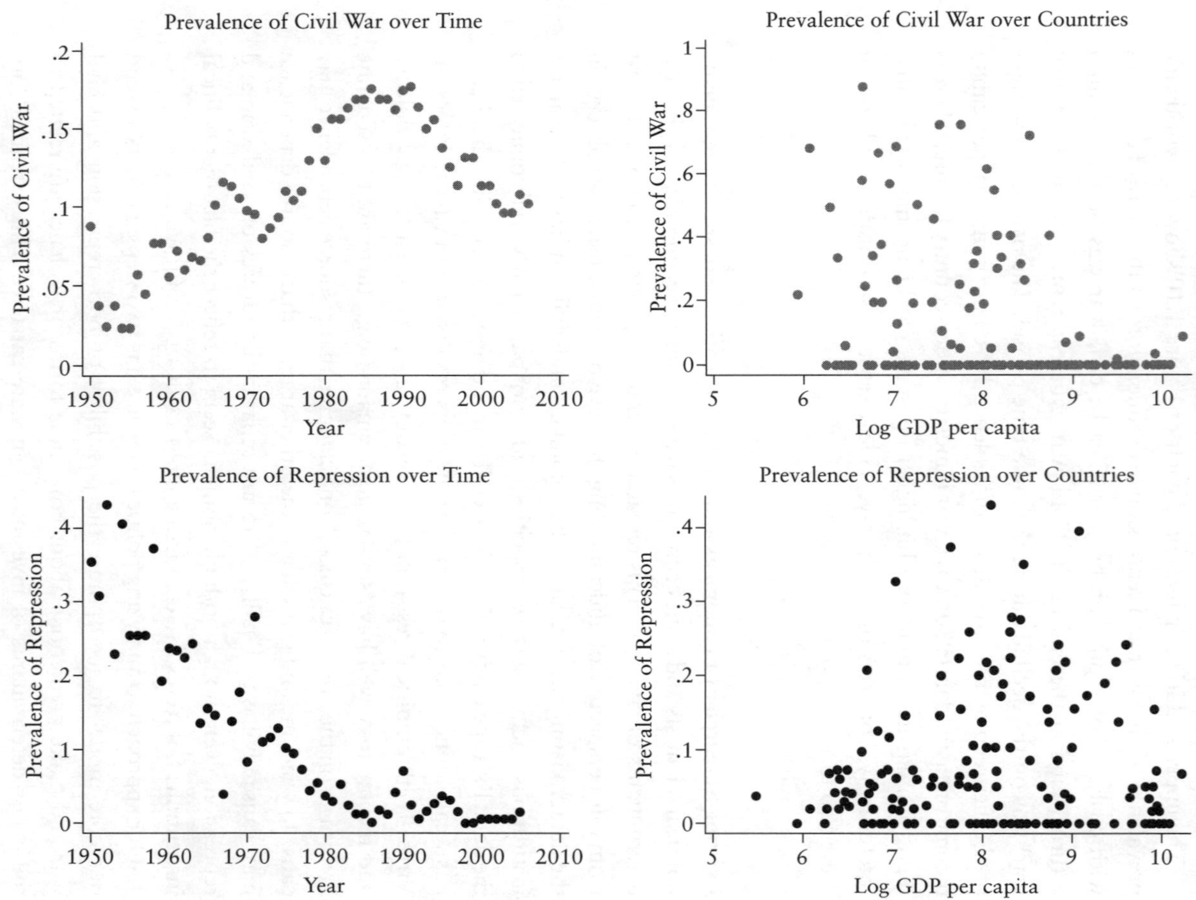

Figure 1.10 Prevalence of civil war and repression.

Basic Theoretical Approach Thus we start out in Chapter 4 with the same two-group, two-period model as in Chapter 3, although we take state-capacity investments and therefore income per capita as given. On the other hand, we allow both groups to invest in violence. The opposition group can invest in armed forces in period 1, so as to try and take power in period 2. The incumbent group can also invest in armed forces to raise its probability of remaining in power. Absent conscription, soldiers are hired at prevailing wages: the opposition has to raise the necessary resources from its own group, whereas the incumbent uses revenue from the public purse. Both groups then face a trade-off: the costs of investing in violence must be weighed against a higher probability of holding power and controlling the opportunity to redistribute in the group's favor. In this simple setting, we can analyze two central questions. (1) When do we observe violence rather than peace, and if so which type of violence? (2) Which economic, political, and institutional variables determine one-sided (repression) and two-sided (civil war) violence?

Three Possible Violence States Given the "conflict technology" that we posit, both groups' propensity to invest in violence is increasing in a common latent variable, namely the ratio of expected marginal benefits to the marginal cost of investment. We show that three conflict outcomes are possible and that these outcomes are ordered in the latent variable. When the ratio of expected benefits to cost is low, no group finds it worthwhile to invest in violence and we observe a *peaceful* outcome. As this ratio becomes somewhat higher, the incumbent but not the opposition takes to violence, and we observe *repression;* the incumbent's violence threshold is lower than the opposition's threshold because we assume that the incumbent has an advantage in terms of lower costs or higher effectiveness of fighting. At high benefit-cost ratios, finally, both groups invest in violence and we observe *civil war.*

Determinants of Political Violence What are the roots of repression and civil war that this simple theory identifies? A first and simple insight is that the three violence outcomes are ordered in the same latent variable. This means that their determinants should be common and strongly suggests that the research on repression and civil war ought to be integrated. Another set of results, of more direct relevance for development clusters, follows when we relate the likelihood of conflicts to the determinants of state capacity studied in Chapters 2 and 3.

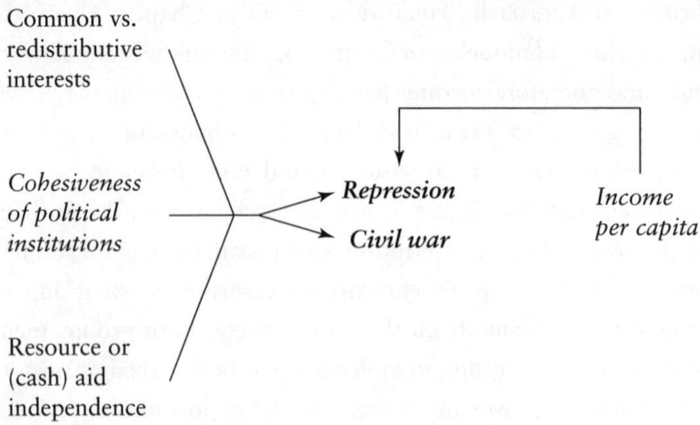

Figure 1.11 Scope of Chapter 4.

To explain the results, we have to explore the expected marginal benefits and costs of investments in violence in more detail. Given that a larger investment in violence of any group raises its probability of holding power and setting policy, the marginal benefit is the share a winner can expect to grab of the total expected redistributive pie, i.e., expected future revenue minus spending on public goods. The marginal cost is simply the real wage paid to the soldiers.

Consider Figure 1.11, where the determinants of state capacity are listed as prospective determinants of violence. When common interests are low, it is expected that less of future revenue will be spent on public goods, which raises the expected benefit of investing in violence to boost the probability of holding office. When political institutions are noncohesive, the winner gets a larger share of any redistribution, which also raises the expected benefit of fighting. A higher level of expected resource rents or cash aid also raises the expected benefit of fighting, as this increases the available redistributive pie. Finally, a lower level of income per capita diminishes the real wage, which cuts the cost of investing in violence. Recalling the discussion around Figure 1.7, we reach a striking conclusion: all factors that diminish the incumbent's motives to invest in the state tend to raise the two groups' motives to invest in violence. To what extent these stronger motives will actually translate into realized repression or civil war depends on the levels of the incumbent's and the opposition's violence thresholds. These, in turn, reflect factors such as the incumbent's and the opposition's relative costs of raising resources for violence and their relative capabilities in fighting.

Extensions of the Basic Framework Chapter 4 also looks at a few extensions of the political-violence framework. One of these is to reintroduce political heterogeneity or polarization in the same way as in one of the extensions considered in Chapter 2. Generally, a higher degree of heterogeneity diminishes the common interests in society, which raises the gain to holding power, and this, in turn, boosts the incentives for both groups to invest in violence. This extension provides a way to study the greed and grievance motives for conflict [see Collier and Hoeffler (2004)] in the same analytical setting.

Another extension picks up the predation theme from one of the extensions in Chapter 3. If the investments in violence by the incumbent group are made by a small elite that is also the main benefactor of predation by the state, there are additional motives for staying in power. As a result, the society's propensity for repression as well as civil war goes up, and this effect is stronger the less institutions constrain the ruling elite from infringements on other citizens.

Empirical Support In the remainder of Chapter 4, we show how one may go from theoretical predictions to serious empirical testing. The first step uses the basic model, together with assumptions about what variables and parameters are observable and unobservable in the data, to derive a set of testable predictions. The second step finds credible sources of exogenous time variation in the determinants suggested by the theory. Using the occurrence of natural disasters for shocks to real wages and aid flows and revolving memberships on the U.N. Security Council for shocks to aid flows, we find quite strong econometric support for the model predictions. The exogenous shocks affect the likelihood of observing government repression as well as civil war *within* each country. In particular, we find that exogenous hikes in aid significantly raise the probability of both types of conflict.

1.6 *State Spaces*

Having used essentially the same core model to study the investments in fiscal and legal capacity in Chapter 3 and investments in political violence in Chapter 4, the next step is to put these pieces together. We do this in Chapter 5, where the state-capacity investment problem is revisited with political stability being endogenously determined by the investments in violence. The flowchart in Figure 1.12 illustrates this analysis schematically.

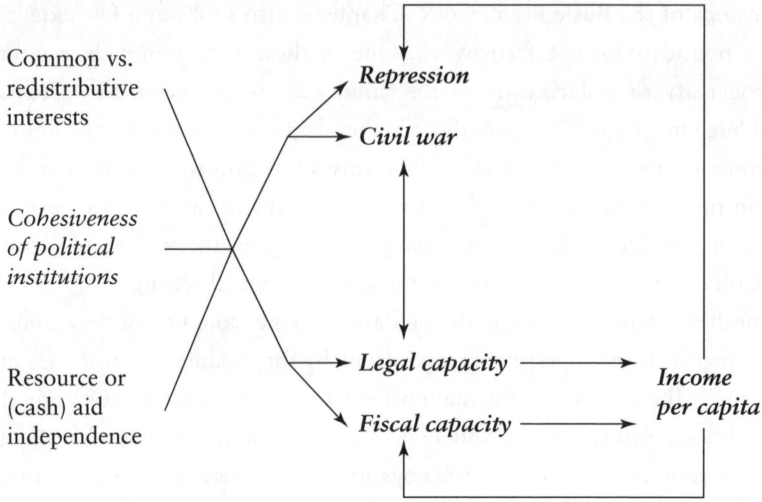

Figure 1.12 Scope of Chapter 5.

State Capacity and Political Violence The analysis in Chapter 5 suggests three channels whereby state capacity and political violence become related. First, as we have just seen, a set of common variables drives both of these outcomes, although in opposite directions. Second, there is a magnification effect: other factors that raise the risk of internal conflict may raise the perceived political instability for the incumbent, something that generally diminishes the motives to build strong institutions. Third, the framework entails feedback effects, whereby investments in state capacity alter the likelihood of conflict—these can go in either direction.

Based on these insights, we expect state capacity and political violence to become negatively correlated. Figure 1.4 suggested that the raw data are indeed consistent with this expectation. Figure 1.13 goes one step further by plotting the partial correlations (computed as in Figures 1.8 and 1.9) between the prevalence of civil war from 1950 to 2000 and fiscal or legal capacity, respectively. Whereas the corresponding correlations with external war (reproduced in the upper panels of the figure) are positive, the correlations with civil war (in the lower panels) are indeed negative. But there is certainly no claim of causality here. Via the three channels mentioned earlier, state capacity and internal violence are very much jointly determined.

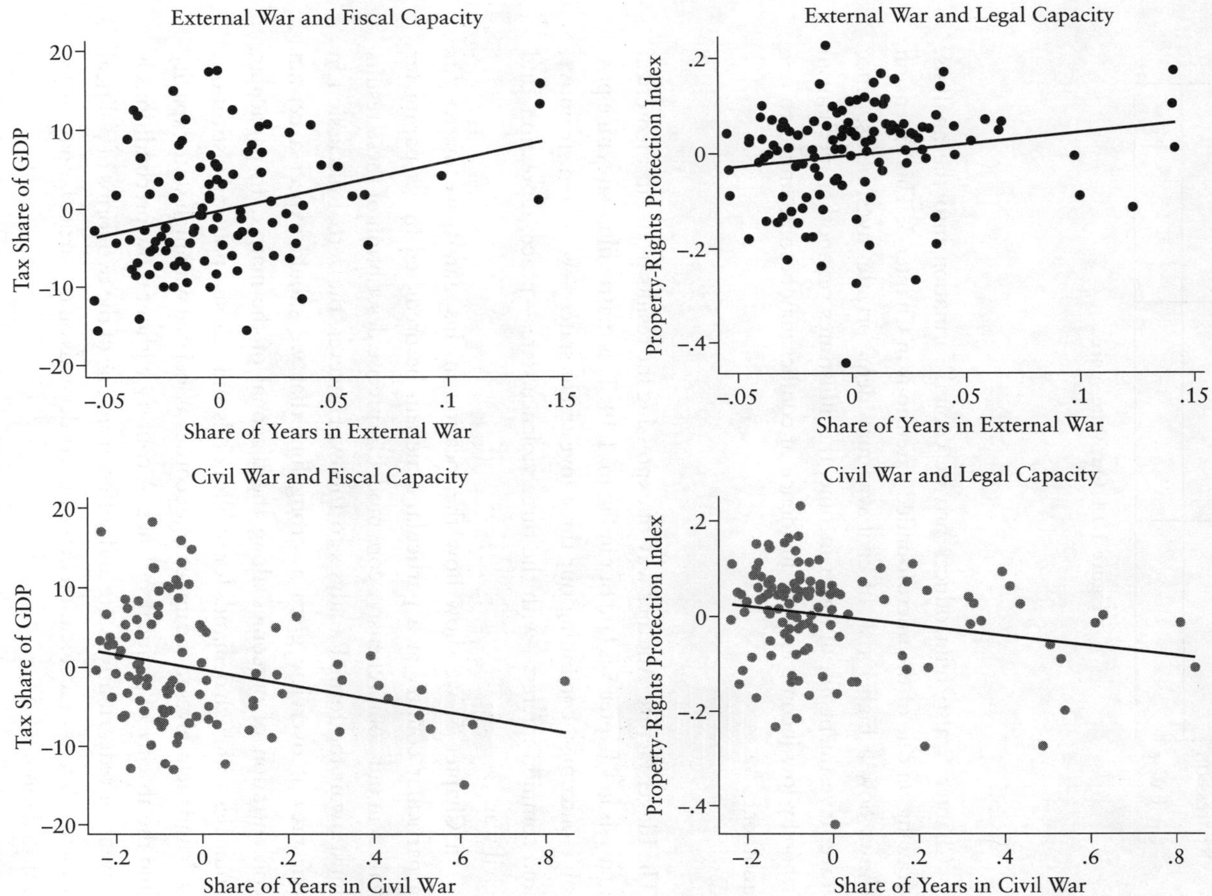

Figure 1.13 State capacity and external and civil war.

	Weak	Redistributive	Common Interest
Peace			
Repression			
Civil War			

Figure 1.14 Our state space.

Chapter 5 also reintroduces private capital formation into the analysis, drawing on one of the microfounded extensions in Chapter 3. This extension shows how a higher risk of civil war may deter private investments. Since lower investments mean lower income, this illustrates yet another mechanism whereby low income and the incidence of conflict may become linked to one another.

The Bigger Picture Another way of expressing the results from our theoretical analysis in Chapter 5 is laid out in Figure 1.14. This matrix illustrates nine possible outcomes, combining our three investment states—weak, redistributive, and common-interest—with the three violence states—peace, repression, and civil war.

In Chapter 5, we show how the location in this state-space matrix for a particular country at a particular time can be predicted by its parameter values in our comprehensive core model. A precise description of these results must await the formal analysis to follow. However, the verbal discussion in our present overview gives a strong hint that we should expect a certain concentration of outcomes along the diagonal of the matrix. In particular, countries with high demands for public goods and cohesive political institutions will find themselves in the upper-right corner associated with high state capacity and the absence of political violence. A country without those preconditions is a weak or redistributive state and suffers from one of the two forms of political violence, but its exact location in the matrix depends on its particular parameter constellation.

Once we have filled out the matrix in Figure 1.14, we refer to the results as an *Anna Karenina principle of development*, based on the first sentence of Leo Tolstoy's 1870s novel: "All prosperous countries resemble each other; every nonprosperous country is nonprosperous in its own way."

1.7 *Development Assistance*

Whether foreign aid helps or hurts development or whether it all depends has been a subject of constant discussion over the last few decades in the academic community as well as the development community. Some optimists have argued that aid can promote prosperity, whereas others have contended that it can even have a pernicious effect on state building and conflict.

Different Types of Interventions in Different Types of States In Chapter 6, we put our modeling machinery to work in analyzing that specific question. We show how our analytical framework can be used to analyze different types of foreign interventions: cash aid, project aid, technical assistance, peace keeping, or postconflict resolution. Figure 1.15 illustrates the scope of this analysis. Our framework allows us to discuss the equilibrium responses to different foreign interventions of policy, state-building, conflict, and—ultimately—welfare.

Having filled in the matrix in Figure 1.14, we discuss how the response to development assistance is affected by the preconditions. Fragile states—those that have poor state effectiveness and are prone to political violence—are particularly complex. But our modeling framework can, at least, pose these dilemmas in a sharp way. Although we do not reach any definitive conclusions, we believe that our approach advances the discussion beyond the current state of the art.

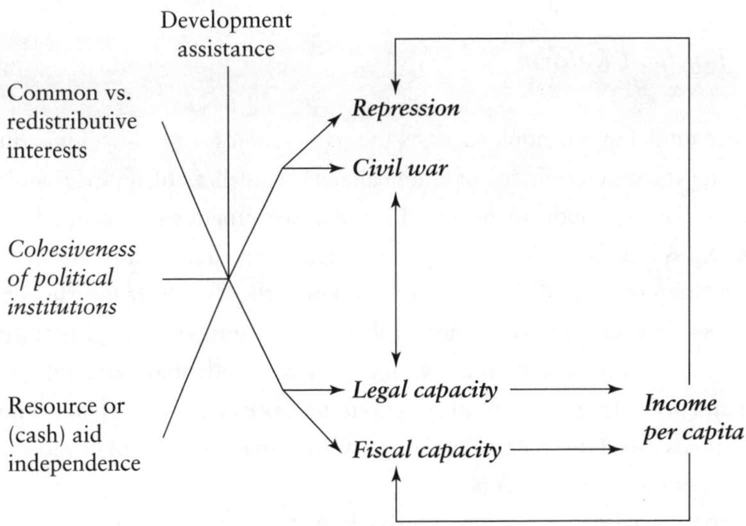

Figure 1.15 Scope of Chapter 6.

Symptoms versus Determinants Ongoing discussions about assistance to weak states are not founded in any underlying theory, which explains why they tend to mix up symptoms and determinants. For example, fragile-state indexes frequently include low income per capita as a criterion. Although low income may certainly strengthen the motives to invest in violence ceteris paribus, it is only an intermediate factor. Our approach implies that the fundamental determinants of fragile states are such things as the strength of common interests in society, the structure of political institutions, the degree of resource or aid dependence, or the technologies for organizing and conducting violence. Other phenomena such as civil war, repression, low spending on public goods, low taxation, weak enforcement of property rights, and corruption are all symptoms.

The Bauer Paradox Overall, Chapter 6 shows how the likely effects of foreign intervention depend on the type of aid, as well as the situation of the receiving country. One of our overall conclusions resonates with the somewhat pessimistic paradox suggested by Peter Bauer—that aid is most likely to work well in countries that do not really need very much aid anyway. Our approach can be seen to fuel either aid pessimism or optimism. The possibility that aid can have negative consequences that reduce its impact may fuel a pessimistic view, especially as such responses are poorly understood from an empirical point of view. However, it is also clear that designing interventions well can make aid more effective.

1.8 Political Reform

The core model in our book suggests that cohesiveness of political institutions is an important determinant of state capacity as well as of political violence, and an important condition for the effect of development assistance. Of course, cohesiveness is a theoretical concept without an immediate real-world counterpart. In Chapter 7, we discuss how one can map theory into reality. In general, we expect democracies to be more cohesive than autocracies; parliamentary forms of government to be more cohesive than presidential forms of government; and proportional electoral systems to be more cohesive than majoritarian electoral systems. However, federal governments may or may not be more cohesive than unitary governments.

As noted earlier, our gradual approach in this book takes the cohesiveness of political institutions as given up to Chapter 6. Given the importance of

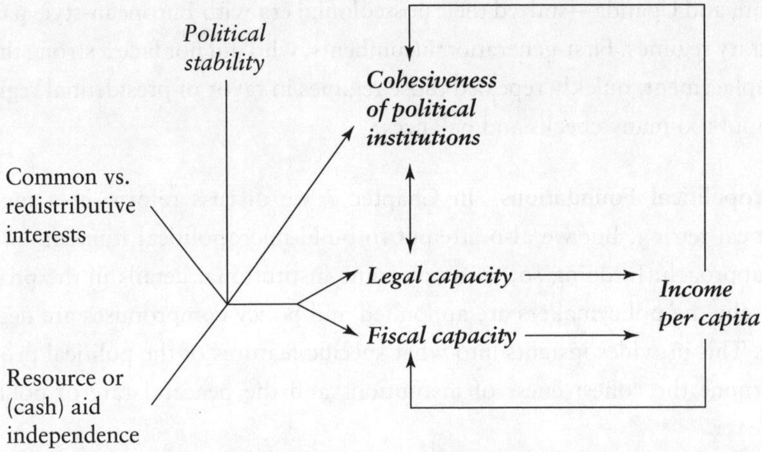

Figure 1.16 Scope of Chapter 7.

political institutions in our argument and the fact that these institutions are also subject to change over time, Chapter 7 makes a start on the difficult task of endogenizing the choice of institutions. We discuss normative as well as positive models of political reform along the lines suggested by Figure 1.16.

Different Horizons We first derive a normative benchmark result when institutions are designed once and for all at a constitutional convention behind a veil of ignorance. In this case, the conveners will always create cohesive political institutions because such institutional arrangements provide the best incentives for creating state capacity.

We then look at the choices for period 2 made by the period-1 incumbent. In this case, we show that choosing cohesive institutions requires a considerable degree of competition for political power. This may shed some light on political reforms in Europe in the decades around the turn of the nineteenth century. Several countries with conservative or liberal governments—such as Denmark, Sweden, and the Netherlands—followed up universal suffrage with reforms toward full parliamentary democracy and/or proportional representation elections, as the labor movement grew stronger in pace with ongoing industrialization and the landed and industrial elites were too divided to work toward a common purpose.

We also obtain the flipside of this result: reform toward less consensual institutions becomes more likely if the incumbent faces little competition for power. This result provides a way of thinking about the decade after independence in Africa. Incumbent rulers in several African countries—such as Nigeria,

Sudan, and Uganda—started their postcolonial era with European-style parliamentary regimes. First-generation incumbents, who did not face a strong threat of replacement, quickly repealed those regimes in favor of presidential regimes without too many checks and balances.

Micropolitical Foundations In Chapter 7 we discuss reform in a macropolitical setting. But we also attempt to build micropolitical foundations for the approach. In doing so, we study some institutional details in the process whereby the policymakers are appointed and policy compromises are negotiated. This provides insights into what specific features of the political process determine the cohesiveness of institutions and the peaceful rate of political turnover.

We show that a latent possibility of violence introduces a trade-off in the building of cohesive political institutions. Such institutions are more desirable for incumbents in that they reduce the costly use of violence. However, since violence also creates the possibility of entrenchment in power, this force will tend to reduce incentives for creating cohesive institutions.

Our macro analysis of incumbent behavior neglects features that create inertia in the choice of institutions. In Chapter 7, however, we show that formal supermajority requirements will tend to make cohesive institutions more sustainable. We also discuss the possible role of trust in supporting cohesiveness.

Finally, we turn to a different dimension of political institutions, introduced in our extension in Chapter 3 on corruption and predation. This concerns the possibility that an incumbent can improve governance to make predation more difficult. As in the case of cohesive institutions, a low probability of turnover makes improvements in governance less likely. But a new factor also plays a very important role: entrenched elites, which make up only a small fraction of the population, will typically resist such governance reform as it threatens their rents from holding power.

1.9 *Main Themes*

In the preceding sections we sketched the contents of the book, chapter by chapter. Here, we describe some of the main themes that run through the book in parallel as the full story unfolds. This description serves as a reading guide to those interested in particular aspects of our analysis.

The Core Model Many of our ideas are presented through the lens of the comprehensive symmetric two-group, two-period model, the gradual development of which we have just described. The perspective here is macroeconomic and macropolitical, meaning that most of the analysis focuses on the investment decisions made by the incumbent (in state capacities and political violence) and opposition groups (in political violence), whereas the result of all other economic and political behavior is represented in reduced form.[7] This model and its results are contained in the first sections of Chapters 2 through 7, which all carry a title involving "the Core Model."

The reader who is interested in the gist of our theoretical argument can follow the gradual building and extension of this core model by reading these sections in sequence. Microeconomic and micropolitical foundations for the behavioral relations in the core model are discussed in the following section of each chapter, generally under the title "Developing the Model." These auxiliary sections also contain various extensions, which relax or modify the assumptions underlying the core model.

Polarization and Inequality In the core model, the main political actors are two completely symmetric groups. This is very convenient for the formal analysis, but of course the symmetry assumption is a gross oversimplification. In reality, phenomena such as polarization, income inequality, and groups of different sizes are parts of economic and political life. One subtheme of the book explores the implications of these phenomena. In particular, they appear in Subsections 2.2.3–2.2.5, 3.2.2, and 4.2. At the risk of oversimplifying, the general result we find is that greater polarization and more income inequality tend to diminish the motives for investments in the state, but boost the motives for investing in political violence.

The Predatory State Many developing countries are governed by small and, often, strongly entrenched elites. This causes tensions not only among groups, but also within groups, between elites and rank-and-file members. Such tensions constitute an important theme that spans a great deal of recent research on development, in economics as well as in political science. We pick this up in some of our extensions of the core model, notably in Sections 3.2.4, 4.2.4, 5.4, and 7.2.6. Our general findings on this theme underscore the possibility of a

7. For a seminal macropolitical analysis of government applied to stabilization policy, see Lindbeck (1976).

predatory state that raises higher hurdles for investments in the state, creates stronger motives for investing in violence, and poses additional obstacles for welfare-enhancing political reform.

Resource and Aid Dependence Resource dependence and aid dependence are important issues in the research community as well as the development community. In particular, the notion of the "resource curse" appears in one literature to label the hypothesis that an abundance of natural resources (or aid) may actually serve to reduce income. But it also appears in another, separate, literature to label the hypothesis that resource abundance may promote violence. Resource dependence appears throughout the book, most notably in the core model as it is developed in Chapters 2 through 5, culminating in our finding—described in Section 5.2—that both hypotheses may come out of a single comprehensive model. Chapters 4 and 6 focus on the effects of development assistance, theoretically as well as empirically.

Private Accumulation To emphasize the most novel parts of the analysis, our modeling generally zooms in on the accumulation decisions by incumbent governments and abstracts from private accumulation of physical capital, human capital, and productive knowledge. This simplification is not only unrealistic, but misses the possibility of making contact with traditional growth theory. For these reasons, we devote some microfounded extensions to reintroducing private capital accumulation. In particular, Section 3.2.3 considers the interactions between individual private investment and government investment in state capacity and Section 5.2 considers the interactions between individual private investment and the risk of conflict, given the collective investments in violence. In both cases, private investments tend to magnify the effects predicted by our simpler models, effectively adding a multiplier to the effects on aggregate outcomes of interest.

Data Although we are trying to break new theoretical ground in much of the book, we are also trying to stay closely connected to the data. Thus, the introduction to each chapter includes some salient facts, typically displayed as correlations or patterns in the raw data. Moreover, almost all the chapters end by revisiting the data. Typically, each visit to the data takes the form of studying some partial correlations in light of the predictions from the theory developed in the chapter. But in Chapter 4, we take a longer tour into empirical territory, deriving a more credible econometric strategy from our theory and applying it to more serious empirical testing than in other chapters.

Notes on the Literature Throughout our journey, we try to acknowledge the adventures of traveling companions, whose work is either prior or parallel to our own. In some cases, we discuss this in situ at the appropriate point in the text. But we try to not break the flow with literature reviews. Instead, we collect a broader summary of themes and contributions in a short section at the end of each chapter, called "Notes on the Literature."

1.10 *Final Remarks*

Chapter 8 summarizes the main things we will have learned. Taking stock of the findings is a bit premature at this early stage, however. Let us very briefly preview some general answers, in the abstract, to the three questions about development clusters that we posed at the beginning of this chapter.

1. What forces shape the building of different state capacities and why do these capacities vary together? According to this book, the answer lies in some common determinants and a crucial complementarity between investments in different parts of the state. The book also identifies conditions, investment traps, under which no motives for state building exist.
2. What factors drive political violence in its different forms? Our answer is that, to a significant extent, these factors are largely the same as those factors, including income, that help determine state capacity.
3. What explains the clustering of state institutions, violence, and income? The book says that the answer lies partly in common positive determinants or lack thereof and partly in the two-way feedbacks between income and state capacity and between income and violence.

In addition to an abstract theoretical discussion of the main messages of the book, Chapter 8 also takes stock of our findings in a concrete empirical way. Based on the main outcome variables emphasized in our theory, we define and compute our own Pillars of Prosperity index for some 150 countries. Moreover, using empirical counterparts to the theoretical determinants of state capacity and political violence, we discuss how well one can predict the outcomes on this index by a small set of socioeconomic and political variables. Comparing actual and predicted outcomes for individual countries yields an interesting perspective on development clusters, but also suggests several shortcomings in our theoretical framework.

Whatever the value of its findings, our book only takes a few steps toward a fuller understanding of the observed clustering among income, institutions, and violence. The final chapter ends by listing a number of issues where more research might follow.

1.11 *Notes on the Literature*

Influential contemporary commentaries on government policy (national and international) in developing countries include Collier (2007), Easterly (2006), Sachs (2005), and Stern, Dethier, and Rogers (2005). The different perspectives offered in these works serve as useful background reading to the debates reflected in this book. Collier and Gunning (1999) and Sachs et al. (2004) discuss the origins of Africa's poor economic performance.

A long-standing debate concerns the proper role of the state in economic development. Chenery (1975) nicely summarizes the discussions that shaped development policy in the postwar period, identifying a set of important structural features of developing economies where state intervention could, in principle, generate better economic performance. Bauer (1972) was a fervent critic of this view and its implications for aid.

Myrdal (1968) saw the problem of weak institutions early on; the "soft state"—facing a multidimensional problem with lacking legislation, weak enforcement, collusion, and corruption—is indeed a recurring theme in his *Asian Drama*. Bates (1981) offers a perceptive account of how government failure lies at the heart of many policy problems in Africa. Nowadays, it is commonplace to put politics at the heart of our understanding of development, seeing economic and political development proceeding in step. Recent works on development that put political economics at center stage include Acemoglu and Robinson (2005), Bueno de Mesquita, Morrow, Siverson, and Smith (2003), and North, Weingast, and Wallis (2009). Bockstette, Areendam, and Putterman (2002), Chanda and Putterman (2004), and Putterman (2008), which link state antiquity to contemporary economic performance with an emphasis on institutional factors, are also related works. A strong statement about the importance of institutions for development can be found in Rodrik, Subramanian, and Trebbi (2004).

State failure has become a central concept in discussions about development. Collier (2008) focuses on the consequences of trying to introduce democracy in poor countries. Bates (2008, 2009) discusses the problems encountered in building effective states in Africa. As discussed at the beginning of the chapter, an extensive policy literature deals with the problems of weak and failing states [see ERD (2009), OECD (2010a), Rice and Patrick (2008), and USAID (2005)].

The economic-history literature has produced numerous explanations for development patterns. A major concern has been to explain the rise in incomes in Western Europe from the beginning of the nineteenth century. A series of largely complementary explanations has emerged, which stresses the importance of different factors. Thus, North and Thomas (1973) offer an explanation based on institutions, Landes (1998) and Clark (2008) give greater weight to cultural change, whereas Mokyr (1990) emphasizes the role of technology. Rosenberg and Birdzell (1986) stress flexibility of market organization, as well as the interplay between economics and politics.

Strayer (1970) is an important contribution to our understanding of the central role played by fiscal and judicial institutions in the development of European states in medieval times. Dincecco (2011) looks at weak and strong states in historical perspective, and Ma (2010) provides an account of state development in China based on incentives to build state capacities. Mann (1986, 1993) is an influential account of sources of power and the development of the state from a sociological perspective. Gellner (1983) is a classic reference emphasizing the importance of nationalism in preceding state development. As noted in the text, Posen (1993) argues that European states strategically developed common nationalistic interests so as to facilitate warfare against rival states.

Fiscal capacity and state building more generally and their relation to war have constituted a major theme in the literature on economic and political history, such as in the work of Brewer (1989), Hintze (1906), and Tilly (1985). However, weak states were late to enter the academic economics literature. Acemoglu (2005) develops a formal model, where rulers in weak states have short time horizons and spend too little on productive public goods, which diminishes their ability to raise future taxes, whereas rulers in strong states have blunt accumulation incentives owing to their security of tenure. Besley and Persson (2009b, 2010a) study fiscal and legal capacity building as a joint investment problem and derive a general complementarity result. Acemoglu, Ticchi, and Vindigni (2011) study the role of bureaucracies in creating (in)effective states.

CHAPTER 2

Fiscal Capacity

The fiscal history of a people is above all an essential part of its general history. An enormous influence on the fate of nations emanates from the economic bleeding which the needs of the state necessitates, and from the use to which the results are put.

Joseph Schumpeter, *The Crisis of the Tax State,* 1918

Following on from the general overview in Chapter 1, we now begin our presentation of an intellectual framework for understanding state capacity and the forces that shape its creation and maintenance. In this chapter, we introduce some of our principal ideas in a formal model, but with an exclusive focus on building fiscal capacity. The crucial component in this approach is the idea that fiscal capacity constitutes a capital investment, which makes it feasible to raise more taxes in the future.

A government can choose levels of redistributive transfers and the provision of public goods. The necessary revenue comes from an income tax, but the level of taxation is constrained by fiscal capacity. In our core model, which has only two time periods, the incumbent government in period 1 makes a decision as to whether to increase fiscal capacity for period 2. Politics plays an important role in the theory through two channels. Political institutions are a key element in that they affect the use of tax revenue, in particular how much of the available revenues an incumbent government can allocate to its own group of supporters. Politics also enters via the process of political turnover. The model delivers a prediction about investments in fiscal capacity as a function of political institutions and the likelihood that the government will be replaced. Economic structure also features in the model and helps to determine fiscal-capacity investments via the level of income and the government's access to nontax revenue, such as resource rents or foreign aid.

Our core model is very streamlined to make a number of points as clearly and concisely as possible. The role of fiscal capacity is specified as a reduced form, but later on in the chapter we show how our simple formulation can be given microeconomic foundations. In a sequence of extensions, we relax a number of the simplifying assumptions in the core model and show the consequences for the main results.

Before going on to model the building of fiscal capacity formally, we present some basic facts and a very brief sketch of the existing literature.

Some Basic Facts The growth of the fiscal state is an incontrovertible fact of the nineteenth and twentieth centuries, at least in the now developed countries. To make this growth possible, revenues had to be raised, which meant introducing new taxes and extending the outreach of those already in place.

Figure 2.1 gives a very partial picture of how fiscal capacity has evolved *over time*. It plots the distribution of two kinds of upgrading of tax systems for a sample of 75 countries since 1800.[1] Black lines demarcate the introduction of the income tax and gray lines whether or not a country has a VAT. Although the sample is limited, it illustrates clearly how such investments in tax collection have evolved over time. Income taxes began appearing in the mid-nineteenth century and are fully prevalent in the sample in the interwar period. VAT was lagging further behind, with adoption still incomplete by the end of the twentieth century. The model developed in this chapter is designed to explain the forces that shape such changes in the tax system. One feature of the changes illustrated in Figure 2.1 is that they required investments in administrative structures that support tax collection.[2]

The narrow sample selection in Figure 2.1, however, ignores many of the poorer countries in the world. We would also like the model in this chapter to analyze how fiscal capacity varies *over countries*. From Figure 1.3 in the first chapter, we already know that richer countries tend to raise more tax revenue as a share of national income than poorer countries. Other measures of fiscal capacity tell the same story. It is interesting to look at the relative uses of different types of taxes, differentiated by the investments required for them to be collected. Arguably, trade taxes and income taxes are two polar opposite cases. To collect trade taxes requires being able to observe trade flows at major

1. The sample is limited by the set of countries for which we have confirmed data on when the income tax was introduced.

2. Aidt and Jensen (2009a) study the factors, such as spending pressures and extensions of the franchise, behind the introduction of the income tax in panel data for 17 countries from 1815 to 1939.

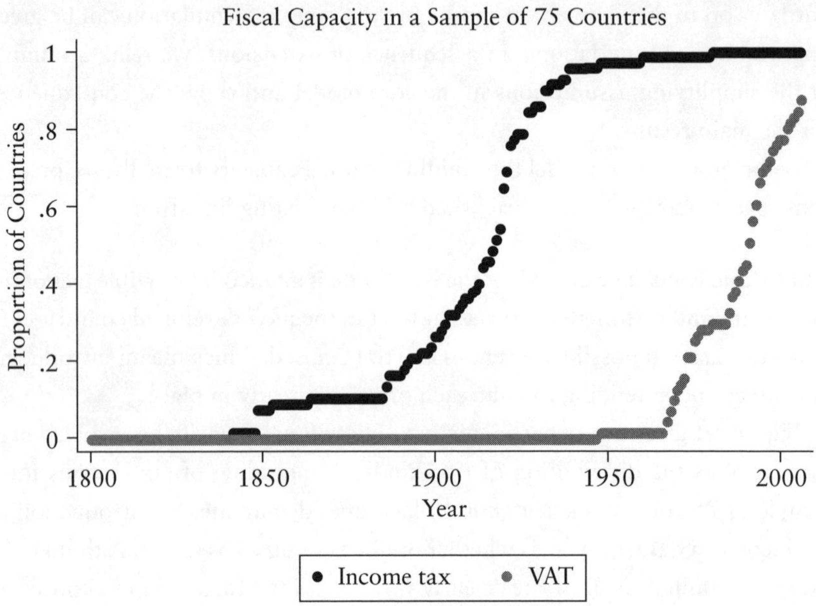

Figure 2.1 The historical evolution of fiscal capacity.

shipping ports. Although such tax allocations may encourage smuggling, it is a much easier proposition than collecting income taxes. The latter requires major investments in enforcement and compliance structures throughout the entire economy.

We can thus obtain an interesting indication of fiscal capacity by holding total tax revenue constant, and asking how large a share of it is collected from trade taxes and income taxes, respectively. These shares are plotted against each other in Figure 2.2.[3] Both the income-tax and trade-tax shares in total tax revenue are measured as late as possible (both in 1999), based on data from the IMF (the omitted categories are consumption taxes, business taxes, and capital taxes). The income-tax share is shown on the vertical axis and the trade-tax share on the horizontal axis. We observe a clear negative correlation: countries with a higher reliance on income taxes tend to have less reliance on trade taxes. The figure also shows a striking pattern by income. High-income countries

3. Other taxes not included in either trade or income taxes include indirect taxes such as VAT, property and corporate taxes.

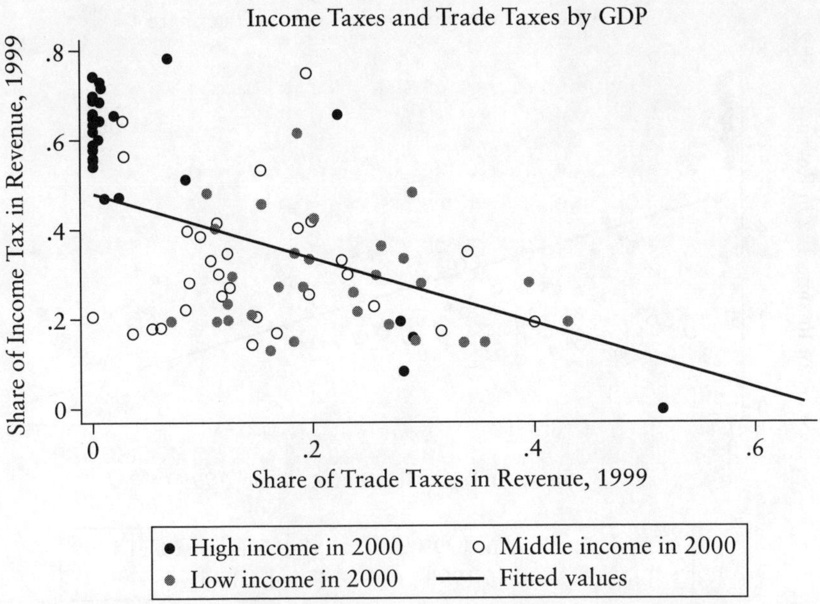

Figure 2.2 Income taxes and trade taxes conditional on income.

tend to depend more on income taxes, whereas middle- and, in particular, low-income countries depend more on trade taxes.

Figure 2.3 also demonstrates the relationship between income taxes and trade taxes at the end of the 1990s. But now the data are broken down by the total tax take in GDP. We separate the observations into three groups: countries that raise more than 25% of taxes in GDP, countries that raise 15–25% of taxes in GDP, and countries that raise less than 15%. The countries in the high-tax group again look markedly different, raising much more of their tax revenues in the form of income taxes.

Existing Research on the Building of Fiscal Capacity Economists have not devoted a great deal of attention to fiscal capacity. As noted in Chapter 1, most normative and positive theories of taxation hardly ever touch upon the lack of administrative infrastructure as an important constraint on the taxes that governments can raise.

Public-finance economists have certainly paid some attention to the compliance and enforcement structures that facilitate efficient tax collection and deter tax avoidance [see, e.g., Slemrod and Yitzhaki (2002) for an overview]. However, this body of research has a normative orientation and does not study the

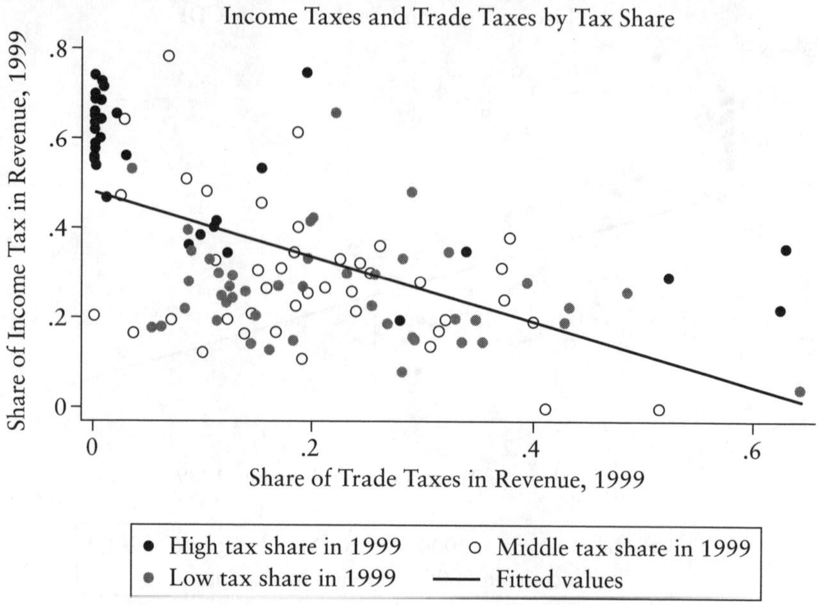

Figure 2.3 Income taxes and trade taxes conditional on total tax take.

building of such structures as a purposive, forward-looking activity by politically motivated incumbents. In this sense, our approach is related to the seminal theoretical and empirical work by Cukierman, Edwards, and Tabellini (1992) on how the use of seigniorage depends on the efficiency of the tax system and how the strategic choice of the latter depends on factors such as political stability and polarization.

The greater reliance on trade taxes (and seigniorage) relative to income taxes in developing countries has, of course, been noted and discussed by many authors [see Burgess and Stern (1993), Hinrichs (1966), and Tanzi (1992) for early contributions]. More recently, Gordon and Li (2009) describe the tilted tax structures as a puzzle that has to be understood. Their proposed explanation relies on an interplay between informality and undeveloped financial systems, but these features are basically taken as given and not seen as equilibrium outcomes of a dynamic process.

In Chapter 1, we noted the extensive work by political and economic historians on the state's fiscal capacity, the crucial role of wars in stimulating the demand for such capacity, and the importance of this aspect of state building for the successful development of nation states. This research has yielded many interesting historical case studies such as Brewer (1989). But there also attempts at broader generalizations, as in the work by Schumpeter, quoted at the beginning of this chapter, as well as Levi (1988) and Tilly (1985). Tilly, in particular, aims at explaining European exceptionalism. His work appears to have been greatly inspired by the encyclopedic scholarship of the German historian Otto Hintze (1906). Some authors, such as Centeno (1997), have claimed that Latin America may be an exception to the Tilly hypothesis that war was a major driving force in the building of fiscal capacity.

Development scholars such as Migdal (1988) have emphasized the problem of weak states in developing countries. Such states often lack the capacity to raise revenue and to govern effectively. Others, such as Herbst (1990, 2000), have ventured the hypothesis that some countries in Africa might have been able to strengthen their weak states if external wars on the continent had been more frequent.

Plan of the Chapter In the next section, we lay out our bare-bones core model of fiscal-capacity building. Having specified the model, we first provide a normative benchmark, based on the policies and investments a social planner would undertake. We then show that, depending on the constellation of parameters, three types of states can emerge—a common-interest state, a redistributive state, or a weak state.

In Section 2.2, we begin by providing some microeconomic foundations for the reduced-form of fiscal capacity used in the basic model. We also show how the basic model can be developed and extended in several different directions to increase the realism of our approach. Thus, we introduce more general models of public goods, polarization between groups, income inequality, group-size differences, tax distortions, multiple tax bases, and an infinite number of time periods—features that are all absent in the basic model of Section 2.1.

Section 2.3 discusses some of the empirical implications of our theory and shows some partial correlations in the data. Section 2.4 concludes the chapter and, as usual, the very last section has some notes on related literature.

2.1 *The Core Model*

We now introduce a workhorse model that we keep extending throughout the book. Several of the economic and political factors that are represented as parameters in this first version of the model are thus turned into endogenous variables as we proceed. However, even in this chapter, the model is dynamic. In fact, its main novel feature is that it gives governments the opportunity to invest so as to improve the workings of the state, in addition to setting standard policy instruments.

2.1.1 Basic Structure

There are two time periods $s = 1, 2$ with two groups of individuals, A and B, each of which comprises half the population. No private savings or government debt enter the model. Total population size is normalized to 1. Every individual has income ω. Income is an exogenous parameter throughout this chapter, but in Chapter 3 it becomes an endogenous variable with appropriate microeconomic foundations.

At the beginning of period 1, one group holds power and we refer to it as the incumbent group, which we denote by $I_1 \in \{A, B\}$. The other group is the opposition and we denote it by $O_1 \in \{A, B\}$. With exogenous probability γ, there is a peaceful transition of power between periods 1 and 2. Thus, parameter γ is a measure of political instability. Such instability is a parameter throughout this chapter and the next. However, in Chapter 4 it is made endogenous by developing a model of conflict. Moreover, some micropolitical foundations for the peaceful transition rate are discussed in Chapter 7.

Utility functions are (quasi-) linear:

$$u_s^J = c_s^J + \alpha_s V(g_s), \tag{2.1}$$

where the first term on the right, c_s^J, denotes private consumption of a typical group-J member in period s and g_s is a public good. Private consumption in period s depends on the net of tax income and transfers received. It is given by

$$c_s^J = (1 - t_s)\, \omega + r_s^J ,$$

where t_s is the income-tax rate and r_s^J is a transfer awarded to group J in period s.

Public Goods In the second term of u_s^J, $V(g_s)$ is the utility from consumption of public goods and α_s (a shifter in) the value of such goods. The function $V(\cdot)$ is smooth, increasing, and concave. In our core interpretation, we have in mind an interpretation of g_s as an archetypal public good. A classic example that we refer to throughout the book is "defense," in which case α_s can be thought of as "external conflict (or not)." In practice, many transfer programs observed in modern welfare states are reasonably well proxied by g since benefits are universal, typically a form of insurance against sickness or unemployment and benefits accrue more or less universally over the life cycle.

We assume that the value of public goods is stochastic: α_s has a two-point distribution $\alpha_s \in \{\alpha_L, \alpha_H\}$, where $\alpha_H > 2 > \alpha_L > 1$, and $\text{Prob}[\alpha_s = \alpha_H] = \phi$. The shocks to α are assumed to be identically and independently distributed over time with the realization of α_s known when policy is set in period s. The particular values of α are chosen so as to make public goods more or less valuable relative to transfers in a way that depends on the structure of political institutions (see more further on). The parameter ϕ plays an important role in the analysis as a measure of the demand for public goods. In the defense example, we can think of ϕ as "the threat of external conflict."

Two convenient special cases are used to get specific insights: (a) a linear case, where $V(g_s) = g_s$, and (b) a nonstochastic case, where $V(\cdot)$ is smooth, increasing, and concave, satisfying the Inada condition, and $\phi = 1$ with $\alpha_H = \alpha$. Special case (a) is the mainstay of the analysis, although some important economic effects are best illustrated in case (b).

Fiscal Capacity The income tax is constrained by existing fiscal capacity, i.e., $t_s \leq \tau_s$, which we treat like a capital stock. As discussed further in Section 2.2.1, this can be given microfoundations by supposing that an individual can earn a share of her income $(1 - \tau_s)$ in the informal sector. The initial stock τ_1 is given, but it can be augmented to achieve fiscal capacity τ_2 by investing $\tau_2 - \tau_1(1 - \delta)$ at $s = 1$, where $\delta \in [0, 1]$ is the depreciation rate. For the time being, it is best to think about such investments as building the administrative institutions necessary for efficient implementation of an income tax.

A limiting feature of this simple model is that (labor) income is the only tax base. In practice, one of the greatest challenges for tax systems around the world is to find ways of taxing capital rather than labor income. Many of the attempts to limit tax avoidance and tax evasion are designed precisely to limit arbitrage between tax bases.

We posit a convex cost, $\mathcal{F}(\tau_2 - \tau_1(1 - \delta))$, for investing in fiscal capacity, where $\mathcal{F}_\tau(0) = 0$, i.e., the marginal cost is negligible when there is no investment.[4] A fixed-cost component could be added without affecting the essence of the main results. As we shall see, a possible outcome is a weak state in which

4. Here, and elsewhere, subscripts on functions denote partial derivatives.

the incumbent invests nothing. Adding a fixed cost would only serve to increase the prevalence of such states. Note also that the income level ω does not affect the cost of investing; we discuss this possibility later in Section 2.1.3.

For now, we assume that investments in fiscal-capacity building are irreversible, i.e., such investments cannot be negative, beyond depreciation. One of the extensions in Section 2.2 allows for negative investments, where fiscal capacity can be "eaten" or purposefully destroyed between periods.

Government Budget Recalling that each group is half the population, we give the government budget constraint at date s is given by

$$R + t_s \omega = g_s + m_s + \frac{r_s^I + r_s^O}{2},$$

where

$$m_s = \begin{cases} \mathcal{F}(\tau_2 - (1-\delta)\tau_1) & \text{if } s = 1 \\ 0 & \text{if } s = 2 \end{cases}$$

represents the investment costs in period 1 and R is an additional time-independent revenue source accruing only to the government. We interpret R as natural resource rents or foreign (cash) aid. Like α, we allow R to be stochastic.[5] However, it is assumed to be realized before any policy decisions are made and is then held fixed throughout the two time periods that we study.

Political Institutions Political institutions constrain the incumbent's allocation of transfers. For now, we assume no agency problem within the incumbent group; whoever holds power on behalf of the group cares about the average welfare of the whole group. Such agency problems are introduced in the next chapter, where we introduce an elite within the ruling group that governs in its own interests. The constraint on transfers is modeled as a requirement that the incumbent group must give a fixed share σ to the opposition for any unit of transfers awarded to its own group. It is convenient to work with the parameter $\theta = \frac{\sigma}{1+\sigma} \in [0, \frac{1}{2}]$ to represent more "cohesive" institutions; the closer θ is to its maximum value of 1/2, the more cohesive the political institutions.

5. The stochastic structure for R is not always important for our argument, and R could actually be treated as parametric in many cases. However, since we do make use of it in interpreting the data, we conduct the analysis throughout with the possibility of a random draw of R by nature as part of the timing that we outline below.

This is an extremely simple, tractable but reduced-form way of looking at politics. We interpret a higher value of θ in one of two broad ways. One real-world counterpart might be minority protection by constitutional checks and balances on the executive as a result of some separation of powers. Furthermore, in practice, we expect democracies to impose greater constraints on the executive than do autocracies. An alternative real-world counterpart might be stronger political representation of the interests of losers in policy decisions through proportional representation elections or parliamentary democracy. The literature on the policy effects of constitutional rules suggests that both of these institutional arrangements tend to induce policymakers to internalize the preferences of a larger share of the population [see, e.g., Aghion, Alesina, and Trebbi (2004), Persson, Roland, and Tabellini (2000), or Persson and Tabellini (2000)].

The parameter θ can also be thought of as representing the extent to which policymakers can commit in the dynamic setting that we explore in what follows. In effect, a high θ allows institutional commitment to a more-or-less equal division of future public resources, whereas with θ close to zero, there is no commitment possible as the winner will take all. Any limited commitment power as embodied in θ will motivate the desire of policymakers to hold on to power in our framework.[6]

As we will see later, θ is one of the key parameters that affect policy decisions, state capacity investments, and investments in violence. We keep it constant and exogenous throughout most of the book. However, in Chapter 7, we discuss different ways of giving micropolitical foundations for this parameter in detail. In that chapter, we also deal with the implications of making θ (or the underlying institutional features) endogenous, which allows us to explore the incentives for political reform.

Timing Events in the core two-period model evolve as follows:

1. We begin with an initial stock of fiscal capacity, τ_1, and an incumbent group, I_1. Nature determines α_1 and R.
2. I_1 chooses a set of period-1 policies $\left\{t_1, g_1, r_1^I, r_1^O\right\}$ and determines (through investment) the period-2 stock of fiscal capacity τ_2.

6. Since we are working in a two-period setting, increasing commitment through repeated play is not an option. But obviously this is an interesting possibility for future extensions of the framework.

3. I_1 remains in power with probability $1 - \gamma$, and nature determines α_2.

4. I_2 chooses period-2 policy $\left\{t_2, g_2, r_2^I, r_2^O\right\}$.

We solve for a subgame perfect equilibrium in policy and fiscal capacity investments. This means solving the model backward, beginning at stage 4.

2.1.2 Politically Optimal Policy

The simple structure of the core model allows us to solve for the optimal policy chosen by an incumbent for any given level of fiscal capacity. The latter, along with the identity of the incumbent group, are the "state variables" of the model. Whoever holds power chooses the policy vector $\{g_s, t_s, r_s^I, r_s^O\}$ to maximize their own within-period payoff,

$$\alpha_s V\left(g_s\right) + \left(1 - t_s\right)\omega + r_s^I,$$

subject to

$$t_s \leq \tau_s, \; r_s^O \geq \sigma r_s^I \tag{2.2}$$

and the government budget constraint. The first constraint in (2.2) is due to limited fiscal capacity, whereas the second is imposed by the structure of political institutions. Optimal policy in each period can be described in terms of its three components: the income-tax rate, transfers, and spending on public goods. We first solve for the optimal t_s. We then solve for r_s^J and plug this into the incumbent's objective, which we maximize to determine g_s.

Equilibrium Taxes and Transfers First, observe that the equilibrium tax rate is set to exhaust fiscal capacity, i.e.,

$$t_s = \tau_s.$$

This is because the gain to the incumbent from a higher tax rate is at least $2\left(1-\theta\right)\omega$ (the gain from larger transfers on the margin) and the loss is ω (the reduction in private income). Thus the result follows since $2\left(1-\theta\right) \geq 1$.

Second, we look at the optimal transfer paid to each group. The incumbent will wish to make her group's transfer as large as possible all else being equal. Using the government budget constraint, we get the following solution:

$$r_s^J = \beta^J\left[R + t_s\omega - g_s - m_s\right] \quad \text{for } J \in \{I, O\}, \tag{2.3}$$

where $\beta^I = 2(1-\theta)$ and $\beta^O = 2\theta$. These transfers are a residual item after netting out the spending on public goods and investments in fiscal capacity, to be determined later. The parameter θ governs the way in which the residual revenues are divided between the groups. If $\theta = 1/2$, transfers are shared equally, whereas a completely unconstrained incumbent, $\theta = 0$, captures all available revenue for her own group.

Equilibrium Public-Goods Provision Third, we look at politically optimal public-good provision by defining the function $\hat{g}(\alpha, x)$ from the equation

$$\alpha V_g\left(\hat{g}(\alpha, x)\right) = x, \tag{2.4}$$

where it is clear that $\hat{g}$ is increasing in α and decreasing in x. The level of public goods provided is then given by

$$G(\alpha, \tau_s) = \begin{cases} R + \tau_s\omega - m_s & \text{if } \alpha V_g\left(R + \tau_s\omega - m_s\right) \geq 2(1-\theta) \\ 0 & \text{if } \alpha V_g(0) < 2(1-\theta) \\ \hat{g}(\alpha, 2(1-\theta)) & \text{otherwise.} \end{cases} \tag{2.5}$$

There are two possible corner solutions. If public goods are extremely valuable so that $\alpha V_g\left(R + \tau_s\omega - m_s\right) \geq 2(1-\theta)$, then all tax revenue not allocated to investing in fiscal capacity is spent on public goods. This is more likely to be the case when the value of public goods, α, is larger and/or θ is closer to 1/2.

We have the opposite corner solution if $\alpha V_g(0) < 2(1-\theta)$, i.e., if public goods are not very valuable. In this case, all spending is devoted to transfers, with the level of spending determined by setting $g_s = 0$ in equation (2.3). This is most likely to happen when α is low (e.g., it is bound to happen if $\alpha = 0$) and/or when θ is close to zero. The latter observation reflects the fact that with weak institutional constraints, transfer spending is highly attractive to the incumbent.

Between these two corner solutions is a possible interior solution determined by (2.4), where the marginal value of public goods is set equal to the marginal cost in terms of foregone transfers, which is given by $2(1-\theta)$.

As mentioned earlier, we frequently make use of the tractable linear case where $V_g = 1$. This permits only two of the three possibilities described in (2.5)—the corner solutions. Thus, we have a so-called "bang-bang" solution with all public spending devoted either to public goods or to transfers. This assumption is certainly not realistic. But it does make the model very easy to analyze, as there is a threshold value of $\alpha = 2(1-\theta)$, which depends on the cohesiveness of institutions, above which all spending is on public goods. For α below this threshold, the incumbent only provides transfers.

Indirect Utilities Substituting these politically optimal policies into the utility function (2.1), we derive the following "indirect payoff" function for group $J \in \{I, O\}$ in period s:

$$W(\alpha_s, \tau_s, m_s, \beta^J) = \alpha_s \mathrm{V}\left(G\left(\alpha_s, \tau_s\right)\right) \\ + (1 - \tau_s)\omega + \beta^J [R + \tau_s \omega - G\left(\alpha_s, \tau_s\right) - m_s]. \quad (2.6)$$

For future reference, it is also useful to define two "value functions":

$$U^I\left(\tau_2\right) = \left[\phi W\left(\alpha_H, \tau_2, 0, \beta^I\right) + (1 - \phi)\, W\left(\alpha_L, \tau_2, 0, \beta^I\right)\right]$$

for the incumbent and

$$U^O\left(\tau_2\right) = \left[\phi W\left(\alpha_H, \tau_2, 0, \beta^O\right) + (1 - \phi)\, W\left(\alpha_L, \tau_2, 0, \beta^O\right)\right]$$

for the opposition group. These depend on τ_2 and the expected value of public goods as represented by ϕ. The model's symmetry implies that the only thing that differentiates the period-2 value is the incumbency status of the group.

Putting all of these pieces together, the expected period-2 utility of group J, as seen from period 1, is

$$W(\alpha_1, \tau_1, m_1, 2\,(1 - \theta)) + [1 - \gamma]\, U^I\left(\tau_2\right) + \gamma U^O\left(\tau_2\right)$$

for the incumbent, and

$$W(\alpha_1, \tau_1, m_1, 2\theta) + \gamma U^I\left(\tau_2\right) + [1 - \gamma]\, U^O\left(\tau_2\right)$$

for the opposition. These sum the period-1 realized payoff with an expected future payoff, which depends on whether or not the incumbent expects to survive in power, an event that occurs with probability $(1 - \gamma)$.

2.1.3 Fiscal-Capacity Investments

We now explore the decision to invest in fiscal capacity. To obtain sharp results, we focus on the case where utility is linear in public goods, i.e., $V(g) = g$. We discuss what happens if this assumption is relaxed in Section 2.2.2.

The optimal fiscal-capacity investment is determined by maximizing

$$W(\alpha_1, \tau_1, \mathcal{F}(\tau_2 - (1-\delta)\tau_1), 2\,(1-\theta)) + [1-\gamma]\,U^I\,(\tau_2) + \gamma U^O\,(\tau_2)\,,$$

by choosing τ_2. This results in an investment "Euler equation," which equates the foregone consumption (in the form of transfers or public goods) from greater investment in fiscal capacity to the future gains of being able to implement a higher income-tax rate.[7] This Euler equation is given by

$$\begin{aligned} -W_m(\alpha_1, \tau_1, m_1, 2(1-\theta))\mathcal{F}_\tau\,(\tau_2 - (1-\delta)\,\tau_1) \\ = (1-\gamma)\,U^I_\tau\,(\tau_2) + \gamma U^O_\tau\,(\tau_2) \\ \text{c.s. } \tau_2 - (1-\delta)\,\tau_1 \geq 0, \end{aligned} \tag{2.7}$$

where c.s. stands for complementary slackness, recognizing the possibility that the investments in fiscal capacity can be zero.

The period-1 cost is dependent on the marginal cost of public funds,

$$\lambda_1 \equiv -W_m(\alpha_1, \tau_1, m_1, 2(1-\theta)) = \max\left\{\alpha_1, 2\,(1-\theta)\right\}.$$

The expression for λ_1 reflects two possibilities in period 1. If $\alpha_1 \geq 2\,(1-\theta)$, then the marginal cost of public funds is the opportunity cost of spending on public goods with value α_1. If instead $\alpha_1 < 2\,(1-\theta)$, the opportunity cost is from foregone transfers. This can be seen by inspecting equation (2.5).

Using the specific model structure, we can simplify the Euler equation (2.7) to

$$\begin{aligned} \omega[E(\lambda_2) - 1] \leq \lambda_1 \mathcal{F}_\tau\,(\tau_2 - (1-\delta)\,\tau_1) \\ c.s.\tau_2 - (1-\delta)\,\tau_1 \geq 0, \end{aligned} \tag{2.8}$$

where

$$E(\lambda_2) = \phi\alpha_H + (1-\phi)\lambda_2^L \tag{2.9}$$

is the *expected* value of period-2 public funds with

$$\lambda_2^L = \begin{cases} \alpha_L & \text{if } \alpha_L \geq 2(1-\theta) \\ 2[(1-\theta)(1-\gamma) + \gamma\theta] & \text{otherwise.} \end{cases} \tag{2.10}$$

7. We use the term Euler equation to draw a parallel with a framework suitable for studying a multiperiod (i.e., more than two-period) model. We develop such a model for fiscal capacity later in Section 2.2.8.

The trade-off involved in the investment decision is transparent in equation (2.8). The right-hand side is the marginal cost weighted by λ_1 representing the marginal value of foregone period-1 tax revenue.

The left-hand side of (2.8) is the "marginal benefit" of fiscal capacity. It has two parts, one positive and one negative. The negative term is represented by $-\omega$ on the left-hand side of (2.8). This is the loss of private earnings because taxation has increased.

The positive term $\omega E(\lambda_2)$ is the future value of public revenues owing to increased fiscal capacity. It depends on how revenues are allocated. Since $\alpha_H > 2 > 2(1-\theta)$, a high realization of the value of public goods always results in spending on public goods. The only question is what happens when $\alpha_2 = \alpha_L$. If public revenues are allocated to public goods even when $\alpha_s = \alpha_L$ then $E(\lambda_2) = \phi\alpha_H + (1-\phi)\alpha_L$. But if they are allocated to transfers, because $\alpha_L < 2(1-\theta)$, then $E(\lambda_2) = \phi\alpha_H + (1-\phi)2[(1-\theta)(1-\gamma)+\gamma\theta]$. The expression $2[(1-\theta)(1-\gamma)+\gamma\theta]$ is the expected value of transfer spending viewed from the perspective of a period-1 incumbent who does not know whether her group will be in office in period 2. With probability $(1-\gamma)$, she survives and earns $2(1-\theta)$ of the available revenue as a transfer, whereas with probability γ, she does not survive and receives only 2θ (<1) of revenues as transfers.

Recalling our assumption that $\mathcal{F}_\tau(0) = 0$, we can see that the logic of comparing the marginal benefit and marginal cost as we have just discussed immediately reveals that a necessary and sufficient condition for a positive level of investment in fiscal capacity is that $E(\lambda_2) - 1 \geq 0$. Essentially, this condition requires that future public funds be valuable enough relative to foregone private consumption. Equation (2.8) makes it plain that this depends on our key parameters: $\{\phi, \alpha_H, \alpha_L, \theta, \gamma\}$. Our next task is to understand how investment decisions depend on these parameters and how this dependence can be interpreted. In Section 2.3, we discuss the empirical implications of the model in a more careful way.

2.1.4 Normative Benchmark: A Pigouvian Planner

Before discussing the positive implications of the model, we study a normative benchmark against which to judge the equilibrium outcome. Specifically, we define optimal policy and fiscal-capacity investment in world where a Pigouvian social planner maximizes expected utility weighting the payoffs of the two groups equally. This Utilitarian criterion seems natural here and mirrors the standard normative approach to policy taken in many public-economics textbooks, such as Atkinson and Stiglitz (1980).[8]

Conveniently, the Utilitarian objective is embedded in our model of politically optimal policy as a special case where $\theta = 1/2$ and $\gamma = 0$. In this case, the model predicts that no transfer spending is optimal, i.e., $r_s^I = r_s^O = 0$ in both periods. With linear utility, a Pigouvian planner would never wish to redistribute resources between the two groups. This allows us to identify precisely the policy failure implicit in politically optimal policy when $\alpha_L < 2(1-\theta)$. In this case, the incumbent spends on transfers when she should optimally spend on public goods. Thus, there is a potential for undersupply of public goods and oversupply of transfers. However, there is no tax distortion in this simple model, as the planner and the incumbent group would both set $t_s = \tau_s$.

The outcome is summarized in the following proposition:

Proposition 2.1: *Suppose that the fiscal-capacity investment is made by a Pigouvian planner with Utilitarian preferences. Then:*

1. *There is positive investment in fiscal capacity.*
2. *Higher ϕ or ω (or higher α_H and α_L) increases investment in fiscal capacity.*

The first part of the proposition follows by observing that $E(\lambda_2) = \phi\alpha_H + (1-\phi)\alpha_L > 1$ since, under our assumptions, a planner spends all taxes on public goods. In words, public spending is sufficiently valuable to justify foregoing a greater loss of private income owing to higher taxation. There is, of course, nothing inevitable about this, as it depends on the quality of public projects that are identified and the ability to adopt equally good projects at any scale without diminishing the marginal value of public goods.

If we had assumed that the value of public goods was $V(g)$ with $V(\cdot)$ increasing and concave, then eventually a planner would not wish to increase fiscal capacity beyond the point where the marginal value of increased public spending minus the loss of private incomes is zero. The efficiency with which public projects can be delivered is also a potential issue in a more general model.

8. In the core model, adding a preference for equality in the planner's payoff would not affect the results.

Thus the normative benchmark that we have set up here is for illustrative purposes only. However, it serves well to fix ideas when we explore how politically optimal investment decisions may diverge from those chosen by a planner. Certainly, we believe that large gains from investing in fiscal capacity to achieve collective benefits is a plausible idea for many of the poorer countries in the world where the state fails to deliver basic public health benefits such as sanitation and clean water. The recent literature on randomized-controlled trials in development economics has produced many examples of high-return projects, such as deworming and vaccination programs [see, e.g., Duflo, Glennerster and Kremer (2007) for an overview], which could be increased in scale. These programs may not be pursued owing to lack of available public funding, a problem exacerbated by low fiscal capacity. The failure of many countries to achieve decent levels of personal security through establishing law and order is another example where there is some potential for welfare-enhancing public provision through greater taxation.

The comparative statics in part 2 of Proposition 2.1 are discussed in the next section.

2.1.5 Three Types of States

In this subsection, we discuss for the first time a theoretical implication of our model that resurfaces frequently throughout this book. We show that the model predicts that one of three types of states can emerge as an equilibrium. Under each of these types, we also discuss the relevant comparative statics with respect to key parameters. Which type of state emerges depends primarily on two critical conditions:

Cohesiveness: $\alpha_L \geq 2\,(1-\theta)\,.$

This requires that θ be close enough to 1/2, i.e., political institutions are sufficiently consensual with enough checks and balances or minority representation.

Stability: $\phi\alpha_H + (1-\phi)\,2\,[(1-\gamma)\,(1-\theta) + \gamma\theta] \geq 1.$

This will be relevant only when the cohesiveness condition fails. Whether it holds depends on the equilibrium level of political turnover as represented by γ. It is more likely to hold if γ is low, i.e., when political turnover is low.

Figure 2.4 illustrates the conditions under which each of these conditions holds in terms of two key parameters: θ and γ. The figure is drawn for the special

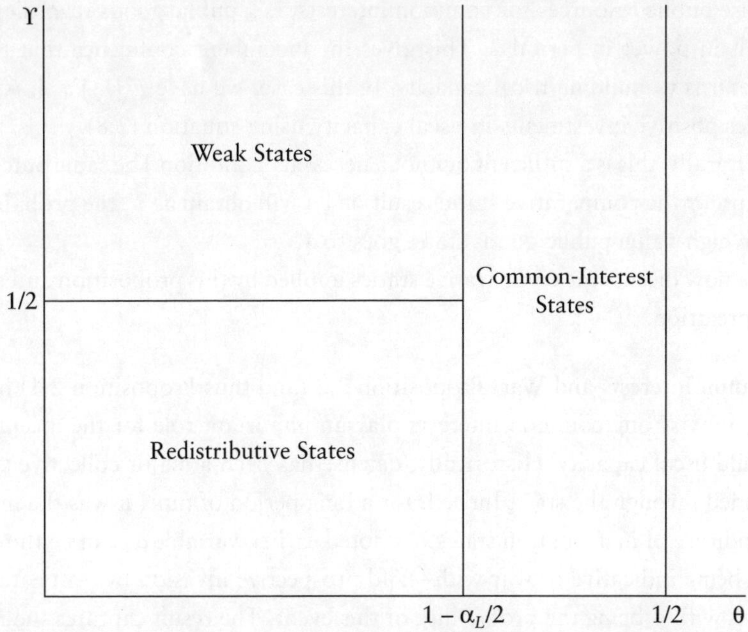

Figure 2.4 Parameters and different types of states (when $\phi = 0$).

case when $\phi = 0$. When ϕ becomes positive, the horizontal line describing the stability condition shifts up and acquires positive slope, whereas the vertical line describing the cohesiveness condition is unaffected.[9] We now show how the equilibrium investment in fiscal capacity depends on these two conditions.

A Common-Interest State We begin with the case where the cohesiveness condition holds. In this case, we have the following result:

Proposition 2.2: *If Cohesiveness holds, then the outcome is exactly as in Proposition 2.1.*

For this result to hold, we require that θ be close enough to 1/2 so that marginal public revenues in period 2 are allocated to public goods whether α_s is high or low. In this case, the incumbent in period 1 is reassured that the state

9. In the general case, the parameter combinations for which the stability condition is satisfied with equality are given by the following curve:

$$\gamma(\theta) = \frac{1 - \left(\frac{1-\phi\alpha_H}{2(1-\phi)}\right) - \theta}{1 - 2\theta}.$$

will use public resources for common interests, i.e., public goods regardless of who is in power in period 2. This gives the incumbent confidence that there are returns to building fiscal capacity. In this case, we have $E(\lambda_s) > 1$, which implies positive investments in fiscal capacity using equation (2.8).

Naturally, this is a sufficient but not a necessary condition The same outcome (except for the comparative static result on ϕ) will obtain as ϕ, the probability of the high-value public goods state, goes to 1.

We now discuss the comparative statics implied by this proposition and their interpretation.

Common Interests and War Proposition 2.2 (and thus Proposition 2.1) highlights how strong common interests play an important role for the incentives to build fiscal capacity. Historically, defense has been a major collective good provided through the state. Indeed, for a long period of time, it was the major expenditure of many nation states. As noted earlier, variable α_s can be thought of as being indicative of war with—and prospective invasion by—an external power, with ϕ being the probability of this event. The result captures the need for spending to deter such conflict and the greater likelihood that a common-interest state (or a social planner) would invest in response to war risk.[10]

As discussed earlier, the desire to build military power has frequently been cited as a key element behind the rise of the fiscal state. The model makes plain how this can be captured by ϕ. The comparative statics in the second part of Proposition 2.1 thus capture the classic war-making incentive for building state capacity discussed by Hintze (1906), Tilly (1985, 1990), and others. Dincecco and Prado (2010) use premodern war causalities to explain fiscal capacity today (measured as direct taxes as a share of total taxes), and then go on to relate GDP per capita to fiscal capacity.

This result has relevance for those seeking high-return public projects in the developing world. If public interventions can be found through randomized-controlled trials and scaled-up to achieve large aggregate returns, we expect this to assist in the creation of common-interest states. Arguably, finding high-return public projects has been the process through which Western welfare states have become the engine of state development during times of peace. Creating effective public health-care systems seems like an especially important

10. Naturally, if Pigouvian planners actually existed and were truly benevolent, they would presumably get together in godlike fashion to resolve all international disputes. But our planner in the previous section has a more limited domain, supporting the national interest of a country faced by an external threat.

example. Such systems persist essentially because the returns are perceived by citizens as common-interest spending.

Income The second comparative static result in Proposition 2.1 says that investing in fiscal capacity becomes more attractive in a common-interest state (or for the planner) when wages or incomes, ω, are higher. This follows naturally from the fact that higher incomes expand the tax base. Therefore, it is consistent with the observation in Chapter 1 that higher income per capita is associated with a larger tax take in GDP.

However, there are reasons to doubt that our simple core model offers a compelling justification for this correlation. First, income is exogenous and many things that the state does, including its investment in state capacity, can have positive or negative effects on income levels. Therefore, it is not particularly reasonable to treat ω as exogenous. We explore these issues in detail in the next chapter.

Second, the costs of investing in our formulation are not affected by ω in any way, but it is plausible to think that this may not be the case. For example, if labor were the only factor of production and $\mathcal{F}(\cdot)$ expressed investment costs in terms of labor requirements, the cost would plausibly be $\omega\mathcal{F}\left(\tau_2 - (1-\delta)\,\tau_1\right)$. But then, ω would appear multiplicatively on both sides of the Euler equation (2.8), and increases in income would have no effect on fiscal-capacity investments because costs and benefits would be affected in equal proportion.

More generally, the cost of investing in state capacity might depend on the factor mix, and the nature of technological progress might affect investment costs and private incomes. This is reminiscent of debates about unbalanced growth, which Baumol (1967) took as a starting point for his famous cost disease. If public-sector activities, as Baumol argued, benefit less from labor-saving technological change, then the costs of running the public sector would tend to rise over time. This would include both the cost of providing g and the cost of investing in τ. Thus, a higher ω might lead to a disincentive to provide g and to invest in τ. But this disincentive would have to be weighed against the higher benefits through higher incomes captured by Proposition 2.1. Clearly, a more thorough discussion of these issues requires a multiperiod model, where the investment technology is modeled in more detail.

Resource Dependence Finally, the result also helps us to think about how the *share* of natural resources in GDP is likely to correlate with fiscal-capacity investments. To see this, observe that the GDP share of natural resources, or aid, $R/(R+\omega)$, is decreasing in ω. It follows that countries with higher R, as we hold total income $(R+\omega)$ constant, should have lower levels of investment in fiscal capacity. If we interpret R as natural resource rents, then their indirect effect given the level of ω rests on it being relatively less expensive to enforce compliance with taxing natural resources than taxing market incomes. This is a plausible assumption for most prominent natural resource flows. The prediction thus provides one possible reason why some resource-rich countries in Africa and Central Asia have underdeveloped tax systems. In Section 1.2.2 we show that this result holds even more strongly when there is curvature in the value of public goods. Jensen (2010) presents econometric evidence consistent with this notion, using country-specific price indexes constructed for natural gas and oil and weighted by respective shares in total national energy production. He finds (using panel data) that a 1% increase in the share of natural resource rents in total government income is associated with a 1.4% decrease in the fiscal capacity of a country.

A Redistributive State In a redistributive state, the Cohesiveness condition fails while the Stability condition is satisfied. The latter implies that fiscal-capacity investment is positive. We now have the following proposition:

Proposition 2.3: *If Cohesiveness fails and Stability holds, the state is redistributive with public revenues used to finance transfers when $\alpha_s = \alpha_L$. Then:*

1. *There is investment in fiscal capacity.*
2. *An increase in ϕ or ω raises investments.*
3. *A lower value of γ unambiguously raises investments, whereas an increase in θ raises (cuts) investments if γ is above (below)* 1/2.

In this case, the failure of the cohesiveness condition implies that a public-goods value of α_L causes the government to spend on transfers. The decision to invest in fiscal capacity is thus partly motivated by the prospect of future transfers. But to earn rewards from this prospect requires that the probability of retaining office be sufficiently high. Therefore, the model predicts that the incentive to invest in fiscal capacity is at its strongest when $\gamma \to 0$ and $\theta \to 0$. Thus, conditional on institutions being noncohesive, political stability may foster investment incentives; the ruling group is a classic residual claimant on the state and has a long time horizon. Such incentives could even be sustained as $\phi \to 0$, i.e., without any common-interest motive for investing in fiscal capacity.

With enough stability, an incumbent may, in fact, invest more than a Pigouvian social planner (with the same α_L). This is reminiscent of the kind of excessively large state that has been discussed extensively in the public-choice literature, as in Buchanan (1967) and Buchanan and Tullock (1962). However, the mechanism here through fiscal-capacity building is somewhat different. Having a low θ is akin to the kind of political failures discussed by Buchanan (1967), as policies do not satisfy Wicksellian unanimity when $\alpha_s = \alpha_L$.[11]

The comparative statics results on the importance of common interests and income (ϕ and ω) corroborate those in a common-interest state. However, the third part of Proposition 2.3 reveals some state-dependent comparative statics.

Political Stability Conditional on institutions being noncohesive, political stability, as represented by a lower γ, fosters investment incentives by lengthening the horizon of rulers.[12]

A good historical case study for how political stability can shape investment in state capacity in a nondemocratic political system comes from England after the Glorious Revolution in 1688, this led to the political dominance of the Whigs in Parliament between 1715 and 1759 [see Stasavage (2007, Table 1)].[13] Mathias and O'Brien (1976) calculate that taxes as a share of GDP rose from 16 to 20% of GDP over this period. Moreover, the administrative institutions put in place during the same period meant that, after 1713, excises and indirect taxes levied on domestically produced goods and services accounted for more than three quarters of the tax revenue (O'Brien, 2005). The considerable investment in state capacity by this dominant elite culminated in the introduction of an income tax, underpinned the fiscal superiority of the British over the French during the Napoleonic wars, and assisted Britain in credibly raising the public debt to fight those wars. In the years from 1803 to 1812, the British government had accumulated sufficient fiscal capacity to raise taxes equal to a remarkable 36% of GDP (Mathias and O'Brien, 1976).

11. The criterion proposed by Wicksell and developed by Buchanan is that policies should be unanimously preferred to a status quo of no spending. This automatically rules out any spending on transfers in our setting.

12. This is similar to an argument made in Dunning (2010) in which a low probability of political survival causes an incumbent not to invest in extracting natural resource rents.

13. Of course, this argument assumes that the Whigs anticipated their political dominance over this period when building fiscal institutions.

Political Institutions The other state-dependent comparative-static result concerns the cohesiveness of political institutions, as represented by the parameter θ. Here, the result is ambiguous and depends on the degree of political stability. When the incumbent can be fairly sure of surviving, i.e., γ is low (below 1/2), more cohesive institutions reduce the incentive to invest. Since investments are driven by the desire to redistribute, a higher θ—which means sharing more of transfers with the opposition group—reduces the motive for investing in fiscal capacity. In the opposite case of political instability, when the opposition is more likely than not to take over (γ above 1/2), a higher value of θ works as insurance against this possibility, and the incumbent becomes more willing to invest in fiscal capacity.

Local and Global Comparative Statics These state-specific comparative statics illustrate two aspects of the theory. The result for γ generates a specific prediction, namely that political stability should only matter for investments when political institutions are insufficiently cohesive to create a common-interest state. Empirically, this implies that we should see an interaction effect between proxies for θ and γ in the data, something we return to in Section 2.3.

The result for θ illustrates another aspect of the model's predictions. Some of the model parameters affect investments in more ways than one. On the one hand, the value of θ determines which type of state prevails: a high enough value of θ is sufficient to create a common-interest state, which indirectly affects fiscal-capacity investment. We refer to these kinds of effects as global comparative statics, as they determine the type of state. Local comparative statics, by contrast, are like those stated in Proposition 2.3. They represent the direct effect on investment, conditional on being in a given type of state. The global and local comparative statics may potentially be in tension with each other and pull in different directions. This is illustrated by the possibility that a higher value of θ may lower the investment in fiscal capacity (when political instability, γ, is low). This local/global distinction is important in thinking about the model's predictions about the data and we return to it below.

A Weak State This is the case where both the cohesiveness and the stability conditions fail together. The following result summarizes the behavior of a weak state in the model:

Proposition 2.4: *If Cohesiveness and Stability fail, the state is weak. There is no incentive to invest in fiscal capacity.*

The fact that the stability condition fails now implies that the marginal benefit of investing in fiscal capacity is negative. The absence of cohesive institutions together with high political turnover mean that any fiscal capacity investments are likely to be used by the opposition group when in office to fund transfers, and this deters the incumbent from making an investment to increase fiscal capacity. Given that the depreciation rate δ is positive, fiscal capacity is actually falling in this case. If we were to include a fixed-cost component into the cost of fiscal-capacity investment, then this would further increase the likelihood that the state is weak. The net marginal benefit on the left-hand side of the Euler equation (2.8) would not only have to be above zero, but it would also have to be large enough to outweigh the fixed cost of investing.

To summarize, weak states suffer from three types of malaise: low θ, so that political institutions do not safeguard common interests; high γ, so that political instability is high; and low ϕ, so that common interests are weak. This parameter combination implies that incentives to grow the tax base are weak.

Clearly, there are no local comparative static results to discuss in the weak state since the investment level is always zero. But θ and γ can have global and local effects on investment. In this case the θ and γ effects go in the same direction: high γ raises the probability that the society ends up with a weak state and, within a redistributive state, high γ decreases investment (as noted in Proposition 2.3).

2.1.6 Taking Stock

Taken together, the predictions of the simple model are quite sharp. Several of the parameters—θ, γ, and ϕ—should influence the type of state that we observe in equilibrium and, hence, the investment that government makes in fiscal capacity. Some parameters—ω and ϕ (and indirectly R)—should have a local effect on investment only in the common-interest and redistributive states. Others—γ and θ—should have a local effect only in the redistributive state. Finally, none of the parameters should have a local effect on the investment level in a weak state.

What can we say about the welfare economics of the three states? We have already observed that only the common-interest state replicates the Pigouvian outcome. This outcome is therefore always Pareto efficient. The main failure of the redistributive state is that one group is favored and, hence, uses the state as an extractive device based on its entrenchment in power. But the allocation in this type of state is still Pareto optimal.

A weak state is more interesting since there exists a policy-cum-investment vector that is Pareto superior. An incumbent group would be willing to invest in fiscal capacity if it could be sure that there would be equitable sharing of the revenues raised. The equilibrium therefore constitutes a political failure in the sense of Besley and Coate (1998). In the language of Acemoglu (2003), the weak state is an example of a failure of the Political Coase theorem.[14] For both groups to be better off, it would require that they be able to commit themselves not to exploit their ability to use the state as an instrument for lopsided redistribution whenever they have a hold on power. But they are unable to make such commitments beyond any institutionalized commitments embodied in the parameter θ. Naturally, this raises the question of why we do not observe political reform to ensure this, a question that we return to in Chapter 7.

2.2 *Developing the Model*

The core model in the previous section is certainly simple. Furthermore, owing to the many simplifications we have made analyzing its implications is straightforward. But these simplifications have a cost in that they abstract from potentially relevant features of the world that could shape state investments in practice. However, it is reasonably easy to extend the model in a variety of ways to expand its realism and relevance. This section discusses a number of such extensions and their implications.

2.2.1 Microfoundations for Fiscal Capacity

The basic framework has a rudimentary reduced-form model of how fiscal capacity is determined. To go into greater depth, suppose that there is an outside option of working in the informal sector, where the wage is $\underline{\omega}$. Further, let d_s be the expected punishment for failing to pay taxes. If agents make a rational calculation of whether to pay or to avoid taxes, the maximally enforceable tax rate becomes

$$\tau_s = \frac{\omega + d_s - \underline{\omega}}{\omega}.$$

14. This idea goes back to the seminal paper on negotiation toward an efficient solution in the provision of public goods [Coase (1960)].

Investments in fiscal capacity are then administrative investments that increase the government's taxing authority. Compliance structures, infrastructure to enforce the income tax (or impose a value added tax), can now be represented as an increase in d_s. The cost of fiscal capacity would then simply be a reflection of investments in fines and detection, as in classic models of tax enforcement such as Allingham and Sandmo (1972). Thus, $\mathcal{F}(\cdot)$ is driven by the enforcement costs associated with d_s.

The costs of enforcement could also be affected by features of the economic structure. For example, Kleven, Thustrup Kreiner, and Saez (2009) argue that formal employment in firms leads to the possibility of cross-reporting to tax authorities by firms and workers. This reduces the cost of tax compliance and lowers the need for direct monitoring by tax authorities. Changes in the production structure that lower the cost of collecting taxes through cross-reporting could be arguments of the function $\mathcal{F}(\cdot)$.

Less Than Full Tax Compliance Our core model assumed that tax compliance is complete and universal. But there could well be heterogeneity in compliance. A simple way to introduce this realistic feature is to let the impact of punishment vary in the population according to preferences or opportunities for evasion. Suppose that the cost of not complying is $q(d_s, \varkappa)$, where $\varkappa$ is uniformly distributed in the population and normalized so that $\varkappa \in [0, 1]$ with $q_\varkappa > 0$ so that a higher $\varkappa$ means that it is more costly/less desirable to evade taxes. For example, we could have $q(d_s, \varkappa) = \varkappa d_s$, where $\varkappa$ represents an opportunity-dependent probability of being detected and having to incur the punishment of d_s. Or else, $q(d_s, \varkappa)$ could represent the personal stigma or shame of being caught cheating, with a higher $\varkappa$ representing a greater stigma and/or shame.

For a fixed d_s, a citizen of type $\varkappa$ will comply with an income tax of t_s if

$$\frac{\omega + q(d_s, \varkappa) - \underline{\omega}}{\omega} \geq t_s,$$

and the proportion of citizens who pay taxes will be $1 - \hat{\varkappa}(t_s, d_s)$, where

$$\frac{\omega + q(d_s, \hat{\varkappa}(t_s, d_s)) - \underline{\omega}}{\omega} = t_s,$$

if we assume an interior solution. For a high enough d_s, there could still be complete compliance. It is clear that $\hat{\varkappa}(t_s, d_s)$ is increasing in t_s and decreasing in d_s, i.e., fewer taxes are raised when the tax rate is higher and more taxes are paid when the penalties/detection are greater. Specifically, the tax revenues raised from a tax rate of t_s are

$$(1 - \widehat{\varkappa}(t_s, d_s))\, t_s \omega.$$

We can now express fiscal capacity as

$$\tau_s = \hat{\tau}(d_s) = \max_t \left\{(1 - \widehat{\varkappa}(t, d_s))\, t\omega\right\}.$$

Once again, investments that increase d_s will increase tax revenue for a given tax rate t_s by increasing compliance.

Tax Morale The model becomes more interesting if we consider a role for social norms in affecting the level of tax compliance. Suppose that the cost of cheating is $q\left(d_s, \varkappa, \widehat{\varkappa}\right)$. Thus as well as being a function of one's own compliance cost, the cost depends on the equilibrium fraction of those who choose to comply: $\widehat{\varkappa}$. A plausible interpretation of this formulation is as a model of stigma/shame, where the perceived stigma/shame from being caught cheating depends on how many others chose to comply. If $q_{\widehat{\varkappa}} < 0$, i.e., an increasing fraction of cheaters lowers the perceived cost of cheating, then there is a possibility of multiple compliance equilibria. This could suggest a role for tax culture in affecting the level of compliance. A country with a strong culture of compliance may find it much cheaper to achieve a similar level of fiscal capacity compared to one where the norm is unfavorable. This issue has been discussed by economists and political scientists, e.g., Levi (1998), Rothstein (2000), and Torgler (2007).

Naturally, what goes into $q(\cdot)$ and how it behaves as a function of its arguments is somewhat open. One could, e.g., assume that the willingness to cheat on taxes depends on the taxpayers' perception of how the money is allocated. Suppose, for instance, that the willingness to cheat depends negatively on the expected level of public goods provided, g_s. In such a setting, $\widehat{\varkappa}$ would depend negatively on g_s and, hence, indirectly on θ. That is to say, a country with more cohesive institutions would achieve higher tax compliance in equilibrium, everything else being equal. This would create a complementarity between higher θ and the costs of investing in fiscal capacity. It also hints at the idea of complying with taxation as a form of contract between citizens and government, where public goods are provide in exchange for greater compliance.

This discussion has been speculative and sketchy. But the issue of tax morale is certainly important and it is plausible that it contributes to the high tax take in many European countries. The idea of tax morale also goes to the heart of debates about state legitimacy, a concept we do not touch on further in the present book. But the interactions among norms of compliance, state legitimacy, fiscal capacity, and institutions constitute an interesting and important topic for further research.

2.2.2 More General Models for Public Goods

We derived the results of fiscal-capacity investments under the assumption that the preferences for public goods were linear with a value of public goods that was stochastic with a two-point distribution. In this subsection, we investigate some implications of relaxing this assumption.

Quasi-Linearity To see the implications of the linearity assumption, assume that preferences are quasi-linear with

$$u_s^J = c_s^J + \alpha V(g_s),$$

where $V(\cdot)$ is a concave function and α is a known and constant parameter in each period. This formulation captures the natural feature of diminishing marginal utility of public goods. As noted in our discussion of equation (2.5), we now have the possibility of an interior solution to the level of public-goods provision. If $V_g(0) \to \infty$ as $g \to 0$, then the solution is always interior. This adds greater realism, as the government allocates resources to achieve a mix of transfers and public-good spending.

A key observation in this case is that the marginal value of public funds becomes

$$\lambda_s = \max\left\{\alpha V_g\left(G\left(\alpha, \tau_s\right)\right), 2\left(1-\theta\right)\right\}.$$

New Euler Equation This formulation of the demand for public goods does not change the basic insights of the model. However, the Euler equation for investing in fiscal and legal capacity does require modification. The expected marginal value of public funds is now

$$E\left(\lambda_2\right) = \gamma\lambda_2 + (1-\gamma)\lambda_2^L,$$

where

$$\lambda_2^L = \begin{cases} \alpha V_g\left(G\left(\alpha, \tau_s\right)\right) & \text{if } \alpha V_g\left(G\left(\alpha, \tau_s\right)\right) \geq 2\left(1-\theta\right) \\ 2\theta & \text{otherwise.} \end{cases}$$

Once again, there will be a positive demand for investing in fiscal capacity provided that $E(\lambda_2) \geq 1$. Now, define τ_2^* from

$$\omega[\alpha V_g (R + \tau_2^* \omega) - 1] = \mathcal{F}_\tau (\tau_2^* - (1-\delta)\tau_1) \tag{2.11}$$

as the level of fiscal capacity that would be chosen by a Pigouvian planner, assuming that $\tau_2^* > (1-\delta)\tau_1$, i.e., the starting point is one where the state is smaller than would be ideal. It equates the marginal value of public goods in a common-interest state with the marginal cost of investing.

Different Types of States The cohesiveness condition is now modified to

Cohesiveness: $\alpha V_g (R + \tau_2^* \omega) \geq 2(1-\theta)$.

Once more, this is guaranteed to hold for θ close enough to 1/2. When it holds, the Pigouvian level of fiscal capacity is sustainable since all spending is on public goods. The stability condition is modified to

Stability: $2[(1-\gamma)(1-\theta) + \gamma\theta] \geq 1$.

This is bound to hold if θ and γ are close to zero.

We now have a characterization of states comparable to what we found in the core model and the interpretation is similar. As in the core model, a common-interest state only spends on public goods. The cost of investing in fiscal capacity implies that the optimal government size in the common-interest state always falls short of that implied by the Lindahl-Samuelson rule, which in this context would satisfy $\alpha V_g(g) - 1 = 0$. This is because the cost of building the state has to be taken into account in determining the optimal size of government. However, such cost-of-building effects are typically not considered in standard public-finance models.

Redistributive and weak states allocate marginal fiscal capacity to transfers. A redistributive or weak state spends on a mixture of public goods and transfers, and even less is spent on public goods in such states. The logic of weak states is the same; it is not worthwhile to build fiscal capacity when it is likely to be spent on transfers paid to the other group.

Natural Resources This version of the model makes an even sharper prediction about the impact of natural resource intensity on the incentive to invest in fiscal capacity. Differentiating (2.11), we observe that

$$\frac{\partial \tau_2^*}{\partial R} = \frac{\alpha V_{gg}\left(R + \tau_2^* \omega\right)}{\frac{\mathcal{F}_{\tau\tau}\left(\tau_2^* - (1-\delta)\tau_1\right)}{\omega} - \alpha\omega V_{gg}\left(R + \tau_2^* \omega\right)} < 0,$$

i.e., the demand for fiscal capacity by a Pigouvian government is lower when natural resources are greater.

The model suggests the possibility of an extreme rentier state if the following condition is satisfied:

$$\alpha V_g\left(R\right) < 2\left(1 - \theta\right).$$

In this case, we have a state that has so many natural resources that it is already spending as much on public goods as it would like to given the quality of its institutions. If such a state builds fiscal capacity further, then it is *only* for the purpose of enhancing its redistributive capacity as would be the case in a redistributive state.

This argument illustrates how natural resources can have both local and global comparative statics—affecting the type of state that emerges and the level of fiscal capacity within a state type (when the state is common interest). The global effects can be negative or positive, depending on whether the stability condition holds.

A Continuous Distribution of Public-Goods Values We now develop the core model to include a continuous valuation of public goods, but revert to linear demand. Instead of a two-point distribution of α_s, we assume a continuous distribution $\alpha_s \in \left[1, \alpha_H\right]$, with $\alpha_H > 2$ with a distribution function $H\left(\alpha\right)$.[15] In this case, there is a critical value of α equal to $2\left(1 - \theta\right)$ above which all public spending is on public goods.

We now have to modify the expression for (2.9) to

$$\begin{aligned} E(\lambda_2) = {} & \left[1 - H\left(2\left(1-\theta\right)\right)\right] E\left\{\alpha : \alpha \geq 2\left(1-\theta\right)\right\} \\ & + H\left(2\left(1-\theta\right)\right) 2[(1-\theta)(1-\gamma) + \gamma\theta]. \end{aligned}$$

A change in the demand for public goods can now be stated in terms of a first-order stochastically dominating shift in the distribution of α. Such a shift

15. This was basically the model used in Besley and Persson (2009b).

will raise the demand for fiscal capacity and represents an increase in common interests.

A weak state remains a discrete category and arises if $E\left(\lambda_2\right) < 1$. The main change in the analysis is that the concept of a common-interest state becomes less well defined; all economies with $\theta < 1/2$ will have some underprovision of public goods in the sense that the politically optimal choice of public goods is lower than the Pigouvian optimum in the interval $\alpha_s \in [1, 2(1-\theta)]$. One could define a common-interest state in a strict sense as $\theta = 1/2$, but this is possibly too stark a definition. It is better to think about having either stronger or weaker redistributive or common-interest motives for building fiscal capacity. States can then move further away from, or closer to, being a common-interest state depending on the values of θ and γ. As long as $\theta < 1/2$, an increase in γ reduces investment in fiscal capacity.

2.2.3 Polarization/Heterogeneity

Thus far, we have assumed that there is a *common* way of valuing public goods across the two groups. However, this need not be the case, as has been forcefully argued by Alesina, Baqir, and Easterly (1999) among others.

Introducing Polarization in Preferences Studying group-specific values offers a simple way of investigating the effect of polarization/heterogeneity between the two groups. To explore this, we now assume that the demand for public goods can be imperfectly correlated across the two groups. This may be due to cross-cutting cleavages in society such as ethnicity, language, or religion.[16] To make things clean, we allow the incumbent and opposition groups to have different valuations, but assume that these are drawn from the same two-point distribution $\{\alpha_H, \alpha_L\}$. Thus, let $\{\alpha_s^I, \alpha_s^O\}$ be the realizations of the valuations of public goods for groups I and O in period s and let the parameter

$$(1-\iota) = \text{Prob}\{\alpha_s^O = z | \alpha_s^I = z\} \leq 1$$

measure the correlation between the valuations. Now, we can capture greater polarization by higher values of ι, because this means that it is less likely that interests will be aligned. This generalizes our baseline model which implicitly assumed that $\iota = 0$.

16. This could be microfounded by allowing the incumbent to choose a mix of public goods.

In this discussion and what follows, we refer to polarization and heterogeneity interchangeably. This makes sense in a two-group model like ours, although in a multigroup setting these are conceptually distinct.[17] However, in the empirical analysis that follows, we focus on heterogeneity, specifically a measure of fractionalization that we feel is a reasonable way of capturing the likelihood of preference diversity.

The Marginal Cost of Public Funds Revisited With this modification, the realized marginal cost of public funds in period s is $\lambda_s = \max\{\alpha_s^I, 2(1-\theta)\}$, i.e., it depends on the incumbent group's valuation of public goods. To see the implications for investing in fiscal capacity, we have to pin down $E(\lambda_2)$, the expected value of public funds for the period-1 incumbent, since this affects the incentive to invest in fiscal capacity via equation (2.8). Now, let ϕ denote the probability that the period-2 value of public goods is high *for whomever is the period-2 incumbent*. Then, the expression for $E(\lambda_2)$ becomes

$$E(\lambda_2) = \phi\left[\alpha_H(1-\gamma\iota) + \alpha_L\gamma\iota\right] + (1-\phi)\lambda_2^L, \tag{2.12}$$

where λ_2^L is now defined as

$$\lambda_2^L = \begin{cases} \left[\alpha_L(1-\gamma\iota) + \alpha_H\gamma\iota\right] & \text{if } \alpha_L \geq 2(1-\theta) \\ 2[(1-\theta)(1-\gamma) + \gamma\theta] & \text{otherwise.} \end{cases}$$

Since the decision rights belong to the incumbent, the probability of retaining political control now has an effect on the expected value of public funds, even when the incumbent chooses to provide public goods. This is because the opposition sometimes has a low valuation of public goods when the current incumbent has a high valuation.

Cohesiveness and Polarization/Heterogeneity When the cohesiveness condition holds, we have that $E(\lambda_2) = \phi\alpha_H + (1-\phi)\alpha_L$, so the unconditional expectation of λ_2 is independent of polarization. However, when the cohesiveness condition fails, we have

$$E(\lambda_2) = \phi\left[\alpha_H - \gamma\iota(\alpha_H - \alpha_L)\right] + (1-\phi)\, 2[(1-\theta)(1-\gamma) + \gamma\theta].$$

17. See Esteban and Ray (1994) for a discussion of how to measure polarization.

If we define $\widetilde{\alpha}_H = [\alpha_H - \gamma\iota(\alpha_H - \alpha_L)]$ as the "effective value of public goods" in the high-value state, we see that more polarization effectively lowers $\widetilde{\alpha}_H$ and, hence, weakens common interests. Thus

$$\frac{dE(\lambda_2)}{d\iota} = -\gamma\phi(\alpha_H - \alpha_L) < 0,$$

i.e., higher polarization lowers the expected value of future public revenue, and this effect is more pronounced when political instability is high. Applying this result to the investment problem for the incumbent, we have the following new result:

Proposition 2.5: *If Cohesiveness fails, increased polarization/heterogeneity, as measured by a higher value of* ι*, decreases fiscal-capacity investments in a redistributive state and raises the likelihood that the economy is in a weak state. Both of these effects are larger when there is greater political instability (a higher value of* γ*).*

Thus, the model now predicts a role for polarization/heterogeneity reducing fiscal capacity investments in noncohesive polities.

This result rhymes with the findings of Alesina, Baqir, and Easterly (1999), who discuss how ethnic divisions result in a weaker incentive to provide public goods. This effect does not appear in our framework with a linear demand for public goods (although it would be easy to modify the model to include this feature). Instead, our model predicts a weaker motive to invest in fiscal capacity, conditional on being in a redistributive state. Thus in such cases we would expect a negative correlation between the level of public-goods spending and polarization. The model also predicts that ethnic (or religious or linguistic) divisions raise the likelihood that we end up with a weak state that does not invest anything in increasing fiscal capacity. Both these effects are stronger the higher is political instability because a shift in power is more fearsome to the incumbent the less correlated the preferences for public goods across groups.[18] In this case, the local and global comparative statics go in the same direction. We return to the prediction in Proposition 2.5 in Section 2.3, when we explore the partial correlations in the data.

18. At a general level, the result is also related to the insight in Alesina and Tabellini (1990) that the incentive to issue debt increases with political polarization.

2.2.4 Income Inequality

The symmetry assumption made in our core model is helpful analytically but is unrealistic. This subsection considers asymmetric income levels and the next looks at asymmetric group sizes.

Naturally, income inequality can also be viewed as a source of polarization in society, as has been argued forcefully by Esteban and Ray (1994). Income inequality can also be closely associated with political instability, as has been shown empirically by Alesina and Perotti (1996). We do not pursue these channels here, but they are interesting avenues for future research.

Income Structure and Taxation In standard models, income inequality is an important determinant of decisions to tax income. A simple model of state-capacity investment in the presence of income inequality is presented in Besley and Persson (2009b). Extensions of that framework with an emphasis on income inequality have been pursued by Cárdenas (2010) and Cárdenas and Tuzemen (2010).

To explore this issue here, we consider a difference in wages between the incumbent and opposition groups with ω^J for $J \in \{I, O\}$. For simplicity, let there be two levels of the wage: $\omega^J \in \{\omega^L, \omega^H\}$. Let ω now denote the average wage, $\omega = (\omega^H + \omega^L)/2$. The transfers out of any residual tax revenue, i.e., the revenue not spent on public goods or creating fiscal capacity, are constrained by political institutions as in the core model.

After we plug in the transfer level, group J's utility function is

$$\alpha_s g_s + (1 - t_s)\omega^J + \beta^J [R - t_s \omega - g_s - m_s],$$

where $\beta^I = 2(1 - \theta)$ and $\beta^O = 2\theta$.

Fiscal capacity is now fully utilized only if

$$\lambda_s \geq \frac{\omega^I}{\omega},$$

i.e., if the marginal value of public funds is greater than the ratio of the incumbent's income share to average income, following the same logic as in Meltzer and Richards (1981). If the period-s incumbent is poorer than average, this will definitely hold and $t_s = \tau_s$ as in the baseline case.

When the incumbent is richer than average, there are three cases to consider:

1. *High inequality:* Rich incumbents will not choose to levy any income tax to fund either transfers or public goods, i.e., $t_s = 0$. This occurs if the value of public goods is too low compared to the cost of taxation, i.e.,

$$\alpha_H < \frac{\omega^H}{\omega}.$$

   In this case $G(\alpha_H) = G(\alpha_L) = 0$, where $G(\alpha_s)$ denotes the politically optimal provision of public goods as a function of the period-s valuation.

2. *Moderate inequality:* An income tax is levied by a rich incumbent (at $t_s = \tau_s$) only when $\alpha_s = \alpha_H$. In this case,

$$\alpha_H \geq \frac{\omega^H}{\omega} > \max\left\{2(1-\theta), a_L\right\}.$$

   We then have $G(\alpha_H) = \tau_s\omega - m_s$ and $G(\alpha_L) = 0$.

3. *Low inequality:* Fiscal capacity is always used maximally by the incumbent, $t_s = \tau_s$. This holds if

$$\max\left\{2(1-\theta), a_L\right\} \geq \frac{\omega^H}{\omega}.$$

   In this case $G(\alpha_H) = \tau_s\omega - m_s$, and $G(\alpha_L) = 0$ if $\alpha_L < 2(1-\theta)$, whereas $G(\alpha_L) = \tau_s\omega - m_s$ if $\alpha_L \geq 2(1-\theta)$. This is essentially the same as in the core model.

We summarize the choice of taxation in these three cases in terms of two functions: $T(\omega^I, \alpha_s)$ for the income tax rate and $G(\alpha_s)$ for public goods.

Fiscal-Capacity Investments Revisited We now consider the implications of income inequality for investing in fiscal capacity. Using the analysis in the previous subsection, we find that the "indirect" payoff function for group $J \in \{I, O\}$ in period s becomes

$$W(\alpha_s, \tau_s, m_s, \omega^J, \beta^J) = \alpha_s G(\alpha_s) + (1 - T(\omega^I, \alpha_s))\omega^J + \beta^J[T(\omega^I, \alpha_s)\omega - G(\alpha_s) - m_s].$$

We can now define value functions for these cases, which now depend on ω^J. These are denoted by

$$U^I\left(\tau_2, \omega^I\right) = \left[\phi W(\alpha_H, \tau_2, 0, \omega^I, \beta^I) + (1-\phi)\, W\left(\alpha_L, \tau_2, 0, \omega^I, \beta^I\right)\right]$$

and

$$U^O\left(\tau_2, \omega^O\right) = \left[\phi W\left(\alpha_H, \tau_2, 0, \omega^O, \beta^O\right) + (1-\phi)\, W\left(\alpha_L, \tau_2, 0, \omega^O, \beta^O\right)\right].$$

The expected two-period utility of the incumbent in period 1 is

$$\begin{aligned} &W(\alpha_1, \tau_1, \mathcal{F}\left(\tau_2 - (1-\delta)\,\tau_1\right), \omega^I, 2\,(1-\theta)) \\ &\quad + [1-\gamma]\, U^I\left(\tau_2, \omega^I\right) + \gamma U^O\left(\tau_2, \omega^I\right). \end{aligned} \tag{2.13}$$

In close analogy with the core model, the optimal level of fiscal capacity maximizes this expression by the choice of τ_2. As we are interested in how equilibrium depends on ω^I, we denote the solution by $\tilde{\tau}_2\left(\omega^I\right)$.

Before proceeding to the detailed analysis, we offer a bird's-eye preview of the results. If the incumbent is poor, $\omega^I = \omega_L$, it will tend to boost his investment in fiscal capacity (compared to the model without any inequality). Intuitively, a poor incumbent pays a smaller share of the cost of fiscal capacity than the average citizen. By the same token, richer incumbents are less keen on fiscal capacity. Whether this leads to greater or smaller fiscal capacity depends on the joint distribution of economic and political power, i.e., whether the incumbents are more likely to be rich or poor.

Modified Euler Equation To flesh this out, observe that maximizing (2.13) by choice of τ_2 yields the following modified version of our Euler equation,

$$\begin{aligned} &\omega[(E(\lambda_2; \omega^I) - \frac{\omega^I}{\omega}] \leq \lambda_1\left(\omega^I\right) \mathcal{F}_\tau\left(\tau_2 - (1-\delta)\,\tau_1\right) \\ &\text{c.s. } \tau_2 - (1-\delta)\,\tau_1 \geq 0, \end{aligned} \tag{2.14}$$

where $\lambda_1\left(\omega^I\right) = \max\left\{\alpha_1, 2\,(1-\theta)\,, \omega^I/\omega\right\}$. As before, $E\left(\lambda_2; \omega^I\right)$ denotes the expected value of period-2 public revenues. This depends on the incumbent's income level, a dependence that we now explore formally. What matters for investment in fiscal capacity is to compare $E\left(\lambda_2; \omega^I\right)$ to an incumbent's income share ω^I/ω; this represents the cost-benefit ratio of an increase in the income-tax rate, i.e., the so-called tax price of public spending.

Low Inequality With low inequality,

$$E(\lambda_2;\omega^I) = \phi\alpha_H + (1-\phi)\lambda_2^L \tag{2.15}$$

for $\omega^I \in \{\omega_L, \omega_H\}$, with λ_2^L defined as in (2.10) above. We now have $\tilde{\tau}_2(\omega^L) > \tilde{\tau}_2(\omega^H)$, i.e., poorer incumbents invest more in fiscal capacity whenever fiscal capacity investments are positive. In this case, inequality has an effect purely via its consequences for the costs and benefits of raising taxes. We call this the *tax-price effect* of inequality. In every case, fiscal capacity is fully utilized.

Moderate Inequality With moderate inequality,

$$E(\lambda_2;\omega^H) = \begin{cases} \phi\alpha_H + (1-\phi)\gamma\alpha_L & \alpha_L \geq 2(1-\theta) \\ \phi\alpha_H + (1-\phi)\gamma 2\theta & \text{otherwise} \end{cases}$$

and

$$E(\lambda_2;\omega^L) = \phi\alpha_H + (1-\phi)(1-\gamma)\max\{\alpha_L, 2(1-\theta)\}.$$

The marginal value of fiscal capacity is reduced for *both* rich and poor incumbents because a rich incumbent does not utilize fiscal capacity when $\alpha_2 = \alpha_L$. This constitutes a further dampener on a rich incumbent's incentive to invest in fiscal capacity since $\lambda_1 = \omega^H/\omega > \max\{\alpha_L, 2(1-\theta)\}$ is the period-1 realization of the value of public goods when $\alpha_1 = \alpha_L$. But the higher inequality will boost the poor's decision owing to a larger tax-price effect than with low inequality.

High Inequality Finally, with high inequality,

$$E(\lambda_2;\omega^H) = \begin{cases} \gamma\left[\phi\alpha_H + (1-\phi)\alpha_L\right] & \alpha_L \geq 2(1-\theta) \\ \gamma\left[\phi\alpha_H + (1-\phi)2\theta\right] & \text{otherwise} \end{cases}$$

and

$$E(\lambda_2;\omega^L) = (1-\gamma)\left[\phi\alpha_H + (1-\phi)\max\{\alpha_L, 2(1-\theta)\}\right].$$

Moreover, $\lambda_1 = \omega^H/\omega > \max\{\alpha_L, 2(1-\theta)\}$ all of the time. Since the rich incumbent does not utilize available fiscal capacity, such capacity is useful only when the incumbent is poor. Again, this will tend to undermine investment efforts by both groups. However, as in the case of moderate inequality, there is a boost to the poor's decision owing to a larger tax-price effect.

Taking Stock Looking at the overall picture, we do not find a clear-cut implication of greater income inequality for the decision to invest in fiscal-capacity. However, things become somewhat clearer if we combine economic inequality with political inequality. A natural case to consider is the one where the rich are in power and expect to remain so that $\omega^I = \omega^H$ and $\gamma = 0$. Here, high inequality will result in a fiscally weaker state and in the case of moderate inequality, this situation can be remedied only by sufficiently strong common interests (high ϕ). This is thus an important caveat to the observation in the core model that political stability would lead to the emergence of a redistributive state. That logic is restored only if inequality is not too great, or the group in power is not rich, or common interests are strong enough.

Cárdenas and Tuzemen (2010) use a similar model and allow for income inequality between two groups, called Elites and Citizens. When the (richer) Elites are in power, in the presence of political instability both income and political inequality lead to lower investment in state capacity. Conversely, if the (poorer) Citizens rule, high political and income inequality results in higher investment in state capacity.

The value of cohesive institutions is also undermined by high levels of inequality, since $\alpha_L \geq 2\,(1-\theta)$ is no longer sufficient for a common-interest state to emerge. Indeed, even if $\theta \to 1/2$ and the rich hold power, there need not be any incentive to invest in fiscal capacity. With income-tax finance, the tax price of public spending for the rich may simply be too high for investing in fiscal capacity to be worthwhile.

The bottom line in this subsection is that there are good reasons to expect income inequality to play an important role in the development of fiscal capacity. Even though the effects are not completely straightforward, our considered expectation is that low inequality is more likely to foster large investments in fiscal capacity. Given that a high level of income inequality curtails the investment incentives particularly for a rich incumbent, this conclusion is strengthened if we are willing to assume that economic power and political power tend to go hand in hand.[19] Cárdenas (2010) considers the question empirically, using

19. We have assumed in this discussion that the rich cannot destroy fiscal capacity. But if they could, it would sometimes be optimal for them to do so.

cross-sectional data for more than 100 countries and finds that political and (especially) economic inequality appears to be associated with lower incentives to invest in state capacity. He uses income inequality to explain Latin America's generally underdeveloped fiscal capacity.

2.2.5 Differences in Group Size

To consider another source of asymmetry, which is not present in the basic framework, suppose that the two groups differ in size. In our structure, the relevant consideration is the fraction of the population in the group represented by the incumbent. Thus, let ρ^J, $J \in \{I, O\}$ be the fraction of the population in each group.

The main effect on the model from this type of asymmetry works through the incentive to allocate transfers. The government budget constraint at date s becomes

$$R + t_s\omega = g_s + m_s + \rho^I r_s^I + \left(1 - \rho^I\right) r_s^O .$$

Given our institutional constraint, i.e., that $r_s^O \geq \sigma r_s^I$, we now have

$$\begin{aligned} r_s^I &= \frac{1}{\rho^I + (1-\rho^I)\,\sigma}\left[R + t_s\omega - g_s - m_s\right] \\ &\equiv 2\left(1 - \theta^I\right)\left[R + t_s\omega - g_s - m_s\right], \end{aligned}$$

where $\theta^I \in \left[\frac{\rho^I - 1/2}{\rho^I}, \frac{1}{2}\right]$ and

$$r_s^O = 2\theta^O\left[R_s + t_s\omega - g_s - m_s\right],$$

with $\theta^O \equiv \sigma\left(1 - \theta^I\right) \in \left[0, \frac{1}{2}\right]$.

By sticking to the θ representation of institutions, the comparison with the core model is clearer. The main difference is that now we have separate parameters for the incumbent and the opposition determining their share of transfers as a function of the size of their group.

Policy There is now the possibility that if $\rho^I < 1/2$, then we can have $\theta^I < 0$ if σ is low enough. This would imply that $2\left(1 - \theta^I\right) > 2$. Intuitively, when a small group is in office, making transfers becomes more attractive. For a given σ, a dollar of tax revenue devoted to transfers goes disproportionately to the incumbent group. At the other extreme, where $\rho^I \to 1$, there is essentially one large group so that $\theta^I = 1/2$ even if $\sigma = 0$. A group that makes up close to the full population finds it unattractive to redistribute via transfers because it pays for such transfers out of its own pocket.

Using these new definitions of θ^J, we find it fairly straightforward to derive the implications for politically optimal policy and state-capacity investments. Whether a government now chooses to spend on public goods depends on whether $2\left(1-\theta^I\right) \leq \alpha_s$. For a given σ, this is more likely if a large group is in office compared to the core model. The flipside of this is that small elites in power are less likely to pursue common-interest policies, all else being equal. In such a case, there may well be no spending on public goods, even when $\alpha_s = \alpha_H$. We now focus on this case, which arises when $\sigma < 1$ and ρ^I is small enough. This is one way of using the model to think about "corrupt rule" by a small elite. All spending is on transfers to the ruling elite, so we have $\lambda_1 = 2\left(1-\theta^I\right)$. The only possibility is now a redistributive state (at least in period 1).

Fiscal-Capacity Investments The fiscal-capacity Euler equation becomes

$$\omega[2\left[(1-\gamma)\left(1-\theta^I\right)+\gamma\theta^O\right]-1] = \omega[2\left(1-\theta^I\right)[(1-\gamma(1-\sigma))]-1] \quad (2.16)$$

$$\leq 2\left(1-\theta^I\right)\mathcal{F}_\tau\left(\tau_2-(1-\delta)\tau_1\right) \quad (2.17)$$

$$\text{c.s. } \tau_2-(1-\delta)\tau_1 \geq 0,$$

The condition for investment in fiscal capacity is now that $\left(1-\theta^I\right)$ $[(1-\gamma(1-\sigma))] > 1/2$. A fall in ρ^I, a smaller elite in power, now boosts the incentive to invest.

The other side of the coin is that the larger the group in office, the better its incentives to invest. Indeed, a change in political power from a narrow elite to a larger group may move the country from a redistributive to a common-interest state. It is not immediately clear whether this boosts demand for fiscal capacity, since that would depend on ϕ. However, a shift in power will lead to a very different pattern of public spending with resources allocated to public goods rather than to transfers favoring a narrow elite.

2.2.6 Tax Distortions

The core model assumes that levying an income tax has no disincentive effect. This is easily modified by introducing a variable labor supply. Let preferences be

$$u_s^J = c_s^J + \alpha_s g_s - \frac{\epsilon}{\epsilon+1}\left(l_s^J\right)^{\frac{\epsilon+1}{\epsilon}},$$

where l_s^J is labor supply by a member of group J in period s and ϵ is the labor-supply elasticity. This formulation continues to neglect income effects in labor supply, which allows us to study policy and investment decisions separately.

Labor Supply and Tax Revenue The labor-supply function associated with the previous preferences is

$$l_s^J = [(1 - t_s)\,\omega]^{\epsilon}\,.$$

The response of labor supply to net wages leads to a standard deadweight loss associated with a higher income-tax rate. The indirect utility function is modified to

$$\alpha_s g_s + \frac{(\omega\,(1 - t_s))^{1+\epsilon}}{1+\epsilon} + r_s^I,$$

and the revenue from income tax is

$$t_s\,(1 - t_s)^{\epsilon}\,\omega^{1+\epsilon}.$$

Using these, we modify the government budget constraint to

$$R + t_s\,(1 - t_s)^{\epsilon}\,\omega^{1+\epsilon} = g_s + m_s + \frac{r_s^I + r_s^O}{2}.$$

The Optimal Income Tax Rate Determining the optimal income-tax rate now resembles a more or less standard problem. Using the observation that

$$r_s^I = 2\,(1 - \theta)\left[R + t_s\,(1 - t_s)^{\epsilon}\,\omega^{1+\epsilon} - m_s - g_s\right],$$

we choose the public-goods level and the income-tax rate to maximize

$$\alpha_s g_s + \frac{(\omega\,(1 - t_s))^{1+\epsilon}}{1+\epsilon} + 2\,(1 - \theta)\left[R + t_s\,(1 - t_s)^{\epsilon}\,\omega^{1+\epsilon} - m_s - g_s\right],$$

subject to $t_s \leq \tau_s$. This yields a politically optimal income tax of

$$t_s^* = \min\left\{\tau_s, \frac{[\lambda_s - 1]}{[\lambda_s\,(1+\epsilon) - 1]}\right\},$$

with $\lambda_s = \max\left\{\alpha_s, 2\,(1 - \theta)\right\}$. The public-goods choice is exactly the same as in the core model.

This income tax is increasing in the shadow value of public revenue, λ_s, which depends on whether the marginal unit of public revenues is allocated to transfers or public goods. Two cases can arise. If λ_s is high enough, then all fiscal capacity is utilized and $t_s^* = \tau_s$. Alternatively, we can have an interior solution, $t_s^* < \tau_s$, where the level of the income tax is chosen to trade off the value of public spending, as represented by λ_s, against the deadweight loss. The result is a standard inverse elasticity (Ramsey) rule that a larger labor-supply elasticity is associated with a lower optimal tax rate.

Underutilization of Fiscal Capacity? The second possibility of an interior optimal tax rate raises a question. Given that there is a cost in building it up, would a government ever wish to have a level of fiscal capacity where some of that capacity is left unused? To understand this, we have to revisit the investment decision. Suppose, first of all, that

$$\min\left\{\alpha_L, 2(1-\theta)\right\} \geq \left(1 - \frac{\tau_1 (1-\delta)\epsilon}{1-\tau_1(1-\delta)}\right)^{-1}.$$

This condition is bound to hold if the initial fiscal capacity level is low. This says that if there is no investment in fiscal capacity, then the incumbent group will fully utilize all of the fiscal capacity available to it in period 2.

Now define $T(z)$ from

$$\omega^{1+\epsilon}(1-T(z))^{\epsilon}\left[z\left(1-\frac{T(z)\epsilon}{1-T(z)}\right)-1\right] \leq \mathcal{F}_\tau\left(T(z)-(1-\delta)\tau_1\right)\lambda_1$$
$$\text{c.s. } T(z)-(1-\delta)\tau_1 \geq 0. \tag{2.18}$$

This is the value of period-2 fiscal capacity that solves the fiscal-capacity Euler equation when z is the expected value of fiscal capacity.[20] It is clear that $z \leq E(\lambda_2)$, where $E(\lambda_2)$ is defined in (3.6).[21] A sufficient condition for some investment in fiscal capacity is that

$$z \geq \frac{1}{\left(1-\frac{\tau_1(1-\delta)\epsilon}{1-\tau_1(1-\delta)}\right)}. \tag{2.19}$$

20. Formally:

$$T(z) = \arg\max_\tau \left\{\frac{(\omega(1-\tau))^{1+\epsilon}}{1+\epsilon} + z\left[\tau(1-\tau)^{\epsilon}\omega^{1+\epsilon}\right] - \lambda_1\mathcal{F}\left(\tau-(1-\delta)\tau_1\right)\right\}$$

21. The fact that $z \leq E(\lambda_2)$ is due to the possibility of unused fiscal capacity in period 2.

To understand this condition, observe that if there is no investment the amount of fiscal capacity left over after period 1 is $(1-\delta)\,\tau_1$. Since the right-hand side of (2.19) is more demanding than $z \geq 1$, the deadweight loss from taxation makes investing in fiscal capacity less desirable. So the value of period-2 public goods has to make the value of an extra dollar of public revenue more valuable when we allow for any deadweight loss from the income tax.

In any investment optimum, there will be full utilization of all fiscal capacity when $\alpha_2 = \alpha_H$. Otherwise, the marginal value of investing in additional fiscal capacity would be zero, i.e.,

$$1 = \alpha_H \left(1 - \frac{\tau_2 \epsilon}{1-\tau_2}\right) > E\,(\lambda_2) \left(1 - \frac{\tau_2 \epsilon}{1-\tau_2}\right) \geq z \left(1 - \frac{\tau_2 \epsilon}{1-\tau_2}\right),$$

so that (2.19) cannot hold. This has interesting consequences for the standard optimal income-tax model, which ignores investment costs. Our model predicts that, since it is costly to build fiscal capacity, the government will sometimes be constrained in the income-tax rate that it sets.

However, on other occasions, the unconstrained optimum income tax, i.e., underutilization of fiscal capacity, may be chosen by the period-2 incumbent. A sufficient condition for an optimum where fiscal capacity is not fully utilized when $\alpha_2 = \alpha_L$ is that

$$\frac{\left[\min\left\{\alpha_L, 2\,(1-\theta)\right\} - 1\right]}{\left[\min\left\{\alpha_L, 2\,(1-\theta)\right\}(1+\epsilon) - 1\right]} < T\,(\phi\alpha_H).$$

This will hold if $\phi\alpha_H$ is large enough, i.e., there is a strong enough desire to build fiscal capacity in anticipation of a high demand for public goods, as would be the case under a high risk of war or a deep economic crisis.

In general, the upper bound on fiscal capacity predicted by the model is given by

$$\tau_2 = \frac{\left[E\,(\lambda_2) - 1\right]}{\left[E\,(\lambda_2)\,(1+\epsilon) - 1\right]}.$$

This level is below the fiscal capacity needed to pursue the revenue-maximizing income-tax rate, i.e., the Laffer rate, which is $\tau_2 = 1/\,(1+\epsilon)$.

In summary, this extension of the core model does not lead to any important changes in logic. But it does incorporate more standard limits on the size of government owing to considerations of deadweight loss. Specifically, a greater elasticity of the tax base with regard to the tax rate will tend to diminish the demand for fiscal capacity, at least fiscal capacity as generated via the income tax.

2.2.7 From Trade to Income Taxes

We now discuss what happens in the presence of an additional tax base. Given the raw data presented in the introduction to this chapter, it is of particular interest to study taxation of trade. This will allow us to think about an important issue in fiscal-capacity building: the move from reliance on trade taxes to reliance on income taxes in the process of economic development. For simplicity, we revert to the simple case of no deadweight losses in the income tax, although these could be retained at the cost of some algebraic complexity.[22]

Goods and Prices To explore this issue, we formulate a different utility function to that in the core model, namely

$$u_s^J = \alpha_s g_s + x_s^{A,J} + \frac{\varepsilon}{\varepsilon - 1}\left(x_s^{M,J}\right)^{\frac{\varepsilon-1}{\varepsilon}},$$

where $x_s^{K,J}$ is the demand for good $K \in \{A, M\}$ in period s. To fix ideas, think of A as an agricultural good and M as a manufactured good. These goods can both be imported and exported. Labor produces ω units of agricultural goods and $\frac{\omega}{\kappa}$ units of manufactures where $\kappa > 1$. We have in mind a world in which manufactures are imported and the government is able to tax these imports. The price of the agricultural good is normalized to 1. The time-invariant world price of manufactures, P, is assumed to lie in the interval $P < \kappa + \psi$, where ψ represents trade costs.

We suppose that there is a ready technology for freely raising revenues from tariffs and that, as earlier, fiscal capacity increases the ability to raise revenue from an income tax. The consumer price of manufactures differs from the world price, owing to a tariff z_s, and is denoted by $Q_s = P - \psi + z_s$. Since the parameter ψ represents trade costs, we can interpret its inverse as a measure of "natural" openness.

Trade and Tariff Revenues The demand for manufactures is given by

$$x_s^{M,J} = Q_s^{-\varepsilon}.$$

22. This section is based on Besley and Persson (2010c) who consider deadweight losses from both tax bases.

As in our treatment of labor supply, we simplify by not allowing for an income effect on the demand for the taxed good. The tariff revenue from imported manufactures is therefore

$$z_s \left(P - \psi + z_s\right)^{-\varepsilon}$$

and the government budget constraint is modified to

$$R + t_s\omega + z_s \left(P - \psi + z_s\right)^{-\varepsilon} = g_s + m_s + \frac{r_s^I + r_s^O}{2}.$$

The only change from the core model is the additional revenue source in the form of trade taxes. The government is limited in its ability to raise tariff revenue by the fact that when the tariff rate becomes too high, it becomes attractive to produce manufactures domestically and the trade tax base collapses. This will happen if $P - \psi + z \geq \kappa$. Assume that

$$-\mathbf{z}\varepsilon \left[P - \psi + z\right]^{-(1+\varepsilon)} + (P - \psi + z)^{-\varepsilon} > 0 \quad \text{for all } z \in [0, \kappa - P + \psi].$$

This condition says that tax revenue is always increasing in the level of the tariff up to the "choke price," $\kappa - P + \psi$. The tariff revenue limit is therefore reached at $z = \kappa - P + \psi$.

Equilibrium Taxes The incumbent group's transfers now become

$$r_s^I = 2\left(1 - \theta\right)\left[R + t_s\omega + z_s \left(P - \psi + z_s\right)^{-\varepsilon} - m_s - g_s\right].$$

For the same reasons as in the core model, it remains optimal to set $t_s = \tau_s$. Thus it follows that the provision of public goods and the tariff rate will maximize

$$\alpha_s g_s + \frac{(P + z)^{1-\varepsilon}}{\varepsilon - 1} + 2\left(1 - \theta\right)\left[R + \tau_s\omega + \mathbf{z}_s \left(P - \psi + z_s\right)^{-\varepsilon} - m_s - g_s\right].$$

Defining $Z(\lambda)$ from:

$$\lambda\left[-Z\varepsilon\left[P - \psi + Z\right]^{-(1+\varepsilon)} + \left[P - \psi + Z\right]^{-\varepsilon}\right] - \left[P - \psi + Z\right]^{-\varepsilon} \leq 0 \qquad \text{c.s. } Z \geq 0,$$

we can state the optimal tariff rate as

$$z_s^* = \min\left\{\kappa - P + \psi, Z\left(\lambda_s\right)\right\}.$$

As in the case of the income tax in the previous subsection, this follows standard Ramsey-taxation logic. The tariff is set to raise revenue for either transfers or public goods. Whenever the upper bound is not attained, the optimal tariff solves

$$\frac{z_s^*}{P + z_s^*} = \left[\frac{\lambda_s - 1}{\lambda_s}\right]\frac{1}{\varepsilon},$$

which is inversely related to the demand elasticity. Clearly, the tariff is higher when the value of public funds, λ_s, is higher. As before, the latter equals either α, when public goods are provided, or $2(1-\theta)$, when public revenues finance transfers.

Trade-Tax and Income-Tax Shares To examine the shares of the two tax bases in total tax revenue, define

$$\eta_s = \frac{z_s^*\left(P - \psi + z_s^*\right)^{-\varepsilon}}{R + z_s^*\left(P - \psi + z_s^*\right)^{-\varepsilon} + \tau_s \omega} \tag{2.20}$$

as the ratio of tariff revenue to total government revenue. It is clear that this is decreasing in τ_s.

In this very simple model, the condition for the optimal investment in fiscal capacity τ_s is essentially identical to that in the core model. So our predictions about investment levels for three types of states carry over directly and now become predictions about the share of tariff revenue in total tax revenue. The model thus predicts that an increase in fiscal capacity raises total revenue and decreases the revenue share of tariffs. This prediction is consistent with the patterns observed in the raw data and illustrated in Figure 2.3. Intuitively this happens because we have assumed that fiscal-capacity accumulation only increases the capacity to tax incomes.

It is worth remarking on what happens if we reintroduce curvature in the value of public goods. As in Section 2.2.2, let the value of public goods be $\alpha V(g)$, where $V(\cdot)$ is increasing and concave. Then, the demand for public goods is given by

$$\alpha V_g\left(\hat{g}_s\right) = 2(1-\theta),$$

assuming an interior solution. Public-goods demand will be at $\hat{g}_s$ if fiscal capacity is great enough. Otherwise, all taxes will be devoted to spending on public goods. The marginal value of public funds is therefore

$$\lambda_s = \max\left\{\alpha V_g\left(R + \tau_s\omega + z_s\left(P - \psi + z_s\right)^{-\varepsilon} - m_s\right), 2(1-\theta)\right\}.$$

In this case, as fiscal capacity τ_s accumulates and the economy is constrained, there is a reduction in the optimal tariff rate since this depends positively on λ_s. Tariffs reach a minimum at $Z(2(1-\theta))$, which goes to zero as $\theta \to 1/2$, i.e., when political institutions are fully cohesive. This is because a common-interest state has no redistributive reason to levy a tariff. The declining tariff-rate prediction reinforces the switch from tariff revenues to income-tax revenues that we previously obtained solely through an increase in τ_s in the denominator of (2.20). Note that the switch from tariffs to income taxes will be diminished if incumbents have more revenue from natural resources or aid, R, available to them.

2.2.8 An Infinite-Horizon Model

Given that we are studying only a two-period structure, our appeal to dynamics might be viewed with some suspicion. Thus, we now explore what happens when the model is extended to an infinite-horizon setting.[23] We simplify on other fronts to make this tractable and so assume nonstochastic quasi linear preferences for public goods, with a constant α multiplying $V(g_s)$; a linear investment technology for fiscal capacity, $\mathcal{F}_\tau = f$; and the absence of any nontax revenue, so that $R = 0$.

Time Structure Time is now infinite with time periods denoted by $s = \{1, 2, \ldots\}$. As in the two-period model, at any given date, s, one group is the incumbent, denoted by $I_s \in \{A, B\}$, and the other group is the opposition, denoted by $O_s \in \{A, B\}$. At the beginning of each period, there is an exogenous probability γ of a peaceful transition of power, so that $I_s \neq I_{s-1}$. With probability $1-\gamma$, the incumbent remains in power so that $I_s = I_{s-1}$. These transition probabilities are independently and identically distributed over time.

Fiscal Capacity Income is constant over time and given by ω. An incumbent enters period s with an accumulated stock of fiscal capacity, τ_s, which constrains the choice of the current tax rate on income $t_s \leq \tau_s$. We impose an upper bound $\bar{\tau} < 1$, which may be interpreted as the highest *technologically* feasible tax rate, as opposed to the highest *institutionally* feasible tax rate, which is τ_s. Fiscal capacity depreciates at a rate δ in each period and the investment cost for one unit of fiscal capacity is constant at f. In this case, we assume that fiscal

23. This section is based on Besley, Ilzetzki, and Persson (2010).

capacity can be scrapped and "consumed," i.e., fiscal capacity investments can be negative. Throughout, we suppose that $\omega > 2\delta f$. This assumption will hold as long as the cost of maintaining the current stock of fiscal capacity is low enough relative to the existing per capita endowment.

Policy and Indirect Utility The within-period political institutions constraining transfers are identical to those in the core model. The government budget constraint per period is

$$t_s\omega \geq g_s + f\left(\tau_{s+1} - (1-\delta)\,\tau_s\right) + \frac{r_s^I + r_s^O}{2}. \tag{2.21}$$

The transfers accruing to each group are

$$r_s^J = \beta^J\left[t_s\omega - g_s - f\left(\tau_{s+1} - (1-\delta)\,\tau_s\right)\right],$$

where, as above, $\beta^I = 2\,(1-\theta)$ and $\beta^O = 2\theta$. As in the core model, it is always optimal for the incumbent group to use all available fiscal capacity fully and therefore to set $t_s = \tau_s$.

Given an inherited level of fiscal capacity τ_s, the indirect utility of group J in period s is now

$$W\left(\tau_s, g_s, \tau_{s+1}, \beta^J\right) = \alpha V\left(g_s\right) + \beta^J\left[\tau_s\omega - g_s - f\left(\tau_{s+1} - (1-\delta)\,\tau_s\right)\right] + \left(1-\tau_s\right)\omega. \tag{2.22}$$

The Decision Problem We study a Markovian optimization problem for the incumbent, where τ is the single state variable (conditional on the group that holds power), using a particular equilibrium concept detailed in what follows.[24]

The value function of the incumbent, $U^I(\tau)$, can be defined recursively from

$$U^I(\tau) = \max_{\tau', g}\left[W\left(\tau, g, \tau', 2\,(1-\theta)\right) + (1-\gamma)\,U^I\left(\tau'\right) + \gamma U^O\left(\tau'\right)\right] \tag{2.23}$$

$$\text{subject to } \omega\tau \geq g + f\left(\tau' - (1-\delta)\,\tau\right) \tag{2.24}$$

$$\text{and } \tau' \leq \bar{\tau}. \tag{2.25}$$

From here on, we suppress the time subscripts and let τ' denote the state capacity left for the following period.

24. An interesting extension for the future would be to consider subgame perfection and a role for history-dependent strategies.

We denote the policy functions that solve the incumbent's problem by $T(\tau)$ and $G(\tau)$. Using these, we can also define the opposition's value function recursively from

$$U^O(\tau) = W(\tau, G(\tau), T(\tau), 2\theta) + \gamma U^I(T(\tau)) + (1-\gamma) U^O(T(\tau)). \tag{2.26}$$

This expression recognizes that policy is governed by $G(\tau)$ and $T(\tau)$ and that political power alternates with probability γ of the opposition becoming the next government.

Equilibrium Definition Following Besley, Ilzetzki, and Persson (2010), we look for a continuous symmetric Markov perfect equilibrium. This equilibrium notion is formally stated as follows:

Definition: A continuous symmetric Markov perfect equilibrium (CSMPE) of the dynamic state capacity game is a set of functions $U^I(\tau)$, $U^O(\tau)$, $G(\tau)$, and $T(\tau)$ that satisfy the following conditions:

1. $U^I(\tau)$ satisfies (2.23) to (2.25).
2. $G(\tau)$ and $T(\tau)$ are the solutions for G and τ' in the maximization problem (2.23) to (2.25).
3. $U^O(\tau)$ is given by (2.26).
4. The functions $U^I(\tau)$, $U^O(\tau)$, $G(\tau)$, and $T(\tau)$ are continuous for all τ.

The model is a now a fully dynamic game, which we solve by characterizing these functions.

The Generalized Euler Equations To study the equilibrium, observe that the first-order conditions for g and τ' of the incumbent's problem defined by (2.23) to (2.25) are given by

$$\alpha V_g(g) = \lambda + 2(1-\theta) \tag{2.27}$$

and

$$c\alpha V_g(g) \leq (1-\gamma) U^I_\tau(\tau') + \gamma U^O_\tau(\tau'), \tag{2.28}$$

where λ is the Lagrange multiplier on (2.24). Equation (2.28) holds with equality as long as (2.25) is not binding.

Note that $\lambda = 0$ whenever the public good is at $\hat{g}$, defined by

$$\alpha V_g(\hat{g}) = 2(1-\theta), \tag{2.29}$$

which is essentially the interior solution from equation (2.5).

There is a cutoff point $\tau = \hat{\tau}$ at which government expenditures coincide with $\hat{g}$, as defined in (2.29). Above $\hat{\tau}$, the incumbent optimally makes transfers.

State capacity evolves according to a generalized Euler equation, a nonlinear second-order differential equation, which is discontinuous at $\tau = \hat{\tau}$. We split this equation into two, the first holding for choices of $\tau' \geq \hat{\tau}$ and the second holding for $\tau' < \hat{\tau}$. When $\tau' \geq \hat{\tau}$, then

$$\begin{aligned} f\alpha V_g(g) = {} & 2(1-\theta)(1-\gamma)[\omega + f(1-\delta)] - \omega \\ & + 2\gamma\theta\left[\omega + f(1-\delta) - fT_\tau(\tau')\right] \\ & - (1-\gamma)\left[\alpha V_g(g'')(\omega + f(1-\delta)) - \omega - 2(1-\theta)f\right]T_\tau(\tau') \\ & + \gamma\left[\alpha V_g(g'')(\omega + f(1-\delta)) - \omega - 2\theta c\right]T_\tau(\tau'). \end{aligned} \tag{2.30}$$

Furthermore, when $\tau' < \hat{\tau}$, then

$$\begin{aligned} f\alpha V_g(g) = {} & \alpha V_g(g')[\omega + f(1-\delta)] - \omega \\ & - (1-\gamma)\left[\alpha V_g(g'')(\omega + f(1-\delta)) - \omega - f\alpha V_g(g')\right]T_\tau(\tau') \\ & + \gamma\left[\alpha V_g(g'')(\omega + f(1-\delta)) - \omega - f\alpha V_g(g')\right]T_\tau(\tau'). \end{aligned} \tag{2.31}$$

Although seemingly complex, these equations are quite intuitive.

In both cases, the left-hand side represents the opportunity cost of accumulating state capacity. The right-hand sides of (2.30) and (2.31) give the marginal value of an additional unit of state capacity.

Pigouvian Benchmark It is worth briefly revisiting the Pigouvian solution in this setting, where $\theta = 1/2$ and $\gamma = 0$. The resulting problem boils down to a more-or-less standard dynamic programming problem, with the value function (2.23) written as

$$U^I(\tau) = \max_{\tau', g}\left\{\alpha V(g) + \omega(1-\tau) - g - f\left(\tau' - (1-\delta)\tau\right) + U^I(\tau')\right\}$$

subject to

$$\omega\tau \geq g + f\left(\tau' - (1-\delta)\,\tau\right).$$

The solution has a unique, globally stable, steady state with

$$\alpha V_g\left(g^*\right) = \frac{\omega}{\omega - f\delta} > 1 \quad \text{and} \quad \tau^* = \frac{g^*}{\omega - f\delta} < \hat{\tau}.$$

If fiscal capacity were costless, the planner would accumulate sufficient fiscal capacity to fund the Lindahl-Samuelson optimal level of public goods. However, that level of public goods requires recurrent expenditures to maintain the necessary stock of fiscal capacity. Indeed, $f\delta$ is the incremental cost of maintaining that level of fiscal capacity. Thus, in the long run, public goods are provided below the Lindahl-Samuelson level. As in the case of a distortionary income tax described earlier, the need to spend resources on the maintenance of the tax infrastructure leads the solution to diverge from that prescribed in traditional normative public-finance models. In the steady state, investment in fiscal capacity is sufficient to support public-goods provision, but no transfers are made by a Pigouvian planner.

Political Equilibria In cases where $\theta < 1/2$ and $\gamma > 0$, there are three possible long-run outcomes mirroring what we showed in the two-period model. Which of these outcomes obtains depends on the following two conditions that suitably modify the cohesiveness and stability conditions from the core model:

Cohesiveness: $2\,(1-\theta) \leq \dfrac{\omega}{\omega - f\delta}$

and

Stability: $(1-\gamma)\,(1-2\theta) + \theta > \dfrac{(1-\theta)\,f + \frac{\omega}{2}}{f\,(1-\delta) + \omega}.$

As in the core model, the cohesiveness condition guarantees that the outcome converges to the Pigouvian optimum. This is a common-interest steady state. We do not require that $\theta = 1/2$ and $\gamma = 0$, but need only the weaker Cohesiveness condition for the planning solution to be implemented. At the Pigouvian level of public goods, no incumbent government would wish to divert resources toward transfers. As can be seen from the cohesiveness condition, this common-interest steady state requires that θ lie above a well-defined benchmark value.

The remaining part of the (θ, γ) space is split into two by the stability condition. This split is similar to that seen earlier in Figure 2.4. A redistributive steady state occurs when the cohesiveness condition fails and the modified stability condition is satisfied. This has $\tau = \bar{\tau}$ and is also globally stable. Here, the steady state has maximal fiscal capacity, public goods provision is at $\hat{g}$, and residual tax revenue is used to make transfers.

Finally, and as before, the weak steady state is the case where the cohesiveness and stability conditions both fail. In this case $\tau = \hat{\tau}$, but the revenue is low enough that the economy is not producing public goods anywhere near the Lindahl-Samuelson level. This outcome is also globally stable.

We refer the interested reader to Besley, Ilzetzki, and Persson (2010) for details on the dynamics and the steady states. The take-away message for the reader is that the general insights of the two-period analysis are preserved in this multiperiod setting.

2.3 *Empirical Implications and Data*

We end this chapter by taking a look at the cross-sectional data in light of the implications of the theory that we have presented so far. Although we present a number of partial correlations, it is important to point out that these are no more than correlations. Thus, our empirical exploration is not intended as a convincing test of the model's predictions and we are not claiming to be uncovering causal patterns in the data. Convincing tests of the theory would require a more credible empirical strategy, one that isolates exogenous variation in the predicted determinants of fiscal capacity. That said, we believe that the empirics presented here do breathe life into the theory. Moreover, the theory in this chapter does prove to be a useful guide for thinking about measurement.

Measuring Fiscal Capacity To measure fiscal capacity, the variable τ in the model, we use five different proxies, four of which rely on data from the IMF.[25] Some of them have already been taken into account in the figures that we presented in Chapter 1 and earlier in this chapter.

From the IMF data, we take the ratio of total tax revenue to GDP, measured at the end of the 1990s. Although it is not necessarily a measure of fiscal

25. The data are from Baunsgaard and Keen (2005).

capacity, we think that this variable is highly likely to be correlated with such capacity. To hold the total tax take constant, we also use the IMF data to measure the share of revenue from income taxes in total taxes, also at the end of the 1990s. Since the model is about building the capacity to charge an income tax, this is a natural measure of fiscal capacity. As argued in Section 2.2.7 on the basic model extended with trade taxes, a decline in trade taxes is likely to be an important part of the accumulation of fiscal capacity. Drawing on that discussion, we use the IMF data to measure the share of *nontrade* taxes in the 1990s. Finally, we use these data to compute the difference between the income-tax share and the trade-tax share as a fourth measure of fiscal capacity.

Recalling the discussion about the microfoundations for fiscal capacity in Section 2.2.1, the size of the informal economy is likely to be inversely related to the ability of the government to enforce taxes. Hence, a larger size of the formal economy is likely to be indicative of greater fiscal capacity. We gauge the size of the formal economy as one minus the share of the informal economy in GDP as measured by the World Bank in 2006.

In all of these cases, the variable we construct is thus higher the higher the fiscal capacity. We rescale each variable by dividing by the standard deviation in the sample, such that the regression coefficients we estimate are comparable for the different versions of the dependent variable. Table 2.1 shows the correlation coefficients among these different measures of fiscal capacity. As expected, they are all positive and relatively high, suggesting that our proxies indeed pick up some common component. Generally, the correlation among the IMF measures is higher, between 0.7 and 0.95, than the correlations between with the formal-sector share and the tax shares, which lie between 0.55 and 0.62. A possible explanation is that the formal sector is measured in a noisier way than the other variables.

Measuring Parameters of the Model Next, we have to find empirical counterparts to the core parameters that determine fiscal capacity in the model. For all variables, we use values from before 2000, so that they can be viewed as predetermined at the point at which we measure our outcome variables. Naturally, this does not guarantee that the independent variables are not correlated with the error. But it makes it less likely.

To proxy for the demand for common-interest spending, parameter ϕ in the model, we compute the proportion of years in external war from 1816 (or when

Table 2.1 Correlations among fiscal-capacity measures

	Tax revenue share in GDP	Income-tax share	Nontrade-tax share	Income-tax bias	Formal sector share
Tax revenue share in GDP	1.000				
Income-tax share	0.815	1.000			
Nontrade tax share	0.729	0.693	1.000		
Income-tax bias	0.846	0.954	0.878	1.000	
Formal sector share	0.564	0.587	0.580	0.624	1.000

a country became independent) until 2000, as measured by the Correlates of War (COW) database (in each year, we use the sum of the binary indicator variables "interstate war" and "extrastate war"). Thus the idea is that a high prevalence of war was associated with a high risk of war, which the theory identifies as a positive determinant of fiscal-capacity investment (at least in some types of states).

Another aspect of the demand for common-interest spending was highlighted in Section 2.2.3. There we argued that polarization/heterogeneity between groups in their valuations of public goods served to reduce $\widetilde{\alpha}_H$, defined as the effective value of public goods in the high-value state from the perspective of the period-1 incumbent. Empirically, we use the extent of ethnic divisions in society as a proxy for this parameter. In particular, we gauge ethnic divisions from the degree of ethnic fractionalization, as measured in Fearon (2003). As other measures of ethnic fractionalization, this variable reflects the probability that two randomly selected people in society belong to two different ethnic groups. It ranges from 0 (perfectly homogeneous) to 1 (highly fragmented). To measure a higher value of $\widetilde{\alpha}_H$, and thus less (polarization) heterogeneity and a higher investment incentive, we take one minus this fractionalization measure to obtain a measure of ethnic homogeneity.

To gauge cohesive institutions for each country, the parameter θ in the model, we compute the average value from 1800 (or independence) to 2000 for its constraints on the executive, as coded in the Polity IV database (the variable "Xconst," measured on a scale from 1 to 7 in each year). We believe that this variable is a reasonable proxy for the constraints faced by the incumbent in our model, and we normalize the country scores to lie between 0 and 1.

As for political stability, the parameter $1-\gamma$ in the model, we use the average values over the same period for open and competitive recruitment of the executive. That is to say, we assume that in a country where the recruitment of the executive is selected out of a small group through a closed process, an incumbent becomes more entrenched in her (expected) hold on power. The data we utilize are also from the Polity IV data (the combined score on variables "Xrcomp" and "Xropen," which take values between 2 and 7 in any given year). To get a measure of political stability we invert these average values and once more scale them to lie between 0 and 1.

For income, the parameter ω in the model, we use the logarithm of GDP per capita measured in the year 2000 according to the Penn World Tables (variable "Real GDP per capita in constant 2005 international prices," in version 6.3 of this database).

Income inequality was discussed in Section 2.2.4. To proxy for a value of ω^I/ω close to 1 in the model, we construct a binary indicator for a low level of income inequality, measured as late as possible, in the Deininger and Squire (1996) data (our specific measure is a Gini coefficient in the lower third of the countries in the database).

As the observant reader will have noted, we have defined all the right-hand-side variables such that the theoretical prediction is for a positive association with fiscal capacity, i.e., a positive regression coefficient in the results to follow.

Basic Correlations We begin by showing some basic partial correlations among the five fiscal-capacity measures and the proxies for parameters $\phi, \theta, (1-\gamma)$, and $\widetilde{\alpha}_H$. Column (1) in Table 2.2 shows that, as expected from the theory, our proxies for all four parameters—past wars, high executive constraints, political stability, and ethnic homogeneity—are positively and significantly correlated with the share of total taxes in GDP. With very few exceptions, the same correlation pattern is also present for all the other measures of fiscal capacity.

What do the sizes of these coefficients imply? As an example, the estimated coefficient for the prevalence of war fluctuates just below 2. This means that a country history that entails 25%, rather than 0%, of the last 200 years (or the time since independence) spent in wartime is associated with higher fiscal capacity in the present by about half a standard deviation in the sample. By a similar calculation, a country with a 25% higher historical value of its constraints on the executive constraints score is associated with a higher present fiscal capacity of about half a standard deviation in the sample. Concretely, half

Table 2.2 Fiscal capacity and covariates: simple correlations

	(1) Tax revenue share in GDP in 2000	(2) Income-tax share in 2000	(3) Nontrade-tax share in 2000	(4) Income-tax bias in 2000	(5) Formal sector share around 2000
Prevalence external war before 2000	1.897*	1.213	2.387**	1.972**	1.671**
	(1.142)	(0.952)	(0.915)	(0.965)	(0.690)
Average executive constraints before 2000	2.130***	2.309***	1.135***	2.001***	1.768***
	(0.374)	(0.335)	(0.312)	(0.307)	(0.356)
Average nonopen executive recruitment before 2000	1.080**	1.254***	0.541	1.054***	1.490***
	(0.432)	(0.451)	(0.391)	(0.392)	(0.447)
Ethnic homogeneity (1 – ethnic fractionalization)	1.058***	0.438	0.656**	0.606**	0.709**
	(0.300)	(0.271)	(0.304)	(0.270)	(0.298)
Observations	104	104	103	103	109
R-squared	0.503	0.465	0.301	0.482	0.317

Notes: Robust standard errors in parentheses: * significant at 10%; ** significant at 5%; *** significant at 1%.

a standard deviation is equal to about 5 percentage points of taxes in GDP and 10 percentage points of income taxes in total taxes.

Interaction Effects However, the correlations in Table 2.2 do not really engage with the predictions of the model, particularly those that we discussed in connection with the global and local comparative statics derived in Section 2.1. Thus, we should expect that an increase in ϕ raises fiscal capacity, τ, in line with the Hintze-Tilly hypothesis, only in a common-interest or redistributive state, but not in a weak state, and that there is a stronger effect of war (high ϕ) when cohesiveness (θ) is high. Similarly, our model predicts that political instability $1-\gamma$ has an impact on the decision to invest in fiscal capacity. However, these local comparative statics are only present when θ is high enough and for the range of γ where the stability condition holds. Thus we would expect higher political stability to have a positive effect on the decision to invest in fiscal capacity when cohesiveness is low, but to have no effect when cohesiveness is high. Moreover, by the global comparative statics, we expect high values of θ to raise the likelihood of a country being in the common-interest or redistributive state and, hence, undertaking positive investments in fiscal capacity.

To study these issues, we construct a binary variable for high versus low cohesiveness by splitting the countries into two groups, depending on whether their (normalized) average score on the executive constraints variable is above or below 0.5. For countries below that value, we code the binary cohesiveness variable as low (a value of 0). This applies to about two-thirds of the countries in our sample. For the remaining third, with an average score above 0.5, the binary variable is coded as high (a value of 1).

We then add two terms to the specification in Table 2.2, namely the binary high-executive constraints indicator times the continuous measure of past wars and the binary low-executive constraints indicator times the continuous measure of past political stability. (We also add the binary executive constraints variable by itself, but this is never significant and is not shown in the table.)

Table 2.3 shows our estimates when this more theory-driven specification is applied to the five measures of fiscal capacity. The basic parameters in the theory continue to be significantly associated with the fiscal-capacity measures. In particular, the average value of executive constraints continues to have a strongly positive and significant correlation with all measures of fiscal capacity. But the interaction terms rarely display the pattern expected from the theory. Although this is somewhat disappointing, we want to stress a point made earlier; cross-sectional correlations such as these are not reliable enough for any meaningful test of the theory. At best, they can serve as useful diagnostics. Thus, the estimates should be taken with a grain of salt. It seems likely that more convincing tests of the theory will exploit time-series variation in a more convincing manner rather than relying solely on cross-sectional variation.

Income and Income Inequality As we noted in Section 2.1, the model also makes predictions on the link between income and fiscal capacity. All else being equal, a higher ω raises state capacity in common-interest and redistributive states in our basic two-period model. In the infinite horizon model of Section 2.2.8, higher income also raises the likelihood of a redistributive state and higher fiscal capacity. Given this, we should expect higher income per capita to be positively correlated with fiscal capacity when executive constraints are high. We may also be concerned that the right-hand-side variables of the regressions in Tables 2.2 and 2.3 are correlated with income per capita, and it would be good to know whether these findings are robust.

Table 2.3 Fiscal capacity and covariates: interaction terms

	(1) Tax revenue share in GDP in 2000	(2) Income-tax share in 2000	(3) Nontrade-tax share in 2000	(4) Income-tax bias in 2000	(5) Formal sector share around 2000
Prevalence external war before 2000	3.136	1.221	7.819***	4.604**	−1.029
	(2.928)	(3.076)	(2.426)	(2.288)	(2.790)
External war* high executive constraints dummy	−1.539	−0.134	−6.204**	−3.096	3.176*
	(3.030)	(3.180)	(2.449)	(2.421)	(2.880)
Average nonopen executive recruitment before 2000	1.934*	2.074***	1.053*	1.834***	1.125**
	(1.167)	(0.683)	(0.536)	(0.635)	(0.562)
Nonopen executive recruitment* low executive constraints dummy	−1.425	−1.176	−0.838	−1.156	0.961
	(1.140)	(0.774)	(0.636)	(0.701)	(0.630)
High executive constraints dummy	0.495	0.169	0.010	0.080	−0.572
	(0.388)	(0.371)	(0.516)	(0.365)	(0.460)
Average executive constraints before 2000	1.083*	1.790***	1.078**	1.679***	2.772***
	(0.596)	(0.543)	(0.516)	(0.501)	(0.658)
Ethnic homogeneity (1 – ethnic fractionalization)	0.774**	0.233	0.472	0.389	1.021***
	(0.312)	(0.285)	(0.358)	(0.291)	(0.352)
Observations	104	104	103	103	109
R-squared	0.550	0.490	0.337	0.503	0.352

Notes: Robust standard errors in parentheses: * significant at 10%; ** significant at 5%; *** significant at 1%.

Adding income to the regressions does raise other issues, however. In the next chapter, we argue that a specification with income on the right-hand side is problematic. The reason for this is that we expect a productive role for government to generate a positive correlation between income per capita and fiscal capacity. Moreover, this correlation is driven by the other determinants isolated by the theory.

Nevertheless, the first three columns in Table 2.4 add log income per capita to the same specification as in Table 2.2 for the tax share of GDP, the income-tax share in total taxes, and the size of the formal sector. (We have also tried to add income interacted with high executive constraints with mixed

Table 2.4 Fiscal capacity and covariates: additional controls

	(1) Tax revenue share in GDP	(2) Income-tax share in total revenue	(3) Formal sector share	(4) Tax revenue share in GDP	(5) Income-tax share in total revenue	(6) Formal sector share
Prevalence external war before 2000	1.536 (1.076)	0.884 (0.867)	1.203* (0.660)	0.819 (1.341)	0.583 (0.860)	1.484** (0.659)
Average executive constraints before 2000	1.595*** (0.415)	1.757*** (0.383)	0.891** (0.397)	1.163** (0.452)	1.240*** (0.402)	1.131** (0.429)
Average nonopen executive recruitment before 2000	0.686* (0.408)	0.866** (0.410)	0.989** (0.428)	0.891* (0.474)	0.473 (0.396)	1.249** (0.475)
Ethnic homogeneity (1 – ethnic fractionalization)	0.718* (0.368)	0.085 (0.339)	–0.010 (0.372)	0.423 (0.384)	0.024 (0.322)	0.084 (0.397)
Log(GDP per capita) in 2000	0.209** (0.105)	0.221** (0.099)	0.398*** (0.106)	0.350*** (0.112)	0.342*** (0.083)	0.378*** (0.117)
Low value of inequality				0.513* (0.297)	0.321** (0.151)	–0.182 (0.191)
Observations	103	103	109	83	83	90
R-squared	0.531	0.496	0.404	0.591	0.570	0.480

Notes: Robust standard errors in parentheses: * significant at 10%; ** significant at 5%; *** significant at 1%.

results.) The results for income are as expected from the theory and from the empirical clustering already identified in Chapter 1. That is, income per capita is strongly positively correlated with all three measures of fiscal capacity. Almost all of the other parameters maintain the same sign as in Table 2.2, but only the correlations with average executive constraints and nonopen and noncompetitive executive recruitment are statistically significant.

The final three columns add our measure of low income inequality to the same specification. Generally, low inequality is correlated with high fiscal capacity. As argued in Section 2.2.4, this is consistent with the most likely prediction of the theory, especially if we are willing to assume a positive relation between economic and political power. The other correlations are not very much affected.

The empirical results that we have presented are purely illustrative. However, they do suggest that some of the determinants highlighted by the theory may be relevant to understanding the cross-country patterns in fiscal capacity. A great deal remains to be done, however, to bring the theory to the data in a more serious way. In particular, there is scope for trying to explain the within-country variation in the data, such as the introduction of new tax bases like the income tax, by way of historical events, including wars and political reforms.

2.4 *Final Remarks*

In this chapter, we have explored the forces that shape investments in fiscal capacity. We have set out a core model that shows how this aspect of state building is influenced by economic and political factors, such as common interests and political institutions. A key feature of the model has been to delineate the types of states that can emerge in equilibrium. We have also shown that the model can be given microeconomic foundations and demonstrated how it can be extended in a number of directions that lead to more realism.

The main focus of the chapter has been on the extractive role of government and on some of the issues raised in traditional public-finance models. This has laid the groundwork for the analyses to come. The models in the chapter rest on many simplifying assumptions, and although analytically tractable, these assumptions come at a price. In particular, we have kept the level of productivity in the economy fixed, and have thus treated income per capita as exogenous. This is an important omission, given that one of our main ambitions in the book is to understand the clustering of state capacity and income at different levels of development. Moreover, many actions by government in its productive role do affect private-sector income, either directly or indirectly through the working of markets. The next chapter shows how these actions can be brought into the framework.

2.5 *Notes on the Literature*

The core model used here is based on Besley and Persson (2009b, 2010b). Many of the underlying ideas are developed verbally by Hintze (1906) and

Tilly (1985, 1990). Cukierman, Edwards, and Tabellini (1992) develop an early model in which investment in income taxes (fiscal capacity) reduces reliance on seigniorage. They also spell out the implications of polarization and political instability.

There is a vast literature on taxation and development, which relates to the general issues in this chapter. Burgess and Stern (1993) and Kaldor (1963) provide overviews of taxation in low-income countries and the ways that tax collection can be restructured and improved. Collections of articles on taxation and development issues include Bird and Oldman (1980), Gordon (2010), and Newbery and Stern (1987). Keen (2010) gives an up-to-date review of the policy experience and more recent literature.

Many influential contributions have studied the forces that have shaped the tax system in history. These often emphasize the importance of political institutions in shaping this process. Bonney (1999) is a collection of essays that look at a variety of historical experiences with the different paths taken all over Europe. Dincecco (2011, Chapter 1) provides a comprehensive overview of the historical literature. Hoffman and Rosenthal (1997) offer an overview of the issues relating public finance to warfare. For a specific discussion of U.K. public finances with a central role for war see Brewer (1989) and O'Brien (2001, 2005). Mathias and O'Brien (1976) contrast the historical experiences of France and the United Kingdom, bringing out the differences in economic and political structure. Karaman and Pamuk (2011) discuss the evidence from early modern Europe.

Schumpeter (1918) is a classic reference in fiscal sociology and our opening quote is from his work. A large modern literature links taxation to culture, politics, and governance, including Bräutigam, Fjeldstad, and Moore (2008), Levi (1988), and Moore (2004). Increasingly this taxation is seen as part of a broader state-building agenda. Levi (1988) discusses the idea that a tax system can be viewed as a contract between citizens and government, linking trust in government and taxation together. This idea is developed formally in Perroni and Scharf (2007), who use a repeated game framework with collective punishments.

At the heart of building fiscal capacity is the idea of expanding tax enforcement and compliance. The earliest formal paper in the tax-enforcement literature is Allingham and Sandmo (1972), which models the gamble that people take when deciding to pay their taxes, facing a probabilistic fine if they do not comply. Cowell (1990) and Slemrod and Yitzhaki (2002) survey the key models and the evidence, which mainly takes off from the Allingham-Sandmo approach. Kleven, Thustrup Kreiner, and Saez (2009) consider the role of firms in transmitting taxation as a means of reducing compliance costs and argue that this was an important factor in shaping the large increases in tax revenue raised by government in the twentieth century.

There is growing interest in the idea that tax morale is central to understanding tax compliance and Torgler (2007) surveys the theoretical and empirical contributions, which draw on psychology and economics in explaining why people pay their taxes. This literature tends to move away from the rational-gambler model toward a wider interpretation of motivation by tax payers. Zolt and Bird (2005) is a useful overview of the issues involved in extending the domain of personal-income taxation in developing countries, where compliance is a more serious problem.

Tanzi (1987) remains a useful quantitative overview of patterns of taxation and development. For a comprehensive overview of the evidence on the choice of tax levels and tax bases see Kenny and Winer (2006). A number of studies have looked at the adoption of specific taxes. Aidt and Jensen (2009a) develop an event study of factors influencing the introduction of an income tax. Berry and Berry (1992) study the factors leading to adoption of income taxes in the context of U.S. states. Scheve and Stasavage (2010) look at inheritance taxation in historical perspective, highlighting the importance of both economic and political developments. Keen and Lockwood (2010) study the factors that have influenced the adoption of a VAT. Aizenman and Jinjarak (2008) argue that political instability makes tax collection from a VAT less effective. Gordon and Li (2009) stress the fact that developing countries rely heavily on trade taxes and suggest a theoretical explanation. Baunsgaard and Keen (2005) consider the impact of trade liberalization on taxes, and Jensen (2010) studies the relationship between tax revenues from oil wealth and other forms of taxation. Dincecco (2011) is a broad historical study of how taxation interacted with political reform, especially fiscal centralization and limited government, in several West European countries.

Cárdenas (2010) and Cárdenas and Tuzemen (2010) extend the model in Besley and Persson (2009b) to study the impact of income inequality on fiscal-capacity investments, theoretically and empirically. Gradstein (2008) and Chong and Gradstein (2007) also consider the link between inequality and state capacity. The impact of polarization on public finance was studied by Alesina, Baqir, and Easterly (1999), who argue that greater polarization is associated with lower public-goods provision. Esteban, Ray, and Duclos (2004) study a variety of polarization measures theoretically and empirically.

Overviews of the political economy of taxation and public-goods provision include Hettich and Winer (1999) and Persson and Tabellini (2002). There is a large emerging literature on dynamic public finance and political economy related to the models developed in this chapter. Golosov, Tsyvinski, and Werning (2006) survey the normative literature. Acemoglu, Golosov, and Tsyvinski (2008, 2009), Azzimonti (2009), Bai and Lagunoff (2011), and Battaglini and Coate (2007, 2008), among others, have studied dynamic political equilibria with government turnover. The dynamic public-goods model in Battaglini and Coate (2007) has many formal similarities with the infinite-horizon model studied in Section 2.2.8. These papers are related to the literature on strategic public debt by Aghion and Bolton (1990), Alesina and Tabellini (1990), and Persson and Svensson (1989), who all study strategic issue of debt in the presence of political turnover.

CHAPTER 3

Legal Capacity

The public good is in nothing more essentially interested, than in the protection of every individual's private rights.

William Blackstone, *Commentaries on the Laws of England*, 1765–1769

This chapter adds an important new dimension to the picture—government efforts to improve the operation of private markets, an intervention that we call legal capacity. This productive role for government can improve the efficiency of resource use and shape the incentives to accumulate capital, issues that tend to surface frequently in academic and policy discussions. Indeed, the need to create a better business climate has been a constant refrain in the development economics literature.

Standing back for a moment, we note that economists hold two broad views on the big question of why some countries are poor, whereas others are rich. The first view, as developed, e.g., in Aghion and Howitt (1998), links poverty to technology: poor countries remain poor because they cannot access or implement modern technologies. This is the modern incarnation of a research program rooted in Solow (1956), where technological change is the engine of long-run growth. The second view, as exposited, e.g., in Banerjee and Duflo (2005), links poverty to resource misallocation: the root of low income is the fact that countries fail to use stocks of capital, labor, and other scarce factors of production in the most efficient manner. This latter view emphasizes structural features that inhibit development and growth and represents the modern incarnation of a research program rooted in Lewis (1954).

Our approach in this chapter takes off from the second view of development and growth. Thus, we put resource misallocation owing to poorly working economic institutions at the heart of poor economic performance. Our treatment of resource misallocation has both static and dynamic aspects.

Static resource misallocation means that an economy with given human and physical capital does not exploit these stocks in the most productive way owing to frictions in contracting or in the protection of property rights. Reducing the extent of such frictions would raise national income for a given capital stock and technology level. This possibility is at odds with the standard neoclassical model and modern endogenous growth theory, where factors of production are assumed to be put to their most productive uses.

Dynamic resource misallocation is then due to the fact that static resource misallocation creates poor incentives for factor accumulation by lowering the return to capital. Moreover, frictions might also inhibit structural change.

In the process of development, improvements in economic institutions can thus help to raise the level and growth of income endogenously. Understanding the incentives governments may have to undertake such improvements is therefore central to understanding economic prosperity and possible barriers to progress.

To explore these issues, we continue developing our core model in this chapter by adding in contractual frictions or badly protected property rights associated with low legal capacity. We then consider why governments may or may not try to alleviate these problems. As with fiscal capacity in the previous chapter, we allow the government to invest in legal capacity, which we think of as better economic institutions. Throughout, we study these investments jointly with investments in fiscal capacity, so that the model now has two state variables—fiscal capacity and legal capacity. As higher legal capacity makes the economy work better, this extended framework also serves to endogenize income.

In the core model, fiscal and legal capacity are complements. This makes the model extremely tractable and allows us to generate a number of testable predictions on the coevolution of fiscal and legal capacity. The complementarity also gives us immediate insights into the reasons why fiscal and legal capacity may be clustered in the raw data, as we observed in Chapter 1.

Having extended this reduced-form framework, we explore the microeconomic foundations of legal capacity. Specifically, we build a simple general-equilibrium model with labor and capital and use it to illustrate how the government can build economic institutions. These institutions can help to improve the economy's resource allocation and raise its income by improving the contracting environment for the private sector. Such institution building is a core example of an investment in legal capacity.

Using this simple general-equilibrium model, we consider how a lack of fiscal capacity can affect incentives to grant equal access to legal capacity to different groups, i.e., to establish the rule of law. We show how additional complementarities between legal and fiscal capacity may arise: governments in an economy with a greater power to tax prefer to use efficient redistributive instruments (taxes and transfers) rather than inefficient ones (production inefficiency leading to reallocation of quasi-rents). We relate this to the Diamond and Mirrlees (1971) production-efficiency arguments.

Moreover, we expand the model to include private capital formation, which leads to further complementarities that can help to magnify the effect of the standard growth-enhancing mechanisms in the economy.

Finally, we analyze an alternative role for legal support to private production when there is the possibility of predation, either by other citizens or by a kleptocratic bureaucracy. Legal capacity now enables governments to protect private property rights against such predation. As we show, however, it is far from clear that legal capacity will be fully exploited for this purpose, especially when government decisions are taken by small elites who are able to capture the main fruits of predation. In fact, the incentives of such rent-seeking elites may cause a predatory weak state, which is caught in a legal-capacity trap.

Some Basic Facts Before proceeding with the model development, we remind the reader of the clustering patterns discussed in Chapter 1. Figure 1.3 showed a strong positive correlation between fiscal capacity, measured by the total tax take in GDP, and legal capacity, measured by an index of property-rights protection. In addition, these measures of state capacity were both strongly correlated with income.

Essentially the same pattern also shows up for other measures of state capacity. For example, we can use one of our alternative measures of fiscal capacity in Chapter 2, namely the share of income taxes in total taxes at the end of the 1990s. We plot this against one of the alternative measures of legal capacity to be used in this chapter, namely an index of contract enforcement (from the World Bank's Doing Business Survey, applying to the early 2000s). As the name suggests, that index focuses on the enforcement of contracts rather than on the enforcement of property rights. The resulting scatterplot is shown in Figure 3.1, which, like Figure 1.3, conditions on country income per capita in the upper, middle, and lower thirds of the 2000 world income distribution. Fiscal and legal capacity are, obviously, also positively correlated

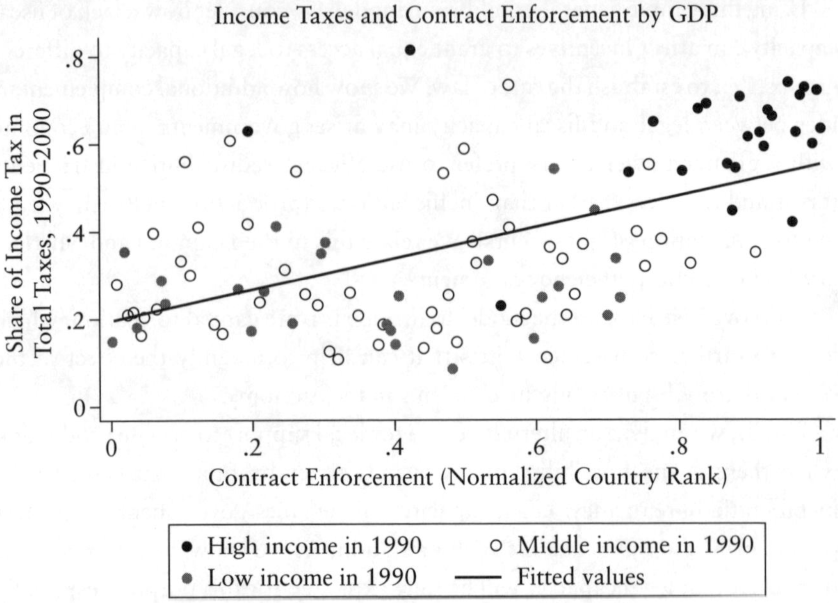

Figure 3.1 Income taxes and contract enforcement conditional on GDP.

when measured by these two alternative indexes. As in Figure 1.3, both legal and fiscal capacity are positively correlated with income. Clearly, any model that we develop should be consistent with such correlations.

Existing Literature A large literature related to this chapter studies the incentives for governments to create market-supporting institutions. In a seminal contribution, North and Weingast (1989) argue that political reform during the Glorious Revolution in England was the *sine qua non* for the development of a market economy. Similar ideas are also key to the interpretation offered by Acemoglu, Johnson, and Robinson (2001) for the observed correlation between income per capita and settler mortality in former colonies. Similarly, Engerman and Sokoloff (2002) argue that factor endowments, leading to income inequality, shaped different development patterns in the Americas via their effect on institutions.

An important strand of literature is focused on the institutions that support financial markets, such as the protection of minority shareholders or private property rights—see, e.g., Acemoglu and Johnson (2005), La Porta, Lopez de Silanes, Shleifer, and Vishny (1998), Pagano and Volpin (2005), and Rajan and Zingales (2003). An early contribution by Svensson (1998) argues theoretically and empirically that political instability and polarization hamper the incentives for governments to develop protection of property rights and that this feeds back to private investment. In line with this literature, we treat market-supporting institutions as endogenous. But a key difference of our approach is that we study market-supporting institutions together with taxation.

Many researchers have found a positive correlation between measures of financial development, or property-rights protection, and economic growth [see, e.g., Hall and Jones (1999) and King and Levine (1993)]. However, those expecting to find a negative relation between taxes and growth have basically come up empty-handed [see, e.g., the overview in Benabou (1997)].

Since the appearance of the work by La Porta et al. (1998), a large literature has emerged that studies how a country's legal origin shapes aspects of its economic development. The leading interpretation of these findings is that legal systems influence how contracts are written and enforced in different societies.

Plan of the Chapter The structure of the chapter is as follows. In Section 3.1, we expand the core model framework from Chapter 2 to include legal capacity. Here, the government's ability to support markets and production is modeled on reduced form. We study investment decisions by incumbent governments, showing how the basic analytical approach from Chapter 2 carries over to a two-dimensional conception of state building. We also develop some comparative statics, showing that the determinants identified in Chapter 2 now become joint determinants of both forms of state capacity.

Section 3.2 broadens and deepens the core model in a number of directions. A first subsection model lays microeconomic foundations for legal capacity in the form of contract enforcement in a two-period, two-group, two-sector, two-factor model. Apart from providing underpinnings to the core model, the microeconomic foundations allow us to explore a number of additional issues. In Subsection 3.2.2, we ask whether a given level of legal capacity will always be fully utilized and whether that situation is likely to persist. Subsection 3.2.3 adds private capital accumulation and observes that this becomes a complement to legal-capacity building. In Subsection 3.2.4, we provide a model with an alternative interpretation of legal capacity, namely as stronger protection of property rights against predation, and how this setup can be used to think about rule by a small corrupt elite. This last extension shows the possibility of a legal-capacity trap, where a weak state becomes rooted not so much in political instability but in the rent-seeking incentives of ruling elites.

Section 3.3 discusses empirical implications of the theory developed in the chapter and extends the empirical results from Chapter 2 to include legal capacity. In Section 3.4, we offer concluding comments, before providing some notes on related literature in Section 3.5.

3.1 *The Core Model with Legal Capacity*

Suppose now that income for group J is no longer given parametrically, but by a function $y = y\left(p_s^J\right)$, for $J \in \{I, O\}$, where $y(\cdot)$ is increasing and concave with $p_s^J \leq \pi_s$. The variable p_s^J represents productivity-enhancing group-specific legal support and π_s is legal capacity that constrains a government's ability to offer such support. In Section 3.2.1, we discuss alternative microfoundations for this formulation and explore their implications further. We also discuss what is specific about this formulation compared to general productivity-enhancing investments. In the formulation used here, the income level of a group depends solely on the legal support granted to that group. We assume that legal capacity does not depreciate and that it can be augmented for period 2 by period-1 investments according to the increasing, convex cost function $\mathcal{L}(\pi_2 - \pi_1)$ with $\mathcal{L}_\pi(0) = 0$. Examples of spending to increase legal capacity include building court infrastructure and training and employing judges, as well as building institutions to enforce court judgments, such as employing bailiffs and setting up regulatory agencies.

Analyzing the implications of legal-capacity investment requires only two fairly minor modifications to the model formulated in Section 2.1. As in Chapter 2, taxation applies to income $y\left(p_s^J\right)$, which can now be in the form of wages or returns to ownership of other factors such as land or capital. Private consumption of group J in period s now becomes

$$c_s^J = (1 - t_s)\, y\left(p_s^J\right) + r_s^J.$$

This is increasing in p_s^J since private incomes are higher with better legal support for that group.

The government budget constraint at date s is modified to

$$R + t_s \frac{y\left(p_s^I\right) + y\left(p_s^O\right)}{2} = g_s + m_s + \frac{r_s^I + r_s^O}{2}. \tag{3.1}$$

Here, it is apparent that taxable income is higher if p_s^J is higher for either group. As the budget constraint makes clear, policy on legal support $\{p_s^I, p_s^O\}$ and fiscal policy through $\{r_s^I, r_s^O\}$ can be used in a discriminatory fashion across groups.

We also have to incorporate two additional features into government policy choices. First, we must consider government policy on legal support for each group for a given amount of legal capacity, i.e., the decision over $\{p_s^I, p_s^O\}$. Second, we have to consider the decision to invest in legal capacity, π_s, alongside investment in fiscal capacity.

Timing The timing structure of the model is essentially the same as in the previous chapter. However, for completeness, we remind the reader here:

1. We begin with initial stocks of state capacities $\{\tau_1, \pi_1\}$and an incumbent group I_1. Nature determines α_1 and R.
2. I_1 chooses a set of period-1 policies $\{t_1, r_1^I, r_1^O, p_1^I, p_1^O, g_1\}$ and determines (through investments) the period-2 stocks of fiscal and legal capacity $\{\tau_2, \pi_2\}$.
3. I_1 remains in power with probability $1 - \gamma$, and nature determines α_2.
4. I_2 chooses chooses period-2 policies $\{t_2, r_2^I, r_2^O, p_2^I, p_2^O, g_2\}$.

As in the previous chapter, we look for a subgame perfect equilibrium in policy and state-capacity investments.

3.1.1 Politically Optimal Policy

The incumbent chooses $\{g_s, t_s, p_s^I, p_s^O, r_s^I, r_s^O\}$ to maximize

$$\alpha_s g_s + (1 - t_s)\, y\left(p_s^J\right) + r_s^I$$

subject to

$$t_s \le \tau_s,\ p_s^J \le \pi_s \text{for } J \in \{I, O)\}\,, \quad \text{and} \quad r_s^O \ge \sigma r_s^I, \tag{3.2}$$

and the government budget constraint (3.1). These are just the familiar requirements that the state-capacity constraints are respected and that the government is constrained by institutions when it chooses transfers.

Public-goods provision, taxes, and transfers are determined as in the basic framework analyzed in Chapter 2. Fiscal capacity is fully utilized; transfers are set so that the incumbent receives a residual claim of $2(1-\theta)$ times the revenue that has not been spent on public goods or investments in state capacity; all tax revenue, minus the costs of building the state, is devoted to public goods if $\alpha_s \geq 2(1-\theta)$ and to transfers otherwise.

The new policy issue is the choice of legal support, p_s^J. Here, we have the following result:

Proposition 3.1: *For $s \in \{1, 2\}$ any incumbent I_s and any α_s, all legal capacity is fully utilized, $p^{I_s} = p^{O_s} = \pi_s$.*

Thus the government offers full legal support, within the constraint of its legal capacity, to both groups. This is an obvious implication of our model and has a simple logic. Since $y(\cdot)$ is increasing in p^J, there are gains to increasing legal support in terms of private goods, as well as through the government budget constraint. In a simplified sense, therefore, the result is related to the famous Diamond and Mirrlees (1971) production-efficiency result.

This result parallels the finding for fiscal capacity, at least in our core model, that all capacity that has been created is in fact used. But crucial properties of the model driving this result are that $y(p)$ is increasing and depends only on the "own group's" legal protection p_s^J. In Section 3.2, we revisit this in a microfounded model and explore when it may be optimal for incumbents to restrict the opposition group's access to legal capacity.

3.1.2 Investments in State Capacity

Having shown that legal capacity will be fully deployed, we can now plug the full set of politically optimal policies into the incumbent's and opposition's payoff functions to derive the following "indirect" payoff function for group $J \in \{I, O\}$ in period s:

$$W(\alpha_s, \tau_s, \pi_s, m_s, \beta^J) = \alpha_s G(\alpha_s, \pi_s, \tau_s) + (1-\tau_s) y(\pi_s) + \beta^J [\tau_s y(\pi_s) - G(\alpha_s, \pi_s, \tau_s) - m_s]. \quad (3.3)$$

When we study the optimization problem of the period-1 incumbent, we now have to consider two state variables $\{\tau_2, \pi_2\}$. We can rewrite the new investment objective of this incumbent as

$$W(\alpha_1, \tau_1, \pi_1, \mathcal{F}(\tau_2 - \tau_1) + \mathcal{L}(\pi_2 - \pi_1), 2(1-\theta))$$
$$+ (1-\gamma)U^I(\tau_2, \pi_2) + \gamma U^O(\tau_2, \pi_2),$$

where $U^J(\tau_2, \pi_2)$ are the value functions for $J \in \{I, O\}$.[1] These are defined by

$$U^I(\tau_2, \pi_2) = \left[\phi W\left(\alpha_H, \tau_2, \pi_2, 0, \beta^I\right) + (1-\phi)\, W\left(\alpha_L, \tau_2, \pi_2, 0, \beta^I\right)\right]$$

and

$$U^O(\tau_2, \pi_2) = \left[\phi W\left(\alpha_H, \tau_2, \pi_2, 0, \beta^O\right) + (1-\phi)\, W\left(\alpha_L, \tau_2, \pi_2, 0, \beta^O\right)\right]$$

for the incumbent or the opposition group in period 2, depending on the two state variables.

As will be clear to the reader, very little modification of the core model has been necessary to introduce a productive as well as an extractive role for government. We now consider the implications for investments in both forms of state capacity.

Euler Equations The Euler equations (first-order conditions) for legal and fiscal capacity are now given by

$$y(\pi_2)[(E(\lambda_2) - 1] \leq \lambda_1 \mathcal{F}_\tau(\tau_2 - \tau_1) \qquad (3.4)$$
$$\text{c.s. } \tau_2 - \tau_1 \geq 0$$

and

$$y_\pi(\pi_2)[1 + (E(\lambda_2) - 1)\tau_2] \leq \lambda_1 \mathcal{L}_\pi(\pi_2 - \pi_1) \qquad (3.5)$$
$$\text{c.s. } \pi_2 - \pi_1 \geq 0.$$

As in the previous chapter,

$$\lambda_1 = \max\{\alpha_1, 2(1-\theta)\}$$

is the realized value of period-1 public funds and

$$E(\lambda_2) = \phi\alpha_H + (1-\phi)\lambda_2^L \qquad (3.6)$$

1. For symmetry, we assume that, like legal capacity, fiscal capacity does not depreciate, so that the costs of fiscal-capacity investments are simply $\mathcal{F}(\tau_2 - \tau_1)$.

is the *expected* value of period-2 public funds, with

$$\lambda_2^L = \begin{cases} \alpha_L & \text{if } \alpha_L \geq 2(1-\theta) \\ 2[(1-\theta)(1-\gamma)+\gamma\theta] & \text{otherwise.} \end{cases} \tag{3.7}$$

Equation (3.4) is essentially of the same form as in Section 2.1, whereas (3.5) is new.

The left-hand side of (3.5), which is the marginal benefit of a small increase in legal capacity, has two parts. The first is $y_\pi(\pi_2)$, which represents the direct impact on productivity in period 2. The second is $y_\pi(\pi_2)\,\tau_2\left[E(\lambda_2)-1\right]$, which represents an additional "indirect" effect of investing in legal capacity, which accrues via increased public resources owing to the expansion of the tax base.

Complementarity One important aspect of the model emerges immediately. Fiscal and legal capacity are *complementary* investments whenever $E(\lambda_2)-1 \geq 0$, i.e., when investing in one form of state capacity increases the marginal return to investing in the other. To see this, note that the left-hand side of (3.5) is increasing in τ_2 and the left-hand side of (3.4) is increasing in π_2.

Intuitively, an increase in legal capacity increases incomes and hence tax revenues making fiscal capacity more valuable on the margin. An increase in fiscal capacity increases the value of raising private incomes if the marginal value of public resources is high enough, since there is a return on the margin in the form of greater tax revenue.

As well as being interesting in its own right, this property is analytically convenient since the payoff function is *supermodular* and we can exploit results on monotone comparative statics. Specifically, any factor that raises the value of the left-hand side of both (3.5) and (3.4) will increase investments in both forms of state capacity.[2] More formally, suppose that we write an objective function in "reduced form" as $n(\tau_2, \pi_2; \varphi)$ for relevant "parameters" φ and suppose that $n(\cdot)$ is supermodular in (τ_2, π_2). Then (τ_2, π_2) is monotonically increasing in φ if $\partial^2 n(\cdot)/\partial\tau_2\partial\varphi \geq 0$ and $\partial^2 n(\cdot)/\partial\pi_2\partial\varphi \geq 0$. This is exactly the condition wherein a change in a certain parameter increases the left-hand side of both (3.5) and (3.4).

2. See Theorems 5 and 6 in Milgrom and Shannon (1994). This result was originally due to Topkis and was generalized in Milgrom and Shannon (1994, Theorem 4).

Equilibrium Investments and Different Types of State We now ask under what conditions both investments are positive. Given the assumption that there are no fixed costs, $\mathcal{F}_\tau(0) = \mathcal{L}_\pi(0) = 0$, a sufficient condition is that $E(\lambda_2) - 1 \geq 0$. The necessary condition for legal capacity is weaker, however, because of the direct benefit from legal-capacity investments according to the first term on the left-hand side of (3.5).

As in Chapter 2, we still have three types of states and the conditions for them to arise are exactly the same. If the cohesiveness condition holds ($\alpha_L \geq 2(1-\theta)$) and/or ϕ tends to one, then we have a common-interest state that invests in both capacities. Again, this will correspond to the Utilitarian optimum. If the cohesiveness condition fails and ϕ is not near one, but the stability condition holds ($\phi\alpha_H + (1-\phi)\,2\,[(1-\gamma)(1-\theta) + \gamma\theta] \geq 1$), then we have a redistributive state, which also invests in both forms of state capacity. Finally, if the cohesiveness and stability conditions both fail, then we have a weak state. The weak state does not invest in fiscal capacity, but it may still invest in legal capacity. However, even if it does, the legal-capacity investments are lower than in a common-interest or a redistributive state, all else being equal. This is because when $E(\lambda_2) < 1$, the second term on the left-hand side of (3.5) is negative.

3.1.3 Comparative Statics

We now explore the implications of this richer model for state building, as measured by the pace of investment in fiscal and legal capacity. This is done in a series of comparative statics results, which we relate to discussions in the literature by economists and historians.

Value of Public Goods Our first result concerns the impact of having a high demand for public goods.

Proposition 3.2: *A higher expected demand for public goods raises investments in state capacity in common-interest and redistributive states:*

$$\frac{\partial E(\lambda_2)}{\partial \phi} = \alpha_H - \lambda_2^L > 0.$$

Common interests make fiscal capacity more valuable. This result can be utilized to make sense of the Hintze-Tilly hypothesis on the importance of war in building state capacity. However, it clearly applies more widely to any public goods that are national in character, such as broad health-care programs or building a welfare state. These are common-interest activities, but they have to be financed. If demand for such public goods or services is expected to be high, then there is a strong incentive to invest in fiscal capacity, and also—by complementarity—to invest in legal capacity.

Political Instability and Cohesiveness We next look at the stability and cohesiveness of political institutions.

Proposition 3.3: *If institutions are not cohesive and we are in a redistributive state, then investments in fiscal and legal capacity are promoted by lower political instability.*

Formally, this can be seen by observing that a lower γ raises the likelihood that Stability holds. Moreover, λ_2^L is decreasing in γ if this condition holds. This effect is stronger, the more noninclusive the political institutions. As in Chapter 2, more cohesiveness has an uncertain effect on state capacity within the redistributive regime, but if θ rises above the value implied by $\alpha_L = 2\,(1-\theta)$, it moves the economy across the boundary to the common-interest regime.

In Chapter 2, we referred to Great Britain in the century following the Glorious Revolution as an historical example of how political stability—a long period of parliamentary rule for the Whigs—in a noncohesive political system can lead to considerable investments in fiscal capacity. War threats at the time, a high value of ϕ, should have pulled in the same direction. According to the extended model in this chapter, this building of fiscal capacity should also have been followed by investments in legal capacity, i.e., in the support of markets.

In fact, a recent study by Klerman and Mahoney (2005) documents a series of reforms of the British legal system during the eighteenth century. In stepwise reforms, Parliament increased judicial independence by making it harder to remove judges from office (in 1701) and increasing their tenure beyond the rule of a certain monarch (in 1761). Parliament also substantially increased the salaries of judges on three occasions during the century (in 1758–1759, 1779, and 1799, respectively). Klerman and Mahoney show in event-study fashion that equity returns went up at the time of these reforms, indicating that the reforms were indeed perceived as a strengthening of property rights.

The British case in the eighteenth century thus appears consistent with the broad thrust of our model, inclusive of the complementarity. The Glorious Revolution increased the power of Parliament—a rise in θ in terms of our model.[3] When faced with constant threats of war against France—a high ϕ in terms of our model—the stable coalition dominating Parliament implemented reforms that increased the state's ability to raise taxes, as well as reforms to provide more credible and better legal services in support of private markets—increases in τ and π in terms of our model.

Costs of Investment How do factors that determine investment costs affect investment decisions? This is answered in the following proposition:

Proposition 3.4: *Lower costs of either legal or fiscal capacity increase investments in both legal and fiscal capacity in common-interest and redistributive states.*

This can be thought of in terms of a downward multiplicative shift in $\mathcal{L}(\cdot)$ or $\mathcal{F}(\cdot)$, which cuts the right-hand side of (3.5) and (3.4) for given π_2 and τ_2.

Many recent studies of institutions, following La Porta et al. (1998), emphasize the importance of legal origins. Our model suggests a straightforward theoretical role for legal origins via the cost function $\mathcal{L}(\cdot)$. If some legal origins affected the ease with which contracting could be done, we would expect this to boost investments in legal capacity. Perhaps less trivially, we would also expect the same legal origins to affect investments in tax systems in the same direction through the basic complementarity between the two forms of state capacity.

Income and Growth Suppose that there are exogenous productivity differences, which vary over countries or over time. We model these as a shifter on the $y\left(p_s^J\right)$ function, i.e.,

$$y_s^J = \Lambda_s y\left(p_s^J\right).$$

Different values of Λ_s could represent natural productivity differences between countries, owing, say, to geography or to Hicks-neutral improvements in productivity. We now have the following:

Proposition 3.5: *More productive economies (higher Λ_2) choose greater investments in fiscal and legal capacity in common-interest and redistributive states.*

3. This depends on the micropolitical foundations of θ, which we discuss further in Chapter 7.

This comes from observing that a higher Λ_2 will increase the left-hand side of both (3.5) and (3.4). Given the complementarity, this increases investment in both forms of state capacity. This result has both cross-sectional and time-series implications.

Turning to implications for cross-country income differences, we should expect countries with inhospitable geographical environments to have less investment in state capacity. Such investments will tend to magnify these underlying differences, as they feed back to income. Moreover, the generated income differences are likely to be the largest when political institutions are weak, i.e., θ is low enough to imply a weak state because weak states do not invest much in any form of capacity.

When we look at time-series differences, our model predicts that positive productivity shocks—owing, say, to new technology—will also tend to be magnified by accompanying improvements in institutions. At least this will be the case when the state is not weak and the economy is institutionally constrained. Growth will be slower in weak states, which will not benefit from the magnification effect we have identified.

Changes in Λ_2 generate "exogenous" growth. But even if such shifts are absent, the model exhibits "endogenous" growth owing to institutional development through the accumulation of legal capacity. To see this, we define aggregate income by

$$Y(p_s^I, p_s^O, R) = R + \frac{\Lambda_s(y(p_s^I) + y(p_s^O))}{2}.$$

Then, the growth rate predicted by the model in this section is

$$\frac{Y(\pi_2, \pi_2, R) - Y(\pi_1, \pi_1, R)}{Y(\pi_1, \pi_1, R)}.$$

If $\pi_2 > \pi_1$, the growth rate is positive, even if all standard sources of growth, e.g., technological improvement and capital accumulation, are absent.

By improving the contracting or property-rights environment, and hence resource allocation, the government is the engine of growth. Moreover, by complementarity, (expected) government size grows together with legal capacity and income. It follows from the earlier comparative statics results that this rate of endogenous growth is influenced by political institutions and political stability: (θ, γ).

3.1.4 Taking Stock

The comparative statics results are interesting, given the correlations in the raw data shown in Figures 1.3 and 3.1. It is pretty clear that the complementarity of fiscal and legal capacity may help explain the strong correlation between them that we observe in these graphs.

When it comes to the positive correlation between income and state capacity, the picture is somewhat more complex. Legal capacity may be closely related to financial development (in the microfounded model to be presented in the next section, e.g., private credit to GDP is proportional to π). Financial development owing to better institutions can thus cause endogenous growth in income, as discussed earlier. But the relationship can easily go the other way: according to Proposition 3.5, higher income through exogenous growth increases the incentives to invest in legal capacity, leading to financial development.

The complementarity between fiscal and legal capacity also has interesting implications for the relationship between taxation and income growth. If greater legal capacity is driven by the determinants suggested in this section, we would expect it to go hand in hand with greater fiscal capacity. Variation in these determinants would tend to induce a *positive* correlation between taxes and growth. Even in weak states, where $E(\lambda_2) < 1$ (and investment in fiscal capacity is zero), legal capacity and national income are still positively correlated even though taxation and growth are uncorrelated.[4]

These observations relate to recent empirical findings in the macroeconomics of development. Many researchers have found a positive correlation between measures of financial development, or property-rights protection, and economic growth [e.g., Hall and Jones (1999), King and Levine (1993), and many subsequent papers], although Proposition 3.5 warns us that such correlations may not reflect a causal effect of financial markets, but rather reverse causation. But many researchers who expected to find a negative relation between taxes and growth found nothing [see, e.g., the overview in Benabou (1997)]. Simple though it is, our model suggests a possible reason for these findings.

4. However, recall the discussion of income distribution in Chapter 2. Besley and Persson (2009a) show that changes in income distribution generally drive fiscal and legal capacity in opposite directions, inducing a *negative* correlation between taxes and growth.

3.2 *Developing the Model*

This section is designed to deepen and broaden our understanding of the core model with legal capacity. We begin by showing how to give microeconomic underpinnings to the analysis in Section 3.1 in a simple general-equilibrium model. Then, this model is extended in several directions to investigate the consequences of quasi-rents to capital owners, private capital accumulation, and legal capacity as a means of protecting private agents against predation.

3.2.1 Microeconomic Foundations

So far, we have just posited a reduced-form function $y\left(p_s^J\right)$. We now put some microeconomic structure beneath this function and study the implications of doing so. For example, an important feature of the reduced-form specification is that income in group J depends solely on legal support granted to that group and is unaffected by what is offered to the other group. We explore when this assumption is justified. To approach this issue and others like it, we begin by formulating a model without legal capacity and then consider how legal capacity can be introduced.

A Two-Sector Economy The model in Section 3.1 did not specify any kind of production structure, stating simply that income per capita in group J and period s is given by $y\left(p_s^J\right)$. In this section, we set up a model economy with capital and allow individuals to own capital as well as labor. We also assume that some individuals have entrepreneurial talent. If they do, they can acquire capital and hire labor in the economy's factor markets. These markets may work more or less well depending on the extent of contractual frictions. Demands for capital and labor determine factor prices: the equilibrium wage and rental rate on capital. The government can support the economy by providing legal support to reduce market frictions.

This framework will be the parable of the classic dual-economy approach, first introduced by Lewis (1954) and extended by Fei and Ranis (1964). Following that approach, we refer to the two as the "advanced" and "traditional" sector. Unlike earlier contributions, however, we give institutions a central place in fostering the development of the advanced sector. The role of the dual-economy parable is to generate an outside option in traditional production, which provides an outside wage, $\underline{\omega}$.

Production Technologies The advanced sector uses labor and capital in a constant-returns, Cobb-Douglas production function:

$$H_s(K, L) = K^{\eta} L^{(1-\eta)}, \tag{3.8}$$

where K and L are the amounts of capital and labor employed. A fraction of citizens, κ^J, in group J are able to operate this technology. Let $\kappa = \frac{\kappa^A + \kappa^B}{2}$ be the economy-wide fraction of the population with such abilities. Implicitly, this formulation thus includes a third unpriced factor, "entrepreneurial talent," which is endowed by nature.

Production in the traditional sector uses only labor and offers a wage of $\underline{\omega}$. We can think of the analysis in Chapter 2 as an economy where $\omega = \underline{\omega}$, i.e., there is only traditional production.

Factor Endowments and Prices Each member of group J has an endowment of capital of K_s^J at date s, which is exogenously given for the time being (we add private capital accumulation in Section 3.2.3). Unlike the reduced-form model in Section 3.1, this allows output to be heterogeneous across groups. Let

$$K_s = \sum_J \frac{K_s^J}{2}$$

be the economy-wide capital stock per capita. Thus, we can have between-group inequality, even though there is no within-group inequality. We assume that individuals can unilaterally earn a return, $\underline{\rho}$ via some backstop technology. The backstop could be putting the money under a mattress, in which case $\underline{\rho} < 1$ if there is a risk of theft or inflation. It could also be the return to U.S. Treasury Bills, traditionally regarded as a safe investment, in an open world capital market. The economy has two factor prices: ρ is the price of capital traded, when individuals choose to lend to the advanced production sector, and ω is the wage rate. Obviously, for any advanced-sector production to take place, we must have $\rho \geq \underline{\rho}$ and $\omega \geq \underline{\omega}$.

A Neoclassical Benchmark Economy We first consider a frictionless world with these production technologies and factor endowments. This is the standard world of neoclassical economics, where markets work perfectly.

Following standard practice, it is useful to work with a production function in intensive form, which relies on $k = K/L$, i.e., the capital intensity of advanced production. With factor prices (ρ, ω), an advanced-sector producer chooses $\{k, L\}$ to maximize

$$L\left[(k)^{\eta} - \rho k - \omega\right].$$

If we denote the solution by $\left\{\hat{k}, \hat{L}\right\}$, it is straightforward to see that it must fulfill

$$\rho_s = \eta\left(\hat{k}\right)^{\eta-1} \quad \text{and} \quad \omega_s = \left(\hat{k}\right)^{\eta} - \rho_s\hat{k}. \tag{3.9}$$

The marginal product of capital equal to the rental rate and the wage rate exhausts all surplus. With common factor prices, all firms in the advanced sector behave in the same way. What is not immediately clear from (3.9) is whether there is any traditional sector production. To understand this, it is necessary to solve for the general equilibrium and the associated factor prices.

Four Possible Neoclassical Equilibria It is relatively straightforward to show that there are four possible general-equilibrium outcomes, depending on whether some factor prices are set by their outside options. To examine these possibilities, it is helpful to define $\bar{k}$ from

$$\eta\left(\bar{k}\right)^{\eta-1} = \underline{\rho}$$

as the maximal amount of capital per worker that will be employed in the advanced sector given the available outside option.

Case 1: $\rho_s = \underline{\rho}$ and $\omega_s = \underline{\omega}$. This will hold if $K_s \geq \bar{k}$ and $(1-\eta)\left(\underline{\rho}/\eta\right)^{\frac{\eta}{\eta-1}} \leq \underline{\omega}$. In this first case, there is production in both sectors and some capital is devoted to its outside option. This will happen in an economy where either capital is plentiful or the outside return to capital is high. Consequently, the returns to capital and labor in the advanced sector are bid down to their reservation prices. This case is not a possibility (at least when capital stocks are finite) if $\underline{\rho}$ is too low.

Case 2: $\rho_s = \underline{\rho}$ and $\omega_s > \underline{\omega}$. We get this outcome if $K_s \geq \bar{k}$ and $(1-\eta)\left(\underline{\rho}/\eta\right)^{\frac{\eta}{\eta-1}} > \underline{\omega}$. In Case 2, we see only advanced-sector production. However, some capital is allocated to its outside option. Once more, this can only happen when capital is plentiful and $\underline{\rho}$ is not too low.

Case 3: $\rho_s > \underline{\rho}$ and $\omega_s = \underline{\omega}$. This occurs when $K_s < \bar{k}$ and $(1 - \eta) \left(K_s\right)^\eta < \underline{\omega}$. Here, as in Case 1, there is positive production in both sectors. However, capital is fully utilized in the advanced sector. This is the case of a fairly productive traditional sector, which can compete successfully with advanced production. In this world, capital is fairly scarce.

Case 4: $\rho_s > \underline{\rho}$ and $\omega_s > \underline{\omega}$. The final possibility occurs if $K_s < \bar{k}$ and $(1 - \eta) \left(K_s\right)^\eta > \underline{\omega}$. In this case, production is only positive in the advanced sector, and both factors earn returns in excess of their outside options. Case 4 is the one that will prevail when advanced-sector production is sufficiently profitable relative to traditional production. Effectively, this economy works like a one-sector model. Each entrepreneur runs an advanced-sector firm, each of which uses the same share K_s/κ of the capital stock and $1/\kappa$ of the workforce. Hence, the factor prices are given by

$$\rho_s = \eta \left(K_s\right)^{\eta-1} \quad \text{and} \quad \omega_s = \left(K_s\right)^\eta - \rho_s K_s = (1 - \eta) \left(K_s\right)^\eta .$$

The level of the capital stock determines these factor prices as well as the level of income per capita, namely $y_s = \left(K_s\right)^\eta$.

This neoclassical economy has a level of national income that is determined entirely by technology and factor availability, where institutions do not seem to matter. In effect, however, we have implicitly assumed an important role for institutions by supposing that all transactions are frictionless, property rights are perfectly enforced, and there is no theft or predation. These are all very strong assumptions in any economy, especially in economies at an early stage of development. Our next task is to explore the consequences of institutional imperfections. This will focus our minds on how legal capacity might improve the functioning of an economy.

An Institutionally Constrained Economy The neoclassical economy is reminiscent of the standard textbook model of a market economy, where institutions to enforce contract or protect property rights are taken for granted. We now offer a simple modification of the model, which brings these assumptions into the daylight and opens a role for legal capacity to improve resource allocation. The alternative economy is institutionally constrained, as it operates less efficiently than the frictionless neoclassical world. However, the institutional constraints imply that the government can potentially improve the efficiency of the economy by reducing frictions through investments in legal capacity. In a sense, the examples we consider are illustrations to breathe life into the idea of legal capacity. But they are important in order to get an idea of the precise way in which higher legal capacity may improve incomes.

Capital-Market Imperfections There is a long tradition in development economics to see capital-market constraints as a central and important characteristic of poor economies.[5] We follow this tradition as a way of getting into the market-supporting role of government. Specifically, we assume that there is limited enforcement in borrowing, since a borrower can potentially walk away, i.e., fail to repay from any uncollateralized loan. Thus, an individual can only borrow in proportion to his/her initial wealth, which is used as collateral. Formally, we have

$$K \leq \left(1 + p_s^J\right) K_s^J, \tag{3.10}$$

where $p_s^J \in [0, \pi_s]$. This collateral constraint effectively restricts an entrepreneur from borrowing more than a specific fraction of his wealth denoted by $p_s^J K_s^J$. As suggested by the notation, we consider the legal support of the government as raising the amount of effective collateral that can be pledged by borrowers. The legal capacity constraining such legal support can readily be interpreted, e.g., as the number of courts and qualified judges, and the existence and quality of a government credit registry.

Labor Demand and Capital-Market Constraints If the capital constraint binds, optimal labor demand in group J, denoted by $\tilde{L}_s^J$, solves

$$\omega_s = (1 - \eta) \left(\frac{\left(1 + p_s^J\right) K_s^J}{\tilde{L}_s^J} \right)^{\eta} \quad \text{for } J \in \{I, O\}, \tag{3.11}$$

This means that production in the advanced sector earns quasi-rents.

We focus on the extreme case where $\underline{\rho} = 0$, so that all capital in the neoclassical economy would be deployed in the advanced sector (Case 3 or 4 described earlier).[6] This means that the supply price of capital to the advanced sector is effectively zero. In the absence of institutional constraints, as we

5. See Banerjee (2003) and Banerjee and Duflo (2010) for overviews.

6. This considerably simplifies the algebra. It is straightforward to incorporate the more reasonable case where $\underline{\rho} > 0$, but the basic analytics remain the same as long as we are in Cases (3) and (4).

just saw, the capital operated per advanced-sector firm is K_s/κ. However, the entrepreneur is limited to operating $\left(1+p_s^J\right)K_s^J$. Thus if

$$\kappa^J K_s^J\left(1+p_s^J\right)<K_s,$$

the institutional constraint is binding for group J. An economy is institutionally constrained for both groups if

$$1+\pi_s<\min\left\{\frac{K_s}{\kappa^I K_s^I},\frac{K_s}{\kappa^O K_s^O}\right\}.$$

In other words, π_s is small enough so that neither group can access sufficient capital for the neoclassical economy outcome to be attained. In the symmetric case, this boils down to the simple condition that $\left(1+\pi_s\right)\kappa<1$.

We now assume that both groups are indeed so constrained and examine the resulting output levels and how they depend on p_s^J. There are two cases to consider depending on whether the wage rate is set by the traditional-sector outside option or not.

Case 3′: Some traditional production. This is the baseline case, which we highlight in what follows. The relevant case is when

$$\left(\frac{\sum_J \kappa^J\left(\left(1+p_s^J\right)\right)K_s^J}{2}\right)^\eta(1-\eta)\leq\underline{\omega}. \tag{3.12}$$

That is, if all available labor (hypothetically) were to be deployed in the advanced sector—and existing legal capacity is maximally employed in both groups—the marginal product of labor would be below the wage in the traditional sector.

The equilibrium wage rate is then pinned down by the traditional wage, $\underline{\omega}$, and the general equilibrium is one where labor works in both the traditional and the advanced sectors. This is like Case 3 in the previous section. Labor is allocated between the two groups to solve (3.11) at $\omega_s=\underline{\omega}$.

The per capita income of group J is then

$$y^J\left(p_s^J\right)=\kappa^J\left[\left(\left(1+p_s^J\right)K_s^J\right)^\eta\left(\tilde{L}_s^J\right)^{1-\eta}-\underline{\omega}\tilde{L}_s^J\right]+\underline{\omega} \tag{3.13}$$

$$=\eta\left[\frac{\underline{\omega}}{(1-\eta)}\right]^{\left(1-\frac{1}{\eta}\right)}\left(1+p_s^J\right)\kappa^J K_s^J+\underline{\omega} \tag{3.14}$$

using (3.11). The first term is the quasi-rent, owing to the fact that institutions constrain the allocation of capital.

Now, consider an improvement in the contracting environment for group J, such that it can borrow a larger amount for any given collateral. Owing to the linear utility in private consumption (and hence risk-neutrality), we can interpret this improvement as a higher likelihood that a typical court will enforce a debt contract if it is called upon to do so. The effect is given by[7]

$$\begin{aligned} y_p^J\left(p_s^J\right) &= \kappa^J \eta \left(\left(1+p_s^J\right) K_s^J\right)^{\eta-1} \left(\tilde{L}_s^J\right)^{1-\eta} \\ &= \eta \left[\frac{\omega}{(1-\eta)}\right]^{1-\frac{1}{\eta}} \kappa^J K_s^J > 0, \end{aligned} \tag{3.15}$$

which is proportional to the capital ownership of group J.

This microfoundation therefore supports the basic model in Section 3.1 in the case of equal ownership of capital across groups. Legal support increases production by improving the contracting environment, decreasing the friction in capital markets, and enhancing the scope for entrepreneurial activities. But each group's income depends only on its own access to legal support.

Case 4′: No traditional production. We now consider what happens if (3.12) does not hold. All labor is now in the advanced sector and the wage rate is given by

$$\omega_s\left(p_s^I, p_s^O\right) = (1-\eta)\left(\sum_J \frac{\kappa^J}{2}\left(1+p_s^J\right) K_s^J\right)^{\eta}. \tag{3.16}$$

In this case, access to legal support of both groups affects equilibrium wages and, hence, there is a (pecuniary) externality between the groups. Here,

$$\frac{\partial \omega_s\left(p_s^I, p_s^O\right)}{\partial p_s^J} = (1-\eta)\,\eta \frac{\kappa^J}{2} K_s^J \left(\sum_J \frac{\kappa^J}{2}\left(1+p_s^J\right) K_s^J\right)^{\eta-1} > 0.$$

With greater access to capital, labor demand increases, as does the wage rate.

The income in one group now depends on the legal support offered to both groups. Average income per capita in group J is

7. This calculation uses the envelope condition and equation (3.11).

$$y^J\left(p_s^I, p_s^O\right) = \kappa^J\left[\left(\left(1+p_s^J\right)K_s^J\right)^\eta\left(\tilde{L}_s^J\right)^{1-\eta} - \omega_s\left(p_s^I, p_s^O\right)\tilde{L}_s^J\right] + \omega_s\left(p_s^I, p_s^O\right)$$
$$= \left(\sum_J \frac{\kappa^J}{2}\left(1+p_s^J\right)K_s^J\right)^\eta\left[\eta\frac{\kappa^J\left(\left(1+p_s^J\right)K_s^J\right)}{\sum_J \frac{\kappa^J}{2}\left(1+p_s^J\right)K_s^J} + (1-\eta)\right], \tag{3.17}$$

where we have used (3.11) and (3.16). Once again, the first term is the quasi-rent earned by entrepreneurs in the advanced sector.[8]

Now consider the effect of increasing p_s^I and p_s^O on the income per head of the incumbent group. This is given by

$$\frac{\partial y^I\left(p_s^I, p_s^O\right)}{\partial p_s^I} = \left(1-\kappa^I\tilde{L}_s^I\right)\frac{\partial\omega_s\left(p_s^I, p_s^O\right)}{\partial p_s^J}$$
$$+\kappa^I\eta\left(\left(1+p_s^I\right)K_s^I\right)^{\eta-1}\left(\tilde{L}_s^I\right)^{1-\eta} \text{ for } J = I \tag{3.18}$$

and

$$\frac{\partial y^I\left(p_s^I, p_s^O\right)}{\partial p_s^O} = \left(1-\kappa^I\tilde{L}_s^I\right)\frac{\partial\omega_s\left(p_s^I, p_s^O\right)}{\partial p_s^J} \text{ for } J = O. \tag{3.19}$$

There are two effects to consider. Both (3.18) and (3.19) include an effect owing to the change in the equilibrium wage. As already observed, the wage rate increases as more capital is deployed in advanced production. Whether this benefits the incumbent group on the margin depends upon whether that group is a net demander or supplier of labor. If $\kappa^J\tilde{L}_s^J = 1$, the group is self-sufficient and hence changes in the wage rate lead to within-group redistribution but no between-group redistribution. However, even if both groups are identical ex ante, in terms of fractions of entrepreneurs and capital holdings, they will not be identical ex post if $p_s^I \neq p_s^O$. Thus the allocation of legal support can change a group from being self-sufficient to being either a net demander or a net supplier of labor.

The second effect only appears in (3.18) and is the same as in (3.15), reflecting the increase in quasi-rents from extending the amount of capital in use. It is always positive up to the point where all capital is deployed in advanced production.

8. Observe that if the groups are identical and have equal access to property rights then $y^J\left(p_s, p_s\right) = \left(\kappa\left(1+p_s\right)K_s\right)^\eta$, which is below the neoclassical output for this case if $\kappa\left(1+p_s\right) < 1$.

Observe that national income per capita is

$$
\begin{aligned}
Y\left(p_s^I, p_s^O\right) &= \frac{y^I\left(p_s^I, p_s^O\right) + y^O\left(p_s^I, p_s^O\right)}{2} \\
&= \left(\sum_J \frac{\kappa^J}{2}\left(1 + p_s^J\right) K_s^J\right)^\eta . \qquad (3.20)
\end{aligned}
$$

It is therefore clear that

$$
\frac{\partial Y\left(p_s^I, p_s^O\right)}{\partial p_s^J} > 0 \text{ for } J \in \{I, O\} . \qquad (3.21)
$$

Thus, national income is unambiguously increased by a full extension of legal support to both groups. Changes in wages make one group gain and the other group lose, but this is purely a transfer between the groups and so leaves the national income unaffected. What increases the national income is the fact that more legal support brings more capital into productive use.

Legal Capacity and Total Factor Productivity We now show that changes in legal capacity can be thought of as changes in total factor productivity (TFP). For this purpose, we use the model of capital-market imperfections, where wages in the advanced sector exceed $\underline{\omega}$ (Case 4′). Suppose that $\left\{p_s^I, p_s^O\right\}$ is the access that the two groups have to the legal system. Income per capita in the economy $Y\left(p_s^I, p_s^O\right)$ is as in (3.20).

For given factor endowments, capital, K_s, and the unit labor endowment, we have already shown how income varies with access to legal services. Moreover, if $p_s^J = \pi_s$ for both groups, then increased investment in legal capacity raises an economy's income per capita. Indeed, comparing income on two dates, we find that this can be a source of growth.

Productivity-Enhancing Legal Capacity To see how legal capacity can be a source of growth, consider an economy with capital K_s and labor endowment 1. Then, the maximum potential output per capital is $\left(K_s\right)^\eta$. Write actual output as

$$
Y\left(p_s^I, p_s^O\right) = \lambda\left(p_s^I, p_s^O\right)\left(K_s\right)^\eta ,
$$

where $\lambda\left(p_s^I, p_s^O\right) \leq 1$ is a measure of the distance from the production-possibility frontier owing to capital-market imperfections and hence, indirectly, to suboptimal institutions.

As national income is given by (3.20), we have

$$\lambda\left(p_s^I, p_s^O\right) = \left(\sum_J \frac{\kappa^J}{2}\left(1+p_s^J\right)\frac{K_s^J}{K_s}\right)^\eta .$$

Suppose, for the sake of illustration, that we are in a symmetric case, where $K_s^J = K_s$ and $\kappa^J = \kappa$ for $J \in \{I, O\}$, i.e., there are no differences in capital ownership or entrepreneurial ability between the two groups. Then, if $p_s^I = p_s^O = \pi_s$, such that all legal capacity is deployed, we can write

$$\lambda\left(\pi_s, \pi_s\right) = \left(\kappa\left(1+\pi_s\right)\right)^\eta .$$

Thus, output is below its potential value as long as $\kappa\left(1+\pi_s\right) < 1$. This is an intuitive condition. It says that the amount of capital that can be used by entrepreneurs—namely the fraction κ of entrepreneurs scaled up by the quality of institutions $\left(1+\pi_s\right)$—is less than the capital available in the whole population, the size of which we have normalized to one.

Note also that in an equilibrium of this economy, the ratio of total credit to GDP can be written as

$$\frac{\pi_s}{\left(1+\pi_s\right)^\eta}\frac{\left(K_s\right)^{1-\eta}}{\kappa^\eta}.$$

This ratio, which is a central measure in the literature on financial development, is thus monotonically increasing in the economy's legal capacity. We return to this measure in Section 3.3 when we address the empirical implications of the model.

Interpretation The discussion of the level of national income illustrates how, all else being equal, changes in legal capacity would be measured as improvements in TFP. However, these are not technological changes; they are simply improvements in the efficiency of resource allocation owing to better market institutions.

This view—that growth can be stimulated by institutional improvements fostering a more efficient use of resources—is part of an older tradition in development economics that we discussed earlier and is somewhat different from the preoccupation with technology that prevails in much of modern growth theory.

In many ways, the approach pursued here is more closely associated with the institution-based perspective on economic growth and development presented by such authors as Acemoglu, Johnson, and Robinson (2001) and North (1990). We are thus able to embed such ideas into our approach and link it to investing in state capacity.

Legal Capacity as a Public Good If access to legal services were a pure private good, then granting more access to one group would have to come at the expense of the other group. If this were the case, decisions about access to legal support would irreducibly be a redistributive policy between the two groups. However, our presumption is that legal capacity has some elements of a public good. A pure public good, as we know, has two properties: it is both nondepletable and nonexcludable.

In our formulation, extending legal rights as embodied in p_s^J assumes that π_s is a nondepletable but excludable good, so that more access by one group does not reduce the amount that is available for the other. We capture this formally by supposing that $p_s^J \leq \pi_s$ for $J \in \{I, O\}$. This parallels the way in which we modeled fiscal capacity in the previous chapter. Even though there is no directly redistributive issue, there is still a question of whether each group is granted full access to legal capacity, i.e., whether $p_s^J = \pi_s$.

Excludability and the Rule of Law If legal capacity were a pure public good, no discrimination between groups would be possible, as it would then be both nondepletable and nonexcludable, and we would necessarily have $p_s^J = \pi_s$ for $J \in \{I, O\}$. This would correspond to a case where it is impossible to exclude anyone from contracting in the shadow of the law once courts and other forms of protection/enhancement infrastructure have been built. If groups were completely identical this might be the natural assumption. But if groups differ in their geographic location, sectoral composition, or ethnicity, it is certainly possible for incumbents to adapt the legal services rendered by the courts in a way that would benefit certain regions, sectors, or ethnic groups.

Whether it occurs technologically or as the result of a decision made by the incumbent, the case where full legal rights are extended, $p_s^J = \pi_s$, corresponds to the standard interpretation of what it means for a society to have the *rule of law*.[9] Not only should laws and the means to enforce them exist, but all

9. Of course there is more to the rule of law than universality. The concept includes the ideas that legal rules be reasonably known in advance rather than subject to the whim of executive decisionmaking.

citizens should be subject to these laws on an equal basis. In the case where legal capacity is excludable, we are thus able to ask whether the rule of law prevails in a policy equilibrium.

Legal Capacity versus Infrastructure Legal capacity as modeled here does have some distinctive features compared to general productivity enhancing investments in infrastructure. For such cases, it would be natural to suppose that infrastructure such as roads, telecommunications, and bridges directly enter the production function, so that output in the advanced sector would be

$$\Lambda\left(\pi_s\right) K^{\eta} L^{1-\eta},$$

where $\Lambda(\cdot)$ is an increasing concave function and π_s is the stock of infrastructure. This, e.g., is essentially the formulation of state investments in Acemoglu (2005).

It would be natural to think that infrastructure could be targeted geographically to groups and hence we could have group-specific stocks of infrastructure $\left\{\pi_s^J\right\}_{J\in\{A,B\}}$. However, such a model would not be equivalent to the p_s^J decision that we are modeling here, where a decision is made ex post about how the stock of infrastructure is deployed. Hence, whether one group has access to infrastructure would be determined in period $s-1$, rather than by the period s incumbent. This may mean that investments in the incumbent's areas may persist over time, even when the incumbent is out of office. Such infrastructure might depreciate over time, of course, but the incentives will be rather different compared to investing in an asset, the allocation of which has a discretionary ex post component.[10]

Nevertheless, there are many similarities between investing in legal capacity (especially when it is fully deployed) and general productive infrastructure. Thus many of our ideas on productive investments by the government can carry over to traditional infrastructure investments.

Additional Complementarities The complementarity on which we focused in Section 3.1 comes entirely through the government budget constraint. But our model suggests an additional source of complementarity. Suppose that, as in Section 2.2.1, $\underline{\omega}$ represents an *untaxed* option in the traditional sector. Suppose further that we are in Case 2 described earlier, with wages in the advanced

10. One should not exaggerate the differences too much. Decisions about access charges and maintenance programs are discretionary ex post.

sector above the reservation wage available in the traditional sector, i.e., the formal sector wage is $\omega_s\left(p_s^I, p_s^O\right) \geq \underline{\omega}$.

Then, the private agent faces a choice between working in the advanced (formal) sector and paying tax or working in the traditional (informal) sector and not paying tax. Simple tax arbitrage implies that an individual in the advanced sector will pay an income-tax rate of t_s only if

$$t_s \leq \frac{\omega_s\left(p_s^I, p_s^O\right) + d_s - \underline{\omega}}{\omega_s\left(p_s^I, p_s^O\right)},$$

where d_s, as in Section 2.2.1, is any direct punishment incurred by someone who gets caught cheating on his/her taxes. As explained in Chapter 2, we can think about the investments in fiscal capacity as raising d_s. Now define

$$\tau_s = \frac{\omega_s\left(p_s^I, p_s^O\right) + d_s - \underline{\omega}}{\omega_s\left(p_s^I, p_s^O\right)}$$

as the fiscal-capacity limit on the income tax. In this formulation, fiscal capacity is tied directly to legal capacity and is increasing in p_s^J for either group J. In particular, if $p_s^I = p_s^O = \pi_s$, then

$$\tau_s = \frac{\omega_s\left(\pi_s, \pi_s\right) + d_s - \underline{\omega}}{\omega_s\left(\pi_s, \pi_s\right)}$$

is increasing in π_s. Better advanced-sector opportunities create an incentive to work there and to pay tax. This creates an additional complementarity between fiscal and legal capacity—legal capacity raises wages in the advanced sector, where taxes can be enforced, which raises fiscal capacity.

There are other "administrative" complementarities between fiscal and legal capacity worth mentioning. An important aspect of building legal capacity may be to invest in an institution such as a land registry, to be better able to enforce private property rights over land, or a credit registry, to be better able to enforce debt contracts. But having such registries also creates information about the ownership of land and financial assets. This information, in turn, makes it easier to use land or assets as tax bases. Investments in such registries may thus be viewed as a form of "joint production," which increases the government's ability to raise tax revenue as well as the direct benefits in supporting markets. In other words, they increase both legal and fiscal capacity.

3.2.2 The Genius of Taxation

In the core model of Section 3.1, it is always optimal to extend legal capacity maximally to each group. However, as explained in Section 3.2.1, an incumbent group can either raise or lower its income by extending the access of the opposition group to legal capacity. In this subsection, we explore the incentives to extend legal capacity to both groups and thus to uphold the rule of law, i.e., a situation in which access to legal protection is universal.

The Policy Problem Revisited The issues are more complicated once we let taxation and redistribution re-enter the picture. Whether the incumbent benefits or loses by changing the legal support to the opposition group also involves the effects on public revenue. We now explore this further and uncover yet another important complementarity between taxation and legal capacity, which we call the *genius of taxation* effect.

To explore this, we now allow y^J to depend on the vector (p_s^I, p_s^O) as in equation (3.17) from Case 4′ in Section 3.2.1. Hence, the policy payoff of the incumbent in period s is

$$\alpha_s g_s + (1 - t_s)\, y^I \left(p_s^I, p_s^O\right) + r_s^I .$$

If the incumbent group demands more labor than the opposition group then $\partial y^I \left(p_s^I, p_s^O\right) / \partial p_s^O < 0$. As we explained in Section 3.2.1, the negative effect on the incumbent group's income is due to the fall in the quasi rents that are earned by the entrepreneurs in the group when the common wage rises owing to greater labor demand. The government budget constraint is now modified to

$$R + t_s Y \left(p_s^I, p_s^O\right) = g_s + m_s + \frac{r_s^I + r_s^O}{2}.$$

Plugging in the level of government transfers and assuming that the income tax is set at its maximal level, we can write the incumbent's payoff as

$$\alpha_s g_s + (1 - \tau_s)\, y^I \left(p_s^I, p_s^O\right) + 2\,(1 - \theta) \left[R + \tau_s Y \left(p_s^I, p_s^O\right) - g_s - m_s\right]. \tag{3.22}$$

Fiscal-Capacity Limits to the Rule of Law We now make the following observation:

Proposition 3.6: *Suppose that* $\kappa^I K_s^I > \kappa^O K_s^O$*; then there exists* $\hat{\tau}(\alpha)$ *with* $\hat{\tau}(\alpha_H) < \hat{\tau}(\alpha_L)$ *such that for all* $\tau_s \geq \hat{\tau}(\alpha)$*, all legal capacity is fully utilized, i.e.,* $p^{I_s} = p^{O_s} = \pi_s$*. But if* $\tau_s < \hat{\tau}(\alpha_s)$*, then* $p^{I_s} = \pi_s$ *and* $p^{O_s} = 0$.

Proof: Differentiating (3.22) with respect to p_s^J yields

$$(1-\tau_s)\frac{\partial y^I(p_s^I, p_s^O)}{\partial p_s^J} + \tau_s\lambda_s\frac{\partial Y(p_s^I, p_s^O)}{\partial p_s^J}, \tag{3.23}$$

where $\lambda_s = \max\{\alpha_s, 2(1-\theta)\}$. For $J = I$, it is clear that this is increasing so $p_s^I = \pi_s$. Then with (3.17), for $J = O$, the first term has the sign of

$$1 - \frac{2\kappa^I K^I(1+\pi_s)}{\kappa^I K^I(1+\pi_s) + \kappa^O K^O(1+p_s^O)},$$

which is negative for all $p_s^O \in [0, \pi_s]$ if $\kappa^I K_s^I > \kappa^O K_s^O$. The second term in (3.23) is positive. Now define $\tilde{\tau}(\lambda_s) \in [0,1]$ such that

$$(1-\tilde{\tau}(\lambda_s))\frac{\partial y^I(p_s^I, p_s^O)}{\partial p_s^O} + \tilde{\tau}(\lambda_s)\lambda_s\frac{\partial Y(p_s^I, p_s^O)}{\partial p_s^O} = 0.$$

Observe that $\tilde{\tau}(\lambda_s) < 1$. Now let

$$\begin{aligned}\hat{\tau}(\alpha_L) &= \tilde{\tau}(\max\{\alpha_L, 2(1-\theta)\}) \\ &> \tilde{\tau}(\max\{\alpha_H, 2(1-\theta)\}) = \hat{\tau}(\alpha_H).\end{aligned}$$

This proves the proposition. ■

This result says that an incumbent from the group with more entrepreneurs denies the opponent access to the legal system unless fiscal capacity is sufficiently high. This is because she prefers lower wages and can ensure this by keeping p_s^O low. Taxation creates a demand for collective consumption in the form of public goods, g, and hence socializes the gains from increasing income per capita. The cutoff value of taxation thus depends positively on the strength of demand for public goods. The reason for this is that a higher demand for public goods raises the value of public funds and hence encourages the incumbent to set improved property rights for the opposition group to generate higher wages, which create benefits through the tax system. This common-interest motive reduces the temptation for inefficiently keeping down the opposition's wages and the economy's income per capita.

The cutoff value of τ also depends on the extent of inequality in entrepreneurial activity across groups. When there is more concentration of entrepreneurs in the incumbent group, the cutoff for fiscal capacity is higher. The proposition does not hold when the groups are identical, as then lower wages no longer benefit the incumbent since income per capita is lower.[11] Proposition 3.6 also shows why even small differences in $\kappa^I K^I$ and $\kappa^O K^O$ can be magnified through decisions to allocate legal protection differentially across the groups. This increases the degree of inequality.

Proposition 3.6 suggests a further complementarity between taxation and efficiency. By undertaking redistribution through the tax-transfer system, the government is encouraged to pursue the rule of law, extending market support for the society as a whole, rather than furthering the narrow interests of its own group. Moreover, the case for the rule of law is stronger when the common-interest motive for the use of the state is stronger.[12]

Implications for State-Capacity Investments The possibility that legal capacity is not fully utilized affects incentives to invest in fiscal and legal capacity. We look first at fiscal-capacity investment in isolation and then consider implications for legal capacity.

A first effect on fiscal-capacity investment comes from the observation that failure to fully extend legal protection to both groups, as illustrated in Proposition 3.6, leads endogenously to greater inequality. As we have already observed in Section 2.4.4, adding inequality to the model changes the incentive for investing in fiscal capacity—the low-income group wants more fiscal capacity and the high-income group wants less. These preferences are simply a reflection of the marginal cost of fiscal capacity in terms of foregone private earnings in each group. The larger inequality created by the effect in Proposition 3.6 means that

11. Another way of getting this result without inequality in capital holding is illustrated in Besley and Persson (2011). That analysis supposes that entrepreneurs do not supply any labor. Then, both groups as incumbents might prefer to generate higher incomes through lower wages.

12. The complementarity between efficiency and taxation is a general phenomenon. But if there is a deadweight loss associated with taxation, it may be that taxes will not be high enough to encourage extension of legal protection to the opposition.

this effect will be exaggerated at low levels of fiscal capacity where the result in Proposition 3.6 applies.

The model suggests that having a poorer group in power can now boost incomes if the group invests sufficiently in taxes to cross the threshold $\hat{\tau}(\alpha_s)$. This will lead to a more efficient use of legal capacity and hence raise incomes. Such effects on output will be permanent to the extent that investments in fiscal capacity are irreversible.

The second effect on fiscal-capacity investment is independent of which group is in power. To illustrate this, suppose that $\hat{\tau}(\alpha_H) \leq \tau_2 \leq \hat{\tau}(\alpha_L)$ and Cohesiveness does not hold. Then, the marginal benefit of investing in fiscal capacity is lower for both groups. For a richer incumbent group, this marginal benefit is

$$(1-\phi)(1-\gamma)2(1-\theta)Y(\pi_2, 0) + \left[\phi\alpha_H + (1-\phi)\gamma 2\theta\right] Y(\pi_2, \pi_2),$$

whereas for a poorer incumbent group it is

$$(1-\phi)\gamma 2(1-\theta)Y(\pi_2, 0) + \left[\phi\alpha_H + (1-\phi)(1-\gamma)2\theta\right] Y(\pi_2, \pi_2).$$

Both of these figures are less than $\phi\alpha_H + (1-\phi)2[(1-\gamma)(1-\theta) + \gamma\theta] Y(\pi_2, \pi_2)$, the marginal benefit when legal capacity is fully utilized, since $Y(\pi_2, 0) < Y(\pi_2, \pi_2)$. This reduces the incentive to invest in fiscal capacity and hence enhances the possibility of a weak state persisting when income is low because taxes are low.

Finally, we have to consider what happens to legal-capacity investment. The effect on the underutilization of legal capacity is to lower the return to investing in such capacity.[13] This will lead to less investment in legal capacity all else being equal. If fiscal-capacity investment is also lower, the negative effect on legal capacity will be further compounded by the complementarity between the two forms of state capacity. Thus, we would expect that a state with low taxes and low and biased utilization of legal capacity, as illustrated in Proposition 3.6, also makes fewer investments in legal capacity. This further reinforces the coincidence of low taxation and low income.

13. This is not completely obvious since, with less capital in use, the marginal product of capital is also higher. However, it can be shown that this is indeed the case with our assumed Cobb-Douglas technology.

Implications of the Weak State for Incomes and Growth The discussion of underinvestment in fiscal capacity has important implications for thinking about incomes and growth. As stated before, the growth rate of income per capita is

$$\frac{Y\left(p_2^I, p_2^O\right) - Y\left(p_1^I, p_1^O\right)}{Y\left(p_2^I, p_2^O\right)} = \sum_{J \in \{I,O\}} \left[\frac{y^J\left(p_2^I, p_2^O\right) - y^J\left(p_1^I, p_1^O\right)}{2y^J\left(p_1^I, p_1^O\right)}\right].$$

Even if π_s is fixed over time, an increase in fiscal capacity can lead to growth if it leads to $p_2^O = \pi_2$, i.e., if the economy crosses one of the thresholds spelled out in Proposition 3.6. However, weak states, which do not invest in fiscal capacity, do not escape the fiscal-capacity trap. This creates a strong correlation between taxation and income per capita.

To illustrate these ideas further, consider two states W (for weak) and S (for strong). Assume that they have the same initial legal capacity $\pi_1^W = \pi_1^S = \pi_1$, but that $\tau_1^W < \hat{\tau}(\alpha_L)$ and $\tau_1^S > \hat{\tau}(\alpha_L)$, so that they find themselves on opposite sides of the fiscal-capacity threshold in Proposition 3.6 because of different initial fiscal capacities, $\tau_1^W < \tau_1^S$.

Let us compare income levels in periods 1 and 2. If the incumbent is rich in period 1, then

$$Y_1^S - Y_1^W = Y(\pi_1, \pi_1) - Y(\pi_1, 0) > 0,$$

i.e., in period 1, economy W has a lower income level owing to the inefficient legal protection of the opposition group. If the rich persist in power in period 2, we have

$$Y_2^S - Y_2^W = Y(\pi_2^S, \pi_2^S) - Y(\pi_2^W, 0) > Y(\pi_1, \pi_1) - Y(\pi_1, 0),$$

where the inequality follows from $\pi_2^S > \pi_2^W$.

Owing to its low fiscal capacity, economy W pursues a policy of less efficient legal protection than economy S in period 2. As legal-capacity investments are lower, there is also weaker growth. The stronger state not only has the higher GDP level, but its income advantage compared to the weaker state is growing over time.

These implications of Proposition 3.6 suggest another possible interpretation of the correlations in Figure 1.3. Using the results in Section 3.1, we may observe a weak state together with low income either because the two are jointly determined by other factors or because low income causes a weak state (recall Proposition 3.2). The results in this subsection suggest that a weak state can now actually *cause* low income, to the extent that it encourages policies that distort production.

It is interesting to think about ways out of inefficient legal protection in an investment trap. Our results suggest that exogenous circumstances as well as political reform may play a role. Circumstances such as a higher likelihood or expected severity of external conflict (higher ϕ or α_H) may make it too costly to pursue inefficient legal protection by raising the prospect of a future common-interest state. A reform that diminishes political instability (a lower value of γ) may induce a first-period investment in fiscal capacity. We return to the likelihood of such a reform in Chapter 7.

The Case for an Independent Judiciary This subsection maintains the assumption that the control over legal support, and therefore the decision whether to follow the rule of law, is in the hands of whomever holds political office. If both groups can agree not to exploit their ex post power to extract rents by invoking inefficient and discriminatory legal support across groups, it might lead to ex ante welfare gains for members of both groups. But, naturally, in our model such an agreement would not be credible ex post, once power has been allocated. This suggests that delegating these decisions to an independent judiciary that cares about economic efficiency and/or equal access to legal protection might bring welfare gains to the society.[14] Such delegation would be particularly valuable when the rich have a monopoly of political power. Thus "investing" in judicial independence would be complementary with investments in fiscal and legal capacity.

This discussion gives some additional perspective on the case often made for the beneficial effects of an independent judiciary. However, there are thorny issues to be dealt with here: de jure independence does not necessarily imply de facto independence.[15] And exactly what makes delegation to an independent agency any more credible than an informal agreement between the two groups?

14. The argument is similar to the case for an independent and conservative central bank made by Kydland and Prescott (1977) and Rogoff (1985).

15. Feld and Voigt (2003) offer a good discussion of such issues and provide empirical measures of de jure and de facto judicial independence.

We will return to these issues in Chapter 7 when we discuss political and institutional reform.

Links to Debates about Financial Development It is worth relating the results in this subsection to recent work on the political origins of financial development. As we discussed in the introduction, this work argues that a desire to create or preserve rents can prevent a ruling elite from building the institutions needed for well-functioning financial markets [see, e.g., Pagano and Volpin (2005) or Rajan and Zingales (2003)]. This work generally considers the financial sector without reference to the tax system. Thus, the political-origins argument may implicitly assume a lack of fiscal capacity, which makes it unattractive for the incumbents to invest in markets or maximize income and instead has them carrying out their desired redistribution via taxes and transfers.

As stressed in Acemoglu (2003, 2006), it is important to pose the Political Coase theorem question explicitly, i.e., why the groups involved cannot get together and bargain over the outcome that maximizes income per capita, dividing the gains between themselves. At least, one has to be explicit about the frictions that prevent that outcome. In our analysis, the friction comes from the absence of a credible mechanism to transfer any efficiency gains beyond the institutional commitments entailed in the value of parameter θ. This is because fiscal capacity is low.[16] The key innovation in the approach applied to the political origins of financial underdevelopment is to think about both aspects of state capacity as evolving together endogenously and influencing policy incentives.

We believe that the argument is much more general than the specific example in this subsection. Further research might consider the joint determination of weak states and other policy-induced production distortions that lead to low income, such as tariffs or red-tape regulation.

Complements or Substitutes? In our core model, state capacities are natural complements. There are always forces pushing in this direction, which our model identifies. However, in certain formulations these forces are weaker and we can even have cases where state capacities become substitutes. To illustrate this, we return to the formulation in Section 2.2.2, where there is curvature in

16. Promises by the poor to the rich in exchange for better access to the legal system are assumed not to be credible in the absence of the fiscal capacity/institutions to support them.

the demand for public goods. The expected period-2 marginal value of public funds is now

$$E\left(\lambda_2\right)=\begin{cases}\alpha V_g\left(\tau_2 y\left(\pi_2\right)+R\right) & \text{if } \alpha V_g\left(\tau_2 y\left(\pi_2\right)+R\right)>2\left(1-\theta\right)\\ 2\left[\left(1-\gamma\right)\left(1-\theta\right)+\gamma\theta\right] & \text{otherwise.}\end{cases}$$

The Euler equations remain effectively as in (3.4) and (3.5).

If $\alpha V_g\left(\tau_2 y\left(\pi_2\right)+R\right)\leq 2\left(1-\theta\right)$, then we have complements as in the core model. However, if $\alpha V_g\left(\tau_2 y\left(\pi_2\right)+R\right)>2\left(1-\theta\right)$, then we find that fiscal and legal capacity are complements only if

$$1+\frac{\tau_2 y\left(\pi_2\right)}{\tau_2 y\left(\pi_2\right)+R}\left(\frac{V_{gg}g_2}{V_g}\right)\geq 0.$$

This requires that the elasticity of demand for public goods $\left(-V_{gg}g_2/V_g\right)$ be low enough. Intuitively, the issue arises because the marginal value of public goods falls as more state capacity is accumulated. This lowers the marginal return to investing in state capacity of each type by lowering $E\left(\lambda_2\right)$.

We have focused on comparative statics of determinants that raise the marginal return to investing in one or both state capacities. This may create the false impression that the demands for state capacities by both groups are always aligned. But this need not be true and demands for different kinds of state capacity can shift with political control when demands are not aligned. This happens to be the case with income inequality, as we introduced it in Section 2.2.4. In a very similar formulation, Besley and Persson (2009a) show that higher-income groups have stronger demands for legal rather than for fiscal capacity, and vice versa for poorer groups.

Although both forms of state capacity remain complements, the forms of state capacity are substitutable issues across groups. Our model would then begin to resemble something like traditional class-based politics—one group wants higher taxes and weaker market development, whereas the other wants lower taxes and stronger market development. The evolution of the mix of state capacities would then differ according to which group holds political power and the extent of economic inequality.

3.2.3 Private Capital Accumulation

The basic model in Section 3.1 is dynamic, but the only accumulation concerns the two forms of state capacity. In this subsection, we augment the model to allow for private capital accumulation. For simplicity, we look at one-period capital, so that—absent investments in new capital—the entire period-1 capital stock depreciates before period 2. Naturally, the focus is on the interactions between state capacity and private accumulation.

Model Modifications To home in on the point of interest, we consider the case in Section 3.2.1, where everyone is identical within and between groups and the wage rate exceeds $\underline{\omega}$. Our assumption is that each citizen has a probability κ of being an entrepreneur in each period and has to make his/her accumulation decision before the resolution of this uncertainty. Everyone is thus the same ex ante.

We also suppose that the parameters are such that $p_s^I = p_s^O = \pi_s$, i.e., legal capacity is fully utilized. Then, expected income per capita (making this explicitly dependent on the per capita capital stock K) is

$$y\left(\pi_s; K\right) = \begin{cases} \rho\left(K_2\right) K + \omega\left(K_2\right) + R & \text{if } \kappa\left(1+\pi_s\right) \geq 1 \\ \left(\kappa\left(1+\pi_s\right) K\right)^{\eta} + R & \text{otherwise,} \end{cases} \tag{3.24}$$

where $\rho\left(K_2\right) = \eta\left(K_2\right)^{\eta-1}$ is the market-determined rental price of capital. In the case where $\kappa\left(1+\pi_s\right) \geq 1$, income depends on aggregate capital per head since capital is fully intermediated into the advanced sector. Citizens take the level of capital per head in the population as a whole, K_2, as given and unaffected by their private accumulation decision. In the case where $\kappa\left(1+\pi_s\right) < 1$, it is instead their own holding of capital that matters since that is what determines their access to capital as entrepreneurs.

Using (3.24), we have that

$$y_K\left(\pi_s; K\right) = \begin{cases} \eta\left(K_2\right)^{\eta-1} & \text{if } \kappa\left(1+\pi_s\right) \geq 1 \\ \eta\left[\kappa\left(1+\pi_s\right)\right]^{\eta}(K)^{\eta-1} & \text{otherwise.} \end{cases}$$

Evaluated at $K = K_2$, the marginal return to saving is highest when there is no institutional constraint on the deployment of capital in production because when the institutional constraint is binding $\kappa\left(1+\pi_s\right) < 1$.

To study the accumulation decision regarding K, note that period-1 utility is

$$y(\pi_1; K_1)\left(1-\tau_1\right) + \alpha_1 g_1 + r_1^J - K.$$

Thus accumulation simply reduces private consumption in period 1. Period-2 utility becomes

$$y(\pi_2; K)(1-\tau_2) + \alpha_2 g_2 + r_2^J.$$

Timing The timing of the model is now modified to the following:

1. We begin with initial stocks of state capacities $\{\tau_1, \pi_1\}$, a capital stock per capita of K_1, and an incumbent group I_1.
2. All citizens choose how much capital, K, to accumulate for period 2.
3. Nature determines α_1 and R and which citizens are entrepreneurs in period 1.
4. I_1 chooses a set of period-1 policies $\{t_1, r_1^I, r_1^O, p_1^I, p_1^O, g_1\}$ and determines (through investments) the period-2 stocks of fiscal and legal capacity $\{\tau_2, \pi_2\}$.
5. I_1 stays in power with probability $(1-\gamma)$, and nature determines $\alpha_2 \in \{\alpha_L, \alpha_H\}$ and which citizens are entrepreneurs in period 2.
6. I_2 chooses period-2 policies $\{t_2, r_2^I, r_2^O, p_2^I, p_2^O, g_2\}$.

The only new feature of the model is the decision on private investments for period 2. We have placed this decision before the period-1 realization of α_1 and R. The precise timing is unimportant here, but will be important when we reintroduce private investments in Chapter 5, where collective investments in political violence determine political instability γ.

As usual, we look for a subgame perfect equilibrium.

Optimal Private Investment The public decisions on the choice of public goods, taxation, and transfers are essentially as described earlier. The new interesting decision is over capital accumulation at stage 2. Define

$$W(\alpha_s, \tau_s, \pi_s, m_s, \beta^J; K, K_s) = \alpha_s G(\alpha_s, \pi_s, \tau_s, K_s) + (1-\tau_s) y(\pi_s; K) \\ + \beta^J [\tau_s Y(\pi_s; K_s) - G(\alpha_s, \pi_s, \tau_s, K_s) - m_s],$$

where $\beta^I = 2(1-\theta)$ and $\beta^O = 2\theta$. Observe that expected period-1 utility viewed from stage 2 in the timing above is

$$\phi W(\alpha_H, \tau_1, \pi_1, m_1, \beta^J; K_1, K_1) + (1-\phi) W(\alpha_L, \tau_1, \pi_1, m_1, \beta^J; K_1, K_1) - K.$$

Note that K is simply deducted from the rest of the expression to recognize that the private-consumption cost of investing is the same regardless of α_1.

The period-2 value functions now depend on private capital stocks and the average period-2 per capita capital stock. They are given by

$$U^I\left(\tau_2, \pi_2; K, K_2\right) \\ = \left[\phi W\left(\alpha_H, \tau_2, \pi_2, 0, \beta^I; K, K_2\right) + (1-\phi)\, W\left(\alpha_L, \tau_2, \pi_2, 0, \beta^I; K, K_2\right)\right]$$

for the incumbent and

$$U^O\left(\tau_2, \pi_2; K, K_2\right) \\ = \left[\phi W\left(\alpha_H, \tau_2, \pi_2, 0, \beta^O; K, K_2\right) + (1-\phi)\, W\left(\alpha_L, \tau_2, \pi_2, 0, \beta^O; K, K_2\right)\right]$$

for the opposition.

The optimal capital accumulation decisions are characterized by

$$\hat{K}_2^I = \arg\max_{K\geq 0}\left\{(1-\gamma)\, U^I\left(\tau_2, \pi_2; K, K_2\right) + \gamma U^O\left(\tau_2, \pi_2; K, K_2\right) - K\right\}$$

for the incumbent and

$$\hat{K}_2^O = \arg\max_{K\geq 0}\left\{\gamma U^I\left(\tau_2, \pi_2; K, K_2\right) + (1-\gamma)\, U^O\left(\tau_2, \pi_2; K, K_2\right) - K\right\}$$

for the opposition. Since both groups have the same production function and face the same tax rate in period 2, the outcome is straightforward and has $\hat{K}_2^I = \hat{K}_2^O$.

We now prove the following proposition:

Proposition 3.7: *Suppose that* $\left(1-\tau_2\right)\underline{\omega}^{\eta} < 1$. *Then, the optimal level of period-2 capital solves*

$$\left(1-\tau_2\right) y_K\left(\pi_2; \hat{K}_2^J\right) = 1 \text{for } J \in \{I, O\}.$$

Proof: Observe first that for $\kappa\left(1+\pi_2\right) < 1$, the optimization yields

$$\eta\left[\kappa\left(1+\pi_s\right)\right]^{\eta}\left(\hat{K}_2^J\right)^{\eta-1} = 1.$$

If $\kappa\,(1+\pi_2) \geq 1$, the optimal accumulation decision for an individual with realized period-1 income, y_1, is

$$\hat{K}_2^J\,(K_2, y_1) = \begin{cases} = 0 & \text{if } (1-\tau_2)\,\eta\,(K_2)^{\eta-1} < 1 \\ \in \left[0, (1-\tau_1)\,y_1\right] & \text{if } (1-\tau_2)\,\eta\,(K_2)^{\eta-1} = 1 \\ = (1-\tau_1)\,y_1 & \text{if } (1-\tau_2)\,\eta\,(K_2)^{\eta-1} > 1. \end{cases}$$

We require private investment to be a fixed point of this mapping $\hat{K}_2^J\,(K_2) = K_2$. It is straightforward to see that $\hat{K}_2^J\,(0) > 0$ and, under the assumption in Proposition 3.7, $\hat{K}_2^J\,(\underline{\omega}) < 1$ since $y_1 \geq \underline{\omega}$. As $\hat{K}_2^J$ is continuous, the Intermediate Value theorem implies that we have a fixed point with symmetric investments if

$$(1-\tau_2)\,\eta\left(K_2^J\right)^{\eta-1} = 1,$$

which is the claim in the proposition. ■

The condition makes intuitive sense and says that the net-of-tax return to capital just has to equal the marginal value of period-1 consumption.[17] If this were not the case, then each individual would be able to gain by saving more or less. This condition holds if markets are imperfect and individuals benefit from their own saving if they become entrepreneurs. But it also holds if they are saving in a world where the markets are perfect and determine the rental price for capital, as would be the case in a neoclassical economy.

Complementarity between Private Capital and Legal Capacity By Proposition 3.7, the post-tax marginal return to capital is set equal to one, i.e., the opportunity cost in terms of foregone period-1 consumption. From that condition, it follows that when the economy is institutionally constrained, so that $\kappa\,(1+\pi_2) < 1$, then

$$\frac{\partial \hat{K}_2}{\partial \pi_s} = \frac{\eta}{1-\eta}\frac{\hat{K}_2}{(1+\pi_s)} > 0.$$

In other words, we have a complementarity between better legal institutions and private capital accumulation. This result implies that there is indeed a link

17. The assumption made in the proposition is sufficient to guarantee that there is an interior solution.

between more standard models of investment and growth and our approach where growth is generated by the government's accumulation of legal capacity. This link suggests that we should see a further dimension of clustering in the data between capital intensity in production and legal capacity.

Given this observation, let us derive the effect of an increase in legal capacity on income per capita, taking the complementarity into account. The total effect on income from an increase in π_2 is given by

$$\begin{aligned}\frac{dy\left(\pi_2;\hat{K}_2\right)}{d\pi_2} &= y\left(\pi_2;\hat{K}_2\right)\frac{\eta}{1+\pi_2}\left[1+\frac{1+\pi_2}{\hat{K}_2}\frac{\partial \hat{K}_2}{\partial \pi_2}\right] \\ &= y\left(\pi_2;\hat{K}_2\right)\frac{\eta}{\left(1+\pi_2\right)\left(1-\eta\right)}.\end{aligned}$$

Thus investing in better legal capacity has a multiplier effect on income owing to the additional private capital that it generates.

In terms of empirical predictions, the complementarity means that we should observe similar determinants of private investment rates and the economy's legal capacity. We return to this observation when we discuss empirical implications in Section 3.3

State-Capacity Investments Revisited Now, consider the impact of private accumulation on the decision to invest in legal capacity. Start with the case when τ_s is fixed and exogenous. Referring back to equation (3.5), we see that the incumbent's marginal return to investing in legal capacity is higher than in the case without a multiplier effect.

Naturally, much work remains to fully integrate our model of productivity with standard growth models. But, in general, we should expect improvements in economic institutions to reinforce the standard mechanisms of economic growth. Another application of the same general idea might be to endogenous innovation, which requires institutions to protect intellectual property rights combined with institutions allowing technology to be licensed.

What happens when we endogenize fiscal capacity? The reader will correctly guess that with endogenous capital accumulation, we will get disincentive effects from taxation that parallel those in the analysis of endogenous labor supply in Section 2.2.6. Thus investments in fiscal and legal capacity will tend to operate in competing directions. Once legal capacity has reached the point where $\kappa\left(1+\pi_s\right)\geq 1$, then we only get the standard negative effect of taxation on capital accumulation. However, below that point, the impact of higher taxation will be attenuated by the building of more legal capacity.

3.2.4 Predation and Corruption

The microfoundations for legal capacity in Section 3.2.1 focused on economic institutions to facilitate contract enforcement in the private sector, especially in private capital markets. In this subsection, we take another tack by looking at the economic costs of predation. Predation might be due to private coercive authority because the rule of law is poorly established. It might also be due to the actions of bureaucrats, who abuse their power for self-enrichment. In either case, resources are misallocated as predatory behavior basically works as a tax on production, which leads to production inefficiency.

The state can improve the situation for producers by building economic institutions that strengthen the rule of law and the protection of private property rights via better access to legal systems. It can also invest in the means to curb the power of bureaucrats by giving legal authority to producers to counter maladministration by the state.

We study these phenomena by adapting the two-sector model developed earlier in this chapter. In doing so, we assume that predatory behavior is only an issue in the advanced production sector. Hence, predation operates as a potential deterrent to structural transformation of the economy toward this sector and leads to lower income per capita.

We use the adapted model to study the implications of rule by a rent-seeking class that lives on such predatory behavior. This kind of rule leads to very poor incentives to build protection against predation and can be the source of a legal-capacity trap.

Introducing Predation To study these issues as simply as possible, we focus on a symmetric case where every citizen in the economy has the same (exogenously given) holding of private capital, K, and there is a common fraction of entrepreneurs, κ, in each group.

Predation by private agents or bureaucrats is a form of (informal) taxation, whose technology we specify in what follows. There is a group of identical predators that includes members of both groups in the economy, $J = I, O$. We denote the share of predators coming from group J by $n^J \in [0, 1]$, with $n^I + n^O = 1$. The rents are shared equally among the predators, so a share n^J of the resources extracted through predation accrues to group J. Similarly, predators belonging to group J bear a share n^J of the costs incurred in predation.

This setting can easily capture pure corruption as a special case with $n^I = 1 - n^O = 1$, i.e., all predation rents accrue to the ruling group. (We could also model a case where rents are purely redistributive within group.)

We continue to assume that the incumbent government acts in the interests of its own group by maximizing its average utility. In what follows, we also consider another case, which is perhaps more realistic, where rent extraction is concentrated in the hands of a small subgroup—i.e., in the hands of an elite.

Predation as a Tax Suppose that after there has been production in the advanced sector, a producer in group J faces the possibility that part of her output is subject to "theft" by predators. We model this theft exactly like a tax on output, which we denote by μ. The predators can discriminate among the different groups J in their predation efforts, which they can target depending on the group-specific profitability of predation. The extent of this tax depends on formal protection of the targeted group's property rights p_s^J and efforts by the predators when targeting group J, denoted by χ_s^J. Even though we are assuming that groups have the same underlying productive capabilities, if $p_s^I \neq p_s^O$ predation rates may differ.

We assume a simple functional form in which the tax rate is

$$\mu(\chi, p) = (1 - p)\,\chi.$$

In this case $\mu_\chi = (1 - p) > 0$, i.e., the tax rate is higher with a higher predation rate. If $p = 1$, then there are no returns to predation. As in the previous section, we can assume that $p_s^J \in [0, \pi_s]$, where π_s is the level of legal capacity in the economy.

Objective of Predators Expected output produced in the advanced sector by group J in period s, net of predation, is now

$$\left[1 - \mu\left(\chi_s^J, p_s^J\right)\right] K^\eta L^{1-\eta}.$$

We suppose that χ^J is determined an by effort decision where all predators act in consort. Together, the predators act like a monopolistic "predatory firm" with shares in the firm equal to n^I and n^O held by agents in the incumbent and opposition groups, respectively.

For each targeted sector, we assume that predatory effort costs are given by $C(\chi)$, where $C(\cdot)$ is increasing and convex. Thus the predatory profits (rents) from sector J are

$$\mu\left(\chi_s^{;J}, p_s^J\right) K^{\eta} L^{1-\eta} - C\left(\chi_s^J\right).$$

We focus on the case where

$$\left[1-\mu\left(\chi_s^J, p_s^J\right)\right] \eta\left(K_s\right)^{\eta-1} > \underline{\rho}. \tag{3.25}$$

This means that the return to capital in its outside option is sufficiently low and that all capital is deployed in advanced production. However, given the outside wage available in traditional production, there are two cases to consider depending on whether the following condition holds:

Advanced-Sector Productivity: $\left[1-\mu\left(\chi_s^J, p_s^J\right)\right](1-\eta)\left(K_s\right)^{\eta} > \underline{\omega}.$ (3.26)

This assumption is more likely to hold in a more capital-rich economy, where advanced production is more attractive when the traditional wage is low and when there is relatively little equilibrium predation so that $\mu(\cdot, \cdot)$ is a long way from one.

Some Traditional Production Suppose that (3.25) holds, but that the advanced-sector productivity condition fails. Then, labor demand, $\tilde{L}_s^J$, solves

$$\left[1-\mu\left(\chi_s^J, p_s^J\right)\right](1-\eta)\left(\frac{K_s}{\tilde{L}_s^J \kappa}\right)^{\eta} = \underline{\omega}. \tag{3.27}$$

This is like Case 3 in the neoclassical model of Subsection 3.2.1.

The optimal predation rate toward group J at date s maximizes predatory rents, namely

$$\hat{\chi}_s^J = \arg\max\left\{\mu\left(\chi, p_s^J\right)\left(K_s\right)^{\eta}\left(\kappa \tilde{L}_s^J\right)^{1-\eta} - C(\chi)\right\}.$$

Labor is now partially deployed in the traditional sector. This optimal predation rate equates the marginal benefit from predation effort to the marginal cost and is given by the condition

$$\left(1-p_s^J\right)\left(K_s\right)^{\eta}\left(\kappa \tilde{L}_s^J\right)^{1-\eta} = C_{\chi}\left(\hat{\chi}_s^J\right).$$

There are two effects of increasing the legal support for group J, p_s^J. The first is a *predation effect,* owing to $\hat{\chi}_s^J$ being lower, and the second is a *reallocation effect,* owing to labor moving into the advanced sector to work for group J entrepreneurs, since labor demand is determined by equation (3.27).

No Traditional Production If the advanced-sector productivity condition (3.26) holds, then $\tilde{L}_s^J$, as defined by (3.27), is equal to $1/\kappa$ and all labor is deployed in that sector.

The optimal predation rate targeted toward group J at date s is now

$$\hat{\chi}_s^J = \arg\max \left\{\mu\left(\chi, p_s^J\right)(K_s)^\eta - C(\chi)\right\},$$

for which, if we assume an interior solution, the first-order condition is

$$\left(1 - p_s^J\right)(K_s)^\eta = C_\chi\left(\hat{\chi}_s^J\right). \tag{3.28}$$

In this case, we have only a predation effect, and no reallocation effect, when p_s^J is increased.

The Assignment of Legal Protection We now use the framework to consider the government's decision to set the levels of $\{p_s^I, p_s^O\}$ given the stock of legal capacity π_s.

To determine this, observe first that productive output per head in the advanced sector in group J at s is given by

$$\left[1 - \mu\left(\hat{\chi}_s^J, p_s^J\right)\right]\tilde{y}\left(p_s^J\right),$$

where

$$\tilde{y}\left(p_s^J\right) = \begin{cases} (K_s)^\eta & \text{if } \left[1 - \mu\left(\chi_s^J, p_s^J\right)\right](1-\eta)(K_s)^\eta > \underline{\omega} \\ (K_s)^\eta\left(\kappa\tilde{L}_s^J\right)^{1-\eta} & \text{otherwise.} \end{cases}$$

Net predatory income generated to group J from predation is

$$n^J[\mu\left(\hat{\chi}_s^I, p_s^I\right)\tilde{y}\left(p_s^I\right) + \mu\left(\hat{\chi}_s^O, p_s^O\right)\tilde{y}\left(p_s^O\right) - C\left(\hat{\chi}_s^I\right) - C(\hat{\chi}_s^O)].$$

Putting these expressions together, we have

$$y^I\left(p_s^I, p_s^O\right) = \left[1 - n^O \mu\left(\hat{\chi}_s^I, p_s^I\right)\right] \tilde{y}\left(p_s^I\right) + n^I \mu\left(\hat{\chi}_s^O, p_s^O\right) \tilde{y}\left(p_s^O\right)$$
$$- n^I\left(\Sigma_J C\left(\hat{\chi}_s^J\right)\right) + \left(1 - \kappa \tilde{L}_s^I\right) \underline{\omega}. \tag{3.29}$$

Note that the income generated to group I by predation of its own members, $n^I \mu\left(\hat{\chi}_s^I, p_s^I\right) \tilde{y}\left(p_s^I\right)$, nets out within the group.

A Normative Benchmark Adding this expression to the corresponding expression for group O, we obtain income per capita as

$$Y\left(p_s^I, p_s^O\right) = \frac{\sum_{J \in \{I,O\}} \left(\tilde{y}\left(p_s^J\right) - C\left(\hat{\chi}_s^J\right) + \left(1 - \kappa \tilde{L}_s^J\right) \underline{\omega}\right)}{2}.$$

Since the terms in $\mu\left(\hat{\chi}_s^J, p_s^J\right)$ are pure transfers between predators and their prey, they drop out of this expression.

We now have the following strong normative result:

Proposition 3.8: *Income per capita is maximized when $p_s^I = p_s^O = \pi_s$, i.e., full legal protection is granted to producers, given the available legal capacity.*

Proof: The proof is simple. The gross value of production, $\sum_{J \in \{I,O\}} \left(\tilde{y}\left(p_s^J\right) + \left(1 - \kappa \tilde{L}_s^J\right) \underline{\omega}\right)$, is maximized by minimizing the implicit taxes on advanced-sector production, i.e., by setting $p_s^I = p_s^O = \pi_s$. Moreover, the total deadweight loss from predation, $- \sum_{J \in \{I,O\}} C\left(\hat{\chi}_s^J\right)$, is minimized by deterring predation as much as possible, i.e., by setting $p_s^I = p_s^O = \pi_s$. ■

This result is just like the one we found in the model of Section 3.2.1. The only prospective effect of encouraging predation is redistributive. But since it lowers output, there is no social benefit and it is best to have the lowest possible level of predation for each group, granting the rule of law.

Political Equilibrium The normative result in Proposition 3.8 would continue to hold in political equilibrium if all predation were to be an entirely within-group affair, i.e., with all predation efforts and revenues remaining within the group. This would exactly replicate the logic leading to Proposition 3.1; each group would only care about the predation rate in its own group and would set predation as low as possible.

However, in the predatory case considered here, full legal protection for both groups may no longer be optimal for the incumbent, depending on how rents from predation are allocated. The key point is that no government can commit in our framework to setting $p_s^J > 0$ so that legal capacity may go unused ex post even if it is created ex ante. For example, if the incumbent group has a disproportionate share of the rents, $n^I >> n^O$, it may be better to offer differentiated legal protection to maximize the net incomes available for the incumbent group. If n^I is close to one and n^O is close to zero, it is clear from (3.29) that predation of group I generates mostly deadweight costs, via the term $n^I C\left(\hat{\chi}_s^I\right)$ (since almost all predatory rents are transferred within group I). Thus, it may be best to minimize these costs by maximal deterrence of predation against group I, i.e., to set $p_s^I = \pi_s$. At the same time, predation on group O members generates substantial rents for group I, via the term $n^I \mu\left(\hat{\chi}_s^O, p_s^O\right) \tilde{y}\left(p_s^O\right)$. Thus, it may be best to enable maximal rents to be extracted from group O, i.e., to set $p_s^O = 0$. The complete formal argument is very similar to the one that we rehearsed in Subsection 3.2.2 on the genius of taxation, and it will not be repeated here. Note, however, that our earlier insight on how high fiscal capacity may help rectify distortions in production efficiency by assigning a large enough weight to average income also applies in the present setting.

Implications The analog to the analysis in the discussion of the genius of taxation in Section 3.2.2 suggests yet another observation. There, we argued that the prospective welfare losses to society from opportunistic short-run rent-seeking behavior by incumbents called for delegating the deployment of legal services to an independent judiciary. The same kind of argument can be made here: it may be in the long-run interest of society to delegate the pursuit of predators to an independent body with a clear mission. When the predators are themselves government bureaucrats, the case would call for politically independent (and honest) surveillance of the bureaucracy. But experience from many attempts at fighting corruption in developing (and developed) countries suggests that such reform is easier said than done. Changing social norms and the motivations of enforcement agents is notoriously difficult.

A Predatory State? So far, we have assumed that the returns to rent seeking are widely held and that the incumbents within groups act on the basis of the average income of the group as a whole. These imply a Coasian bargain within each group that is perhaps too optimistic. Intuitively, we often think about a world of rent seeking and predation as one where small dominant cliques run these operations on the basis of their narrow personal interests. This alternative world has much more damaging implications and can serve as the foundation of a predatory state.

Suppose now that the ruling group is a self-interested and corrupt elite, which carries out all the predation and thus monopolizes the predatory rents. To model this situation, suppose that all rents from predation go to a fraction $e^I < 1$ of the incumbent group that also bears the cost of predatory activity. We assume that the predation level is set to maximize the income from predation net of such costs. For simplicity, we assume that both groups are ruled by an elite in the same way and that the size of the elite is the same within each group. Political turnover, if it occurs, is between the rulers in these elites.

Governance In this setup, we may introduce an additional parameter for political institutions to complement θ and γ. We refer to the *governance parameter,* denoted by $\zeta \in [0, 1]$. Think about ζ as a transaction cost imposed on the elite that reduces the rents that they can extract given any level of legal protection, p_s^J. Thus, the *realized* level of per capita rents accruing to the elite is now

$$\frac{\sum_{J \in \{I,O\}} \left[\mu\left(\hat{x}_s^J, p_s^J\right) \tilde{y}\left(p_s^J\right) - C\left(\hat{x}_s^J\right)\right]}{e^I}(1-\zeta),$$

with $\zeta = 0$ being the weakest type of governance and $\zeta = 1$ the strongest. One interpretation of ζ might be the extent to which an independent judiciary holds the government to account. Of course, the qualifier made earlier regarding the possibility of credible delegation to an independent judiciary is still valid.

As in our core model, the citizens from the group in power benefit from official resources allocated through the tax system, in which case the incumbent is constrained by political institutions as represented by θ. In theory cohesiveness, as measured by θ, and good governance, as measured by ζ, concern distinct distributional issues. In reality, however, we would expect θ and ζ to be linked, as both are associated with constraints on the executive.

Indirect Utilities The utility of a nonelite citizen of type J is

$$\alpha_s g_s + (1-t_s)\left[1-\mu\left(\hat{x}_s^J, p_s^J\right)\right]\tilde{y}\left(p_s^J\right) + r_s^J.$$

The utility of a representative member of the elite (always a member of group I by assumption) is

$$\frac{\sum_{J\in\{I,O\}}\left[\mu\left(\hat{\chi}_s^J, p_s^J\right)\tilde{y}\left(p_s^J\right) - C\left(\hat{\chi}_s^J\right)\right]}{e^I}(1-\zeta)$$

$$+\alpha_s g_s + (1-t_s)\left[1-\mu\left(\hat{\chi}_s^I, p_s^I\right)\right]\tilde{y}\left(p_s^I\right) + r_s^I. \tag{3.30}$$

The elite attaches less weight to the general group interest as represented by the second term in (3.30). However, this also depends on the quality of governance ζ. If $\zeta = 1$, then the incumbent cares only about group welfare. This formulation assumes (quite reasonably) that the rents earned from predation are not subject to income taxation because they are informal.

Solving for transfers using the government budget constraint yields

$$r_s^I = 2(1-\theta)\left[R + t_s\left[1-\mu\left(\hat{\chi}_s^I, p_s^I\right)\right]Y\left(p_s^I, p_s^O\right) - g_s - m_s\right]. \tag{3.31}$$

As in the core model of Section 3.1, we still have $t_s = \tau_s$ and public-goods demand determined by a corner solution, depending on the value of α_s compared to $2(1-\theta)$. The only interesting new issue is how legal protection against predation is pursued.

Legal Protection Reconsidered Plugging (3.31) into (3.30) with $t_s = \tau_s$ and the optimal public-goods decision yields the incumbent's payoff function. We assume that the resulting payoff function is concave in $\left(p_s^I, p_s^O\right)$. The choice of p_s^J will maximize this payoff subject to the constraints on legal and fiscal capacity. The first-order conditions are

$$\frac{\partial\left[\mu\left(\hat{\chi}_s^I, p_s^I\right)\tilde{y}\left(p_s^I\right) - C\left(\hat{\chi}_s^I\right)\right]}{\partial p_s^I}[1-\zeta]$$

$$+e^I\left[(1-\tau_s)+\tau_s\lambda_s\right]\frac{\partial\left[1-\mu\left(\hat{\chi}_s^I, p_s^I\right)\right]\tilde{y}\left(p_s^I\right)}{\partial p_s^I} \gtreqless 0 \tag{3.32}$$

$$\text{c.s. } p_s^I \in [0, \pi_s]$$

for the incumbent group and

$$\frac{\partial\left[\mu\left(\hat{\chi}_s^O, p_s^O\right)\tilde{y}\left(p_s^O\right) - C\left(\hat{\chi}_s^O\right)\right]}{\partial p_s^O}[1-\zeta]$$

$$+e^I\tau_s\lambda_s\frac{\partial\left[1-\mu\left(\hat{\chi}_s^O, p_s^O\right)\right]\tilde{y}\left(p_s^O\right)}{\partial p_s^O} \gtreqless 0 \tag{3.33}$$

$$\text{c.s. } p_s^O \in [0, \pi_s]$$

for the opposition, where, as before, $\lambda_s = \max\{\alpha_s, 2(1-\theta)\}$ is the marginal value of public funds.

The first term in both (3.32) and (3.33) is negative and, as p_s^J is increased, represents the marginal loss to the elite from greater rents owing to weaker legal protection. The second term is positive and represents the gain in income from strengthening legal protection. For the incumbent group, this includes the fact that its income is higher as well as the gain coming via the government budget constraint.

Using (3.32) and (3.33), we now have the following result:

Proposition 3.9: *The protection of property rights depends on the strength of governance. There are two thresholds:* $\zeta_H(\tau_s, \pi_s, \lambda_s, e^I) > \zeta_L(\tau_s, \pi_s, \lambda_s, e^I)$ *such that:*

1. *If* $\zeta \geq \zeta_H(\tau_s, \pi_s, \lambda_s, e^I)$*, then* $p_s^I = p_s^O = \pi_s$.
2. *If* $\zeta \in (\zeta_L(\tau_s, \pi_s, \lambda_s, e^I), \zeta_H(\tau_s, \pi_s, \lambda_s, e^I))$*, then* $\pi_s \geq p_s^I > p_s^O \geq 0$.
3. *If* $\zeta \leq \zeta_L(\tau_s, \pi_s, \lambda_s, e^I)$*, then* $p_s^I = p_s^O = 0$.

Proof: First observe by (the envelope theorem) that

$$\frac{\partial\left[\mu\left(\hat{\chi}_s^J, p_s^J\right)\tilde{y}\left(p_s^J\right) - C\left(\hat{\chi}_s^J\right)\right]}{\partial p_s^J} = -\hat{\chi}_s^J\tilde{y}\left(p_s^J\right) < 0,$$

i.e., rents are always higher when p_s^J decreases. Now, define ζ_H from

$$-\hat{\chi}_s^O\tilde{y}(\pi_s)\left[1-\zeta_H\right] + e^I\tau_s\lambda_s\frac{\partial\left[1-\mu\left(\hat{\chi}_s^O, \pi_s\right)\right]\tilde{y}(\pi_s)}{\partial\pi_s} = 0.$$

Since the payoff function is assumed to be concave, $p_s^O = \pi_s$ for for all $\zeta \geq \zeta_H$. Moreover, using (3.32), we also see that $p_s^I = \pi_s$. Observe that ζ_H always exists in the unit interval. Now define ζ_L from

$$-\hat{\chi}_s^I\tilde{y}(0)\left[1-\zeta_L\right] + e^I\left[(1-\tau_s) + \tau_s\lambda_s\right]\frac{\partial\left[1-\mu\left(\hat{\chi}_s^I, 0\right)\right]\tilde{y}(0)}{\partial p_s^I} = 0.$$

Since the function is concave, $p_s^I = 0$ for $\zeta \leq \zeta_L$. For $\zeta_L > 0$, we require e^I to be small enough; otherwise $\zeta_L = 0$. Moreover, it is straightforward to see from (3.33) that $p_s^O = 0$ at ζ_L and a fortiori for all $\zeta \leq \zeta_L$. Finally, observe that for

$\zeta \in [\zeta_L, \zeta_H]$, p_s^I is strictly positive at least for the incumbent. From (3.32) and (3.33), it is also straightforward to see that $p_s^I > p_s^O$. ■

Interpretation Proposition 3.9 gives us three cases. If governance is good $[\zeta \geq \zeta_H(\tau_s, \pi_s, \lambda_s, e^I)]$, then maximal protection against predation is given to both groups and all legal capacity is utilized. If governance is bad $[\zeta \leq \zeta_L(\tau_s, \pi_s, \lambda_s, e^I)]$, neither group is offered any legal protection against predation. Between these two extremes, legal protection favors citizens in the incumbent group. This is like an oligarchic system of property-rights protection, where protection is different for each group, with the incumbent group being favored. However, legal protection still falls short of using all legal capacity.

The striking feature of Proposition 3.9 is that—unlike the model of Section 3.2.1—both groups may be denied access to the legal system. This provides a vivid illustration of how corruption/predation can be economically costly. The point is not just the standard channel of raising $\mu\left(\hat{\chi}_s^J, p_s^J\right)$, but also that corruption reduces the interest of the ruling elite in offering legal support for citizens against such activity. The damage may not stop with this static effect, however, since predation also reduces the incentive to invest in legal capacity. We return to this possibility shortly.

The proof of Proposition 3.9 shows that equilibrium bad governance requires that the elite be small enough. To see this, observe that as $e^I \to 0$, the second term in (3.32) and (3.33) goes to zero, so that gains in rent seeking from worse legal protection dominate any positive effect on private incomes or any effect owing to the government budget constraint. Intuitively, a lower e^I makes the elite less and less representative of the interests of its group and hence brings about greater divergence from a Coasian outcome.

The governance thresholds also depend on λ_s. This is clear from (3.32) and (3.33), which show that the gain from improving property-rights protection comes, in part, from higher public revenues. It is possible, however, that if $\alpha_s = \alpha_H$—with the value of public goods being very large (such as in a war-time economy)—common-interest motives may become strong enough to trigger attempts to stamp out corruption and predation. But for strong and small elites, such a common-interest "shock" would have to be very large indeed. The main hope for restoring incentives to deploy legal capacity efficiently is that ζ will increase.

Finally, observe that one way of undermining these incentives is to try to tax returns from predation and corruption. This seems unlikely by the very nature of the activity. But to the extent that predation returns are taxed, it will have a similar effect to that of improving governance.

Incentives to Invest in Legal Capacity We now explore the implications of bad governance for incentives to invest in improving legal capacity. Let us focus on the case where governance is bad. Following Proposition 3.9, we define the following:

Bad Governance: $\quad \zeta \leq \zeta_L \left(\tau_s, \pi_s, \lambda_s, e^I\right).$

As we saw in Proposition 3.9, under bad governance the government has no incentive to offer legal protection to members of either group. If $p_s^I = p_s^O = 0$, we have $y_\pi\left(\pi_2\right) = 0$. Applying this logic to the legal-capacity Euler equation (3.5) implies that there is no incentive to invest in legal capacity. We refer to this case as a *predatory state,* since it is the unchecked predation of the ruling elite that undermines the incentives to create legal institutions and sustain the rule of law.

We summarize this observation in the following proposition:

Proposition 3.10: *If bad governance holds, the state is predatory and has no incentive to invest in legal capacity. This also reduces the period-1 incumbent's incentive to invest in fiscal capacity.*

The predatory state in some ways parallels the weak state we identified in Sections 2.1 and 3.1, since the incumbent has no incentive to invest in one form of state capacity. There are three important differences, however.

First, weak states were defined by a lack of incentive to invest in *fiscal capacity* because of limited institutional cohesion in allocating government resources. In predatory states, the weakness is due to the rulers benefiting directly from weak legal institutions because of poor governance, i.e., a low value of ζ.

Second, a predatory state can, in principle, coexist with all three kinds of states identified in the last part of Section 2.1. It may even be possible to have a common-interest state that is simultaneously predatory! The rent-seeking problem arises, not predominantly because of a lack of cohesion across groups, but rather because of an "agency" problem within groups. However, given that high θ and ζ are likely to have many common features, it is unlikely that a common-interest state will also be predatory. We thus expect predatory states to arise mainly when the Cohesiveness condition fails, i.e., in weak and redistributive states.

Third, unlike weak states predatory states have direct implications for economic efficiency: such states will have low and inefficient levels of production. This creates a direct link among low legal protection, corruption, and low income.

Given the complementarity we have identified between fiscal and legal capacity, the unwillingness to build legal capacity also results in weaker incentives to invest in fiscal capacity. In a predatory state, none of the elite groups has an incentive to break out of this trap—even if γ is high and power is expected to turn over—since whatever legal capacity might be created will never be deployed. In other words, moves to strengthen the rule of law will simply be emasculated.

Even in the absence of the worst form of bad governance, any situation with $\zeta < \zeta_H \left(\tau_s, \pi_s, \lambda_s, e^I\right)$ will imply weak incentives to invest in legal capacity. Improving governance will therefore be a complement to investing in legal capacity, as well as in fiscal capacity.

Incentives to Invest in Private Capital We can also observe that a predatory state will have extremely poor incentives for private capital accumulation, as the rate of return is reduced by $\left(1 - \mu\left(\hat{\chi}_s^J, p_s^J\right)\right)$. Thus, if we were to introduce private capital accumulation in the same way as in Section 3.2.3, we would also expect predatory states to have lower levels of private accumulation. This effect would not necessarily be related to τ_s because the predatory margin is separate from the standard tax margin. Owing to the lower incentive to build legal capacity in predatory states, we would expect the predatory margin to be more important than the tax margin.

Taking Stock The analysis of the predatory state extends our approach to incorporate a new set of concerns. We stress the usual static distortions of predation and corruption. But we also highlight two other (linked) margins, where predation distorts: (1) incentives to deny citizens access to legal protection, and (2) incentives to create ineffective legal institutions. Thus the predatory state reveals new dimensions of state fragility, which complement the dimension identified earlier.

In Chapter 4, we will see that the presence of a predatory state will also have other negative consequences. In particular, it will strengthen the motives for elites dominating incumbent and opposition groups to invest in violence, so as to maintain or acquire a hold on power.

Moreover, our analysis motivates the need to improve governance as a means of promoting development, a regular theme in the recent development-policy literature. Through the lens of the model in this subsection, the right agenda would be political reform to improve the governance parameter ς. In Chapter 7, we discuss reforms that are designed to reduce elite capture and when we might expect such reforms to come about endogenously.

3.3 Empirical Implications and Data

We end this chapter as we ended Chapter 2—by taking a look at the cross-sectional data in light of the implications of the theory we have presented. As in the previous chapter, what we present here are no more than suggestive correlations. However, as in Chapter 2, we argue that theory is a useful guide to our measurement and the way we interpret these correlations.

Measuring Legal Capacity To measure legal capacity, variable π in the model, we use five different proxies, one from the International Country Risk Guide (ICRG) and four from the World Bank's Doing Business project.[18] Some of these have already figured in the graphs in this chapter as well as in Chapter 1.

From the ICRG, we take the annual measure of government antidiversion policy, which is intended to serve as a catch-all for private investment incentives affected by government. We use the value of this measure in the last year that it is available (1997). As it is quite a broad measure, it is hard to relate precisely to any specific theoretical mechanism. As mentioned in Chapter 1, however, this index has been commonly used in the macroeconomic development literature to gauge the protection of property rights. As it has this connotation, the index resonates well with our theoretical discussion of predation in Subsection 3.3.4. In analogy with some of our measures of fiscal capacity, it is not completely clear whether this is a measure of π_s or of $\{p_s^I, p_s^O\}$.

Our second measure is also quite general. It is a country's (normalized) rank on the Doing Business indicator, an index aggregated across a series of measures that rank the business environment of particular countries. It reflects a whole

18. See www.doingbusiness.org.

Table 3.1 Correlations among legal capacity measures

	Government antidiversion policy	Doing business	Registering property	Obtaining credit	Contract enforcement
Government antidiversion policy	1.000				
Doing business	0.801	1.000			
Registering property	0.508	0.567	1.000		
Obtaining credit	0.668	0.788	0.436	1.000	
Contract enforcement	0.728	0.706	0.385	0.407	1.000

gamut of frictions that governments impose on business. However, we can be fairly confident that there is a strong link to the underlying economic institutions and, hence, a reflection of π_s.

For our third, fourth, and fifth measures, we select specific indicators from the Doing Business project that are closer to the theory. The third measure is a country's (normalized) rank on ease of registering property. This clearly relates to the ease with which assets can be collateralized, which is quite close to the microfounded model in Subsection 3.2.1, where $p_s^J = \pi_s$ allowed entrepreneurs to leverage their wealth. The fourth measure is a country's (normalized) rank in the ease of access to credit, which also relates well to the microfounded model with capital-market imperfections. The fifth measure is a country's (normalized) rank on a measure of enforcing contracts, which should also be relevant to trade in capital markets, but perhaps also to the legal system in general.

Table 3.1 shows a correlation matrix for the five measures of legal capacity. Not surprisingly, these are positively correlated. This reflects the kind of clustering that we have been emphasizing throughout. However, there are clearly some differences among the measures.

Measuring Parameters of the Model For these measures, we proceed exactly as in Chapter 2 and the reader may wish to refresh her memory of how we chose to construct proxies for $\{\phi, \theta, 1-\gamma, \widetilde{\alpha}_H\}$. However, it is worth highlighting two differences between the approach we take here and the one in Chapter 2. Both of these are motivated by the theoretical models in this chapter.

First, in Chapter 2, income per capita was taken as exogenous and used as a regressor in Table 2.4 on the grounds that the model offered predictions about the correlation between fiscal capacity and exogenous income ω. However, this chapter has emphasized the endogeneity of income, which clearly calls into question the interpretation of such regressions. Indeed, the model of this chapter could even be used to argue that income per capita should appear on the left-hand side of the regression.

Second, the models in this chapter suggest that we may want to highlight variables that affect the costs of investing in better legal institutions. As discussed in Section 3.1, this suggests a natural link to the empirical literature on legal origins. Indeed, our models offer a natural interpretation of legal origins through the impact they might have on the $\mathcal{L}(\cdot)$ function. Therefore, we include a set of legal-origin indicators in all the specifications that follow. In fact, the theory suggests that something more than legal origins affect legal capacity. Through the complementarity we have identified, there should be common effects on both the legal and the fiscal capacity of legal origins, as well as other determinants identified by the theory. This tells us something precise about which correlations we should expect to find in the data, and hence we revisit some of our measures of fiscal capacity to see whether the predicted correlation structures are present in the data.

Measuring Other Outcomes Although our focus is on legal capacity, we also want to check whether the suggested determinants of legal capacity are also correlated with other outcomes suggested by the theory. As pointed out in our discussion of the microeconomic model in Section 3.2.1, we should expect private credit to be monotonically related to determinants of legal capacity. Following common practice in the financial-development literature initiated by King and Levine (1993), we measure private credit as a share of GDP in the last year it is available to us (namely 1997).[19]

Referring to Section 3.2.3 and the complementarity between legal capacity and private investment, we should expect private investment to be positively correlated with the determinants of legal capacity. We measure private investment in the year 2006 from the Penn World Tables (variable "ci" in version 6.3 of the database) to parallel the timing of our main measures of legal capacity.

Given the extension on predation and corruption in Section 3.2.4, we should expect realized corruption to be negatively correlated with the determinants of legal capacity. We measure corruption via an index based on several sources of corruption perceptions. This is provided by Transparency International for a

19. We are grateful to Giovanni Favara for providing us with these data.

number of years and once more we use the 2006 outcome.[20] Note that higher values of this index imply less corruption.

Basic Correlations In Table 3.2, we begin by showing the partial correlations between our five legal-capacity measures and the proxies for parameters ϕ, θ, $(1-\gamma)$, and $\tilde{\alpha}_H$, plus the legal-origin indicators. Column (1) shows that—as expected from the theory—past wars, high constraints on the executive, nonopen and noncompetitive recruitment of the executive, and ethnic homogeneity are all positively and significantly correlated with the government antidiversion policy at the end of the 1990s. The same correlation pattern is also present for the other measures of legal capacity, although the correlations are somewhat weaker for registering property. For the four ranks extracted from the Doing Business survey, the estimated coefficient for the prevalence of war fluctuates around 0.5. This means that a country history that entails 25%, rather than none, of the last 200 years spent in wartime is associated with about 12.5% higher performance, i.e., about 20 steps, in the world ranking. By a similar calculation, a country with 20% higher historical average in its historical constraints on the executive score is associated with a higher world ranking of around 10%, i.e., about 15 steps.

Legal origins are also correlated with our measures of legal capacity. Particularly consistent is the positive and significant effect of Scandinavian and German legal origin compared to French legal origin (the omitted category). Perhaps surprisingly, given all the emphasis on common law in the legal-origins literature, British legal origin is less strongly correlated with our legal capacity measures, as is—perhaps less surprisingly—Socialist legal origin.

Interaction Effects As argued in Chapter 2, the correlations in Table 3.2 do not really engage with the detailed predictions of the model, as discussed in connection with the global and local comparative statics of the model. The arguments are essentially the same as those that we discussed in relation to fiscal capacity, but reinforced when fiscal and legal capacity are complements, as in Section 3.1. As a higher ϕ raises legal capacity π only in a common-interest or redistributive state, we expect a stronger effect of war (high ϕ or α) when cohesiveness (θ) is high. As political instability $1-\gamma$ has an impact on legal capacity only when θ is low enough, and for the range of γ where

20. This is their variable CPI. The CPI focuses on corruption in the public sector and defines corruption as the abuse of public office for private gain.

Table 3.2 Legal capacity and covariates: Simple correlations

	(1) Government antidiversion policy	(2) Doing business	(3) Registering property	(4) Obtaining credit	(5) Contract enforcement
Prevalence external war before 2000	1.294** (0.580)	0.427** (0.185)	0.278 (0.441)	0.355* (0.203)	0.749*** (0.230)
Average executive constraints before 2000	2.085*** (0.291)	0.535*** (0.084)	0.222* (0.122)	0.358*** (0.092)	0.287*** (0.108)
Average nonopen executive recruitment before 2000	1.467*** (0.303)	0.235** (0.109)	0.229 (0.152)	−0.082 (0.114)	0.202* (0.09)
Ethnic homogeneity	1.079*** (0.259)	0.241*** (0.073)	0.257*** (0.091)	0.286*** (0.089)	0.104 (0.096)
English legal origin	−0.157 (0.189)	0.148*** (0.050)	0.106* (0.064)	0.062 (0.054)	0.103* (0.054)
Scandinavian legal origin	0.706*** (0.204)	0.276*** (0.067)	0.327*** (0.079)	0.127 (0.081)	0.452*** (0.069)
German legal origin	0.627*** (0.185)	0.280*** (0.054)	0.244*** (0.079)	0.219*** (0.051)	0.365*** (0.063)
Socialist legal origin	0.013 (0.153)	0.062 (0.050)	0.155** (0.059)	−0.007 (0.059)	0.265*** (0.053)
Observations	122	147	147	147	147
R-squared	0.623	0.552	0.293	0.414	0.442

Notes: Robust standard errors in parentheses: * significant at 10%; ** significant at 5%; *** significant at 1%. French legal origin is the omitted category.

the stability condition holds, we expect higher political stability to positively affect legal capacity when cohesiveness is low, but not when it is high. By the global comparative statics, we expect high values of θ to raise the likelihood of a common-interest or redistributive state and larger investments in legal capacity.

We proceed as in Chapter 2 and add two interaction terms to the specification used in Table 3.2: (1) the binary high-executive constraints indicator times the continuous measure of past wars, and (2) the binary low-executive constraints indicator times the continuous measure of past political stability.

Table 3.3 shows our estimates when the more detailed and theory-driven specification is applied to the five measures of legal capacity. The results are of mixed success. Although a number of the correlations go in the expected direction, many are insignificant. However, the findings from Table 3.2 regarding

Table 3.3 Legal capacity and covariates: Interaction terms

	(1) Government antidiversion policy	(2) Doing business	(3) Registering property	(4) Obtaining credit	(5) Contract enforcement
Prevalence external war before 2000	1.369 (1.918)	0.708 (0.518)	1.529*** (0.549)	0.515 (0.659)	1.052* (0.561)
External war* high executive constraints dummy	0.146 (2.062)	−0.299 (0.554)	−1.535** (0.680)	−0.203 (0.676)	−0.320 (0.596)
Average nonopen executive recruitment before 2000	0.547 (0.630)	−0.030 (0.199)	0.151 (0.257)	−0.059 (0.210)	−0.038 (0.229)
Average nonopen executive recruitment* low ex constraints	1.097* (0.657)	0.245 (0.204)	0.028 (0.259)	0.010 (0.212)	0.254 (0.233)
Average executive constraints before 2000	2.147*** (0.561)	0.632*** (0.127)	0.235*** (0.175)	0.613*** (0.147)	0.216 (0.150)
Ethnic homogeneity	1.150** (0.296)	0.256*** (0.070)	0.241*** (0.091)	0.310*** (0.089)	0.102 (0.096)
English legal origin	0.137 (0.171)	0.145*** (0.050)	0.112* (0.065)	0.074 (0.053)	0.092 (0.057)
Scandinavian legal origin	0.931*** (0.286)	0.340*** (0.101)	0.347*** (0.091)	0.171 (0.107)	0.492*** (0.097)
German legal origin	0.714*** (0.286)	0.305*** (0.054)	0.265*** (0.078)	0.227*** (0.059)	0.388*** (0.067)
Socialist legal origin	−0.037 (0.171)	0.061 (0.052)	0.132** (0.062)	0.005 (0.062)	0.254*** (0.056)
Observations	122	147	147	147	147
R-squared	0.635	0.566	0.318	0.441	0.450

Notes: Robust standard errors in parentheses: * significant at 10%; ** significant at 5%; *** significant at 1%. French legal origin is the omitted category.

average executive constraints, ethnic homogeneity, and legal origins continue to hold up in a strong way.

Other Outcome Measures Although legal capacity should be the primary channel through which our institutional variables affect outcomes, these variables should also be related to the other outcome measures suggested by the theory. To the extent that our measures of legal capacity are imprecise, it is worth looking at some reduced-form partial correlations with the three outcomes mentioned earlier: financial development, private investment, and corruption. Indeed, if these correlations did not follow the patterns we found in Tables 3.2 and 3.3, we might be concerned about the mechanisms suggested by the theory. Thus these correlations serve as a further reality check.

The results are presented in the first three columns of Table 3.4, which uses the same specification as Table 3.2. We find a remarkably consistent picture with all determinants—war experience, strong executive constraints nonopen and noncompetitive executive recruitment, ethnic homogeneity, and German legal origin—being positively correlated with the three alternative outcome measures. This is precisely what we would expect if these determinants are indeed working through investments in legal capacity.

Common Determinants of Fiscal and Legal Capacity Finally, we turn to the important prediction of our theory that fiscal and legal capacity are jointly determined. Owing to the complementarity between the two, common factors should drive both legal and fiscal capacity. This is explored in the final columns of Table 3.4, which repeat the correlations from Table 2.2. We use three of our previous fiscal-capacity measures—overall tax take, income-tax share, and the size of the formal sector—as dependent variables. In line with the theory in this chapter, however, we now also include the legal-origins dummies on the right-hand side.

The results in columns (4)–(6) confirm that the pattern of correlations is similar for fiscal and legal capacity when it comes to our proxies for parameters ϕ, θ, $(1-\gamma)$, and $\widetilde{\alpha}_H$, plus German and Scandinavian legal origins. Given the amount of general clustering in the raw data between income and state capacity, this is perhaps not too surprising. But the theory we have developed in this section gives us a precise way of thinking about such clustering, where theory and data are saying the same thing.

Table 3.4 Other outcomes and covariates: Simple correlations

	(1) Private credit to GDP	(2) Corruption perceptions	(3) Private-investment rate	(4) Tax-revenue share in GDP	(5) Income-tax share in total revenue	(6) Formal sector share
Prevalence external war before 2000	2.490*** (0.571)	2.130*** (0.495)	0.132 (0.659)	3.227*** (1.160)	2.056* (1.100)	2.159*** (0.807)
Average executive constraints before 2000	1.729*** (0.331)	1.799*** (0.275)	0.906*** (0.260)	1.491*** (0.420)	1.690*** (0.421)	1.485*** (0.375)
Average nonopen executive recruitment before 2000	1.099** (0.429)	0.870*** (0.310)	0.751** (0.356)	0.640 (0.388)	0.849* (0.473)	1.249*** (0.471)
Ethnic homogeneity	0.489 (0.301)	0.693*** (0.254)	0.991*** (0.216)	0.650** (0.311)	0.171 (0.283)	0.549 (0.353)
English legal origin	0.131 (0.218)	0.078 (0.156)	0.298* (0.161)	0.047 (0.178)	0.225 (0.183)	0.089 (0.233)
Scandinavian legal origin	−0.346 (0.41)	1.719*** (0.212)	0.154 (0.212)	1.966*** (0.348)	1.114*** (0.293)	0.499** (0.215)
German legal origin	1.618*** (0.407)	1.117*** (0.231)	0.272 (0.232)	0.677* (0.359)	1.273*** (0.219)	0.892** (0.221)
Socialist legal origin	N/A	−0.376*** (0.120)	0.268* (0.146)	−1.027*** (0.171)	−0.308 (0.450)	−0.172 (0.239)
Observations	96	147	154	104	104	109
R-squared	0.633	0.643	0.332	0.630	0.554	0.375

Notes: Robust standard errors in parentheses: * significant at 10%; ** significant at 5%; *** significant at 1%. French legal origin is the omitted category.

In the same way as for the correlations given at the end of Chapter 2, the results presented here are only illustrative and suggestive. But they do continue to suggest that our theoretical ideas are relevant to explaining cross-country differences in legal and fiscal capacity. The next phase of empirical research, however, must focus on exploiting the time variation in the data found within countries.

3.4 *Final Comments*

This chapter has focused on the productive role of government in improving the environment for doing business. Improvements in the performance of government are measured as TFP and differences in income across countries can be explained by differences in the quality of their economic institutions. This makes it essential to understand why some countries make the right investments in legal institutions and deploy such legal capacity effectively.

A running theme of the chapter is the possibility of a complementarity between the extractive (taxation) and the productive (supporting markets) roles of government. This is at the heart of the empirical observation that market development and state development move hand in hand. But the key insight from our framework is that we have to understand the incentives of a government to make investments to improve the workings of the economy. The common drivers of state and market development are political institutions as well as natural endowments that affect productivity. The core model we have developed in Chapter 2 and extended here lays bare these common determinants.

Three further sources of complementarity have emerged in this chapter. First, a better ability to redistribute through the tax system makes government less inclined to use inefficient forms of redistribution, such as denying legal services to some groups of entrepreneurs. Second, improved legal systems may bring people out of the informal economy and into the formal economy, which lowers the cost of tax enforcement. These two channels were discussed in Section 3.2.1. Third, increases in legal capacity can encourage capital accumulation and promote growth through the conventional accumulation channel, as discussed in Section 3.2.3.

The framework developed in this chapter also helps us to understand the forces behind the observed clustering between income and both forms of state capacity. On the one hand, some common factors, such as common interests and cohesive political institutions, determine both forms of state capacity. But legal capacity will promote income via the endogenous growth mechanism discussed in Section 3.1 and the complementary private accumulation channel discussed in Section 3.2.3. Moreover, as discussed in Section 3.2.4, higher fiscal capacity may also promote income by stimulating incumbents not to engage in production-distorting rent seeking. On the other hand, Section 3.1 highlighted a force operating from income to state capacity, namely that higher exogenous growth increases prospective tax bases and thus promotes investments in legal as well as fiscal capacity.

It is easy to see that the positive feedbacks entailed in these two-way relations between income and state capacity can generate virtuous or vicious circles. Such circles can help explain an important dimension of the development clusters we observe in the data.

Finally, we explored the role of extralegal taxation (predation). This is most damaging when combined with elite control and highlights the role of governance relations between the elite and the citizenry when predatory rents accrue to the elite. This leads to the possibility of a legal-capacity trap, which we referred to as a predatory state. The predation effects further reinforce the mechanisms identified earlier in the chapter.

3.5 *Notes on the Literature*

Our models of legal capacity in this chapter focus mostly on enforcement of private contracts by a public body. In the terminology of Dixit (2009), we are considering enforcement-based rather than information-based institutions. In particular, we do not deal with self-enforcing agreements between private parties. In the terminology of Greif (2005), we are primarily considering (public-order and designed) contract-enforcement institutions, i.e., government enforcement of agreements between private parties, rather than coercion-constraining institutions, i.e., obstacles to government expropriation of private parties. But the governance institutions we introduced in the predatory state would be of the latter type.

A long-standing tradition in development economics sees reallocation of resources to higher return activities as the main mechanism for raising incomes. Perhaps the most famous statement of this view is in the paper by Lewis (1954), who highlighted the movements of labor from traditional to advanced production as the key mechanism of development. More recent work in this vein has accorded increasing recognition to misallocation in capital markets, as in Banerjee and Duflo (2005).

Hseih and Klenow (2009) stress the aggregate productivity consequences of factor market misallocation using microdata from India and China. Restuccia and Rogerson (2008) also look at aggregate implications of policy-induced resource misallocation. More general implications of these views are developed in Hseih and Klenow (2010), who conclude that 50–70% of income per capita differences between countries can be accounted for by differences in TFP rather than in physical or human capital. Related work on China by Song, Storesletten, and Zillibotti (2011) considers the process of capital accumulation through the entry of new firms as the main source of Chinese growth and argues that this pattern is due to capital-market imperfections.

Acemoglu (2006) underlines the political origins of resource misallocation with a particular focus on adverse factor price effects that lead to inefficiencies in production. This work also highlights the importance of fiscal capacity, although it takes such capacity as given.

Many researchers have emphasized the links between financial development and growth. See Beck (2010) for a useful general overview of the literature on legal institutions and their impact on economic development. Early discussions include Gerschenkron (1962) and Schumpeter (1934). Aghion, Howitt, and Mayer-Foulkes (2005) and King and Levine (1993) offer modern-day tests of these ideas. Levine (2005) provides an overview of the large literature on finance and economic growth.

The factors—economic and political—that shape capital-market development have been an active area of research. The legal-origins tradition pioneered by La Porta, Lopez de Silanes, Shleifer, and Vishny (1998) has emphasized how some legal traditions—particularly those rooted in common law—are more conducive to development of some kinds of capital markets. This body of research is summarized in La Porta, Lopez de Silanes, and Shleifer (2008).

La Porta et al. (1999) discuss the quality of government more generally and a variety of factors—including legal origins—that determine it. They find that larger governments are associated with more effective governments in many dimensions. Chong and Gradstein (2007) and Gradstein (2008) also consider the link between inequality and property-rights protection both theoretically and empirically. Hodgson (2006) finds that fractionalization, measured using Fearon's (2003) measure, is one of the most important and statistically significant variables in explaining differences in post-1989 real GDP growth per capita among ex-Soviet countries.

The importance of the business climate for economic development has been a major theme in much recent research, a great deal of which emphasizes the significance of legal origins. For example Djankov, McLiesh, and Shleifer (2007) find that legal origins are an important determinant of both creditor rights and information-sharing institutions, which, in turn, affect the supply of credit.

Djankov, La Porta, Lopez de Silanes, and Shleifer (2002) find a relationship between the regulation of business entry and legal origins. Cantoni and Yuchtman (2009) study how historical market development patterns within Germany are affected by the availability of legal institutions and try to circumvent the simultaneity problem by using the locations of medieval universities following the Papal Schism in the late 1300s as an instrument for legal institutions.

Rajan and Zingales (2003) and Svensson (1998) emphasize the role of politics in affecting financial-market development, as do Pagano and Volpin (2005) alongside legal origins. Further work in this tradition includes Pagano and Volpin (2001, 2006) and Perotti and von Thadden (2006). Caselli and Gennaioli (2008) develop an interesting political-economics model of institutional reform in financial markets.

A variety of macroeconomic models with political-economic orientations have explored the links between government policy and economic growth. These include Alesina and Rodrik (1994), Krusell and Ríos-Rull (1996), Parente and Prescott (2000), and Persson and Tabellini (1994). Acemoglu (2003) builds the link between these ideas around a Political Coase theorem. Besley and Coate (1998) develop a theory of political failure based on governments not implementing Pareto-improving policies.

There is a now a large microeconomic literature on the role of private property rights in improving resource allocation in developing countries, which is surveyed in Besley and Ghatak (2010). There is also an emerging empirical literature using microdata, which entails work by Banerjee, Gertler, and Ghatak (2002), Besley (1995), Field (2007), and Johnson, MacMillan, and Woodruff (2002).

Barro and Sala-i-Martin (1992) look at conventional links between taxes and growth where taxation is spent on productive investments. There are a number of contributions that have tried to link taxation and growth surveyed in Benabou (1997). More in the spirit of the arguments in this chapter Dincecco and Prado (2010) argue that there is positive link between fiscal capacity and development; they use casualties sustained in premodern wars to instrument for current fiscal institutions.

The predatory state as a constraint on development is an old idea. The notion is reviewed in historical perspective by De Long (2000). Pioneering work by North (1990) and North and Thomas (1973) highlights the central role played by property-rights protection in fostering historical developments in Western Europe. De Long and Shleifer (1993) use city growth in medieval Europe as a testing ground for these ideas. North and Weingast (1989) regard the Glorious Revolution in 1688 leading to the establishment of secure property rights as a pivotal moment in U.K. history. In addition, this set important fiscal and financial changes in motion. Stasavage (2003) discusses their arguments looking at both France and Great Britain.

Acemoglu, Johnson, and Robinson (2001) stress the empirical importance of settler mortality in explaining modern-day income levels by predicting the creation of productive or predatory state institutions. Similar ideas lie behind the empirical work of Hall and Jones (1999). Jellema and Roland (2010) emphasize the clustering of institutions. Seminal studies by Bates (1981, 2009) have explored the importance of state institutions in an African context.

Theoretical models of predatory states have been proposed by many researchers, including Azam, Bates, and Biais (2009), Grossman and Kim (1995), Grossman and Noh (1994), McGuire and Olson (1996), Moselle and Polak (2001), Olson (1993), and Weingast (1997). Within the institutions literature, there is considerable debate about which aspects of institutions are the most important. Acemoglu and Johnson (2005) argue that the most robust finding is that protecting private-property rights rather than promoting contracting institutions is the more important. This would put more weight on the dangers of a predatory state.

Related to studies of the predatory state, there is now a large literature on corruption—its causes and consequences. See Treisman (2000) and Svensson (2005) for overviews of this literature. An early contribution by Mauro (1995) emphasized the negative correlation in the cross-country data between corruption and growth, although the direction of causality is notoriously hard to determine. Hodgson and Jiang (2007) argue that the study of corruption should not be confined solely to the public sector, in part because public/private boundaries are often unclear. This provides a link to the literature on rent seeking since such activity can be either public or private. The original rent-seeking models are due to Krueger (1974) and Tullock (1967). Hillman (2011) offers a recent overview of the main ideas and existing literature on such behavior.

For all the importance attached to institutions, some scholars remain doubtful about how much institutions can help explain economic growth. Bloom and Sachs (1998) and Gallup, Sachs, and Mellinger (1999) stress geography rather than institutions, whereas Glaeser, La Porta, Lopez de Silanes, and Shleifer (2004) stress human capital rather than institutions.

CHAPTER 4

Political Violence

A prince ought to have two fears, one from within, on account of his subjects, the other from without, on account of external powers.

Niccolo Machiavelli, *The Prince,* 1513

In Chapters 2 and 3 we developed a framework for analyzing how the extractive and productive capabilities of the state are built, with particular emphasis on investments in fiscal and legal capacity. Politics certainly played an important role in that argument, but we modeled the forces of politics with two simple parameters, capturing the nature (cohesiveness) of political institutions and the rate of political turnover (stability). Although analytically useful, this approach kept the mechanisms for resolving political conflicts in the background. It is now time to explore these issues in more detail.

Our purpose in this chapter is to take a first step toward a better understanding of the observed clustering of development with political violence. Studying the causes of political violence is important in and of itself. Thus we begin by isolating the likely determinants of internal political violence, drawing on—and extending—the existing literature. Furthermore, political violence ties in closely with our previous modeling in at least two ways.

First, the theory in Chapters 2 and 3 suggests that the risk of *external* violence, i.e., the risk of war, can promote state building by enhancing common interests relative to redistributive interests across different groups in society. The risk of *internal* political violence appears to be different. Conditions that sow the seeds for internal violence are hardly a sign of common interests but rather of an extreme form of redistributive struggle across domestic groups. Intuitively, the risk of internal political violence may therefore drive incentives for state building in a different direction than the risk of external violence. Thus, we might expect the incumbent's two fears, highlighted by Machiavelli in the opening quote, to be associated with different consequences for state-capacity investments.

Second, the theory that we have proposed suggests that political *instability*—parameter γ in previous chapters—may be an important hurdle for investments in the state, especially outside the realm of common-interest states (recall the stability condition). Manifestations of political violence such as insurgencies and civil wars are important determinants of political instability in countries where they take place.

For both of these reasons, it is essential to explore the determinants of political violence both theoretically and empirically—the main goal of this chapter.[1] That exercise will serve to endogenize the previously parametric γ, and this will allow us to revisit investments in state capacity in a more general setting, which is the task of Chapter 5. Before delving into the theory and empirics of political violence, we discuss some background facts about different forms of violence and give a brief overview of some of the existing research in political science and economics.

Background Facts Political violence is a hallmark of weakly institutionalized polities. The starkest manifestation of such violence is outright conflict in the form of civil war. The Armed Conflict Dataset (ACD) codes any year in a given country as a year of civil war if a conflict between a national government and some insurgent group(s) claims more than 1000 battle deaths. When we apply that definition to all countries and years since 1950 where data are available, the average yearly prevalence of civil war is more than 10%, with a peak higher than 15% in the early 1990s. The upper-left panel of Figure 1.10 illustrates the variable trend in the worldwide prevalence of civil war by year, according to the ACD. The upper-right panel of the same figure displays the prevalence of civil war by country (since 1950 or independence, if later) against GDP per capita in 1980, showing how civil wars have been disproportionately concentrated in the poor countries of the world. The cumulated death toll of these conflicts exceeds 15 million people.[2]

1. Chapter 4 is closely related to Besley and Persson (2009a) and especially (2010b), although both the modeling and the empirical work in those papers are somewhat different. The idea that external and internal violence may drive state capacity in different directions appears in Besley and Persson (2008).

2. See Lacina and Gleditsch (2005).

A key feature of civil war is two-sided violence between an insurgent and the government. However, many citizens also suffer consequences of one-sided political violence, owing to government repression through a variety of infringements of human rights. The Banks (2005) data set reports a stark form of repression, namely purges—i.e., the removal, by assassination or arrest, of political opponents considered undesirable by the incumbent government. To create nonoverlapping measures of repression and civil war, we code any year in a country when it has no civil war (according to the ACD definition), but a positive number of purges in the Banks data. By this measure, some 7% of all country-years since 1950 are associated with repression. The lower-left panel in Figure 1.10 shows the worldwide development of purges, absent civil war, over time. Interestingly, up to the early 1990s, the repression series is almost a mirror image of the civil-war series in the earlier graph.[3] The lower-right panel completes the picture by plotting the prevalence of repression by country against 1980 GDP per capita and showing that repression has been most common in countries with somewhat higher incomes than in those where civil war has been prevalent.

Both the variation across time and the variation across countries in Figure 1.10 suggest that the two forms of violence tend to be substitutes for one another.

The analysis to follow is designed to identify determinants of violence and we show that some variables, such as cohesive political institutions, are common elements behind both one-sided and two-sided political violence. Naturally, outright conflicts and government repression come in different forms and intensities. Our focus here is on large-scale and serious manifestations of violence, i.e., civil war rather than civil conflict and major rather than minor acts of government repression.[4] In contrast to much of the civil-war literature, we focus on the *incidence* of violence (for both civil war and repression) rather than the *onset* and *duration* of violence, since our theory has much less to say about the latter two.

3. We show in Section 4.4 that this mirror image is not a mechanical consequence of a large number of overlapping observations with both purges and civil war.

4. We also ignore other forms of violence such as riots and political intimidation. See, e.g., Urdal (2008) or Bohlken and Sergenti (2010) for some recent work on how such violence relates to economic factors in India.

Table 4.1 reveals the countries that hide behind the dots in Figure 1.10. It lists the countries that have been basically free from conflict, as well as those that have experienced repression, civil war, or both types of violence. For civil war, the line between the left and right parts of the table is drawn between no year versus some year or years of civil war, since 1950 or independence (if later). For repression in the absence of civil war, the line between the upper and lower parts of the table is drawn at 5%—alternatively at 0%—of all years since 1950 (or independence). The table shows that 67 out of the 149 countries in the table have been violence-free according to the 5% definition of repression. This number becomes 40 when the repression cutoff is set at 0% of the years—countries in the upper part of the table that had in between 0 and 5% of all years in repression are marked by italics. Of the others, 39 countries have experienced both civil war and repression and 35 have experienced repression but no civil war, whereas only 8 have seen repression without civil war; these numbers become 44, 62, and 3 when the repression cutoff is set at 0%. Thus, the number of countries that have had a civil war but no separate instance of repression is much lower than the number that have experienced repression but no civil war. This is consistent with the idea that repression and civil war are ordered variables and suggests that government repression may often serve as a prestage to full-scale civil war.

Existing Research on Civil War and Repression The analysis in this chapter builds on earlier research, which, although comparatively recent, has developed both in its scope and its sophistication. By now, there is a large body of empirical work by both political scientists and economists on the causes of civil war. This literature has progressed from mainly cross-sectional inference using country-level data to panel-data studies, which exploit within-country variation [see the survey by Blattman and Miguel (2009)]. A largely independent literature [surveyed by Davenport (2007)], has explored the determinants of government repression and violations of human rights. [See, however, Collier and Rohner (2008) for the connection between repression and civil war.]

The main focus in both these strands of work has been on exploring empirical regularities, in some cases searching for credibly exogenous sources of variation. But the links between theoretical models of conflict and violence are limited. In fact, the surveys of Blattman and Miguel (2009) and Davenport (2007) both lament the fact that so few empirical findings forge links between the theory and data.[5] Thus, the former pronounce:

> the theoretical and empirical conflict literatures have too often run along parallel paths, informing each other, yes, but seldom directly intersecting; greater efforts need to be made to identify and test the precise empirical implications of the leading theoretical frameworks.

In this chapter, we argue that theory indeed provides a natural way of joining our understanding of the common pathology of civil war and repression. This will be seen clearly, as we approach the data.

Virtually all empirical research takes income as given. The correlation between civil war and poverty is commonly seen as a relation from income to civil war, with two leading interpretations; Collier and Hoeffler (2004) see it as a reflection of a low opportunity cost of fighting at low levels of income, whereas Fearon and Laitin (2003) understand it as a reflection of low-income countries having poorer state capacity. Taking income as given is problematic, though, since violence and income may well have common determinants. For example, there are two separate literatures on the "resource curse," one claiming that resource dependence may cause low income and low growth and the other arguing that resource dependence may cause civil war. On top of this, realized civil wars are likely to exert a negative impact on income.[6] Moreover, as we argued at the outset of this chapter, political violence and its effects on political instability may also affect investments in state capacity.

Plan of the Chapter The empirical links among political violence, income, and state capacity are likely to reflect a complex web of multidirectional relations. An explicit theoretical framework is an indispensable tool if we wish to untangle this web and interpret the patterns observed in the data.

5. There are certainly exceptions, however, such as Dube and Vargas (2008), who build explicitly on the theoretical framwork developed by Dal Bó and Dal Bó (2006). See also Fearon (2008).

6. See Collier (1999) for a discussion of the effects of civil war on income and Skaperdas (2010) for a more general overview of the various losses owing to civil war. Some recent work, beginning with Miguel, Satyanath, and Sergenti (2004) has addressed the reverse causality problem by isolating exogenous variation in income, e.g., through instrumenting income growth with weather shocks.

Table 4.1 Repression and civil war by country

	Some civil war			No civil war				
Less than 5% repression	Bosnia			Australia	*Cyprus*	*Jamaica*	New Zealand	Switzerland
	Cameroon			Bahamas	Czech Republic	Kuwait	*Norway*	Tanzania
	Guinea-Bissau			Bahrain	*Denmark*	*Lesotho*	Oman	*Togo*
	Liberia			Barbados	Djibouti	*Luxembourg*	*Panama*	Trinidad-Tobago
	Nepal			Belize	*Equatorial Guinea*	*Madagascar*	New Guinea	Tunisia
	Rwanda			Benin	Fiji	*Malawi*	Qatar	*United Kingdom*
	Sierra Leone			Bhutan	Gabon	*Malaysia*	*Saudi Arabia*	Uzbekistan
	Yemen			Botswana	Gambia	Maldives	*Senegal*	
				Brunei	*Guinea*	*Mali*	*Singapore*	
				Burkina Faso	Guyana	Malta	Slovak Republic	
				Canada	*Honduras*	Mauritania	Slovenia	
				Cape Verde	Iceland	Mauritius	Solomon Islands	
				Central African Republic	*Ireland*	*Mongolia*	Suriname	
				Costa Rica	*Israel*	Namibia	Swaziland	
				Croatia	Ivory Coast	Netherlands	*Sweden*	
More than 5% repression	Afghanistan	India	South Korea	Albania	Ghana	Taiwan		
	Algeria	Indonesia	Sri Lanka	Austria	Greece	Thailand		
	Angola	Iran	Sudan	Bangladesh	Haiti	Uruguay		
	Argentina	Iraq	Syria	Belgium	Hungary	Venezuela		
	Burundi	Laos	Turkey	Bolivia	Italy	Zambia		
	Cambodia	Lebanon	Uganda	Brazil	Japan			
	Chad	Libya	United States	Bulgaria	Jordan			
	China	Morocco	Vietnam	Chile	Kenya			
	Colombia	Mozambique	Zimbabwe	Comoros	Mexico			
	Congo	Nicaragua		Dominican Republic	Niger			
	Cuba	Nigeria		Ecuador	Paraguay			
	El Salvador	Pakistan		Egypt	Poland			
	Ethiopia	Russia		Estonia	Portugal			
	France	Somalia		Finland	Romania			
	Guatemala	South Africa		Germany	Spain			

Note: Countries with fewer than 5%, but more than 0%, of all years (since 1950 or independence) in repression are printed in italics.

We turn to building a theoretical structure in Section 4.1. In that section, we add investments in political violence to the core state-capacity model as formulated in Section 3.1. These investments affect the allocation of political power in period 2. In the present chapter, we do not fully solve that model, but focus on the solutions for violence while treating state-capacity investments as given. Section 4.2 develops the extended core model in a few directions, allowing for asymmetries, polarization, and predation along the same lines as the extensions in Chapters 2 and 3.

Having solved for the determinants of violence theoretically, we take a somewhat lengthy detour into empirical territory. In Section 4.3, we discuss how the theoretical model, together with specific assumptions about observability and time variation, allows us to design an empirical strategy that can be used to test the theoretical predictions. Section 4.4 then approaches the data with this strategy in hand. Unlike the empirical sections in Chapters 2 and 3, the ambition here is to isolate causal relationships. Thus, we exploit only the within-country variation in the data and arguably exogenous variation in the variables suggested by the theory. Section 4.5 concludes the chapter, before the customary notes on the literature.

After this empirical detour, Chapter 5 returns us to the theory and explores the joint determination of investments in state capacity and violence. It also includes a further discussion of the empirical clustering among violence, state capacity, and income.

4.1 *The Core Model with Political Violence*

4.1.1 Model Modifications

We take a starting point in the two-period, two-group, state-capacity framework of Chapter 3. In this chapter, we provisionally keep the legal and fiscal capacities in each period fixed, postponing the study of their endogenous determination until Chapter 5. Thus, not only are fiscal capacity and legal capacity, τ_s and π_s, taken as given, but so are wages and income levels, $\omega(\pi_s)$ and $y(\pi_s)$. As before, we treat exogenous government income, R, as stochastic and drawn from a distribution with finite support $[R_L, R_H]$. This variable has not played a particularly important role in the previous two chapters. But as we shall see soon, it now enters center stage.

Violence and Transitions of Power The most important feature of this chapter is that we replace the exogenous transition of power, summarized in the parameter γ, with the outcome of a potential conflict that is triggered by investments in violence by the incumbent and the opposition. In particular, the opposition group in period 1, O_1, can mount an insurgency with an army of size $L^O \leq \overline{L}$. This investment is paid for within the group, at some exogenously given marginal cost of funds ν. Analogously, the incumbent group I_1 can invest in an army of size $L^I \leq \overline{L}$. This investment is paid out of the public purse, at marginal cost λ_1 (given endogenously by the realized cost of funds in period 1). There is no conscription; each soldier must be paid the period-1 wage, $\omega(\pi_1)$.

The probability that the opposition wins office in period 2 depends on these investments, according to a conflict technology $\gamma(L^O, L^I; \xi)$, which is increasing in L^O and decreasing in L^I, with ξ denoting a set of parameters governing this technology. Later, we impose some further conditions on the technology $\gamma(\cdot)$ and relate these conditions to common assumptions in the literature on contest functions. If nobody arms, the probability of a peaceful transition is $\gamma(0, 0; \xi)$. Notwithstanding whether the transition takes place peacefully or violently, the winner becomes next period's incumbent, $I_2 \in \{A, B\}$ and the loser becomes next period's opposition, $O_2 \in \{A, B\}$.

Timing of Events The timeline of events in this more comprehensive model is identical to that in Section 3.1, except that we add the investments in violence by the first-period incumbent and opposition, which we assume to take place simultaneously with the other choices in period 1:

1. We begin with initial stocks of state capacities $\{\tau_1, \pi_1\}$ and an incumbent group I_1. Nature determines α_1 and R.
2. I_1 chooses a set of period-1 policies $\{t_1, r_1^I, r_1^O, p_1^I, p_1^O, g_1\}$, and determines (through investments) the period-2 stocks of fiscal and legal capacity $\{\tau_2, \pi_2\}$. I_1 and O_1 simultaneously invest in violence levels L^I and L^O.
3. I_1 remains in power with probability $1 - \gamma(L^O, L^I, \xi)$, and nature determines α_2.
4. I_2 chooses period-2 policies $\{t_2, r_2^I, r_2^O, p_2^I, p_2^O, g_2\}$.

Eventually, we will study a full subgame-perfect equilibrium in policy, violence, and state-capacity investments. Since the problem is recursive, we are able to study these three parts separately. In this chapter, we look at the choices of policy and investments in violence, in that order, taking the levels of state capacity as given. Chapter 5 goes on to the complete analysis with endogenous state-capacity investments.

The Source of Conflict Models that generate outright conflict as an equilibrium outcome rely on either imperfect information or inability of the parties to commit. The key friction in our model is of the second type—an inability of any prospective government to offer postconflict transfer credibly and an inability of potential insurgents to commit to not using their capacity to engage in conflict. In other words, if at stage 2 the incumbent and opposition could make a binding agreement not to exploit their (peacefully obtained) hold on power to redistribute resources in their own favor at stage 4, costly conflict might be avoided. But in the present model such agreements are infeasible, beyond the institutional commitments entailed in the value of θ.

4.1.2 Policy

As in Chapter 3, there are four dimensions of policy: regulation, transfers, taxation, and public goods, and the period-s incumbent chooses the optimal policy vector $\{g_s, t_s, p_s^I, p_s^O, r_s^I, r_s^O\}$ so as to maximize

$$\alpha_s g_s + (1 - t_s)\, y\left(p_s^I\right) + r_s^I, \tag{4.1}$$

subject to $t_s \leq \tau_s$, $p_s^J \leq \pi_s$, and $r_s^O \geq \sigma r_s^I$ and the government budget constraint. The government budget constraint is identical to equation (3.1) in Chapter 3, except that investment expenditures m_s include not only the costs of any (given) investments in state capacity but also the incumbent's investments in violence,

$$m_s = \begin{cases} \mathcal{F}(\tau_2 - \tau_1) + \mathcal{L}(\pi_2 - \pi_1) + \omega(\pi_1)L^I & \text{if } s = 1 \\ 0 & \text{if } s = 2. \end{cases} \tag{4.2}$$

As the incumbent's problem continues to be recursive, the fact that the objective function and the constraints are identical implies exactly the same solution as in Section 3.1. Thus, the group-specific extension of property-rights protection exhausts any available legal capacity with $p_s^I = p_s^O = \pi_s$. The income tax is set at its maximum $t_s = \tau_s$. Public goods satisfy one of two corner solutions given by

$$g_s = G(\alpha_s, \tau_s) = \begin{cases} R + \tau_s y(\pi_s) - m_s & \text{if } \alpha_s \geq 2(1-\theta) \\ 0 & \text{otherwise.} \end{cases} \tag{4.3}$$

Finally, transfers are determined residually as shares of the (tax plus other) revenue not spent on public goods or investments,

$$r_s^J = \beta^J [R + \tau_s y(\pi_s) - G(\alpha_s, \tau_s) - m_s], \tag{4.4}$$

where the shares reflect the cohesiveness of political institutions: $\beta^I = 2(1-\theta)$ and $\beta^O = 2\theta$.

Indirect Payoffs When we plug these optimal policies into (4.1), we obtain the "indirect" payoff function

$$\begin{aligned} W(\alpha_s, \tau_s, \pi_s, R, m_s, \beta^J) = \alpha_s G(\alpha_s, \tau_s) + (1-\tau_s) y(\pi_s) + \\ \beta^J [R + \tau_s y(\pi_s) - G(\alpha_s, \tau_s) - m_s] \end{aligned} \tag{4.5}$$

for being the incumbent or opposition group in period s depending on the state variables $\{\tau_s, \pi_s\}$. As in Chapter 3, we define "value functions"

$$U^I(\tau_2, \pi_2) = \left[\phi W\left(\alpha_H, \tau_2, \pi_2, R, 0, \beta^I\right) + (1-\phi) W\left(\alpha_L, \tau_2, \pi_2, R, 0, \beta^I\right)\right]$$

and

$$U^O(\tau_2, \pi_2) = \left[\phi W\left(\alpha_H, \tau_2, \pi_2, R, 0, \beta^O\right) + (1-\phi) W\left(\alpha_L, \tau_2, \pi_2, R, 0, \beta^O\right)\right]$$

for being the incumbent or opposition group in period 2 depending on the state variables $\{\tau_2, \pi_2\}$.

When we put these together, the expected period-2 utility of group J in period 1 becomes:

$$\begin{aligned} & W(\alpha_1, \tau_1, m_1, \beta^J) \\ & + (1-\gamma(L^O, L^I, \xi)) U^I(\tau_2, \pi_2) + \gamma(L^O, L^I, \xi) U^O(\tau_2, \pi_2) \end{aligned} \tag{4.6}$$

for the incumbent group and

$$\begin{aligned} & W(\alpha_1, \tau_1, m_1, \beta^J) - \nu\omega(\pi_1) L^O \\ & + \gamma(L^O, L^I, \xi) U^I(\tau_2, \pi_2) + \left[1 - \gamma(L^O, L^I, \xi)\right] U^O(\tau_2, \pi_2) \end{aligned} \tag{4.7}$$

for the opposition group. For the opposition, we have deducted the private cost of violence: $\nu\omega(\pi_1) L^O$, whereas for the incumbent, violence is funded from the public purse and thus embodied in the definition of $W(\alpha_1, \tau_1, m_1, \beta^J)$.

4.1.3 Investments in Political Violence

Preliminaries We now characterize the Nash equilibrium in violence levels denoted as $\left\{\hat{L}^O, \hat{L}^I\right\}$. These maximize (4.6) and (4.7). The first-order conditions are

$$-\gamma_I(\hat{L}^O, \hat{L}^I, \xi)\left[U^I(\tau_2, \pi_2) - U^O(\tau_2, \pi_2)\right] - \lambda_1\omega(\pi_1) \le 0, \tag{4.8}$$

where—as in Chapters 2 and 3—$\lambda_1 = \max\{\alpha_1, 2(1-\theta)\}$ is the realized marginal value of tax revenue for the period-1 incumbent, and

$$\gamma_O(\hat{L}^O, \hat{L}^I, \xi)\left[U^I(\tau_2, \pi_2) - U^O(\tau_2, \pi_2)\right] - \nu\omega(\pi_1) \le 0. \tag{4.9}$$

This way of writing the first-order conditions makes it clear that the marginal benefit of investing in violence comes from the increased probability of being the incumbent in period 2 and that the marginal cost is the resources needed to finance additional violence, whether from public or private funds. For both groups, this marginal benefit is proportional to $[U^O(\tau_2, \pi_2) - U^I(\tau_2, \pi_2)]$, the value of being an incumbent in period 2. The parameter λ_1 is the opportunity cost of public funds to the incumbent.

A key observation to motivate the result that follows is that the common positive term in the two first-order conditions, (4.8) and (4.9), can be expressed as

$$U^I(\tau_2, \pi_2) - U^O(\tau_2, \pi_2) = \omega(\pi_1)\, 2(1-2\theta)\, Z, \tag{4.10}$$

where

$$Z = \frac{R + \tau_2 y(\pi_2) - E(G(\alpha_2, \tau_2))}{\omega(\pi_1)} \tag{4.11}$$

and the expectations are taken over the uncertain future value of public goods (since α_2 is stochastic).

In the definition of Z, the numerator is the expected size of the redistributive "pie" in period 2 and the denominator is the wage in period 1. The marginal benefit of investment in violence for both groups is thus proportional to the numerator of Z, whereas the marginal cost of investment for both groups is proportional to the denominator of Z. It follows that Z can be interpreted as a benefit-cost ratio from the use of violence. As can be seen from (4.10) and (4.11), the term $\omega(\pi_1)$ appears in both terms of (4.8) as well as (4.9) and thus drops out of the first-order conditions.

The Conflict Technology We impose the following restrictions on the conflict technology

Assumption 4.1: *For all* $L^J \in [0, \overline{L}^J]$, *we have:*

(a) *if* $\gamma \in (0,1), \gamma_O > 0, \gamma_I < 0, \gamma_{OO} < 0, \gamma_{II} > 0,$

(b) $\dfrac{-\gamma_I\,(0,0;\xi)}{\gamma_O\,(0,0;\xi)} \geq \dfrac{\alpha_H}{\nu}$, and

(c) $\dfrac{\gamma_I \gamma_{OO}}{\gamma_O} \geq \gamma_{IO} \geq \dfrac{\gamma_O \gamma_{II}}{\gamma_I}.$

Condition (a) just says that fighting always has positive returns for both groups, albeit at a decreasing rate. The property in (b) ensures that the incumbent has a higher marginal return to fighting when neither party invests in violence. It guarantees that the incumbent has a sufficient advantage in military terms vis-à-vis the rebels. Finally, (c) restricts the extent of any strategic complementarities or substitutabilities in the conflict technology. These conditions are discussed further after the proof of Proposition 4.2.

Nash Equilibria We now study properties of the equilibrium investments (4.8) and (4.9) for each group and how these violence decisions depend on some key parameters. Our first result is the following proposition:

Proposition 4.1: *If (1)* $\alpha_L \geq 2(1-\theta)$, *or (2)* $\phi \to 1$, *no group invests in violence, i.e.,* $\hat{L}^I = \hat{L}^O = 0$.

Proof: Suppose first that $\alpha_2 = \alpha_H > 2 > 2(1-\theta)$. In that state, $G\left(\alpha_2, \tau_2\right) = R_2 + \tau_2 y(\pi_2)$ and no transfers are paid. Then, clearly if the probability of state α_H goes to 1, i.e., $\phi \to 1$, then $Z \to 0$. It follows that both (4.8) and (4.9) become strictly decreasing in L^J, and none of the groups invests anything, as the marginal benefit of investments in violence goes to zero.

Suppose, alternatively that $\alpha_L > 2(1-\theta)$. Then, cohesiveness holds and any incumbent spends nothing on transfers independently of which value of α_2 is realized. Thus, we have $Z = 0$. Again, neither the incumbent group nor the opposition group invests anything in violence as the marginal benefit of investments in violence is equal to zero. ■

This proposition says that as long as institutions are sufficiently cohesive or there is a high permanent demand for public goods, there is never any political violence. We recognize (1) and (2) as the conditions for a common-interest state from earlier chapters. The intuition is simple. If condition (1) holds, all future revenue will be spent on public goods. If (2) holds, transfers are paid when $\alpha_2 = \alpha_L$, but the probability of this state goes to zero. Therefore, expected transfers, and from (4.11) Z, are zero or go to zero. Neither group invests in violence, since investing in violence carries a cost but yields no return.[7]

We now explore what happens when the conditions in Proposition 4.1 do not hold.

Proposition 4.2: *If Assumption 4.1 holds, $\alpha_L < 2(1-\theta)$ and $\phi < 1$, there are two thresholds $Z^I(\theta,\xi)$ and $Z^O(\theta;\xi)$,*

$$Z^I(\theta;\xi) = -\frac{\lambda_1}{\gamma_I(0,0;\xi)\,2(1-2\theta)}$$

$$< Z^O(\theta;\xi) = \frac{\nu}{\gamma_O(0,0;\xi)\,2(1-2\theta)},$$

such that:

1. *If $Z \leq Z^I$, there is peace with $\widehat{L}^O = \widehat{L}^I = 0$.*
2. *If $Z \in (Z^I, Z^O)$, there is repression with $\widehat{L}^I > \widehat{L}^O = 0$.*
3. *If $Z \geq Z^O$, there is civil conflict with $\widehat{L}^I, \widehat{L}^O > 0$.*

Moreover, $\widehat{L}^O$ and $\widehat{L}^I$, whenever positive, increase in Z.

Proof: In this case, all spending is on transfers when $\alpha_2 = \alpha_L$, such that the wage-adjusted expected redistributive pie becomes $Z = (1-\phi)\,[R + \tau_2 y(\pi_2)]/\omega(\pi_1)$. The complementary-slackness conditions for the problems faced by L^I

7. This bang-bang solution for transfers is a stark but convenient consequence of the linear utility function in our core model. However, using the alternative formulation from Chapter 2 with concave utility $V(g)$ of public goods yields very similar results to those obtained here.

and L^O, assuming that $L^I > 0$ and $L^O > 0$, are

$$-\gamma_I\left(L^O, L^I; \xi\right) xZ - \lambda_1 \lesssim 0$$

$$\text{c.s. } \bar{L}^I \geq L^I \geq 0$$

and

$$\gamma_O\left(L^O, L^I; \xi\right) xZ - \nu \lesssim 0$$

$$\text{c.s. } \bar{L}^O \geq L^O \geq 0,$$

where we use the shorthand $x = (1 - 2\theta)$.

First, we show that, at any interior solution, resources devoted to fighting by both groups are increasing in Z. To see this, observe that differentiating and using the first-order conditions when they hold with equality yield

$$\begin{bmatrix} -\gamma_{II}xZ & -\gamma_{IO}xZ \\ \gamma_{IO}xZ & \gamma_{OO}xZ \end{bmatrix} \begin{bmatrix} dL^I \\ dL^O \end{bmatrix} = \begin{bmatrix} \gamma_I x dZ \\ -\gamma_O x dZ \end{bmatrix}. \tag{4.12}$$

Define $\Omega = \left[-\gamma_{II}\gamma_{OO} + (\gamma_{IO})^2\right] x^2 Z^2 > 0$. Solving (4.12) using Cramer's rule yields

$$\frac{dL^I}{dZ} = \frac{x^2 Z\left[\gamma_I \gamma_{OO} - \gamma_O \gamma_{IO}\right]}{\Omega} > 0$$

and

$$\frac{dL^O}{dZ} = \frac{x^2 Z\left[\gamma_{II}\gamma_O - \gamma_I \gamma_{IO}\right]}{\Omega} > 0,$$

where we have used both parts of Assumption 4.1c.

We now derive two trigger points for violence. Define $\hat{L}(Z)$ from

$$-\gamma_I\left(0, \hat{L}(Z); \xi\right) xZ - \lambda_1 \lesssim 0$$

$$\text{c.s. } \bar{L}^I \geq \hat{L}(Z) \geq 0.$$

It is simple to check that this is an increasing function of Z under Assumption 4.1b. Clearly with $L^O = 0$, $L^I = \hat{L}(Z)$. We can define $Z^I(\theta; \xi)$ from $\hat{L}(Z) = 0$, i.e.,

$$Z^I(\theta; \xi) = \frac{-\lambda_1}{\gamma_I(0, 0; \xi)\, x}.$$

Next, define $Z^O(\theta;\xi)$ implicitly from

$$\gamma_O\left(0, \hat{L}(Z^O(\theta;\xi)\right) x Z^O(\theta;\xi) = \nu.$$

The expression for $\frac{dL^O}{dZ}$ implies that for $Z \geq Z^O$, we must have $L^O > 0$.

As the next step, we prove that $Z^O(\theta;\xi) > Z^I(\theta;\xi)$. Suppose not, then

$$\gamma_O(0, 0; \xi)\, x Z^O(\theta;\xi) = \nu.$$

If so,

$$Z^O(\theta;\xi) = \frac{\nu}{\gamma_O(0, 0; \xi)\, x} \leq Z^I(\theta;\xi) = \frac{-\lambda_1}{\gamma_I(0, 0; \xi)\, x}$$

or

$$\frac{-\gamma_I(0, 0; \xi)}{\gamma_O(0, 0; \xi)} < \frac{\lambda_1}{\nu} \leq \frac{\alpha_H}{\nu},$$

which contradicts Assumption 4.1c for all values of θ.

Finally, it is easy to see from the explicit definition that $Z^I(\theta;\xi)$ is an increasing function. Using the implicit definition of $Z^O(\theta;\xi)$ and the fact that $\hat{L}\left(Z^O(\theta;\xi)\right)$ is (weakly) increasing, we find that this function is increasing as well. This concludes the proof of the proposition. ■

The proposition describes three states of political violence. When Z is below Z^I, no conflict erupts as both the incumbent and the opposition accept the (probabilistic) peaceful allocation of power, where the opposition takes over with probability $\gamma(0, 0; \xi)$. When $Z \in [Z^I, Z^O]$, the government invests in violence to increase its survival probability, but the opposition does not invest in conflict. It is natural to label this case government repression. Finally, when $Z > Z^O$, the opposition mounts an insurgency, which is met with force by the incumbent group, and we have civil war. Variation in Z may reflect variation in factors such as exogenous income R or period-1 wages $\omega(\pi_1)$, whereas variation in the thresholds Z^I and Z^O may reflect variation in the costs of raising revenues λ_1 and ν or in the efficiencies of fighting as captured by ξ.

Discussion Although the results in Proposition 4.2 may be intuitive, it is important to discuss the specific assumptions behind them. Assumption 4.1b rules out an undefended insurgency. It says that the return to fighting is strong enough for the incumbent, given the threat of political transition under peace. If this assumption does not hold, we may have a range of Z where the incumbent does not bother to fight the opposition when it rebels. This might be true, for instance, if $\gamma(0,0;\xi)$ is very close to zero and $\frac{-\gamma_I(0,0;\xi)}{\gamma_O(0,0;\xi)}$ is close to zero, so that the incumbent is not very much threatened by a transition and/or has low competence in defending against it. We find it natural to rule out undefended insurgencies, since we think such a phenomenon is rare. But as shown in Section 4.2, such insurgencies can be encompassed as a theoretical possibility in our framework.

Assumption 4.1c guarantees that the fighting propensities of both the incumbent and the opposition increase in the "prize of winning," as measured by Z. Given that a civil war is under way, this ensures that a higher Z does not make either party give up. This will be true as long as the marginal return to fighting is not strongly affected by the fighting decisions of the other group, placing bounds on γ_{IO}, not allowing a too strongly positive or strongly negative cross-partial.[8] In fact, under the assumption, both parties fight harder as Z goes up.

We have presented the results for a general conflict technology, or contest function. But the analysis works with a number of reasonable and commonly used specific contest functions. For example, it works in the logistic formulation [see Hirshleifer (1989)] if[9]

$$\gamma\left(L^O, L^I;\xi\right) = \frac{\exp[\xi_O L^O]}{\exp[\xi_O L^O] + \exp[\xi_I L^I]}$$

and $\frac{\xi_I}{\xi_O} \geq \alpha_H$. The same argument also holds in the popular ratio formulation [see Skaperdas (1992) and Tullock (1980)] if

$$\gamma\left(L^O, L^I;\xi\right) = \frac{\xi L^O}{\xi L^O + L^I},$$

where (scalar) parameter $\xi \geq 1$. It also holds in the semilinear formulation

$$\gamma\left(L^O, L^I;\xi\right) = \gamma_O + \xi_1\left[h\left(L^O\right) - \xi_2 h\left(L^I\right)\right],$$

8. We could make the weaker assumption that $\frac{\partial}{\partial\lambda}\left(\frac{-\gamma_I(\lambda x,(1-\lambda)x)}{\gamma_O(\lambda x,(1-\lambda)x)}\right) \geq 0$ for $\lambda \in [0,1]$ and $x \geq 0$, which is implied by Assumption 4.1c. This amounts to saying that the conflict technology is quasi-concave, i.e., it has level sets that are convex in $\left(L^O, L^I\right)$ space. This makes total spending on conflict by the two parties monotonic in Z, but not necessarily the spending by each group. In economic terms, this could lead to a resumption of repression or undefended insurgency at high levels of Z as one group drops out of the fight.

9. By l'Hopital's rule: $\gamma(0,0;\xi) = \frac{\xi}{\xi+1}$.

where $h(\cdot)$ is an increasing bounded and concave function, with $h_L(0) > 0$, a function that describes how investments in arms translate into violence, with the parameter restrictions $\xi_1 > 0$, $\xi_2 \geq \alpha_H/\nu$ and $1 - \xi_1 h(\bar{L}) > \gamma_O - \xi_1\xi_2 h(\bar{L}) > 0$.

4.1.4 Empirical Implications

Our results have some striking empirical implications when the logic of political violence is expressed as a function of latent variable Z. As explained earlier, Assumption 4.1 rules out undefended insurgencies and any of the parties dropping out of a civil war as Z gets higher. Under that assumption, our theory predicts an *ordering* in Z of the three violence states: peace, repression, and civil war.[10] This ordering is particularly interesting against the backdrop of Figure 1.10 and Table 4.1, which suggest that repression and civil war have been substitutes for one another, at least for some of the time and in some of the countries in the postwar world.

In countries where $\alpha_L < 2(1-\theta)$ and $\phi < 1$, transfers are paid, but only in the state when $\alpha_2 = \alpha_L$. Then, we can write the latent variable as

$$Z = \frac{(1-\phi)\left[R + \tau_2 y(\pi_2)\right]}{\omega(\pi_1)}.$$

This expression summarizes a few important determinants of violence, which we introduce in the following corollaries. We state these in terms of likelihoods, implicitly assuming that some factors are not only uncertain but also unobserved by an outside analyst. A more precise formulation of the empirical predictions—along precisely these lines—is found in the Section 4.3.

Corollary 4.1: *Higher wages, $\omega(\pi_1)$, reduce the likelihood that an economy will experience political violence, i.e., be in repression or civil war, unless political institutions are cohesive or the demand for public goods is high (θ close to $1/2$ or ϕ close to 1).*

The result follows from Proposition 4.2 by observing that $\omega(\pi_1)$ is the denominator of Z. Given the distributions of α and R, when $\omega(\pi_1)$ is higher the whole distribution of Z shifts to the left. Based on this, we can definitely say that higher wages make peace more likely (political violence less likely). We can

10. In an earlier version of Besley and Persson (2010b), we considered a case where the incumbent makes her investment in violence before (rather than simultaneously with) the opposition group and found a similar result.

also definitely say that civil war becomes less likely. But whether repression is more or less likely depends on relative densities (in the p.d.f. of Z; see further Section 4.3). The conditional statement regarding θ at the end of the corollary follows directly from Proposition 4.1.

Naturally, this result reflects a higher opportunity cost of fighting at higher wages and, hence, a lower net gain from winning a conflict to both parties. In the literature on civil war, this effect is well known at least since Grossman (1991) and has been emphasized, in particular, by Collier and Hoeffler (2004). Here, we see that the result extends to political violence more generally.

In the empirical literature, this opportunity cost channel is most often proxied by the level of income per capita. However, whether changes in income per capita are a good proxy for wage changes depends on the underlying source of the shock.[11]

Corollary 4.2: *Higher exogenous income, such as natural resource rents or aid, a higher value of R, increases the likelihood that a country will be in repression or civil war, unless political institutions are cohesive or the demand for public goods is high (θ close to 1/2 or ϕ close to 1).*

The corollary follows from Propositions 4.1 and 4.2, once we note that Z depends directly on the level of expected natural resource rents or exogenous income to the government from other sources, such as aid. In a more general model, with a resource sector that also uses labor, higher available resource rents—triggered, say, by an increase in world market prices—would also drive up the real wage. Such a Dutch-disease effect would (partly) counteract the impact effect in Corollary 4.2 by raising the cost of fighting.

Grossman (1992) argues that foreign aid can increase the probability of insurrection by raising the stakes of holding on to the government. The effect of resource rents has been emphasized in the empirical literature on civil war [see, e.g., Humphreys (2005) and the surveys in Blattman and Miguel (2009) and Ross (2004)], but few papers have derived the theoretical result [see, however, Aslaksen and Torvik (2006) and Olsson and Fors (2004)]. As far as we know, the rent-seeking channel does not figure much in the literature on repression and human-rights infringements.

11. In the two-sector conflict model of Dal Bó and Dal Bó (2006), e.g., world price shocks drive real wages and returns to capital in opposite directions, producing an unclear correlation between wages and income per capita.

Corollary 4.3: *In the range of ϕ for which the equilibrium is not necessarily peaceful, higher expected spending on common-interest public goods, a higher value of ϕ, reduces the likelihood of observing repression or civil war, unless political institutions are cohesive (θ close to* 1/2*).*

This follows because an increase in ϕ raises the expected spending on public goods, which reduces expected transfers and hence reduces Z. To the best of our knowledge, this specific prediction of our model is new to the formal modeling of civil war, since conflict models are typically not embedded in an explicit public-finance context. At a general level, however, the broad selectorate framework in Bueno de Mesquita, Smith, Siverson, and Morrow (2003) considers the split of government revenue into public goods versus redistribution, as well as government repression and civil war, as endogenous outcomes. In their analysis, some institutional variation—such as a larger winning coalition within the selectorate—might produce a correlation between public goods and violence similar to the one in Corollary 4.3.

Although these three implications of the model all reflect variations in Z, other parameters will also influence the likelihood of conflict by changing the two trigger points Z^O and Z^I. Such will be the case with parameters of the conflict technology ξ, but sorting these out requires additional specific assumptions. The two trigger points are also affected by the costs of investments in conflict through ν and λ_1. We postpone to the next chapter the analysis of how these parameters affect conflict risks and political turnover. However, we state here an additional result concerning the effect of political institutions.

Corollary 4.4: *In the range of θ for which the equilibrium is not necessarily peaceful, political institutions with more checks and balances (more minority representation), a higher value of θ, reduce the likelihood of observing repression or civil war, unless the demand for public goods is high (ϕ close to* 1*).*

This follows by observing that $Z^O(\theta;\xi)$ and $Z^I(\theta;\xi)$ in Proposition 4.2 are both increasing functions of θ. Intuitively, more inclusive institutions make control of the state less valuable, and thus shift up the point at which Z triggers violence for both the incumbent and the opposition. Many of the papers in the civil-war and repression literatures discuss and attempt to estimate the dependence of violence on political institutions, typically as a direct effect in line with Corollary 4.4.

However, Propositions 4.1 and 4.2 together imply that Corollaries 4.1–4.3 should only hold in societies and times where θ—the minority protection or representation embedded in political institutions—is below a certain lower bound or where ϕ—the demand for public goods—is below a certain lower bound. Empirically, this does not imply a direct effect of political institutions, but rather an interaction effect between political institutions and other determinants. As far as we know, this specific theoretical insight from our model is also new.

Comparative Statics and the Determinants of State Capacity The corollaries of the model can also be described in terms of the *global* and *local* comparative statics discussed in Sections 2.1 and 3.1. The global comparative statics are associated with the levels of θ and ϕ, which determine whether a country finds itself in a peaceful state with certainty. The local comparative statics are associated with variations in parameters $\omega(\pi_1)$, R, θ, and ϕ, given that the country finds itself potentially outside the peaceful state. There is thus an analytical commonality to the frameworks we have developed in the last three chapters.

Our model of conflict has other comparative statics as well, which are tied to the costs of raising resources and the military capabilities of the incumbent and opponent groups, captured by parameters ν, λ_1, and ξ. Since these parameters were not part of the core state-capacity framework in Chapters 2 and 3, we have not stressed them so far. However, factors such as these do figure prominently in some of the civil-war literature. For example, Fearon (2004, 2008) and Fearon and Laitin (2003) stress how the military capabilities of the government (ξ in our model) relate to outcomes such as income and state capacity. As noted above, we return to the role of these forgotten parameters in Chapter 5.

Since the model framework is common, it is interesting to compare the determinants of political violence with the determinants of state-capacity investments that we isolated in Chapters 2 and 3. When we do so, we find a striking result: basically, all the factors that raise the likelihood of violence tend to drive down investments in state capacity. To see this, consider our earlier typology of states.

In the earlier chapters, common-interest states were defined by the global comparative statics, specifically the *cohesiveness* condition $\alpha_L > 2(1-\theta)$ or the condition $\phi \to 1$. Evidently, those coincide with the conditions in Proposition 4.1 that guarantee a peaceful outcome. When these conditions did not hold in earlier chapters, we had redistributive or weak states. According to Proposition 4.2, those states sometimes experience violence. In Chapters 2 and 3, weak states had no investment in fiscal capacity and little investment in legal capacity.

Redistributive states had some investments, and in those the same variables that raise the likelihood of violence (weakly) decrease state-capacity investments. These are the local comparative statics discussed earlier: more resource or aid dependence (a higher level of R), lower wages [a lower level of $\omega(\pi_1)$ given income $y(\pi_2)$], and a lower demand for public goods (a lower value of ϕ), as well as a lower cohesiveness for political institutions (a lower value of θ).

The distinction between redistributive and weak states was made on the basis of the *stability* condition, however, which included the exogenous stability parameter γ. Drawing such a distinction is no longer straightforward because the rate of turnover is endogenous in the present model. Moreover, our analysis of political violence in this chapter has taken state capacity as given. For both of these reasons, we have to complete the analysis of the model looking at the full-fledged equilibrium outcomes when (potentially violent) political turnover and state capacity are jointly determined. This is exactly what we do in Chapter 5. Before taking on that task, however, we present a few developments of the violence model and then embark on a relatively long detour, discussing how the predictions we have derived about political violence can be taken to the data and what happens when we do so.

4.2 *Developing the Model*

We now sketch a handful of ways in which the basic model can be extended and how this would affect the main conclusions.

4.2.1 Asymmetries

In the basic model presented earlier the two groups are completely symmetric. This feature is very convenient because group decisions do not depend on group characteristics, just on their incumbency status. But there are natural ways of relaxing this rather strong assumption.

First, we could introduce income inequality in the form of asymmetric wages, in a similar way as in Section 2.4.4. Such asymmetry might make the richest group less inclined to violence. This would be the case if there were a "loyalty premium," requiring the high-income group to recruit soldiers from within its own ranks, as that would raise the cost of violence. Ideally, however, rich and violence-motivated groups would wish to hire low-wage mercenaries to carry out violence on their behalf to offset this comparative disadvantage.

Second, one group could be better organized in raising resources for fighting when in opposition. Crudely, this could be captured with groups having different values of ν. One of the groups would then tend to fight more, making civil conflict more likely when the low-ν group is in opposition.

Yet, another possibility—which is discussed in the empirical civil-war literature—would be that the government does not have a full monopoly on natural resource rents. In the model, this could be represented as the opposition group having access to a share of exogenous income, R, perhaps because of its geographical location. Again, the likelihood of observing violence would then depend on the identity of the group in power.

4.2.2 Polarization, Greed, and Grievance

A large literature emphasizes the role of polarization in promoting conflict [see, e.g., Esteban and Ray (1994, 1999) for theoretical foundations and Montalvo and Reynal-Querol (2005) for empirical patterns]. As we saw in Chapters 2 and 3, polarization/heterogeneity in the preferences for public goods reduces common interests and hence affects state-capacity investments. Having identified the importance of common interests in using political violence, it is not surprising to see that it also affects incentives for violence.

To illustrate this, we employ the same modeling as in Section 2.4.4, where $1-\iota$ is the probability that the two groups have the same preferences for public goods. In other words $\iota > 0$ represents polarization or heterogeneity in the demand for public goods; as noted in Chapter 2, it is hard to make a clear distinction between, say, ethnic heterogeneity and polarization in our two-group context. The key observation is that the expression for the expected utility difference between incumbent and opposition in (4.10) is now replaced by

$$U^I(\tau_2, \pi_2) - U^O(\tau_2, \pi_2) = \phi\iota\left[\alpha_H - \alpha_L\right] + \omega(\pi_1)\, 2(1-2\theta)\, Z,$$

where Z is defined as in (4.11).

The first term on the right-hand side is new and reflects the forces of polarization/heterogeneity. In particular, this term is positive whenever parameter ι is positive. Moreover, its magnitude depends on the distance between α_H and α_L. Proposition 4.1 now no longer holds, since as $\phi \to 1$ and/or $\theta \to 1/2$, the polarization/heterogeneity term remains and could be a source of conflict, independently of the mechanism that we have already identified. This is because $\phi \to 1$ is no longer a guarantee of common interests.

Crudely speaking, this extended model captures both of the most widely quoted motives for violence—greed and grievance [see Collier and Hoeffler (2004)]. In our core model, the motives for capturing the state were based on private-goods benefits from redistribution, which corresponds to greed. Polarization/heterogeneity introduces another dimension in connection with the way the state can be used, perhaps reflecting decisions on noneconomic issues such as religion or ethnicity. Moreover, this could be the sole motive for mounting an insurgency, which corresponds to grievance. The extended model sketched here shows how these motives fit together and how they can be considered jointly.

One interesting possibility suggested by the extension would be to allow the incumbent group to pick a leader who is more or less polarizing. One could think of a world where the main issue is religious polarization/heterogeneity and the leader could either be a zealot or a moderate. With a zealot in charge polarization/heterogeneity would be a much bigger issue. The incumbent would then have a choice between, say, setting $\iota = 0$ or $\iota = 1$, knowing that this would affect the incentives for violence. A hardliner who credibly would use violence might sometimes be preferred to a moderate. For example, if having a hardliner in place would result in repression but not in civil war, it would enhance the probability of the incumbent group staying in power. The shift between different types of leaders in Israel and among Palestinian groups suggests that such considerations could have real-world importance.

4.2.3 Anarchy

Assumption 4.1 on the conflict technology implied an ordering from peace to repression and conflict. In particular, we rule out an undefended insurgency, where one social group takes over by raising a military threat against another social group. Note that this would not correspond very well with a bloodless coup d'état, which would be rather a transition of power between members of the same social group, such as the military. We might instead think about an undefended insurgency as a situation close to anarchy, perhaps like the one we observe in today's Somalia. In such an anarchic situation, the incumbent government is so weak that only the opposition invests in violence. Eventually, we would expect the incumbent to lose power. Formally, anarchy is a possibility when we replace Assumption 4.1b with

$$\frac{-\gamma_I(0,0;\xi)}{\gamma_O(0,0;\xi)} < \frac{2(1-\theta)}{\nu}.$$

This is best motivated by thinking of ν as being low and ξ as giving an advantage to the opposition in terms of marginal return.

With this alternative assumption, the motives for insurgency and incumbent investments remain. But one could now have a Nash equilibrium with $\hat{L}^I = 0$ and $\hat{L}^O > 0$. Moreover, increasing Z could now increase political instability by raising $\hat{L}^O$. In this alternative model, we would generally lose our ability to predict an ordering among repression, conflict, and peace, which is a feature of Proposition 4.2. But in a context where undefended insurgencies would be a major empirical phenomenon requiring explanation, our model could certainly be adapted to include it.

4.2.4 Conflict in a Predatory State

We now show how to generalize the model to include the case where the state is governed by a small predatory elite. As we saw in Section 3.2.4, such a predatory state sets $p_s^I = p_s^O = 0$. The rents earned by the incumbent elite are now

$$\hat{\Pi}_0 = \frac{\sum_{J \in \{I,O\}} \left[\mu\left(\hat{\chi}_0, 0\right) \tilde{y}\left(0\right) - C\left(\hat{\chi}_0\right)\right]}{e^I}, \tag{4.13}$$

where $\hat{\chi}_0$ is the corresponding predation level.

To develop the implications for violence, the key observation is that (4.10) is now replaced by

$$U^I\left(\tau_2, \pi_2\right) - U^O\left(\tau_2, \pi_2\right) = \hat{\Pi}_0\left[1 - \zeta\right] + \omega\left(0\right) 2\left(1 - 2\theta\right) Z,$$

where

$$Z = \frac{R + \tau_2 y(0) - E(G(\alpha_2, \tau_2))}{\omega(0)}. \tag{4.14}$$

There are three main implications for the results in Section 4.1.

First, Proposition 4.1 no longer holds since $\hat{\Pi}_0$ remains and if governance is weak, then incentives for violence remain. Similarly, the thresholds Z^I and Z^O in Proposition 4.2 are all shifted down to reflect the additional motive for using violence, namely to capture the state and the ability to extract predatory rents.

Second, compared to a nonpredatory state, we may have an additional wage effect since $\omega\left(0\right) \leq \omega\left(\pi_s\right)$. Whether the wage is strictly lower depends on whether an outside option of working in the traditional sector is binding or not, as discussed in Section 3.2.4. To the extent that wages are indeed lower, this raises Z and hence increases the possibility of violence.

Third, period-2 income will be lower than in a nonpredatory state: $y(0) \leq y(\pi_2)$. Since this expression appears in the numerator of (4.14), this income effect will tend to reduce violence. All things considered, however, we expect predatory states to be more prone to violence, since the shift of income from public resources into the hands of elites will be the dominant effect.

Predatory states are also an interesting context in which to model within-group conflict, since some rank-and-file members of the group may wish to stage a coup d'état to take over as the elite and hence lay their hands on the predatory rents in $\hat{\Pi}_0$. This means that political violence might be used on two fronts, within groups and between groups. To capture this situation more fully would mean extending the model with two dimensions of L^I and two separate conflict technologies, one applying within groups and the other across groups.

4.2.5 Investing in Coercive Capacity

We have taken the parameter ξ, reflecting the relative military advantage of the incumbent government as given. If we adopt the earlier interpretation of public goods as defense, then spending on defense in period 1 might also have the side-effect of being able to engage in more effective violence against an insurgent group. Arguably, the government advantage could also be subject to investment by the government as with other forms of state capacity. Such investments may involve a secret police and/or surveillance, which are typical of authoritarian regimes. We do not model these possibilities formally here, as that would require adding additional stages to the model where ξ would be chosen prior to the conflict stage. But such an approach would bring our modeling closer to the analysis of civil war in Fearon (2004) and Fearon and Laitin (2003), who focus a great deal on the military capabilities of pursuing conflict.

If θ is low this type of extended model could entail another complementarity. Investments by the government in coercive capacity would raise the incidence of repression relative to peace and conflict. They would therefore tend to move an economy toward a redistributive regime, which could make investments in coercive capacity complementary with investments in other forms of state capacity in redistributive regimes.

4.3 *From Theory to Empirical Testing*

We now discuss how the theory in this chapter can inform the empirical study of the incidence of political violence. Although our model in Section 4.1 is extremely simple, it does provide a transparent set of predictions as to how parameters of the economy and the polity shape the incidence of conflict. A clear advantage of beginning from a well-defined theory is that we can clarify and evaluate the assumptions made on the way to empirical testing. Specifically, we must decide which variables and parameters to treat as measurable in the data and which to treat as fixed (at the country level) rather than time-varying. We argue that more reliable inference requires time-varying measures of the determinants suggested by the theory.

Measurement and Observability Our data are in panel form for countries and years from 1950 onward. Hence, consider a particular country at date s. As long as we take state capacity as given, there are no endogenous dynamics and time-independent shocks to wages, resource rents or aid, and public-goods demands are the only sources of time variation. We can thus treat period s as a typical period in a sequence of periods.

Later, we discuss how we can use readily available sources of data to decide whether that country-year is characterized by peace, repression, or civil war. As in previous chapters, we are able to rely on decent proxies for θ, the cohesiveness of political institutions. When it comes to the components of the latent index variable Z_s, we argue that for each country, we can find some time-varying correlates of ω_s, as well as R. With a slight abuse of notation, we label the observations of resource rents or aid by the outside analyst by R_s .

But we find it difficult to measure the demand for public goods, ϕ, which enters into the expression of Z_s, or variation in the realized value of public goods over time. Thus, we give up the possibility of testing the prediction in Corollary 4.3.[12] Moreover, we maintain that it is impossible to measure the returns to

12. It might be argued that we could test this corollary indirectly through observing the provision of public goods over time. Although we might be able to find variables such as government expenditures or government consumption, these include an important component of redistribution. Credible time-varying measures of public-goods provision do not exist for a sufficiently large number of countries for a sufficiently long time period. In previous chapters, we used the prevalence of external war in the *past* as a (time-invariant) measure of past demand for public goods. For a variety of reasons, it would not be suitable to use realized external wars as a time-varying contemporaneous measure of the demand for public goods.

violence, $\gamma_O(0,0,\xi)$ and $\gamma_I(0,0,\xi)$, and the marginal cost components ν and λ_s, which enter into the expressions for Z_s^I and Z_s^O.

Treating the state-capacity levels as given, we thus have several unobserved sources of randomness in the model's determinants of violence. For example, from the viewpoint of an outside analyst, $Z_s - Z_s^I$ becomes a random variable that satisfies

$$Z_s - Z_s^I = \frac{R_s}{\omega_s} - \overline{Z}^I - \frac{\varepsilon_s^I}{\omega_s},$$

where $\overline{Z}^I$ is a constant and ε_s^I an "error term" with c.d.f. $F^I(\varepsilon)$. Similarly, we can write

$$Z_s - Z_s^O = \frac{R_s}{\omega_s} - \overline{Z}^O - \frac{\varepsilon_s^O}{\omega_s},$$

where $\overline{Z}^O$ is another constant and ε_s^O another error term with c.d.f. $F^O(\varepsilon)$.

Conditional Probabilities of Observing Violence Transposing Proposition 4.2 to the current notation, we will observe civil war at date s if

$$Z_s - Z_s^O \geq 0 \Leftrightarrow \varepsilon_s^O \leq R_s - \omega_s \overline{Z}^O .$$

Given the information available to us as analysts, the conditional probability, i.e., the likelihood, of observing civil war is

$$F^O(R_s - \omega_s \overline{Z}^O). \tag{4.15}$$

As predicted by the theory in Corollaries 4.1 and 4.2 , a higher value of R or a lower value of ω both raise the likelihood of observing civil war, *provided* that θ is not close to 1/2.[13]

By similar reasoning, the likelihood of observing peace is

$$1 - F^I(R_s - \omega_s \overline{Z}^I), \tag{4.16}$$

whereas the likelihood of observing repression is

$$F^I(R_s - \omega_s \overline{Z}^I) - F^O(R_s - \omega_s \overline{Z}^O). \tag{4.17}$$

13. Formally, as θ approaches 1/2, Z^I and hence $Z^O > Z^I$ approach infinity. Given the finite support for the distributions of ω and R, the maximum of F^O, namely $F^O(R_H - \omega_L(\pi)\overline{Z}^O)$, is thus equal to 0.

As explained in Section 4.1, the theory gives us distinct predictions about how changes in R and ω shift the distribution of index variable Z and thereby the likelihood of observing peace. We now see clearly, however, that the predictions regarding the conditional probability of observing repression hinge on the relative densities of F^I and F^O. In other words, we have specific predictions about two types of transitions: between civil war and non–civil war (peace cum repression) and between peace and political violence (repression cum civil war).

Another informative way of interpreting expressions (4.15)–(4.17) is that they define the relative probabilities of the three ordered states of political violence. This strongly suggests that the most straightforward way of confronting the theory with data would be to estimate an ordered logit driven by variables that shift the country-specific distribution of Z_s given the country-specific thresholds Z_s^I and Z_s^O.

Cross-Country versus Within-Country Variation What kind of variation in the data should we use to test the model predictions? A good deal of the empirical civil-war literature and virtually all of the empirical repression literature estimate the probability of observing violence from cross-sectional data sets. Expressions (4.15)–(4.17) illustrate clearly why this may not be such a good idea. Cross-sectional data replace time-varying variables of interest—such as R_{s+1} and ω_s in the present context—with their cross-sectional means over some time period. But this makes statistical inference a hazardous exercise, since we run a large risk of confounding the cross-country variation in these variables with cross-country variation in unobserved parameters—such as ξ or ϕ in the present context—something that could seriously bias and invalidate the estimates. We return to this point later.

It is more rewarding to exploit within-country variation in panel data, as in the cross-country panel studies of civil war in Africa by Bruckner and Ciccone (2008) or Miguel, Satyanath, and Sergenti (2004) and the within-country panel studies of civil war by Deininger (2003) for Uganda or Dube and Vargas (2008) for Colombia.[14] For instance, estimating a specification for the likelihood of observing civil war with country fixed effects is equivalent to evaluating

$$F^O(R_s - \omega_s \overline{Z}^O) - E\{F^O(R_s - \omega_s \overline{Z}^O)\}, \tag{4.18}$$

14. Both Collier and Hoeffler (2004) and Fearon and Laitin (2003) do present some fixed-effects estimates in their cross-country studies, although they appear as a robustness check rather than as the main specification.

i.e., the difference between the conditional and the unconditional probability of civil war. Proceeding in this way identifies the effect of resource rents/aid flows R_s and wages ω_s on the incidence of civil war exclusively from the within-country variation of these variables. Any impact of their average values and time-invariant parameters in each country is absorbed by the country fixed effect.

As we saw earlier in Figure 1.10, the worldwide prevalence of civil war and repression has important and irregular time trends. Thus, it is also essential to allow for global shocks, which hit all countries in a common way, through year fixed effects (binary year-indicator variables). The trends in violence are then picked up in a flexible (nonparametric) fashion, and we only use the country-specific yearly variation relative to world-year averages for identification.

Given the theory developed earlier, our specification should also take into account that the predictions about shocks are conditional on the value of θ. Let $\Theta_c = 1$ if political institutions have strong checks and balances (i.e., θ_c close to 1/2) in country c in the period of our data and equal to zero otherwise. We then model the index function in (4.18) for country c in period s as

$$R_{c,s} - \overline{Z}_c^O \omega_{c,s} = a_c(\Theta_c) + a_s(\Theta_c) + b(\Theta_c)\widetilde{Z}_{c,s}, \tag{4.19}$$

where $a_c(\Theta_c)$ is a country fixed effect, $a_t(\Theta_c)$ are year dummies, and $\widetilde{Z}_{c,s}$ are time-varying regressors that reflect changes in $R_{c,s}$ and $\omega_{c,s}$. The theory predicts that the parameter of interest, $b(\Theta_c)$, is heterogeneous with respect to Θ_c, and in particular that $b(0) > b(1) = 0$. To test this prediction, we estimate a model that allows for separate slope coefficients for countries with cohesive and noncohesive institutions.[15]

Concretely, the discussion in this section points clearly toward two strategies by which we may confront the theoretical predictions from Section 4.1 with data. One strategy would be to estimate the time variation across the three violence states by way of an ordered logit specification including country and year fixed effects. An alternative would be to estimate the transition between nonviolence and violence or the transition between non–civil war and civil war by way of a conditional (country and year fixed effects) logit specification. Section 4.4 presents results from both of these econometric strategies.

15. In the specifications reported in Section 4.4, we impose $a_c(1) = a_c(0)$ and $a_t(1) = a_t(0)$. However, the results hold up when we allow for separate country and time effects by estimating the model on separate subsamples, i.e., with $\Theta_c = 1$ and $\Theta_c = 0$.

4.4 *Data and Results*

In this section, we first describe our data. Then, we take a look at some cross-sectional correlations. Finally, we present our econometric estimates based on the empirical strategy discussed at the end of the last subsection.

4.4.1 Data

Political Violence A large body of literature looks at the determinants of civil war. Much of the empirical work deals with the onset and duration of civil war, concepts that are not as closely related to our theory as the incidence of civil war.[16] To define civil war empirically, we use the ACD produced by the peace research institutes in Oslo and Uppsala. More precisely, we use the civil-war incidence measure in this data set, starting in 1950.[17] It takes a value of 1 if—in a given country and year—the government and a domestic adversary are involved in a conflict that claims a death toll of more than 1000 people. As noted earlier, more than 10% of all country-years between 1950 and 2005 are classified as civil war in our sample.[18] Since we want to focus on large-scale political violence, we do not exploit the alternative oft-used incidence of civil conflict (also from the ACD), which only requires a death toll of 25 people.

To measure repression, we use data from Banks (2005), which counts up purges: systematic murders and eliminations of political opponents by incumbent regimes. We create a binary indicator that is equal to one in any year when purges exceed zero. In the 1950–2005 period, on average 7% of all country-years are classified as being in a state of repression, but not in civil war.[19]

16. There are a number of issues involved in the coding of conflicts into civil wars. See Sambanis (2004) for a thorough discussion about different definitions that appear in the empirical literature.

17. Specifically, we use the variable "incidence of intrastate war" in the UCDP/PRIO ACD v.4-2007, covering the years 1946–2006.

18. An alternative measure is available in the Correlates of War (COW) database, but this only runs up to 1997. Given that one of our independent variables relies on Cold-War and post-Cold-War experience, the COW variable would only allow for eight, as opposed to sixteen, observations in the post-Cold-War era. See Sambanis (2004) for a discussion of issues in the empirical measurement of civil war.

19. An alternative would be to exploit the commonly used Political Terror Scale based on the reports on human-rights violations by the U.S. State Department and Amnesty International [see Gibney, Cornett, and Wood (2007)]. This variable is only available from 1976, however, which cuts short the Cold-War period that we can exploit. Moreover, as shown by

Based on these two measures, we construct an ordered variable of political violence that follows the theory in Section 4.1. Specifically—and w.l.o.g., as only the ordinal ranking matters—we assign a value of 0 to peace, a value of 1 to repression in the absence of civil war, and a value of 2 to civil war.[20]

Political Institutions We construct two indicator variables to capture strong political institutions, corresponding to Θ_c in Section 4.3. As in previous chapters, our main measure is based on the assessment of executive constraints in the Polity IV data set. We believe that this variable best captures the thrust of θ in our theory. Executive constraints are coded annually from 1800 or from the year of independence. We do not exploit the high-frequency time variation in this variable, however, as we are concerned that its changes are likely to be correlated with the incidence of political violence. This means that we must leave a test of Corollary 4.4 to future work. The model in Section 7.2.4 treats both political violence and political institutions as endogenous.

To construct a time-independent measure of Θ_c, we adopt quite a conservative approach. First, we evaluate the presample evidence, measuring the fraction of years for which a country had the highest score (of 7) for executive constraints before 1950. Then, we compute the fraction of years for which a country had the top score over the sample period. A country is deemed to have cohesive political institutions, $\Theta_c = 1$, if two conditions are fulfilled. First, the fraction in the presample period is above zero (a country that did not exist before 1950 is assigned a value of zero). Second, the fraction in the sample period is greater than 0.6. This definition implies that just fewer than one-fifth of all countries have cohesive institutions (see further Table 4.3). Marginal changes in the classification criteria have little effect on the results.

As a robustness check, we consider an alternative classification of political institutions, namely the prevalence of parliamentary democracy. Although

Qian and Yanagizawa (2009), Security Council membership during the Cold-War period may have influenced the way the U.S. State department reported on human rights in U.S. allied and nonallied countries.

20. To be precise, we begin from two underlying variables: civil wars as coded in the ACD and the purges variable in Banks (2005). We construct a binary variable based on the latter depending on whether there were any purges in a country at a given date. Since 1950, we have 4841 country-year observations with neither civil war nor government purges. There are 90 observations that entail both a civil war and some purges, 714 observations where there are civil wars but no purges, and 425 observations where there are purges but no civil war. This yields 1229 observations with some violence and 804 with civil war.

high executive constraints are associated with stiffer checks and balances on the government, the alternative measure is intended to capture larger representativeness.[21] We define it analogously, namely as the result of having had a positive prevalence of parliamentary democracy before 1950 and a minimum prevalence of 0.6 in between 1950 and 2005.

Exogenous $\tilde{Z}$-Shocks To test the specific model predictions with the specification in (4.19), we still need credibly exogenous variation in the time-varying regressors $\tilde{Z}_{c,s}$. We use two variables for this purpose. The first is a measure of natural disasters, constructed from the EM-DAT data set.[22] Specifically, we define a variable that adds together the number of extreme temperature events, floods, slides, and tidal waves in a given country and year.[23] Then, we create a binary indicator variable, set equal to one if a country experiences any such event. We expect such a natural disaster to negatively affect the current real wage $\omega_{c,s}$ (and the effect on the current real wage to be larger than the effect on the future tax base that also appears in the expression for Z). Consistent with this hypothesis, a country-year with at least one natural disaster is associated with a 2.5% reduction in income per worker. But part of this could be a productivity effect working through capital.[24] Of course, a natural disaster is also likely to trigger international aid flows of some duration. In terms of our theory, this corresponds to a positive shock to $R_{c,s}$, which affects the likelihood of violence in the same direction as a negative shock to $\omega_{c,s}$.

As a second source of exogenous variation, we use the revolving memberships in the U.N. Security Council (for the nonpermanent members). We expect membership to raise a country's geopolitical importance and therefore its likelihood of receiving international aid from important countries, corresponding to positive shocks to $R_{c,s}$. Indeed, Kuziemko and Werker (2006) find that U.S. aid flows depend on Security Council membership. Similar incentives are likely to

21. See Aghion, Alesina, and Trebbi (2004) or Persson, Roland, and Tabellini (2000) for theoretical arguments and Persson and Tabellini (2003) for empirical evidence.

22. Nel and Righarts (2008) recently used this data set to study civil war.

23. Specifically, we added together the variables "flood," "etemp," "slides," and "wave." Some other EM-DAT coded diaster events, such as epidemics, are not used since they may be endogenous to civil wars.

24. In a more elaborate model, a lower return to capital may also cut the opportunity cost for engaging in conflict and thus have a similar effect on conflict propensity as a lower return to labor.

have applied to other permanent Security Council members. Of course, Security Council membership may change a country's international accountability, reducing the likelihood that its government engages in violence. Membership may also reflect a country's past propensity for violence. Therefore, we pay little attention to the effect of membership per se and instead mainly exploit the *interaction* between membership and time, allowing for a different effect before and after the fall of the Berlin Wall. In particular, we expect the strategic aid motives to be considerably stronger in the period before 1990 because of the stronger geopolitical tensions during the Cold War.[25]

To sort out the importance of these possible channels, we use data on total international aid disbursements from OECD countries and on GDP per capita from the Penn World Tables (PWT).[26]

4.4.2 Cross-Sectional Correlations

Let us briefly look at the correlations in the raw data among the three violence states and some determinants suggested by the theory in this chapter.

According to the theory, the lower a country's wages, the more likely it is to experience political violence, with a greater likelihood of civil war rather than repression at the lowest levels of wages. Suppose we take income per capita (from the 6.3 PWT, 2005 constant international prices) as a proxy for wages ($\omega_{c,s}$ in the model). Are the three violence states naturally ordered in the data, as in the theory? For income per capita, the answer is a fairly clear-cut "yes." Peaceful country-years in our panel data have an average income per capita of \$9,412, repressing countries are poorer with \$5,625 per capita, and those in civil war are the poorest with average incomes of \$3,612.

25. See Bates (2008) for a discussion of how the Cold War affected governments in Africa. Cold-War Security Council membership may have impacted on conflict through a different channel, namely the provision of military aid raising the government's capability of fighting. In the simple semilinear conflict model referred to in Section 4.1, a higher value of ξ_2 can readily be interpreted as the incumbent's advantage in fighting. It can be shown that Z^I (the incumbent's trigger point) is decreasing in ξ_2, whereas Z^O (the opposition's trigger point) is increasing in ξ_2. Adding this channel to the effect of a higher Z via regular aid would mean that Cold-War Security Council membership should definitely raise the likelihood of political violence, whereas it might raise or cut the likelihood of civil war.

26. More precisely, for aid we use the variable "Official Development Assistance, Excl Debt (Constant Prices, 2007 USD millions)" from the OECD Development Database on Aid from DAC Members (subset 2a). For GDP per capita we use the variable "Real GDP per capita (2005 constant price, Chain series)" from PWT 6.3.

Table 4.2 illustrates the unconditional correlation between income and violence in a different way. The table reproduces the two-by-two tabulation of different violence states in Table 4.1, except that countries with the highest 25% of income (from the same PWT data) are now set in italics. Evidently, richer countries are overrepresented in the peaceful upper-right quadrant of the table.

As another example, we would expect a monotonic ranking of violence states, similar to the ranking in income, in our variable for cohesive political institutions based on high executive constraints (θ_c in the model). Using the two-way variable defined earlier, we indeed uncover a striking regularity across political regimes. For the one-fifth of all countries with cohesive institutions, 93% of the annual observations are peaceful, with 3.7% in repression and 2.8% in civil war. For countries with noncohesive institutions, these figures are 77%, 8%, and 15%, respectively.

Table 4.3 illustrates the association between political institutions and violence in an analogous way to Table 4.2: the one-fifth of countries classified as having cohesive political institutions are set in boldface. As with high income, cohesive political institutions are clearly overrepresented in the peaceful upper-right quadrant.

These differences in the unconditional probability of observing political violence are entirely in line with our theory. It is tempting to investigate whether they and other correlations implied by the theory—such as a correlation with ethnic heterogeneity as a proxy for polarization—would hold up, not only in the raw data but also as partial correlations. That is, are they robust to controlling for a number of other prospective determinants of violence? As noted in the introduction to this chapter, this is indeed the approach in most existing empirical research on repression and civil war, which relies on the cross-sectional variation—or the cross-sectional cum time-series variation—in the data. However, as discussed in Section 4.3, such an approach is endangered by statistical pitfalls, so it is not pursued here. Instead, we turn to the more rewarding (time-series) variation within countries.

4.4.3 Econometric Estimates

Basic Results—Ordered Logit Table 4.4 presents the core results when we follow the empirical strategies outlined at the end of Section 4.3 for statistical inference based on the within-country variation in the data.

In column (1), we follow the approach suggested by the theory of estimating a fixed-effect ordered logit. This is not a standard estimation method, but we

Table 4.2 Repression and civil war by country and high income

	Some civil war			No civil war				
Less than 5% repression	Bosnia			*Australia*	*Cyprus*	Jamaica	*New Zealand*	*Switzerland*
	Cameroon			*Bahamas*	*Czech Republic*	*Kuwait*	*Norway*	Tanzania
	Guinea-Bissau			*Bahrain*	*Denmark*	Lesotho	*Oman*	Togo
	Liberia			*Barbados*	Djibouti	*Luxembourg*	Panama	Trinidad-Tobago
	Nepal			Belize	Equatorial Guinea	Madagascar	New Guinea	Tunisia
	Rwanda			Benin	Fiji	Malawi	*Qatar*	*United Kingdom*
	Sierra Leone			Bhutan	Gabon	Malaysia	*Saudi Arabia*	Uzbekistan
	Yemen			Botswana	Gambia	Maldives	Senegal	
				Brunei	Guinea	Mali	*Singapore*	
				Burkina Faso	Guyana	*Malta*	Slovak Republic	
				Canada	Honduras	Mauritania	*Slovenia*	
				Cape Verde	*Iceland*	Mauritius	Solomon Islands	
				Central African Republic	*Ireland*	Mongolia	Suriname	
				Costa Rica	*Israel*	Namibia	Swaziland	
				Croatia	Ivory Coast	*Netherlands*	*Sweden*	
More than 5% repression	Afghanistan	India	South Korea	Albania	Ghana	Taiwan		
	Algeria	Indonesia	Sri Lanka	*Austria*	*Greece*	Thailand		
	Angola	Iran	Sudan	Bangladesh	Haiti	Uruguay		
	Argentina	Iraq	Syria	*Belgium*	Hungary	Venezuela		
	Burundi	Laos	Turkey	Bolivia	*Italy*	Zambia		
	Cambodia	Lebanon	Uganda	Brazil	*Japan*			
	Chad	*Libya*	*United States*	Bulgaria	Jordan			
	China	Morocco	Vietnam	Chile	Kenya			
	Colombia	Mozambique	Zimbabwe	Comoros	Mexico			
	Congo	Nicaragua		Dominican Republic	Niger			
	Cuba	Nigeria		Ecuador	Paraguay			
	El Salvador	Pakistan		Egypt	Poland			
	Ethiopia	Russia		Estonia	*Portugal*			
	France	Somalia		*Finland*	Romania			
	Guatemala	South Africa		*Germany*	*Spain*			

Note: Countries with per capita income above the 75th percentile in 1990, by PWT 6.3, Real GDP per capita (2005 international prices), are printed in italics.

Table 4.3 Repression and civil war by country and cohesive political institutions

	Some civil war			No civil war				
Less than 5% repression	Bosnia			**Australia**	Cyprus	Jamaica	**New Zealand**	**Switzerland**
	Cameroon			Bahamas	Czech Republic	Kuwait	**Norway**	Tanzania
	Guinea-Bissau			Bahrain	**Denmark**	Lesotho	Oman	Togo
	Liberia			Barbados	Djibouti	**Luxembourg**	Panama	Trinidad-Tobago
	Nepal			Belize	Equatorial Guinea	Madagascar	New Guinea	Tunisia
	Rwanda			Benin	Fiji	Malawi	Qatar	**United Kingdom**
	Sierra Leone			Bhutan	Gabon	Malaysia	Saudi Arabia	Uzbekistan
	Yemen			Botswana	Gambia	Maldives	Senegal	
				Brunei	Guinea	Mali	Singapore	
				Burkina Faso	Guyana	Malta	Slovak Republic	
				Canada	Honduras	Mauritania	Slovenia	
				Cape Verde	**Iceland**	Mauritius	Solomon Islands	
				Central African Republic	**Ireland**	Mongolia	Suriname	
				Costa Rica	**Israel**	Namibia	Swaziland	
				Croatia	Ivory Coast	**Netherlands**	**Sweden**	
More than 5% repression	Afghanistan	India	South Korea	Albania	Ghana	Taiwan		
	Algeria	Indonesia	Sri Lanka	**Austria**	**Greece**	Thailand		
	Angola	Iran	Sudan	Bangladesh	Haiti	Uruguay		
	Argentina	Iraq	Syria	**Belgium**	Hungary	Venezuela		
	Burundi	Laos	Turkey	Bolivia	**Italy**	Zambia		
	Cambodia	Lebanon	Uganda	Brazil	**Japan**			
	Chad	Libya	**United States**	Bulgaria	Jordan			
	China	Morocco	Vietnam	Chile	Kenya			
	Colombia	Mozambique	Zimbabwe	Comoros	Mexico			
	Congo	Nicaragua		Dominican Republic	Niger			
	Cuba	Nigeria		Ecuador	Paraguay			
	El Salvador	Pakistan		Egypt	Poland			
	Ethiopia	Russia		**Estonia**	Portugal			
	France	Somalia		**Finland**	Romania			
	Guatemala	**South Africa**		**Germany**	Spain			

Note: Countries with predominantly cohesive political institutions, according to the definition described in the text, are printed in boldface.

Table 4.4 Basic econometric results

Dependent variable	(1) Ordered variable	(2) Ordered variable	(3) Ordered variable	(4) Political violence	(5) Political violence	(6) Civil war	(7) Civil war	(8) Ordered variable
Natural disaster	0.263** (0.107)	0.317*** (0.110)	0.299*** (0.111)	0.278** (0.109)	0.327*** (0.112)	0.370** (0.152)	0.431*** (0.155)	0.263** (0.111)
Security Council member	−1.048*** (0.399)	−1.194*** (0.417)	−1.382*** (0.456)	−1.110*** (0.412)	−1.269*** (0.430)	−1.360** (0.545)	−1.383** (0.547)	−1.048** (0.413)
Security Council member in Cold War	1.275*** (0.439)	1.461*** (0.458)	1.657*** (0.495)	1.267*** (0.453)	1.465*** (0.472)	1.074* (0.633)	1.105* (0.635)	1.275** (0.504)
Natural disaster × strong institutions		−0.701* (0.374)	−0.333 (0.318)		−0.618* (0.376)		−1.233** (0.595)	
Security Council member × strong institutions		1.975* (1.173)	2.940*** (1.123)		2.186* (1.178)			
Security Council member in Cold War × strong institutions		−2.577* (1.375)	−3.379*** (1.247)		−2.746** (1.381)			
Strong institutions measure		High executive constraints 1950–2005	Parliamentary Democracy 1950–2005		High executive constraints 1950–2005		High executive constraints 1950–2005	
Estimation method	FE ordered logit	FE ordered logit	FE ordered logit	FE logit	FE logit	FE logit	FE logit	FE ordered logit
Significance of interactions (p-value)		0.61	0.49		0.66		0.17	
Observations	4251	4251	4251	4251	4251	2061	2061	4251
Number of countries	97	97	97	97	97	49	49	97

Notes: The time period covered is 1950–2006. For definitions of variables refer to the text. Standard errors are in parentheses: * significant at 10%; ** significant at 5%; *** significant at 1%. Robust standard errors are in columns (1)–(7) with bootstrapped standard errors in column (8). The p-value refers to the significance of a test of the hypothesis that coeff_[natural disaster × strong institutions] = −coeff_[natural distaster] and coeff_[Security Council member × strong institutions]= −coeff_[Security Council member] and coeff_[Security Council member in the Cold War × strong institutions] = −coeff_[Security Council member in the Cold War], where coeff_ is the estimated coefficient on the variable in question. The reduced sample size in columns (6) and (7) is due to all countries that never had a civil war during this period being dropped.

implement it in a way proposed by Ferrer-i-Carbonell and Frijters (2004).[27] In addition to the (country and year) fixed effects, the specification includes our exogenous shock variables. The panel for estimation includes the 97 countries that have experienced some kind of political violence since 1950 (for the others, the fixed effect perfectly predicts the absence of violence). All three variables of interest are statistically significant: having a natural disaster is positively correlated with political violence, whereas being a member of the U.N. Security Council is negatively correlated with violence, except during the Cold War when the correlation turns positive. The effect of a natural disaster is nontrivial: the point estimate corresponds to just above a 4-percentage-point higher probability of observing violence, given a sample average of about 17%. The effect of Security Council membership is also around a 4-percentage-point lower probability of political violence.

In general, we are agnostic about the "right" sign for Security Council membership. We expect this variable to perhaps reflect an accountability effect of being temporarily in the international spotlight. Our main interest lies in the interaction of membership with the Cold-War period (in the third row).[28] As stated above, we hypothesize that the strategic geopolitical motives for giving aid (in the form of cash or military assistance) to Security Council members would have been much stronger in the Cold-War period than after 1990. This is indeed what the data suggest.[29]

In columns (2) and (3), we show that these effects are only present in countries with noncohesive political institutions. To do so, we interact our three variables of interest with an indicator for cohesive political institutions, measured either by a high incidence of strong executive constraints or parliamentary democracy (as detailed above). If our exogenous variables have no effect under cohesive institutions, the coefficients for the interacted variables should be opposite in sign and equal in absolute value to the coefficients on the non-

27. The method relies on three steps. First, we compute an average of the ordered violence variable for each country. Second, we define a new binary variable as observations of the ordered variable above or below the country-specific averages computed in step one. Third, we estimate a conditional logit for the binary variable defined in step two. Building on Chamberlain (1980), Ferrer-i-Carbonell and Frijters (2004) show that this three-step procedure implements—in our context—an ordered logit with fixed country effects and country-specific thresholds.

28. We do not include a separate Cold-War indicator in the regression, since any systematic differences between the Cold-War and non-Cold-War periods are captured by the year effects.

29. Two recent studies of the relation between aid and civil conflict are de Ree and Nillesen (2009) and Nunn and Qian (2010).

interacted variables. As shown by the table, the interaction and noninteraction coefficients do have the opposite sign in every case. Moreover, for both our measures of cohesive institutions, we cannot reject the hypothesis of a zero correlation between the exogenous variables and political violence in countries with cohesive institutions: *p*-values for these tests are reported at the bottom of the table. The results in these columns corroborate an important and nontrivial prediction of the theory.

It is reasonable to ask if these interaction effects really capture the impact of political institutions rather than just that of high income. To investigate this point, we use a dummy variable, which is equal to one if a country is in the top quarter (or top half) of the income per capita distribution in 1980. The correlations between this indicator of high income and the executive-constraints and parliamentary democracy measures of good institutions turn out not to be particularly high: 0.35 and 0.28, respectively (0.28 and 0.19, for the top half of income). When we add interactions of high income and shocks to the earlier specifications, all results on the interactions with political institutions—both those above and those below—hold up qualitatively.

Basic Results—Margins of Violence In columns (4) through (7), we consider separately each of the margins where our theory has a clear prediction, namely peace versus some violence (repression or civil war) and non–civil war (peace or repression) versus civil war. In each case, we estimate conditional logits that allow for country (and year) fixed effects. We report two specifications—one without and one with interaction terms for our executive-constraints measure of strong institutions. Columns (4) and (5) show that the earlier results are robust, with signs and magnitudes of the coefficients from the conditional logits being similar to those from the ordered logits. Once more, we cannot reject the hypothesis that political violence in the cohesive-institutions countries displays no significant correlation with the exogenous variables. For the civil-war margin, only 49 countries have some time variation in the left-hand-side variable. We are unable to estimate an interaction effect with Security Council membership, since none of the cohesive-institutions countries that have been (nonpermanent) members of the Security Council ever had a civil war. However, we cannot reject a zero effect for natural disasters on civil war in countries with cohesive political institutions.

These estimates square well with the predictions of our theory. The civil-war result is also consistent with the findings of Miguel, Satyanath, and Sergenti (2004) based on rainfall shocks rather than natural disasters, although here we extend the sample from Africa to the world and widen the scope to include one-sided, in addition to two-sided, political violence. This is also consistent with the findings of Nel and Righarts (2008) who, building on Drury and Olson (1998), argue that natural disasters increase the risk of civil conflict, although our results are based exclusively on the within-country variation in the data (rather than the cross-sectional cum time-series variation).

Columns (1) through (7) all show nonadjusted standard errors. Since the estimation procedures are somewhat involved, the best alternative is probably to bootstrap (by country block) the standard errors. Whenever our bootstrapping procedure converges, it yields standard errors very similar to the nonadjusted standard errors.[30] Column (8) shows this by reporting bootstrapped standard errors for the same specification as in column (1). It is reassuring that the linear-probability estimates in Table 4.5 rely entirely on standard errors that are robust to arbitrary forms of heteroskedasticity and serial correlation (Huber-White standard errors clustered at the country level).

Extended Results—Alternative Estimation Table 4.5 relies on an alternative estimation method and also explores the mechanism at work in more detail.

The first four columns establish that we obtain similar results when running the specifications in columns (4) to (7) of Table 4.4 with a conventional fixed-effect estimator, corresponding to a linear probability model. (Since we do not want to impose a strong cardinality assumption, we focus on the binary variables corresponding to the two margins investigated in Table 4.4.) The standard errors in column (1), as in the whole of Table 4.5, are robust to heteroskedasticity and clustered at the country level.

It is easy to give a direct quantitative interpretation of these estimates: having (at least) one natural disaster raises the probability of political violence by about 2.4 percentage points and the probability of civil war by 2.9 percentage points. Security Council membership during the Cold War raises the probability of political violence by a whopping 9 percentage points, compared to the post-Cold-War period. All these effects appear quite large and consistent with the findings in Table 4.4. The terms that interact these variables with cohesive institutions as measured by executive constraints also display the same sign pattern as in Table 4.4.

30. Performing the bootstrapping is nontrivial owing to the stepwise estimation (see the previous footnote) and the unbalanced panel, especially when the interaction effects in columns (2), (3), (5), and (7) are included.

Table 4.5 Extended econometric results

Dependent variable	(1) Political violence	(2) Political violence	(3) Civil war	(4) Civil war	(5) Log GDP per capita	(6) Log aid disbursements	(7) Political violence	(8) Civil war
Natural disaster	0.024*	0.029*	0.029**	0.043***	−0.005	0.105**		
	(0.013)	(0.017)	(0.013)	(0.016)	(0.003)	(0.043)		
Security Council member	−0.066**	−0.092***	−0.051**	−0.053**	0.009	−0.269***		
	(0.027)	(0.029)	(0.023)	(0.023)	(0.008)	(0.092)		
Security Council member in Cold War	0.090**	0.129***	0.034	0.036	−0.004	0.434***		
	(0.040)	(0.045)	(0.029)	(0.029)	(0.010)	(0.113)		
Natural disaster × strong institutions		−0.024		−0.079***				
		(0.037)		(0.024)				
Security Council member × strong institutions		0.148***						
		(0.054)						
Security Council member in Cold War × strong institutions		−0.205***						
		(0.068)						
Two-year lagged log GDP per capita					0.905***			
					(0.013)			
Log GDP per capita							0.062	0.046
							(0.039)	(0.040)
Log aid disbursements							0.191***	0.161***
							(0.046)	(0.050)
Observations	5880	5880	5880	5880	6300	5067	3914	3914
Number of countries	158	158	158	158	178	150		
R-squared	0.030	0.031	0.056	0.059	0.914	0.136		

Notes: The time period covered is 1950–2006. For definitions of variables refer to the text. Robust standard errors adjusted for clustering by country in parentheses: * significant at 10%; ** significant at 5%; *** significant at 1%. The specification in columns (1)–(6) is OLS. The results in columns (7) and (8) are IV specifications in which natural disaster, Security Council member and Security Council member in the Cold War and two-year lagged log income per capita are used as instruments for log GDP per capita and log aid disbursements.

Extended Results—Inspecting the Mechanism In columns (5) and (6), we look at the mechanisms behind the reduced-form results. Specifically, we ask how our three exogenous variables affect two intermediate variables that the theory suggests could shape political violence: income per capita (for real wages) and aid disbursements. In column (5), we allow natural disasters and Security Council membership to affect income per capita (allowing for income convergence by including the two-year lag of income per capita). The results show no significant correlation with income per capita, although we cannot reject a negative effect. On the basis of this result, we would not wish to argue that the real wage is the main channel by which natural disasters affect the probability of conflict. In column (6), the dependent variable is (the log of) aid disbursements. The estimates show that aid flows increase with natural disasters, are higher during the Cold War when a country is on the U.N. Security Council, and are lower in the post-Cold-War period. This sign pattern is identical to the effects of these variables on political violence.[31]

It is simple to compute the implied (semi)elasticity of political violence, p, with respect to aid, by observing that

$$\frac{\partial p}{\partial \log(aid)} = \frac{\partial p/\partial x}{\partial \log(aid)/\partial x}.$$

Through this formula, the estimated coefficients in columns (1) and (6) give us three estimates of the elasticity of political violence to aid, which are remarkably similar—all in the range between 0.20 to 0.24. Quantitatively, a 10% increase in aid is associated with an increase in the probability of violence by about 2 percentage points. These results are consistent with the recent results on aid and civil conflict presented by Nunn and Qian (2010).[32]

31. We have also interacted these shocks with our institutional measure (available from the authors upon request). For natural resource shocks, we find that they (significantly) increase aid to countries with noncohesive institutions, but (significantly) reduce aid to countries with cohesive institutions. However, Security Council membership has a (significantly) much stronger effect on aid, both during and after the Cold War in countries with cohesive institutions than in countries with noncohesive institutions. The latter result suggests that it is really the difference in institutions that drives the results in Table 4.4, rather than a different response to shocks.

32. Nunn and Qian (2010) use weather shocks in the U.S. wheat belt to instrument for food aid across the world. Their results and those in this chapter are at odds with de Ree and Nillesen (2009), who study civil conflicts in Sub-Saharan Africa. Ree and Nillesen (2009) use shocks to GDP per capita in the United States and a few other donor countries to instrument for ODA in Sub-Saharan Africa. Their dependent variable is also different and they find significant effects only when they study the persistence and onset of civil war.

In light of these results, it is tempting to look further into the mechanism behind the reduced-form results by estimating a two-stage model, where income per capita and aid are instrumented with our exogenous variables and two-year lagged income. The results from this exercise are reported in columns (7) and (8). Not surprisingly, given the results in columns (5) and (6), we find a positive and significant effect of aid disbursements on political violence as well as civil war, but no significant effect of income per capita. Moreover, the effects of aid estimated by the two-stage model are very close to the aid to violence elasticities computed from our earlier estimates.

We do not want to push these IV results, however, since the required identifying assumption is quite strong. For example, and as noted earlier, Cold-War Security Council membership might have affected violence not only through regular aid but also through military assistance (which we cannot measure), thus violating the exclusion restriction.

Taken together, the empirical estimates presented in Tables 4.4 and 4.5 are quite consistent with the theoretical predictions derived in Section 4.1 and operationalized in Section 4.3.

4.5 *Final Remarks*

The analysis in this chapter has taken some steps toward integrating two different strands of research on political violence, developing a theoretical model to analyze the common roots of repression and civil war. Under specific assumptions about the conflict technology, we show that peace, repression (one-sided violence), and civil war (two-sided violence) become ordered states depending on a common underlying latent variable, which is shifted by shocks to the value of public goods, wages, aid, and resource rents. But these effects only emerge when political institutions do not provide sufficient checks and balances on the ruling group or adequate protection for those excluded from power.

The chapter also shows how we can start bridging the gap between theoretical modeling and econometric testing. Under specific assumptions on what can be observed, the predictions from our model can be taken to the data by estimating either an ordered logit or the conditional probability of transition from peace to violence or from non–civil war to civil war. The empirical strategy here is much sharper than in earlier chapters and shows that the kind of theory we are building can help us approach the data in a specific way.

Our identification relies on two sources of, arguably, exogenous variation affecting violence that are part of the mechanism isolated by the theory: natural disasters (affecting real wages and aid flows) and membership on the U.N. Security Council (affecting aid flows). The empirical results are consistent with the theoretical predictions as real wages and aid flows affect the latent variable Z in the model. These exogenous shocks do indeed alter the likelihood of government repression as well as civil war in line with the theoretical priors, but only if political institutions have weak checks and balances or weak minority representation. Inspecting the mechanism, we find that variations in foreign aid seem to drive the bulk of the within-country variation in political violence that we explain.

These findings resonate with previous work that emphasizes the role of institutions, economic development, and natural resources in shaping civil conflict or political violence more generally. However, much work remains to complete the agenda of interpreting empirical results on violence through the lens of well-specified theoretical models. One helpful, but limiting, feature of the current model is the symmetry between incumbent and opposition groups. As discussed in Section 2.2, the general model framework can be extended to incorporate income inequality via heterogeneity in incomes or asymmetry in group size. In Section 4.2, we highlighted how groups might differ in their weighting of national interests (national public goods) against group-specific interests (transfers), which is a way of modeling ethnic, cultural, or religious tensions and how this offers a way to introduce a grievance motive for conflict in addition to the greed motive stressed in Section 4.1.

Our empirical analysis of the *incidence* of violence has not really engaged with the distinction between *onset* and *duration* of violence, which plays an important role in the empirical civil-war literature. Further theoretical progress on this issue requires an underlying source of state dependence. State capacity, to be endogenized in the next chapter, is one obvious source of state dependence and is also emphasized by Fearon (2004) and Fearon and Laitin (2003). We could also get a more dynamic model by introducing asymmetry between groups, along the lines discussed in Section 4.2. The state variable would then be the group in power, making the equilibrium in any given period state dependent. This would naturally lead to an empirical model where political violence and political turnover are jointly determined. Another possibility would be to introduce an economic state variable such as land or capital, with conflict in one period destroying part of this state variable in the next period. The implied dynamics of the real wage would naturally imply some duration dependence in conflict. We take a preliminary look at such a model in Section 5.2.

Studying the joint determination of state capacity and political violence in the next chapter allows us to make further predictions about the links between conflict risk and state capacity. This way, we find a predicted link between conflict risk and income, which is intermediated by investments either in state capacity or in private capital. Altogether, this extended analysis helps improve our understanding of the observed clustering among income, institutions, and violence.

4.6 *Notes on the Literature*

Classic theoretical models of conflict, such as those in Grossman (1991) and Skaperdas (1992), have been applied to understanding civil war. In common with the model developed in this chapter, these authors see conflict as the outcome of an equilibrium process in which the incentives of the various parties are modeled explicitly. Those incentives arise from the technology of conflict, the preferences of the protagonists, and the underlying economic constraints. Grossman (1992) makes the point that foreign aid may increase the propensity of civil conflict for the same reason as the one stressed in this chapter. For excellent reviews of the theoretical literature, see Blattman and Miguel (2009) on general issues and Garfinkel and Skaperdas (2007) on the research that uses contest functions. Dixit (1987) and Skaperdas (1996) survey the use of contest functions more generally, and Aslaksen and Torvik (2006), Azam (2002), Caselli (2006), and Chassang and Padro i Miquel (2009) are more recent theoretical contributions that take somewhat different approaches. Azam (2005) discusses state types in Africa, where the distinction between one-sided and two-sided political violence is important. Parker (1988) is a classic reference on the role of military technology and its historical impact on the organization of the state.

Much progress has been made in this theoretical research, but most of it has been pursued separately from the empirical literature and the models have not generally been formulated with empirical testing in mind. Fearon (2008) is an exception, but he follows a somewhat different modeling approach to the one adopted in this chapter. Another exception is the literature on polarization and conflict, where the theory by Esteban and Ray (1999, 2008a) has both been informing and been informed by empirical work such as Montalvo and Reynal-Querol (2005) and Reynal-Querol (2002).

In recent years, a large empirical literature has emerged that looks at the determinants of civil war, and is reviewed by Blattman and Miguel (2009) and Elbadawi and Sambanis (2002). A robust finding in this body of work is that poor countries are disproportionately involved in civil war, even though the direction of causation may be difficult to establish. But the interpretation of this correlation is open to debate. Fearon and Laitin (2003) see it as reflecting limited state capacity to put down rebellions, whereas Collier and Hoeffler (2004) see it as a reflection of the lower opportunity cost of fighting when incomes are low.

There is also considerable debate about other prospective drivers of civil war, such as ethnic divisions and political institutions. When it comes to natural resources, results diverge as well. Although some researchers have found natural resources to significantly raise the probability of onset and/or duration of civil war, others have failed to find such an effect (see Ross, 2004 for a review of the research on this topic). However, most empirical researchers would probably agree that there is a significant cross-sectional correlation between oil dependence and civil war. A few papers, such as Drury and Olson (1998) and Nel and Righarts (2008), look at the empirical links between natural disasters and civil conflict and very recent studies by de Ree and Nillesen (2009) and Nunn and Qian (2010) explore the links between aid and civil war.

A smaller set of studies focuses on variation in conflict within countries. For example, Deininger (2003) uses community-level data from Uganda, finding that scarcity of economic opportunities (proxied by infrastructure) and the presence of cash crops are correlated with the civil strife. Another within-country study by Dube and Vargas (2008) builds on the theoretical framework developed by Dal Bó and Dal Bó (2006) to explain the incidence of conflict within Colombian municipalities, exploiting the time-series variation in coffee and oil prices.

There is also a considerable literature in political science that aims at finding economic, political, and social variables to explain government repression and violations of human rights. This literature, surveyed in Davenport (2007), is almost exclusively empirical. The literatures on civil war and government repression have been developed largely in parallel, without too much contact with each other, even though civil war sometimes appears as a "right-hand-side" variable in empirical studies of repression. Azam and Hoeffler (2002) show how violence against civilians (repression) can be effective at deterring rebellion and apply this to data on refugees.

CHAPTER 5

State Spaces

All happy families resemble each other; every unhappy family is unhappy in its own way.

Leo Tolstoy, *Anna Karenina*, 1873–1877

In the previous chapter we expanded our core state-capacity model from Chapter 3 to include investments in violence. We used this model to explore the theoretical determinants of repression and civil war and demonstrated that the predictions are consistent with the within-country variation in violence over time. Prior to the empirical detour in the last half of Chapter 4, we observed that political violence and state-capacity investments had several common determinants. Specifically, investments in the state and investments in violence appeared to be substitutes for one another; among the common determinants, every variable that increased investments in violence decreased those in state capacity.

The theoretical analysis in Chapter 4 was incomplete, however, in that we treated the levels of legal and fiscal capacity as given. We now complete the analysis by making them endogenous. Thus, we derive the optimal investments in state capacity by a period-1 incumbent when political (in)stability is endogenous—rather than exogenous, as in Chapters 2 and 3—and driven by the equilibrium investments in violence. This exercise results in a new pair of Euler equations for legal and fiscal capacity, through which state capacity, income, and political violence are jointly determined. Moreover, we take a further step toward endogenizing income by reintroducing private capital formation into the analysis. This suggests a natural negative relation between conflict risk and investment (and thereby income).

Once these remaining tasks have been resolved, we can put the pieces together to obtain a more complete picture of development clusters. As we shall see, our comprehensive core model further helps us in isolating possible explanations for the observed correlations among income, institutions, and violence. In particular, we can combine our findings in Chapters 2 and 3 of a typology with common-interest, redistributive, and weak states with our findings in Chapter 4 of a typology with peaceful, repressive, and civil-war states. This gives us a general state space in the form of a matrix. A country's precise location in this matrix at a given time depends on the parameter values that describe its polity and economy.

Plan of the Chapter In the next section, we summarize the lessons from Chapter 4 in the form of a function that describes endogenous political turnover. This preliminary allows us to study equilibrium investments in fiscal and legal capacity in the comprehensive core model. Section 5.2 develops the model by adding private capital formation along the same lines as in Section 3.2.3, but in a setting where the risk of civil war affects the expected return to private investment. In Section 5.3, we discuss the empirical implications of our comprehensive framework and how it can be used to interpret observed patterns in the data.

Section 5.4 puts the typologies of investment states and violence states together into an Anna Karenina principle of development, an allusion to the Tolstoy quote at the beginning of the chapter. We also briefly revisit the possibility of a predatory state and observe how this enriches our understanding of nonprosperity. As usual, the chapter ends with final remarks and notes on the literature.

5.1 *State Capacity in the Comprehensive Core Model*

Let us return to the core model formulated in Section 4.1, where we conducted the analysis of violence taking fiscal and legal capacities as givens.

5.1.1 Equilibrium Political Turnover

Analyzing the equilibrium investments in state capacity is considerably simplified by the model's recursive structure. Recursivity implies that violence shapes investments only via the equilibrium rate of political turnover, $\gamma(\hat{L}^I, \hat{L}^O; \xi)$.

Preliminaries Let us first recall that the latent variable driving conflict is

$$Z = \frac{(1-\phi)\,[R + \tau_2 y(\pi_2)]}{\omega(\pi_1)}.$$

Let us also replace the general vector ξ in the conflict technology by a scalar parameter ξ. We make the following assumption on how this parameter affects the marginal returns to fighting of the incumbent and opposition:

Assumption 5.1: $-\gamma_{I\xi}\left(L^O, L^I; \xi\right) > 0$ *and* $\gamma_{O\xi}\left(L^O, L^I; \xi\right) < 0$.

This says that ξ indexes the advantage of the incumbent: raising ξ increases the incumbent's marginal return to fighting while reducing the opposition's marginal return to fighting (in terms of each group's probability of holding power in period 2).

Drawing on the results in Propositions 4.1 and 4.2 and plugging the Nash equilibrium values $\{\widehat{L}^I, \widehat{L}^O\}$ into the conflict technology, we find the equilibrium turnover rate:

$$\Gamma(Z, \nu, \xi) = \begin{cases} \gamma\left(\hat{L}^O, \hat{L}^I; \xi\right) & Z > Z^O(\theta, \nu, \xi) \\ \gamma\left(0, \hat{L}^I; \xi\right) & Z^O(\theta; \nu, \xi) \geq Z > Z^I(\theta, \lambda_1, \xi) \\ \gamma(0, 0; \xi) & Z^I(\theta, \lambda_1, \xi) \geq Z. \end{cases} \tag{5.1}$$

Comparative Statics We can easily do comparative statics on the $\Gamma(Z, \nu, \xi)$ function, which are summarized in the following result:

Proposition 5.1: *If Assumptions 4.1 and 5.1 hold, the probability that the incumbent loses office at the end of period 1 varies with (Z, ν, ξ) as follows:*

1. *An increase in Z reduces the probability that the incumbent loses office when there is either repression or civil war.*
2. *An increase in ν reduces the probability that the incumbent loses office when there is civil war.*
3. *An increase in ξ reduces the probability that the incumbent loses office when there is either repression or civil war.*

Proof: Part 1 is proved as follows. First, suppose that there is repression. Then, the result follows, since Assumption 4.1 implies that the incumbent's payoff is concave in L^I and that Z increases the marginal benefit to fighting. Now, suppose that there is civil war. Differentiating (5.1) with respect to Z yields

$$\begin{aligned}\Gamma_Z(Z,\nu,\xi) &= \gamma_I \frac{dL^I}{dZ} + \gamma_O \frac{dL^O}{dZ} \\ &= \frac{\left[(\gamma_I)^2 \gamma_{OO} + (\gamma_O)^2 \gamma_{II} - 2\gamma_I \gamma_O \gamma_{IO}\right]}{\left[-\gamma_{II}\gamma_{OO} + (\gamma_{IO})^2\right] Z} < 0,\end{aligned}$$

where we have used the comparative static result in (4.12) and Assumption 4.1c.

To prove Part 2 of the proposition, observe that under repression, changing ν has no effect on $\hat{L}^I$ since $L^O = 0$. Under civil war, a higher ν affects violence according to

$$\begin{bmatrix} -\gamma_{II}xZ & -\gamma_{IO}xZ \\ \gamma_{IO}xZ & \gamma_{OO}xZ \end{bmatrix} \begin{bmatrix} dL^I \\ dL^O \end{bmatrix} = \begin{bmatrix} 0 \\ d\nu \end{bmatrix}. \tag{5.2}$$

Differentiating (5.1) with respect to ν and using Cramer's rule, we have

$$\begin{aligned}\Gamma_\nu(Z,\nu,\xi) &= \gamma_I \frac{dL^I}{d\nu} + \gamma_O \frac{dL^O}{d\nu} \\ &= \frac{\left[-\gamma_{II}\gamma_O + \gamma_I \gamma_{IO}\right]}{\left[-\gamma_{II}\gamma_{OO} + (\gamma_{IO})^2\right] 2(1-2\theta) Z^2} < 0,\end{aligned}$$

where the sign follows from Assumption 4.1c.

Finally, turn to Part 3. First, suppose that there is repression. Then, the result follows because Assumption 4.1 implies that the incumbent's payoff is concave in L^I and because of the assumption that ξ increases the marginal benefit to fighting. Next, suppose there is civil war. Then, as ξ increases, the effect on violence is given by

$$\begin{bmatrix} -\gamma_{II}xZ & -\gamma_{IO}xZ \\ \gamma_{IO}xZ & \gamma_{OO}xZ \end{bmatrix} \begin{bmatrix} dL^I \\ dL^O \end{bmatrix} = \begin{bmatrix} \gamma_{I\xi}\left(L^O, L^I; \xi\right) xZd\xi \\ -\gamma_{O\xi}\left(L^O, L^I; \xi\right) xZd\xi \end{bmatrix}, \tag{5.3}$$

where $x = (1-2\theta)2$. Differentiating (5.1) with respect to ν and using Cramer's rule, we have

$$\Gamma_\xi(Z,\nu,\xi) = \gamma_I \frac{dL^I}{d\xi} + \gamma_O \frac{dL^O}{d\xi}$$

$$= \frac{\gamma_{O\xi}\left[\gamma_{II}\gamma_O - \gamma_I\gamma_{IO}\right] + \gamma_{I\xi}\left[\gamma_{OO}\gamma_I - \gamma_{IO}\gamma_O\right]}{\left[-\gamma_{II}\gamma_{OO} + (\gamma_{IO})^2\right] Z} < 0,$$

where the sign follows from Assumption 4.1c. This proves the result. ■

Proposition 5.1 is an important result when it comes to studying the impact of violence on state-capacity investments since the likelihood that the incumbent holds on to power affects these decisions when θ is low.

The first part follows from the fact that the incumbent fights relatively harder than the opposition when more is at stake. This is so because, by Assumption 4.1c, γ_I rises faster than γ_O. This comparative-statics prediction is consistent with the results in Smith (2004), who finds that oil-rich states have longer leadership durations than others, ceteris paribus.

The second part of the proposition follows from the fact that it becomes more costly for the opposition to use violence as ν goes up. This reduces turnover when there is a civil war, as the opposition fights less intensively. It is also shifts up the threshold Z^O at which civil war breaks out.

As for the third part, the range of Z associated with repression becomes wider as ξ increases. This is because, by Assumption 5.1, a higher value of ξ cuts the incumbent's trigger point for violence and raises that of the opposition. Within the repression and civil war regimes, a higher value of ξ makes the incumbent invest more in violence, whereas the opposition invests less. Hence, it raises the probability that the incumbent group stays in power.

5.1.2 Investments in State Capacity Revisited

Armed with these preliminaries, let us now consider investments in state capacities $\{\pi_2, \tau_2\}$ in the comprehensive core model of Chapter 4. These investments are determined by the period-1 incumbent at the same time that she invests in violence L^I and, thus, simultaneously with the period-1 opposition group's decision on L^O, which the incumbent takes as given. This simultaneity, together with the linear structure of the model, permits us to analyze the investments in state capacity separately from policy. Moreover, the only connection with the investments in violence runs through the equilibrium turnover rate $\Gamma\,(Z,\nu,\xi)$.

Although different in its details, our analysis is related to the work of Caselli (2006), who considers how the availability of natural resources shapes the discount factor of an incumbent government via the probability of a future coup and how this, in turn, affects the investments made by the incumbent to develop the economy.

The Investment Objective The period-1 incumbent chooses investment levels at stage 2 so as to maximize its two-period utility. As before, let

$$W(\alpha_s, \tau_s, \pi_s, m_s, \beta^J) = \alpha_s G(\alpha_s, \tau_s) + (1-\tau_s)y(\pi_s) + \beta^J[R + \tau_s y(\pi_s) - G(\alpha_s, \tau_s) - m_s] \tag{5.4}$$

be the indirect payoff function within each period.

Replacing the conflict technology $\gamma(L^O, L^I, \xi)$ with the equilibrium turnover rate $\Gamma(Z, \nu, \xi)$ in the incumbent's payoff function from the previous chapter, we can express the investment objective as

$$W(\alpha_1, \tau_1, \pi_1, m_1, \beta^J) + (1-\Gamma(Z, \nu, \xi))U^I(\tau_2, \pi_2) + \Gamma(Z, \nu, \xi)\, U^O(\tau_2, \pi_2), \tag{5.5}$$

where

$$U^I(\tau_2, \pi_2) = \left[\phi W\left(\alpha_H, \tau_2, \pi_2, 0, \beta^I\right) + (1-\phi)\, W\left(\alpha_L, \tau_2, \pi_2, 0, \beta^I\right)\right]$$

and

$$U^O(\tau_2, \pi_2) = \left[\phi W\left(\alpha_H, \tau_2, \pi_2, 0, \beta^O\right) + (1-\phi)\, W\left(\alpha_L, \tau_2, \pi_2, 0, \beta^O\right)\right]$$

are the period-2 value functions.

Optimality Conditions Maximizing (5.5) with respect to π_2 and τ_2 and applying the envelope theorem, we obtain the following Euler equations (first-order conditions) for legal and fiscal capacity

$$y_\pi(\pi_2)[1 + (E(\lambda_2; Z, \nu, \xi, \theta) - 1)\tau_2] \leq \lambda_1 \mathcal{L}_\pi(\pi_2 - \pi_1)$$
$$\text{c.s. } \pi_2 - \pi_1 \geq 0$$
$$y(\pi_2)[(E(\lambda_2; Z, \nu, \xi, \theta) - 1] \leq \lambda_1 \mathcal{F}_\tau(\tau_2 - \tau_1)$$
$$\text{c.s. } \tau_2 - \tau_1 \geq 0,$$

where

$$E(\lambda_2; Z, \nu, \xi, \theta) = \phi\alpha_H + (1-\phi)E(\lambda_2|\alpha_L; Z, \nu, \xi, \theta)$$

is the *expected* value of public funds with

$$E(\lambda_2|\alpha_L; Z, \nu, \xi, \theta)$$
$$= \begin{cases} \alpha_L & \text{if } \alpha_L \geq 2(1-\theta) \\ 2[(1-\theta)(1-\Gamma(Z, \nu, \xi)) + \theta\Gamma(Z, \nu, \xi) & \text{otherwise.} \end{cases}$$

The form of these optimality conditions should be familiar from the core models in Sections 2.1 and 3.1.

In the absence of a corner solution, each condition equates the marginal cost with the marginal benefit of investment, which depends on the expected marginal value of public funds. The only new aspect is that the endogenous turnover rate Γ appears in place of exogenous parameter γ in the expression for $E(\lambda_2; Z, \nu, \xi, \theta)$, where we have replaced our earlier notation λ_2^L to emphasize the fact that $\Gamma(Z, \nu, \xi)$ is now endogenously determined. As before, the equilibrium entails a complementarity between the two types of investment, provided that

$$E(\lambda_2|\alpha_L; Z, \nu, \xi, \theta) - 1 \geq 0.$$

We do not repeat all of the comparative statics from Chapter 3. Instead, we focus on the new insights and implications we can draw from this extended model.

Characterizing the Equilibrium Once again, we have a three-way classification of possible states, depending on two conditions, which we label as in the simpler model. The first of these is identical to its predecessor:

Cohesiveness: $\alpha_L \geq 2(1-\theta)$.

The second condition is similar to its predecessor, but reflects the endogenous turnover rate:

Stability: $\phi\alpha_H + (1-\phi)\,2\,[(1-\Gamma(Z, \nu, \xi))(1-\theta) + \Gamma(Z, \nu, \xi)\,\theta] \geq 1.$

This modified stability condition is more likely to hold if $\Gamma(Z, \nu, \xi)$ is low. Our characterization of how this turnover rate depends on the parameters (Z, ν, ξ) in Proposition 5.1 will therefore be useful whenever the stability condition determines investments.

The conceptual meaning as well as the consequences of the two conditions are exactly the same as in Chapters 2 and 3. For completeness, we restate how they map into the three possible types of states.

Proposition 5.2: *Suppose that Cohesiveness holds or $\phi \to 1$. Then, we have a common-interest state, where*

1. *There are investments in both kinds of state capacity.*
2. *An increase in ϕ increases both fiscal and legal capacity investments, whereas changes in R, ν, or ξ have no effect on investments.*

For this result to hold, we require that θ be close enough to one-half that marginal public revenues are allocated to public goods. In this case, the incumbent in period 1 is reassured that the state will use public resources for common interests, i.e., public goods, regardless of who is in power in period 2. This makes her confident that the state can be developed. Observe that by Proposition 4.1, common-interest states are always peaceful, since there is no redistribution to fight about. A higher value of ϕ raises investments in both aspects of the state by making future government revenue more valuable.

The second possibility is as follows:

Proposition 5.3: *Suppose that Cohesiveness fails and $\phi < 1$, but that Stability holds. Then, we have a redistributive state, where*

1. *There are investments in both kinds of state capacity.*
2. *A higher value of ϕ increases both fiscal- and legal-capacity investments, as do (weakly) higher values of R, ν,* or *ξ.*

In a redistributive state, the incumbent government uses available funds to redistribute when $\alpha_s = \alpha_L$, and it invests in the state as the group is likely enough to stay in power. If the incumbent government finds itself in repression or civil war—i.e., Z is above one or both of the trigger points Z^I and Z^O—parameter changes that raise the intensity of repression or civil war, hence increasing the chances that the incumbent survives, promote higher investments in the state.

A stronger redistributive state may thus go hand in hand with higher levels of repression. Note that, unlike in Chapters 2 and 3, the local comparative statics in common-interest and redistributive states are now different when it comes to changes in R, ν, *or* ξ.

The following result summarizes the third possibility.

Proposition 5.4: *When both Cohesiveness and Stability fail, the state is weak. There is no incentive at all to invest in fiscal capacity, and legal-capacity investment is lower than in a common-interest or redistributive state, all else being equal.*

As the stability condition fails, the marginal benefit of investing in fiscal capacity is negative. The noncohesiveness of political institutions and the high rate of political turnover mean that any fiscal capacity is likely to be used by the opposition group to redistribute away from the current incumbent. This deters investment in the state and we see a weak state together with high political instability driven by political violence.

5.2 *Developing the Model*

So far, our comprehensive model has been developed without any private capital accumulation decisions. However, the model still generates an indirect link between political violence and income, since investments in legal capacity directly raise income and the risk of conflict affects investments in the state. Suppose that θ is low enough to generate a weak or redistributive state. Then, if we have shocks to Z, the correlation between violence and income will be positive. But if we have shocks to ν, the correlation will be negative.

Either way, this is a restrictive perspective on the link between violence and income, as it leaves out the most obvious possibility, namely a reduction in private investment. For example, Goldin and Lewis (1975) estimate that the largest economic cost of the American Civil War in the U.S. South was due to destruction of physical capital. Under that circumstance, any anticipation of conflict will surely lead to less investment. We now show how such a mechanism can be introduced into our model.

Reintroducing Private Investment To model the effect of conflict risk on investment, we augment the model to include a decision to invest in physical capital along the same lines as in Section 3.2.3. However, we do so in the context of our comprehensive core model, which includes investments in political violence. Specifically, we model the individual decisions to invest in the period-2 capital stock, K_2.

To home in on the effect of conflict, we proceed as in Chapter 4 by keeping investments in state capacity fixed. We leave the analysis of the full comprehensive model with both private and public investment in the wake of prospective conflict to further work.

We augment the model with the realistic assumption, confirmed by the analyses in Collier (1999) and Goldin and Lewis (1975), that a *realized* civil war has a lasting effect on the economy's productive capacity by destroying some outstanding private capital. Since destruction is most likely a by-product of all-out conflict, we assume that no such destruction occurs in a state of repression. Formally, we make the following assumption:

Assumption 5.2: *If a civil war takes place then a share $\delta < 1$ of period-2 capital is destroyed.*

Given the timing assumptions to follow, this means that destruction occurs after the savings decision but before production has taken place in period 2. Effectively, private capital will thus be subject to stochastic depreciation.

Timing The timing of the modified model is now:

1. We begin with initial stocks of state capacities $\{\tau_1, \pi_1\}$, a capital stock per capita of K_1, and an incumbent group I_1.
2. All citizens decide how much capital to accumulate for period 2, K.
3. Nature determines α_1 and R.
4. I_1 chooses a set of period-1 policies $\{t_1, r_1^I, r_1^O, p_1^I, p_1^O, g_1\}$ and determines (through investments) the period-2 stocks of fiscal and legal capacity $\{\tau_2, \pi_2\}$. I_1 and O_1 simultaneously invest in violence levels L^I and L^O. If a civil war erupts, there is capital destruction.
5. I_1 remains in power with probability $1 - \Gamma(Z, \nu, \xi)$, and nature determines α_2.
6. I_2 chooses period-2 policies $\{t_2, r_2^I, r_2^O, p_2^I, p_2^O, g_2\}$.

Since private accumulation decisions are made ahead of the realization of R (and α), the probability of conflict can affect the decision to accumulate.

Expected Return to Capital We study the equilibrium in a similar way as in Section 3.2.3. In the notation of Chapter 3, we assume that $\kappa\left(1+\pi_s\right)<1$ so that the institutional constraint is binding and capital is incompletely deployed in the advanced sector. Period-2 expected private income for an individual who saves K is

$$Y\left(\pi_2; K\right)=\left(\kappa\left(1+\pi_2\right) K\right)^\eta .$$

Suppose that the country is prone to civil conflict. Then, we can write the probability that civil war will break out after the realization of wages and natural resource rents, R, as

$$F^O(R-\omega_1\overline{Z}^O)=\text{Prob}\left[Z>Z^O\right]$$

using the same notation as in Section 4.3. For a country that always has high realizations of R and noncohesive institutions, $F^O(R-\omega_1\overline{Z}^O)=1-\phi$. Furthermore, as we discussed in Chapter 4, $F^O(R-\omega_1\overline{Z}^O)$ is equal to zero only in a common-interest state.

The *expected* net-of-tax marginal return to capital is now

$$\left(1-\tau_2\right)\eta\left[\kappa\left(1+\pi_2\right)\right]^\eta(K)^{\eta-1}\left[1-F^O(R-\omega_1\overline{Z}^O)\cdot\delta\right].$$

The final term represents the lower return to capital with $[1-F^O(R-\omega_1\overline{Z}^O)\cdot\delta]<1$ owing to the destruction of capital in a civil conflict.

Optimal Private Investments Following steps analogous to those that led to Proposition 3.7, we can derive an implicit solution for the optimal level of private capital:

$$1=\left(1-\tau_2\right)\eta\left[\kappa\left(1+\pi_2\right)\right]^\eta\left(K^J\right)^{\eta-1}\left[1-F^O(R-\omega_1\overline{Z}^O)\cdot\delta\right],\quad \text{for } J\in\{I,O\}. \tag{5.6}$$

This just says that the marginal product of capital is equal to the value of foregone consumption. The level of accumulation is the same for members of the incumbent and opposition groups because we have assumed that both groups are equally susceptible to capital destruction in the event of a civil war.

The final term in (5.6) is like a stochastic tax on accumulation. Since investors know that their investment returns will be lower if civil war breaks out, they invest less than they would if they were certain of peace.

Taking Stock Several insights follow from the private-investment optimum. First, any factor that raises the risk of civil war—i.e., any factor that raises $F^O(R - \omega_1 \overline{Z}^O)$ in expression (5.6)—must cut private investment. Thus, a lower expected probability of high public-goods demand weakens the incentive for private accumulation.

Second, because period-2 income, $Y(\pi_2; K)$, is increasing in capital, higher civil-war risk also means lower (future) income, as it reduces private investment. This mechanism will thus contribute to the observed negative correlation between the incidence of conflict and income per capita, as will the direct destructive effect of realized war on capital.

Third, a first-order stochastic shift of the distribution for R induces a higher risk of civil war in redistributive or weak states. Together with the two previous observations, this means that higher expected resource rents increase the risk of civil war as well as reduce private income.

These findings are interesting in view of the two largely separate literatures on the resource curse that we discussed in the introduction to Chapter 4. One of these literatures emphasizes the possibility that higher resource rents may cause low income, whereas the other emphasizes that natural resource rents can provoke civil war. The results in this section show how both of these effects can be present simultaneously.

Our analysis also provides insight into the preconditions for these effects in terms of weak common interests, i.e., low ϕ and low θ (or low ethnic homogeneity, high ι). It is these auxiliary parameters, rather than the resources per se, that give rise to both of the resource curses. Although a society such as Nigeria faces a threat from high R, a society with cohesive institutions such as Norway does not.

Our model in this section has focused on the private accumulation of physical capital. Similar arguments could also be developed for other kinds of investments, such as education decisions, and infrastructure could be destroyed.

However, we leave a more complete treatment of this wider range of possibilities for future work.

5.3 *Empirical Implications*

We have modeled the links between political violence and investments in state capacity in Section 5.1 and the links between violent conflict and private capital formation and income in Section 5.2. How can we draw on the theoretical insights to interpret the development clusters observed in the data and discussed at various points in the book?

Links between Income and Violence Recall first the negative correlation between income per capita and the two forms of violence in the raw data from 1950 until today, which we first reported in Figure 1.10 and then discussed at the beginning of Chapter 4. Figure 5.1 reproduces those correlations. The analysis in Chapter 4 showed that low income and, in particular, low wages might cause repression and civil war by decreasing the costs of investing in violence.

However, in light of our theory, this is only one of several possible explanations for the association between low income and violence. Our analysis in Section 5.2 suggested why circumstances with a high risk of civil war might lead to lower income via curtailed incentives for private investment. The analysis in that section built on a direct negative effect of civil war on the productive capacity of the economy. In Section 5.1, on the other hand, we suggested an indirect link, where the risk of conflict is associated with less investment in the state's legal capacity, and hence lower income. The correlations illustrated in Figure 5.1 may thus reflect causation in both directions, as well as common direct or indirect determinants.

Links between State Capacity and Violence What about the negative correlation between political violence and state capacity? Figure 5.2 reproduces the familiar scatterplot of fiscal and legal capacity in the raw data that we highlighted in Chapter 1. The figure classifies the observations into three groups based on the average value from 1950 and onward of the ordered variable analyzed empirically in Section 4.4 (i.e., with 0 for peace, 1 for repression, and 2 for civil war). In particular, gray dots represent little violence (in fact, none at all),

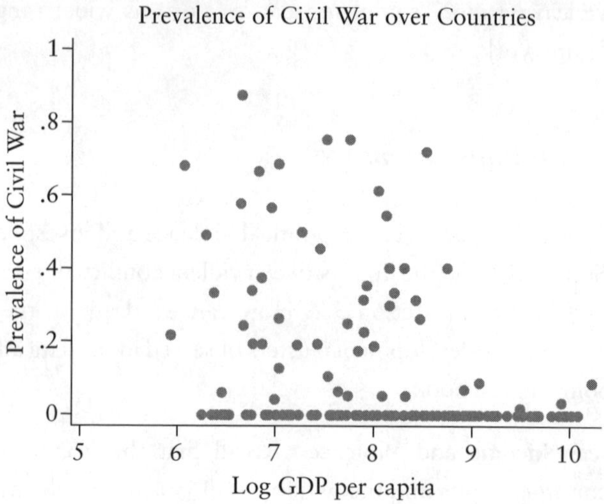

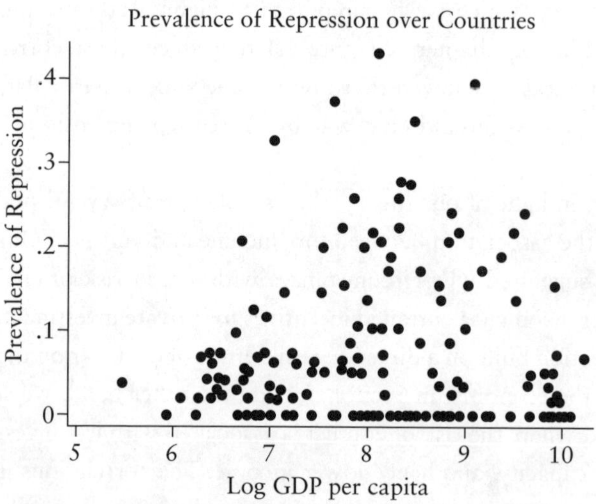

Figure 5.1 Prevalence of civil war and repression by income.

hollow dots represent middle levels of violence, and black dots high levels of violence. Although the correlation is not perfect, the scatter in the uppermost-right part of the graph is dominated by countries with high state capacity in both dimensions that have not experienced any political violence. In contrast, no country among the weak states in the lowermost-left part of the graph has been violence free.

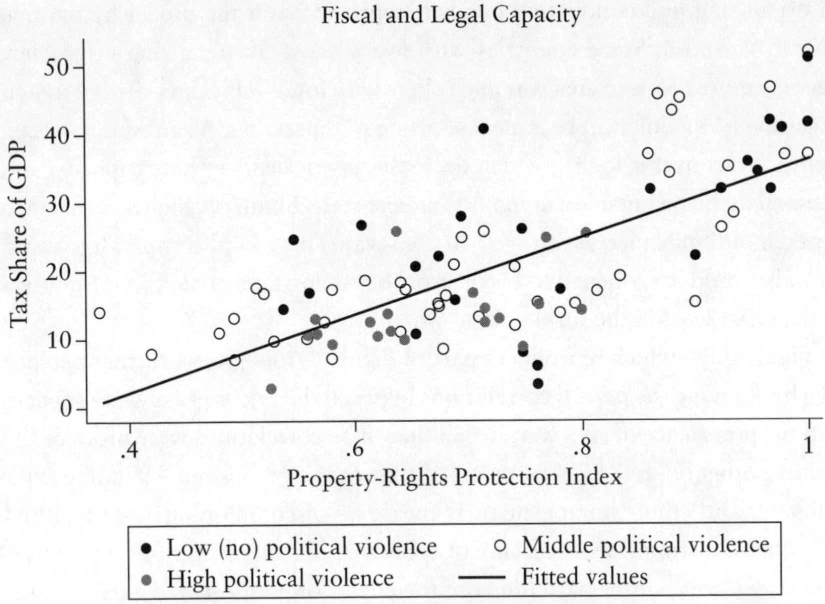

Figure 5.2 State capacity conditional on violence.

The theoretical analysis in Section 5.1 gives us a clear way to interpret these patterns in the data. On the one hand, it suggests some common determinants of state-capacity investments and violence. In particular, these determinants include the strength of common interests and the cohesiveness of political institutions, captured in the core model by parameters ϕ and θ (and in the extended polarization model described in Sections 2.2.4 and 4.2.2 by parameter ι). Countries with high values of ϕ and θ (low values of ι) become common-interest states, which invest in both forms of state capacity and have peaceful outcomes. Countries with low values of ϕ and θ (high values of ι) become redistributive or weak states, with repression or civil war depending on these and other parameter values. These global comparative statics, by determining which type of states we observe, can clearly produce a negative correlation between state capacities and violence.

On the other hand, conditional on being outside the common-interest state, the model also suggests several other determinants of conflict, which shape state capacity indirectly through the risk of political turnover. Examples of such determinants are resource rents or aid and the efficiency and costs involved in organizing and conducting conflict, represented in the model by parameters R, ν, and ξ. Some countries with low ν (cost of organizing insurgency) become more prone to civil war and others with low ξ (efficiency of government investments in violence) become less prone to repression. As a result, expected political turnover is higher, which decreases investments in state capacity, conditional on being outside a common-interest state. Similarly, higher R (resource rents or aid) may increase the risk of civil war. These local comparative statics can also produce a negative correlation between state capacity and political violence, at least in the form of civil war.

Figure 5.3—which reproduces part of Figure 1.13—gives a further perspective by showing the *partial* correlations between the two types of state capacity and the prevalence of civil war. Recall that these correlations were produced by holding other observed determinants of state capacity constant, including external wars and ethnic homogeneity as measures of common interests and high executive constraints as a measure of cohesive political institutions. In terms of the model, we are thus partialing out the effects of parameters ϕ, ι, and θ, i.e., the global comparative statics. But Figure 5.3 shows that a negative correlation between state capacities and civil war remains even when we hold (empirical proxies for) parameters ϕ, ι, and θ constant. This negative correlation suggests that the remaining parameters, ν, ξ, and R, might explain part of the negative correlation in the raw data by increasing (decreasing) political instability, which in turn lowers (raises) investment in both forms of state capacity.

The discussion in this section reveals a major problem with the standard practice in the civil-war literature of treating the level of income as a given. As noted in the introduction to Chapter 4, there are two leading interpretations of the fact that civil wars generally break out in poor countries: these have (1) a low opportunity cost of fighting (Collier and Hoeffler, 2004) or (2) low state capacities (Fearon and Laitin, 2003). Obviously, both interpretations become tenuous if income, state capacity, and the propensity for violence are indeed jointly determined.

To be fair, however, the discussion in Fearon and Laitin (2003) does not really revolve around the fiscal and legal capacities emphasized here, but around the costs and capacities for military action for governments and insurgents and the links of these costs and capabilities to income. In terms of our model, their discussion is thus not about τ and π, which we treat as endogenous variables, but about ν and ξ, which we treat as exogenous parameters. Further research might try to turn these parameters into endogenous variables, theoretically

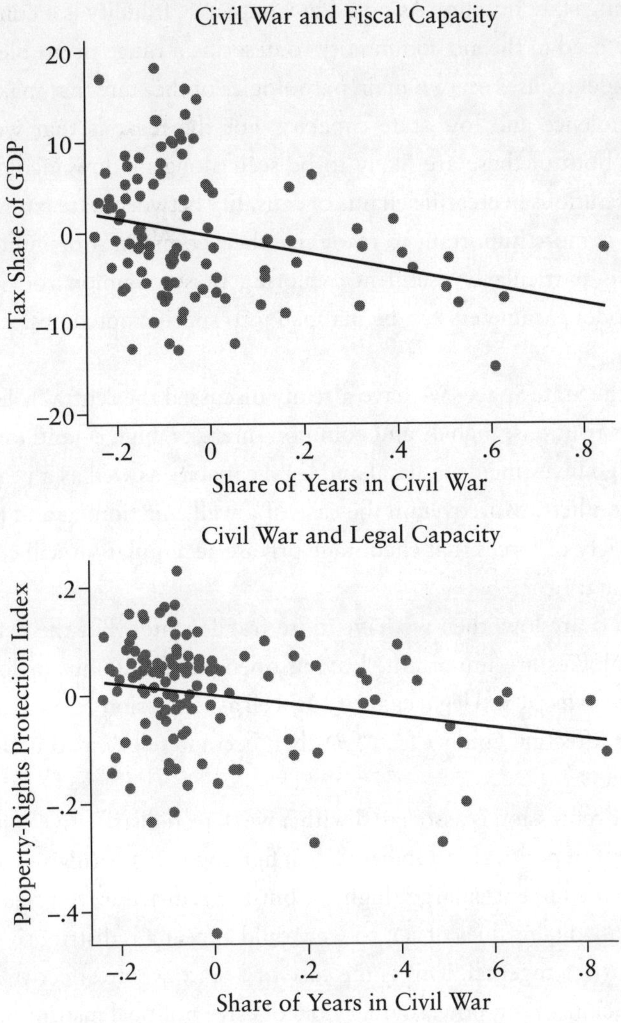

Figure 5.3 State capacity and civil war.

modeling purposeful investments in military capabilities and finding empirical measures for them.

5.4 *Putting the Pieces Together*

Up to this point, we have gradually developed a more complete model of investments in state capacity and violence, which provides us with a framework for analyzing state fragility. As noted in Chapter 1, fragility is a concept that is commonly used in the aid community to describe a range of problems.

Our model focuses on two main pathologies of the state that make it fragile: political violence and low state capacity. For the reasons that we have just discussed, both of these are likely to be seen alongside low income. But one should be cautious in creating chains of causality between state pathologies and income. It is more important to recognize their common roots. Our modeling approach is particularly useful in exploring these common roots, since the various model parameters can be mapped into specific outcomes.

Mapping the State Space We have already discussed the central role played by cohesive institutions, high θ, and common interests, high ϕ (and low ι). These result in high investments in fiscal and legal capacity as well as a peaceful resolution of conflicts. Moreover, in the case of a well-functioning and prosperous state, a variety of forces that encourage private accumulation will complement state building.

If θ and ϕ are low, then we have more fragile states. But the details of the state pathologies are important, leaving open the possibility of low or zero investments in fiscal and legal capacity as well as repression or outright conflict. Parameters affecting conflict (ξ, ν, R) then become relevant to understanding the outcome.

Whether repression is associated with a weak or redistributive state depends on the extent of political instability. When fighting is costly (high ν), the advantage to the incumbent is large (high ξ), but the redistributive prize is not too great (intermediate values of R), so we would expect a redistributive state and repression to go together. This is the case of a state where effective repression keeps an incumbent in power under noncohesive political institutions.

Civil war erupts only in weak or redistributive states. A weak state and civil war may reflect a case where the insurgency is relatively easy to organize (low ν), the government is not effective in fighting it (low ξ), and the economy is highly resource or aid dependent (high R).

We can summarize these global comparative statics indicating the type of state regime that is observed in a two-way table that combines the three possible investment states with the three possible violence states. Table 5.1 and the previous discussion suggest a clear pattern that we can label the Anna Karenina principle of development, by analogy with the first line of Leo

Table 5.1 Our state space

	Weak	Redistributive	Common interest
Peace	Low θ, ϕ, ξ, R High ν	High ϕ Low θ	High θ, ϕ
Repression	Low θ, ϕ, ξ, R High ν	Low θ, ϕ, R High ν, ξ	n/a
Civil war	Low θ, ϕ, ξ, ν High R	Low θ, ϕ, ν High ξ, R	n/a

Tolstoy's famous novel quoted at the beginning of this chapter.[1] "All prosperous countries resemble each other; every nonprosperous country is nonprosperous in its own way." To reflect this observation, we refer to Table 5.1 in what follows as the Anna Karenina matrix.

The Predatory State Redux In Chapter 3, we defined a predatory state as one in which the incumbent does not invest in legal capacity at all, leaving private producers open to predation by elites. The persistence of such states is a function of weak governance—a low value of parameter ζ introduced in Section 3.2.4. In Section 4.2.4, we noted that a predatory state is also likely to be prone to repression and civil war by increasing the benefits and lowering the cost of violence.

As we discussed in Chapter 3, a predatory state can arise (in principle) alongside any kind of state in Table 5.1. Thus, it is an additional dimension of state classification. Visually, this would mean turning our 3×3 matrix into a $3 \times 3 \times 2$ box, where the added dimension would exposit whether governance—as represented by parameter ζ—is good or bad. Bad governance would become a further source of nonprosperity, with a direct negative effect on income and an indirect negative effect on violence and state building.

In practice, we would not expect common-interest states to be predatory, mainly because institutions that create high θ also create high ζ. The mileage

1. Diamond (1997) also refers to an Anna Karenina principle, although with a slightly different meaning. In his version, a certain property (failed domestication of animals) arises whenever any one out of several (necessary) conditions fails. In our version, there is also only one way to succeed, but different kinds of failure lead to (predictably) different outcomes.

offered in terms of state classifications would likely reside in further enriching the description of state pathologies. A state that is both predatory and weak is in the very worst situation, with no incentives for state building and very poor incentives for peace. Political institutions that generate low equilibrium turnover [low $\Gamma(Z, \nu, \xi)$] and little cohesiveness (low θ) may subdivide into predatory and nonpredatory states depending on how well political elites are kept under control.

An exciting challenge for future empirical work would be to see to what extent these different pathologies can be identified empirically and to what extent their implications for government behavior can be understood.

5.5 Final Remarks

The overarching theoretical approach in this chapter sheds some light on the problems of weak and fragile states. We have shown that the pathologies of fragile states are rooted in low common interests, noncohesive political institutions, resource or aid dependence, and technologies that favor the use of violence. Phenomena such as civil war, repression, low income per capita, low spending on common-interest goods, low taxation, and weak enforcement of property rights are all symptoms, rather than determinants, of fragile states.

Most existing approaches to fragile states in the development policy community are not derived from an underlying theory, which explains why they tend to conflate symptoms with causes. For example, low income per capita is frequently used as a criterion in fragility indexes. Although it is true that low income may increase the incentives for violence, everything else being equal, it is only an intermediate factor.

The real challenge posed by the Anna Karenina matrix is twofold. The first challenge concerns foreign intervention. What if anything can the international community do to improve the situation of weak and fragile states? To discuss this challenge, we have to use our framework to study development assistance. The advantage of relying on a specific theoretical structure is that it provides a clear sense of the margins where we might see an equilibrium response should a bilateral or multilateral actor intervene. The framework summarized in the Anna Karenina matrix will thus help us analyze the pros and cons of various forms of development assistance in different types of states. This is the topic of Chapter 6.

The second challenge concerns political institutions. Why do we not see more political reforms taking place to move states out of the lower left-hand part of the matrix? This is a natural question, given the apparent benefits of escaping from the different dimensions of nonprosperity into the prosperous uppermost right corner. Clearly, any attempt to say something about this challenge must rely on an analysis that starts to endogenize political institutions. This is the topic of Chapter 7.

5.6 *Notes on the Literature*

Weingast (2005) provides a classification of state types that shares features in common with our approach. These ideas are further refined and developed in North, Weingast, and Wallis (2009), whose work most closely shares the ambition in this chapter of understanding the development of a state where political violence is a possibility. Bates (2001) discusses the links between establishing peace and prosperity in contemporary Africa.

However, to the best of our knowledge, the joint determination of state capacity, political violence, and income in an integrated formal framework is new. Although many authors have analyzed some of the partial relations in the data, theoretically and empirically, the comprehensive analysis pursued in this chapter does not have any counterpart in earlier research. The closest antecedent known to us is the paper by Caselli (2006) referenced in the text of Section 5.1.2.

The various empirical classifications of countries into weak or fragile states do employ multidimensional criteria, including the main state pathologies we have emphasized here, but often do not distinguish clearly between determinants and outcomes. Rice and Patrick (2008) give an overview of different attempts to measure state weakness or fragility. The heterogeneity of state pathologies and the link to political institutions are discussed by Vallings and Moreno-Torres (2005).

This chapter is related to the large literature on the resource curse. Mehlum, Moene, and Torvik (2006) offer an approach that is intellectually related to the one taken here, linking these arguments to the quality of institutions, theoretically and empirically. The seminal empirical paper on the resource curse, as a problem for income, is Sachs and Warner (2001) [see also Sachs and Warner (1995)]. Torvik (2002) formalizes this argument using a rent-seeking framework and Robinson, Torvik, and Verdier (2006) take a political-economics approach. Torvik (2009) and van der Ploeg (2011) provide useful overviews of the state of knowledge, and the volume edited by Humphreys, Sachs, and Stiglitz (2007) contains a recent collection of essays on the resource curse.

Our discussion in Section 5.2 of how conflict affects investment is linked to the literature on the impact of civil conflict on incomes. Evidence on the negative impact of conflict on economic activity and well-being in various contexts can be found, e.g., in Abadie and Gardeazabal (2003); Besley and Mueller (2010); Blomberg and Hess (2002); Collier (1999); Coyne, Dempster, and Isaacs (2010); Goldin and Lewis (1975); Skaperdas (2010); and Zussman, Zussman, and Orregaard Nielsen (2008).

CHAPTER 6

Development Assistance

In Africa today, we recognize that trade and investment, and not aid, are pillars of development.

Paul Kagame, president of Rwanda, speech in Kigali, 2004

In Chapter 5 we used our framework to focus on the common determinants of state pathologies, particularly those owing to noncohesive political institutions and weak common interests. The findings were summarized in the Anna Karenina matrix of Table 5.1. But the rest of the world does not, for the most part, stand idly by leaving countries in conflict and with poorly functioning states to their own devices. A whole development industry—comprising international organizations, donor governments, and nongovernmental organizations (NGOs)—tries to influence the paths of developing countries and are intent on offering a helping hand. In this chapter, we look at such efforts through the lens of our approach as developed in the first five chapters of the book.[1]

We approach development assistance by supposing that an external agency, such as a donor government or multilateral organization, is considering some form of intervention. The conventional intervention has been foreign assistance in the form of a transfer to increase the recipient government's budget. In the context of our comprehensive core model, such an infusion of resources can be modeled like an increase in natural resource rents. The analysis of cash aid in our core model is novel because it considers the equilibrium responses to larger aid flows on a number of margins: policy choices, investments in state capacity, and investments in political violence. We develop a cost-benefit calculus for additional budgetary support viewed from the donor's perspective when the recipient country's responses are taken into account. This illustrates how the benefits depend on the recipient country's circumstances and institutions.

1. This chapter is closely related to Besley and Persson (2011).

Unrestricted budgetary support is beholden the recipient country's whims. Aid agencies and international organizations typically try to influence policy in such countries. Whether such conditionality is feasible in practice has been widely debated. Our model illustrates the potential benefits of making cash aid conditional on decisions made by the recipient government, It does so by identifying specific pathologies that might be solved by such conditionality. However, given the incentive-compatibility problems involved, we are not able to address whether such conditionality is likely to be effective in practice.

Our framework can also be used to consider the impact of different forms of noncash aid. Some of these are extremely controversial, as in the case of foreign military intervention or supply of weapons to governments or rebels. As our comprehensive core model allows for a margin of behavioral change affecting political violence, we are able to address these issues, in theory at least. We also consider the less controversial area of technical assistance, i.e., foreign interventions aimed directly at increasing the capabilities of the state. Finally, we briefly consider governance reforms. Such interventions tend to arise in postconflict situations in an attempt to reconcile group differences and hence to make peace credible.

Throughout this chapter, we take the nature of political institutions as given, as we have done in the book thus far. In the next chapter, however, we analyze endogenous political reform, and then we again address the question of whether development assistance may have beneficial or harmful effects on political institutions.

Some Basic Facts A large amount of aid is given by rich countries to nations in the developing world. Official Development Assistance (ODA) comes mainly from the 23 members of the Development Assistance Committee (DAC). According to the OECD, the total figure in 2009 was around \$123 billion (this figure, as all those that follow, is in fixed 2008 prices), which is the highest number ever recorded. Although the amount of aid kept increasing in the post-war period, it started falling immediately after the end of the Cold War, but then picked up again. In 2002 it surpassed its previous peak of \$86 billion from 1992, and has been increasing ever since. Aid targets for rich countries have been set at 0.7% of Gross National Income, but very few countries meet these targets and, in fact, the trend is declining over time. The amount of aid from the DAC countries today stands at about 0.31 of their total GDP, as opposed to 0.54 in 1961.

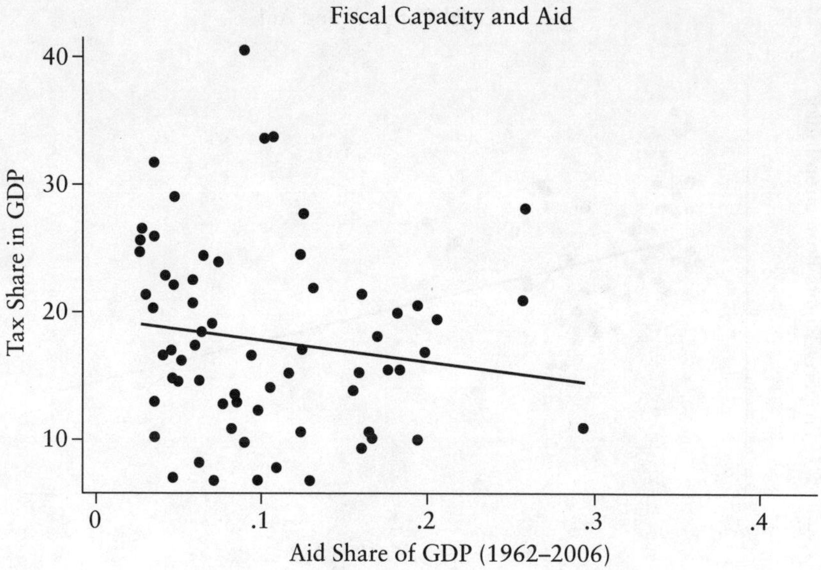

Figure 6.1 Tax share in GDP versus aid share in GDP.

Out of the $120 billion of total ODA given in 2008, some 30% was given indirectly through contributions to multilateral institutions such as the European Union and the World Bank. About one-sixth came in the form of technical cooperation (plus additional indirect amounts through multilateral institutions). On top of ODA, additional aid is given through the private and institutional sector, with more than $20 billion channeled by NGOs. The largest regional recipient of aid is Sub-Saharan Africa, which received 33% of all ODA in 2007–2008, followed by 21% to Middle East–North Africa, about 15% each to South-Central Asia and the rest of Asia, 9% to Latin America, and 4% to Europe.[2]

How does received aid at the country level correlate with the variables of greatest interest in our theory? We saw in Chapter 4 that receiving aid appears to be positively partially correlated with political violence. How does aid correlate with other central outcomes in the raw data? Figure 6.1 plots received aid against fiscal capacity. The vertical axis shows a measure of the average level of aid per capita since the 1990s (based on data from the World

2. See OECD (2010b) for these background figures. Gupta, Pattillo, and Wagh (2006) give an overview of trends in overall aid flows during 1960–2004.

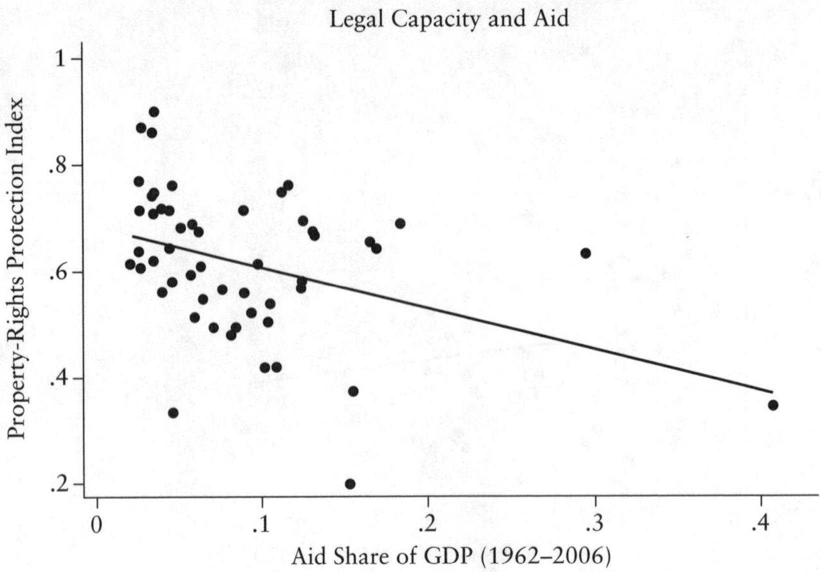

Figure 6.2 Property-rights protection versus aid share in GDP.

Development Indicators). The horizontal axis shows one of our core measures of fiscal capacity—the share of income taxes in total taxes. As expected, these variables are negatively correlated.

Figure 6.2 plots the same aid measure against one of our key measures of legal capacity—from the ICRG data on government antidiversion policy. This also shows a negative correlation with the aid share.

The Context and Different Views on Aid Exactly what can be done to improve the well-being of citizens in poor nations has been a controversial topic throughout the postwar period.[3] As we just discussed, foreign aid flows from rich to poor countries have been the main vehicle for improving the situation of poor countries. But the efficacy of such development assistance remains contested.

A shining example, which buoyed interest and enthusiasm for aid, was the experience of the Marshall Plan for rebuilding post–World War II Germany and other parts of Europe. Between 1948 and 1951, the United States transferred some $13 billion to European economies. This episode created a sense that large-scale resource transfers could make a significant difference to economic

3. See Riddell (2007) for a review. Temple (2010) provides an excellent review of many of the economic debates.

development, a sense that was further underpinned by the so-called Truman Doctrine, which called for a global focus on the plight of the developing world.

Traditionalists The Marshall Plan fueled the belief that lack of resources is the key impediment to economic development and that aid flows are necessary to build public institutions and stocks of capital. A country might eventually achieve a successful development path if left to itself, but a helping hand of international transfers would speed up that progress. This view was institutionalized in a network of development banks, such as the International Bank for Reconstruction and Development (IBRD), known simply as the World Bank; the Asian Development Bank; the Inter-American Development Bank; and the European Bank for Reconstruction and Development. Chenery and Strout (1966) is a key exposition of the underlying ideas, and Sachs (2005) is a modern statement of a similar view.

This "gap-oriented" traditional view of aid is one of the crucial underpinnings of the huge aid flows from developed countries. Cost-benefit analysis is the handmaiden of the traditional view, and the notion is that aid should be spent on the projects with the highest social returns. Whether such analyses are conducted in practice—by donors or recipients of aid—is questionable. Moreover, even if it is, the question remains as to whether all margins relevant to the impact of projects can be captured.

Pessimists The real-world experience has not fulfilled the rather romantic vision of aid traditionalists. Aid pessimists point to the fact that much of the aid advanced would not survive any reasonable cost-benefit test. Domestic political agendas of governments in poor countries have frequently not supported economic development, and these governments often lack the technical competence to spend resources wisely. The result, it is argued, is that much aid is wasted and does not contribute to developmental ends. Bauer (1972, 1975) was an early aid pessimist, and a more modern aid critique is stated strongly in Easterly (2006).[4]

Just what to make of this view of aid is moot. A drastic response would be simply to cut off all aid, in the belief that the long-run prospects for countries would be better in the absence of international transfers. This response is closely

4. Djankov, Montalvo, and Reynal-Querol (2008) argue that aid leads to a deterioration in the quality of institutions.

linked to the resource-curse view, which identifies natural resources with slow development and possibly with decline rather than progress.

Another response to a failure of aid would be to argue in favor of greater conditionality, trying to condition the receipt of aid on specific policies or institutional reforms. But the real aid pessimists are skeptical. Conditionality frequently creates soft conditions and there is overwhelming pressure from the development community to disperse funds allocated to development assistance. Far from being an indication of problems in recipient countries, a failure to disperse ODA is thought of as a failure of the donor countries. Thus committing to aid conditionality is hard or infeasible.

Conditional Optimists More recently, some observers have attempted to reconcile the two views by being more optimistic on conditionality and the ability of analysts to identify the underlying pathologies. Certainly, traditionalists have had a naive view of the workings of political institutions or the ability of aid agencies to navigate around political constraints and allocate resources to high-return projects. Without a more forthright analysis of the institutional environment, it is hard to make progress. Collier (2007) can be seen as an exponent of this revisionist view.

In terms of the Anna Karenina matrix in Table 5.1, a state away from the top right-hand corner may have a variety of potential symptoms and these have a variety of causes. Moreover, the problems may change in response to shocks, such as resource prices and natural disasters. Effective development assistance has to tailor the right form of intervention to circumstances and institutional context. This opens up the menu of possibilities to include the right mix of budgetary, project, military, and technical assistance and to make the right degree of conditionality credible.

Plan of the Chapter The chapter is organized as follows. In Section 6.1, we use the comprehensive core model to analyze aid. We start by taking a close look at cash aid, followed by a brief discussion of conditionality. Then, we go on to various forms of noncash aid, including military intervention. Concluding comments are offered in Section 6.2, followed by notes on the literature.

6.1 The Core Model with Aid

We use our comprehensive core model, formulated in Section 4.1 and solved in Sections 4.1 and 5.1. In the analysis, we assume that the primary objective of the international community is the ex ante welfare of citizens in a country where it intervenes. This neglects the role of strategic objectives, which could explain the willingness of countries to donate.[5] We also assume away coordination problems by analyzing a single intervention rather than the plethora of sometimes uncoordinated actions that characterize the aid industry. Our perspective thus supposes that a foreign government or multilateral organization makes a cash transfer to a developing country. The question is how this affects the behavior of the recipient government, opposition groups, and, ultimately, the welfare of citizens.

Our model suggests a number of natural margins to focus on. First, the *policy dimension*: (g_s, r_s^I, r_s^O). Does development assistance increase or decrease spending on public goods at the expense of redistributive transfers? Second, the *state-capacity dimension*: (π_s, τ_s). In what way do different forms of development assistance influence the incentive to build fiscal or legal capacity? Third, the *political-violence dimension*: (L^I, L^O). How does development assistance affect incentives of both the incumbent and opposition to use violence as a means of winning or securing power?

6.1.1 Cash Aid

We begin by applying a cost-benefit style analysis of cash aid. Suppose that an aid agency considers disbursing some budgetary resources to a particular country at date 2. Let the shadow price of this aid in the donor country be $\hat{\lambda}$, where we assume that $\hat{\lambda} \geq 1$. This means that aid that is transferred to pure private consumption is not worthwhile (or just barely worthwhile). But some readers may think that the donor's shadow price should be set lower than that because of distributional concerns or exigencies of donor aid agencies to expend allocated funds at all cost. Such readers can easily convert the propositions in this chapter from a set of decisionmaking criteria to a ranking of the payoffs to different varieties of aid in different types of countries.

Depending on circumstances and institutions, the additional resources might affect public-goods spending, state-capacity investments, and transfers (or, in a more general model, tax levels). We model cash aid as an increase in the recipient government's budget, which we denote by ΔR. This acts like an increase in Z in the previous model. In the benchmark case, we use the formulation where $V(g) = g$, i.e., utility is linear in public goods. But sometimes we refer to the case studied in Section 2.2.2, with quasi-linear preferences and a concave utility

5. See the discussion in Alesina and Dollar (2000) and OECD (2010a).

function $V(g)$. This is because some additional and interesting margins of behavior are captured in this latter case.

The timing of the model is now modified as follows:

1. We begin with initial stocks of state capacities $\{\tau_1, \pi_1\}$ and an incumbent group I_1. Nature determines α_1 and R.

2. The development assistance agency now considers whether to offer ΔR to be paid in period 2.

3. I_1 chooses a set of period-1 policies $\{t_1, r_1^I, r_1^O, p_1^I, p_1^O, g_1\}$, and determines (through investments) the period-2 stocks of fiscal and legal capacity $\{\tau_2, \pi_2\}$. I_1 and O_1 simultaneously invest in violence levels L^I and L^O.

4. I_1 remains in power with probability $1 - \Gamma(Z, \nu, \xi)$, and nature determines α_2.

5. I_2 chooses period-2 policies $\{t_2, r_2^I, r_2^O, p_2^I, p_2^O, g_2\}$.

We are interested in the impact of ΔR determined at stage 2 of the model. In deciding whether to offer aid, we assume that the aid agency can see through the government's subsequent equilibrium choices and takes the policy responses into account. In effect, the aid agency is applying backward induction to the moves outlined earlier. Thus, our aid agency is both farsighted and rational, the best possible scenario for effective policymaking.

Aid Effects in the Absence of Violence We start by analyzing the situation when the parameters governing violence outcomes outside of the common-interest state, namely R, ν, and ξ, are such that there is no risk of either repression or civil war (we are essentially in the upper row of the Anna Karenina matrix).

We then have the following benchmark result:

Proposition 6.1: *In a common-interest state with linear demand for public goods, cash aid is worthwhile if and only if* $\phi\alpha_H + (1 - \phi)\alpha_L > \hat{\lambda}$.

The logic of this result is clear. If $2(1 - \theta) \geq \alpha_L$, all future spending is devoted to public goods regardless of the realization of α_2. Furthermore, by definition there is also no conflict risk in this case (as showed in Proposition 4.1). In ex ante terms, ΔR will therefore be spent on public goods, with a value of

$\phi\alpha_H + (1-\phi)\,\alpha_L$. This benefit to the receiving society is compared to the cost of $\hat{\lambda} \geq 1$.

In the common-interest state, it would actually not make any difference whether development assistance comes as budgetary aid or as direct support for specific projects. There is complete congruence of interest between the aid donor and the recipient government.

Suppose instead that the cohesiveness condition fails, but that there is no propensity to political violence. When $\alpha_2 = \alpha_L$, the additional resources are spent on transfers rather than on public goods. Then, Proposition 6.1 is modified to the following:

Proposition 6.2: *In a weak or redistributive state with linear demand for public goods, cash aid is worthwhile if and only if* $\phi\alpha_H + (1-\phi) > \hat{\lambda}$.

In this case, the value of aid is lower than in the benchmark case of Proposition 6.1 because with some probability it will just be spent on transfers with an ex ante welfare effect of unity. It is even possible that aid does not yield a gross return above unity, as $\phi \to 0$. This result concurs with the frequently made observation, discussed in Collier and Dollar (2004), inter alia, that the impact of aid is more favorable when institutions are stronger.

The Bauer Paradox Propositions 6.1 and 6.2 allow us to reflect upon an observation made by Peter Bauer, which Temple (2010) has christened the *Bauer paradox*. His view is succinctly stated in the following quote: "A government unable to identify . . . projects or collect taxes is unlikely to be able to use aid productively" (Bauer, 1975, p. 400). Being able to identify projects is like having high α_H and/or high ϕ. As emphasized in earlier chapters, it is countries with more cohesive political institutions (high θ) that are likely to be able to collect taxes (have a high fiscal capacity, τ). Hence, these are the governments where Proposition 6.1 applies. But when θ and ϕ are low, aid is less likely to be used productively and the government is less likely to build fiscal capacity.

Crowding Out of Fiscal Capacity? In the benchmark model, granting cash aid in a common-interest state makes no difference to investments in state capacity. But this is due to the fact that utility is linear in public goods. In the case where $V(g)$ is increasing and concave, this aspect of the model is changed in interesting ways and captures some aspects of the more skeptical view of aid and its impact.

To illustrate this, let us study the case of quasi-linear preferences from Section 2.2.2, where there is only a fiscal-capacity investment. Aid can now yield a resource-curse-style result, in the sense that it does not lead to any increase in investment in fiscal capacity or to additional spending on public goods. In that setting, as we saw in Section 2.2.2,[6] where α_s is not stochastic, optimal fiscal-capacity investment is given by $\hat{\tau}_2$ defined from

$$\alpha V_g \left(R + \Delta R + \hat{\tau}_2 \omega\right) = 1 + \frac{\mathcal{F}_\tau \left(\hat{\tau}_2 - \tau_1\right)}{\omega}. \tag{6.1}$$

It should be clear from (6.1) that the optimal level of fiscal capacity now depends on aid. Using the implicit-function theorem, we have that

$$\frac{\partial \hat{\tau}_2}{\partial \Delta R} = \frac{\alpha V_{gg} \left(R + \Delta R + \hat{\tau}_2 \omega\right)}{\frac{\mathcal{F}_{\tau\tau}(\hat{\tau}_2 - \tau_1)}{\omega} - \alpha \omega V_{gg} \left(R + \Delta R + \hat{\tau}_2 \omega\right)} < 0.$$

In other words, more aid means a reduction in fiscal-capacity investments.

From Section 2.2.2, we also recall that the cohesiveness condition now has to be rewritten as $\alpha V_g \left(R + \Delta R + \hat{\tau}_2 \omega\right) \geq 2\left(1 - \theta\right)$. For a large enough ΔR, this condition could fail, leading to a transition to a weak or redistributive state. Thus aid dependence (like resource dependence) can undermine investments in the state. This argument has quite commonly been made in the literature on aid and taxation and is consistent with the pattern displayed earlier in Figure 6.1.

Crowding Out of Public Goods? As long as the cohesiveness condition continues to hold, all period-2 spending is on public goods. With curvature in the utility function, the effect of an increase in aid on public-goods provision in period 2 becomes

$$\begin{aligned} \frac{dg_2}{d\Delta R} &= \left[1 + \frac{\partial \hat{\tau}_2}{\partial \Delta R} \omega\right] \\ &= \left[\frac{\frac{\mathcal{F}_{\tau\tau}(\hat{\tau}_2 - \tau_1)}{\omega}}{\frac{\mathcal{F}_{\tau\tau}(\hat{\tau}_2 - \tau_1)}{\omega} - \alpha \omega V_{gg} \left(R + \Delta R + \hat{\tau}_2 \omega\right)}\right] \in [0, 1]. \end{aligned}$$

6. Observe that, unlike in Section 2.2.2, we are not assuming any depreciation in fiscal capacity between periods, i.e., $\delta = 0$.

The fact that the derivative is less than one represents a "crowding out" effect, whereby higher aid reduces the investment in fiscal capacity and thus dilutes the aid effect on public goods provision.

When the cohesiveness condition does not hold, spending on public goods is given by

$$\alpha V_g\left(g_2\right) = 2\left(1 - \theta\right).$$

This means that the marginal utility of public goods in period 2 is fixed. Thus, the provision of public goods is also fixed and not affected by aid at the margin. As $\alpha V_g\left(g_2\right)$ is fixed, so is the equilibrium investment in fiscal capacity, independently of ΔR, given that we are in a redistributive state. (As before, the weak state does not invest in fiscal capacity at all.) Any aid in period 2 is therefore entirely spent on transfers.

We can summarize the cost-benefit result on aid as follows:

Proposition 6.3: *Suppose that the government is investing only in fiscal capacity and that there is curvature in the demand for public goods. Then*

1. *In a common-interest state, cash aid is worthwhile if and only if* $\alpha V_g\left(R + \Delta R + \hat{\tau}_2\omega\right) > \hat{\lambda}$.
2. *In a redistributive or weak state, aid has no impact on the provision of public goods and state-capacity investments, so that cash aid is never worthwhile.*

In the common-interest state, the result follows from the crowding-out effects and the fact that the direct effects of the induced change in fiscal-capacity investment drop out of welfare owing to the envelope theorem. The model would be somewhat more complicated if we allowed for investment in both fiscal and legal capacity. However, the essence of the point made here would be the same—aid dependence can show up in lower investment in fiscal capacity.

In the redistributive or weak state, the ex ante welfare effect of aid is equal to one, i.e., the marginal utility of redistributive transfers summed over the two groups, which is no higher than the shadow cost of funds given by $\hat{\lambda}$.

Aid would, of course, be worthwhile if there were a pure redistributive motive for aid captured by $\hat{\lambda} < 1$. But in the redistributive or weak state such aid would be transferred predominantly to the ruling group. In a model where the donor had preferences over distribution within the recipient country, it would care about which groups receive the cash transfer made possible by aid. For example, "maximin" preferences between groups would mean that the donor cared only about the 2θ per unit of transfers going to the opposition group. In this case, cash aid is worthwhile only if $\hat{\lambda} < 2\theta$.

Proposition 6.3 illustrates clearly why donors have to understand the political equilibrium of the country receiving aid. Assistance that appears worthwhile under naive assumptions, e.g., that all policy will remain the same, is no longer welfare improving when changes in policy are taken into account. But it is also clear that second-guessing such equilibrium responses is extremely difficult, and it would be hard to point to any settled body of empirical knowledge that makes this feasible. Moreover, there would not be any point in looking at the average relationship between aid provision and fiscal-capacity building, as any concrete case very much reflects the specific environment of the recipient country. But the fact that we have little evidence is not the same as saying that we know such effects to be unimportant in practice.

Aid Effects in the Presence of Violence We now revert to the model with linear demand for public goods and consider the case where θ is low enough that the cohesiveness condition does not hold and ϕ is low enough that the state is prone to political violence. This adds two considerations to the comparative statics when we assess the effect of cash aid on welfare. There is an impact on the use of political violence, and there is also a new effect, through political stability, on investments in state capacity.

In terms of our earlier analysis, the effect of higher cash aid is an increase in Z, which, as we know from Proposition 4.2, may, in theory, increase the occurrence of political violence. The empirical results in Section 4.4 also give a hint that this dismal prediction may indeed be borne out in practice. In the current framework, a higher value of Z has two effects on welfare. First, it leads to more resources being allocated to violence, a measure that is directly unproductive. Second, when deciding on violence, one group does not internalize this effect on the welfare of the other group, thus leading to a strategic inefficiency. We summarize this as follows:

Proposition 6.4: *In a weak or redistributive state, which is prone to political violence, a small increase in cash aid is welfare improving if*

$$\phi\alpha_H + (1 - \phi) - \omega(\pi_1)\frac{dL}{dZ} > \hat{\lambda}$$

where

$$\frac{dL}{dZ} = \begin{cases} \left[\lambda_1 \frac{dL^I}{dZ} + \nu \frac{dL^O}{dZ}\right] & \text{if } Z > Z^O(\theta; \nu, \xi) \\ \lambda_1 \frac{dL^I}{dZ} & \text{if } Z^O(\theta; \nu, \xi) \geq Z > Z^I(\theta, \lambda_1; \xi). \end{cases}$$

As before, with $\alpha_2 = \alpha_H$ resources are spent on public goods, whereas with $\alpha_2 = \alpha_L$ resources are spent on transfers. The key point is that aid now also has an impact on the equilibrium level of violence.[7] This is reflected in the third term, which is deducted from the value of any public goods and transfers generated by aid. Compared to Proposition 6.2, it is less likely that cash aid is worthwhile, owing to the additional welfare cost of the resources wasted on violence. Indeed, cash aid may very well lower ex ante welfare, especially when ϕ is low and a great deal of the expected aid is dissipated through investments in violence. To get tighter results, we would have to be more specific about the conflict technology.

But more violence affects political stability as directly stated in Proposition 5.1:

Proposition 6.5: *In a redistributive state, which is prone to political violence, cash aid can increase political stability and increase the investments in fiscal and legal capacity.*

This effect comes through the fact that when institutions are not cohesive foreign aid allows incumbents to entrench themselves and cement their control on power. [8] The most clear-cut example is the case of a repressive regime. If aid is given to such a regime, then the incentive to hang on to power is enhanced. Greater repression induces more political stability, which results in more state-capacity investment all else being equal. But the benefits are partly allocated to increased use of military force and accrue disproportionately to the incumbent group.

Conditionality The assumption so far in this analysis is that the donor and the recipient government cannot contract directly over the policy and investment decisions when aid is granted. Conditionality should be thought of as a

7. We showed in Chapter 4 that, under Assumption 4.1, the level of violence used by both groups is increasing in Z.

8. Formally, the result follows from using the state-capacity Euler equations in Chapter 5 and recalling from Proposition 5.1 that $\Gamma(\cdot)$ is decreasing in Z.

contracting problem, where the donor specifies an array of observable and verifiable decisions by the recipient government in exchange for ΔR. As with any interesting contracting problem, the real issue is what can reasonably be supposed to be observed and verified and thus potentially enforced. Enforcement is a particular issue in this context, given that the world has nothing equivalent to an international court that can enforce agreements. Indeed, this is often thought of as a major obstacle to effective aid conditionality.[9]

Nonetheless, it is interesting to see how the results we have derived may help us think about conditionality. Propositions 6.2 and 6.4 highlight the possibility that conditionality that ensures that aid is spent on public goods could be valuable to a donor. In the case of Proposition 6.2, successful conditionality would raise the return to giving aid.

In the case of Proposition 6.4, conditionality might ensure that fewer resources are spent on violence. However, to achieve the desired effect, conditionality would have to be binding on both the incumbent and the opposition.

Proposition 6.3 opens up the door for other forms of conditionality, where an attempt is made to influence the decisions on investments in the state. In this case the giving of aid would have to be dependent on such investments taking place.

Again, these prospective benefits require that conditionality can be credibly enforced. An interesting agenda for future research would be to combine aspects of our framework with explicit modeling of mechanisms that might help achieve credible enforcement, as in Svensson (2003). External players potentially have several prospective instruments, whereby they can give a future prize in return for present and continued good behavior. This could include membership in or association with desirable clubs like the European Union (something used by the European Union to influence political and economic reform in Turkey and earlier in Eastern Europe). Another possibility might involve debt concessions (or free-trade agreements) such as the ones currently negotiated by the European Union with Pakistan and some African countries as well as by the United States with several countries in Latin America.

6.1.2 Technical Assistance

Although budgetary aid is certainly very important, foreign interventions also come in a variety of other forms. In the following subsections, we consider the

9. See Svensson (2000b, 2003) for early analyses of the credibility problems with conditionality.

possibility of development assistance in forms other than cash aid. As we shall see, it is possible to represent these forms of assistance as efforts by donors to influence parameters other than R in the comprehensive core model. We begin by considering technical assistance.

Technical assistance refers to the transfers of skills and knowledge that can be useful in improving the operations of the recipient government. Gupta, Pattillo, and Wagh (2006) discuss the changing composition of aid flows and show that technical assistance has been increasing, both in real terms and as a share of total ODA, since the 1960s. Estimates from the OECD (2010b) suggest that at least one-sixth of direct official aid in 2008 is given in this form. However, some people refer to technical assistance as *phantom aid,* as it is often rendererd by international consultants who reside in the donor country. The evaluation of returns to technical assistance is notoriously difficult. But the returns are likely to be specific to the context and the nature of the intervention under consideration. Technical assistance can come in many forms. Our model suggests a focus on two of these: (1) efforts to increase the benefits or reduce the costs of providing public goods, and (2) efforts to cut the cost of investing in state capacity. We discuss these two cases here and demonstrate how their impact can be thought of in the model framework of this book.

Identifying Good Projects Assistance that helps to identify good projects can be thought of as raising α or ϕ (the value of public goods or the probability of a high-value state). An important line of development research in recent years has been the use of Randomized Controlled Trials (RCTs) to identify the value of public interventions. These can be thought of as trying to find ways of better allocating resources to public goods by identifying high-benefit interventions. [See Duflo et al. (2007) for a discussion of the methodology.]

In our framework, we can think about an RCT as a particular form of experiment to evaluate project effectiveness. Instead of the common two-point distribution of α_s, let us return to the continuous distribution on $[1, \alpha_H]$, where $\alpha_H > 2$ with distribution $H(\alpha)$ that we introduced in Section 2.2.2. Suppose that α_s represents a public project drawn at random from the H distribution in each period. If $\alpha_s \geq 2(1-\theta)$, the project will go ahead, and if not the government will spend on transfers. Further, suppose that before choosing the project, the government conducts N trials of possible interventions, perhaps with the help of J-PAL at MIT. A well-meaning government will then pick the best project based on these trials. Now $\alpha_s = \max\left\{\alpha^1, \ldots, \alpha^N\right\}$, where α_n is the nth independent draw from $H(\alpha)$. In technical terms, α_s becomes the Nth-order statistic (the maximum) of the sample. It follows that an increase in N leads to a first-order stochastically dominating shift in the ex ante value of public goods.

The analyses in Chapters 2 and 3 imply that such an increase in the value of public goods will lead to higher investments in both fiscal and legal capacity, at least in common-interest and redistributive states. Given the results in Chapter 4, the higher value of α_s also makes conflict less likely (for given θ).

Proposition 6.6: *Technical assistance that increases* α_H *or* ϕ *increases welfare and investment in state capacity. It also reduces the likelihood of political violence.*

Technical assistance can also be directed toward raising α_L. In our framework, this could even lead to the creation of a common-interest state, with its virtuous consequences. In the case describe here, the cost of the intervention should thus be weighed against the larger amounts of public goods that will be provided because of both a higher direct return and higher investments in fiscal and legal capacity.

Although these observations are useful, they sweep a host of important problems under the rug. First, there is a scaling-up issue. Can the conditions in small controlled trials really be replicated when they are implemented in a large program by a government? This question is particularly acute since many RCTs are implemented directly by NGOs, with limited contact with the recipient government. Second, in assuming that the government budget will be spent either on public goods or transfers, depending on the value of α, we have not considered any of the issues discussed in Sections 3.2.4 and 4.2.4 associated with a corrupt state run by a small elite.

Improving State Capabilities Another type of technical assistance would be to reduce investment costs—improving state capabilities. Interventions in this spirit are quite common in development assistance and can crudely be represented in the model as shifts in the functions $\mathcal{F}(\cdot)$ and $\mathcal{L}(\cdot)$. Applying Proposition 3.4 to this interpretation, we have the following:

Proposition 6.7: *Technical assistance that reduces the cost of investing in state capacity,* $\mathcal{F}(\cdot)$ *and* $\mathcal{L}(\cdot)$, *increases welfare and investment in state capacity. Such assistance will raise the likelihood of political violence, all else being equal.*

Our framework makes sense of these types of interventions. Examples include giving advice on tax collection and the creation of specialized courts to expedite the resolution of business disputes. Interventions could even mean advice about fundamental changes in the nature of the legal code. The (perhaps surprising) effect on political violence comes from the fact that Z goes up when state-capacity investments increase, which, by Proposition 5.1, may lead to an increase in political violence in redistributive or weak states, as the redistributive value of holding office is now higher.

Taking Stock When it comes to technical assistance, our model shows the same complementarity between the value of aid and cohesive institutions that we saw in the case of cash aid. Technical assistance is more powerful in countries where public resources are more likely to be allocated for the common good. Thus, the return to RCTs might be lower in weak or redistributive states if they are intended to inform the government about the value of good policies.

In the aid community there is indeed considerable debate about the effectiveness of technical assistance. Observers such as Berg (1993), Gupta, Pattillo, and Wagh (2006), and the contributors to UNDP (2002) point to problems where donor-funded institutional capacity building is generally considered less effective than cooperation around hard technical projects. These evaluations confirm that recipient-country governments often do not have much involvement in or control over technical assistance programs.

This critique rhymes well with the challenges we have already mentioned in transposing the results of successful RCTs to the macro level, with a view to generating a self-sustaining effect on overall public-goods provision and investments in state capacity. Nevertheless, this is an important instance where microeconomic and macroeconomic research on development might meet productively. An important issue for further research is thus to analyze how successful interventions can be designed and scaled up, in practice, given the kind of systematic incentive problems that we have emphasized throughout this book.

6.1.3 Military Assistance

We now turn to military assistance, as it is represented in the comprehensive core model. Specifically, think about the recipient government receiving assistance in regard to military technology or strategy as a change in ξ (the marginal return at zero investments in violence for the government relative to the opposition). Such assistance could involve training or provision of weapon systems or intelligence.[10] In principle, this could be offered to opposition groups as well, and external governments could also intervene directly by providing manpower to rebels. Such cases have often occurred in practice, e.g., the U.S. support for the Mujahideen in their insurgency against the Soviets in Afghanistan during the 1980s and the deployment of Cuban troops to support the MPLA rebels in Angola during the 1970s. But here we focus on the case where support is offered to the government.

Our core result, which follows directly from Propositions 4.2 and 5.2, is as follows:

Proposition 6.8: *Military assistance that increases ξ, augmenting the military capacity of the incumbent government, increases the parameter range in which there is repression. This increases political stability and investments in fiscal and legal capacity.*

If institutions are weak, the higher political stability owing to greater repression increases political stability and thereby state-capacity investments. But this comes at the price of increasing the entrenchment of the incumbent. In effect, this can create a rentier state, where the opposition group is frozen out of power. Military intervention to help any incumbent will therefore tend to increase the incentives for the incumbent to invest. But it is not a substitute for more consensual institutions (higher θ). This story seems relevant, perhaps especially for the Cold War, but also for modern-day fragile states with ongoing or latent conflicts.

6.1.4 Postconflict Assistance

Finally, we briefly consider attempts by external actors to assist in the process of promoting peace in postconflict situations. Our model allows us to represent this in a very stylized fashion.

Peace-keeping or disarming the rebels can be thought of as raising ν (the cost for the opposition group of investing in a given level of violence). By Proposition 5.2, this reduces the parameter range in which there is conflict and increases political stability. Many postconflict settlements can also be thought

10. We have in mind forms of assistance that would not ordinarily be available in world markets.

of as efforts to raise θ (diminishing the gain to the winner of the conflict). By Propositions 4.1 and 4.2, this will reduce the risk of violence. However, the latter effect requires that interventions are expected and credible ex ante. A recent example of setting up such a mechanism was attempted after the 2010 Haiti earthquake, where the high influx of aid to the country was disbursed outside of the government structures with former U.S. President Bill Clinton playing a key role. We summarize this in the following:

Proposition 6.9: *Postconflict assistance that raises ν or θ will lead to greater investments in state capacities and reduce the parameter range in which there is violence.*

Naturally, postconflict reconstruction may have a wider remit, part of which could involve direct efforts to increase (or rebuild destroyed) τ and π. However, postconflict assistance generally also comes with a good deal of cash aid. In view of Propositions 6.4 and 6.5, this makes complementary attempts to raise θ and lower ν doubly important.

A related question is whether we can think about a window of opportunity in weak or collapsed states. The issue here is whether—and, if so, under what conditions—external players can be of any help. Can external players—as key internal players like founding fathers at historical moments—assist in designing a political mechanism and/or institutions capable of changing the internal political equilibria in countries such as Iraq, Afghanistan, and Somalia? Historical experience cautions us that a simple export or duplication of existing institutions often does not work. In the nineteenth century almost all of the Latin American states modeled their constitutions on the U.S. document, but with very different results. The Commonwealth countries of India and Pakistan started off with the same constitutional framework, provided by the 1935 Government of India Act, but with very different outcomes.

Changing political mechanisms and institutions would be like changing θ, and thereby potentially altering the type of state. To even pose that question, we obviously have to think about the mapping of concrete rules for the political game into abstract macro parameters such as θ and γ. Moreover, we have to think carefully about the incentives for undertaking endogenous political reform. We make a start on these difficult, but important, questions in the next chapter.

6.2 *Final Remarks*

This chapter has explored the implications of our analytical approach for the design of development assistance. Our model suggests a number of margins on which we would expect such assistance to have an effect. Although we are offering a very stylized picture, the results illustrate the difficulties faced by external donors and actors who are trying to improve the situation in developing countries, particularly in weak and fragile states. Some of the issues are well known, particularly the problem that development support might crowd out rather than crowd in government. It is clear that a great deal more has to be understood about the political equilibrium before any reasoned assessment on aid can be reached. Absent this understanding, the triumph of hope over expectation, so characteristic of more than 50 years of policy experience, is likely to continue.

Some of the aspects suggested by our framework are perhaps more novel. The analysis highlights the oft-discussed trade-off between providing resources through aid and developing domestic fiscal capacity. We have shown how this margin would indeed have to figure in a cost-benefit calculation. We have also considered the violence margin. As noted in Chapter 4, researchers are becoming increasingly aware of the possibility that aid can exacerbate problems of political violence. This is a potentially sobering consequence of international aid, which goes beyond what even the most ardent aid pessimists have tended to suggest.

On a more optimistic note, the value of technical assistance looks promising in our framework. RCTs can help identify more valuable outlets for public resources, which can foster investments in state capacities and reductions in violence. But for this to be the case, it is essential not only that the evidence base acquired by NGOs supporting RCTs be transferred to public projects, but also that these projects can indeed be implemented on a large scale. Inevitably, this will require state cooperation, so the policymaking and investment incentives we have dealt with in this book re-enter into the fray.

Our suggested Anna Karenina principle underlines the importance of heterogeneity. This may, to some degree, reconcile the different positions in the debate on development policy. Our model suggests that some advantageous development policy may always exist. But identifying that policy requires a great deal of knowledge about circumstances and institutions. One might then be an aid pessimist or an aid optimist depending on the form of aid and the ability of aid agencies to understand its impact in specific contexts.

6.3 *Notes on the Literature*

There is an extensive literature on aid in general. Collier (2007), Easterly (2006), and Sachs (2005) all have discussions on the role of the international community in promoting development and offer their own perspectives on both the history of intervention and the prospects for future success. Riddell (2007) surveys the extensive policy literature. For an excellent recent survey of the literature on foreign aid, see Temple (2010), who also coined the term "Bauer paradox" that we used in this chapter.

Chauvet and Collier (2006) put forward a conceptual framework for thinking through the impact of aid in failing states. As we do in this chapter, they emphasize the importance of understanding heterogeneity in responses depending on state pathologies. Political institutions are also at the heart of the analyses of fragility in Vallings and Moreno-Torres (2005), who emphasize the need to build institutions to overcome fragility. McGillivray (2006) surveys the literature on aid to fragile states. He discusses the factors that determine whether states become aid orphans (i.e., cut off from aid) or aid darlings (get extra aid) in response to fragility and the dilemmas faced by the policy community.

Much has been written on the relationship between aid and growth using cross-country comparisons. Reviews emphasizing different aspects of this literature are Collier and Dollar (2004), Easterly (2003), Hansen and Tarp (2001), and Rajan and Subramanian (2008). A meta study can be found in Doucouliagos and Paldam (2008). A more recent literature, following Boone (1996) and Burnside and Dollar (2000), has stressed the heterogeneity in the impact of aid according to the institutional and policy environment in place in a country. Aid conditionality is discussed and modeled in Azam and Laffont (2003) and Svensson (2000b, 2003).

Frey and Schneider (1986), among others, have studied the determinants of multilateral aid. Alesina and Dollar (2000) study the determinants of bilateral aid and find that a significant proportion of the variation in aid-flow disbursements is explained by colonial history and political and strategic interests of donors. Gstoettner and Jensen (2010) study the relationship between multilateral foreign aid flows and the quality of recipient countries' public-finance institutions and argue that higher aid flows lead to a significant deterioration in the quality of public finances.

The idea that aid can lead to a deterioration in institutions is an important theme in Bauer (1972). His critique has been taken up and endorsed more recently in Leeson (2008) and Shleifer (2009), and is explored theoretically in Smith (2006) and Svensson (2000a). Djankov, Montalvo, and Reynal-Querol (2008) and Knack (2001) observe negative correlations between changes in the quality of governance and foreign aid using cross-country data.

Collier et al. (2003) review the issues surrounding aid and conflict. Addison (2003) emphasizes the importance of institutional change in sustaining peace postconflict and discusses the role that international organizations and donors can play postconflict. Coyne (2008a,b) and Coyne and Boettke (2009) discuss postconflict reconstruction and efforts to create democracy after conflict based on foreign intervention. Coyne and Pellillo (2011) discuss lessons from Afghanistan and Iraq.

We have focused on the carrot of aid and development assistance. But whether aid or sanctions is the best policy is an interesting issue in many contexts and is studied in Azam and Saadi-Sedik (2003) and Kletzer (2005).

Banerjee and Duflo (2009) and Duflo, Glennerster, and Kremer (2007) provide comprehensive overviews of the role of RCTs in general and the way such trials can provide an evidence base to guide policy interventions. Banerjee and He (2008) discuss more generally whether evidence-based policymaking shapes the aid agenda and lament the fact that many aid and multilateral organizations pay so little attention to policy evaluation.

CHAPTER 7

Political Reform

What is government itself but the greatest of all reflections on human nature? If men were angels, no government would be necessary. If angels were to govern men, neither external nor internal controls on government would be necessary.

James Madison, *The Federalist* No. 51, 1788

One of the main themes of the book thus far has been that cohesive political institutions are vital for cultivating peace as well as investments in state capacity. But our analysis has kept the details of politics in the background—the exception being strategic decisions on violence to affect political turnover. In this chapter, we peek into this black box and examine the role of political institutions and political reform in our framework more closely. This exercise can help us to understand why some countries end up with cohesive institutions, whereas others fail to do so.

We begin the chapter in a macropolitical mode, by extending the core model of the book to include choice of institutions as reflected in the parameter θ. Our analysis treats this as a problem of constitution design. The closest real-world example where this is relevant is the inception of a new state. The end of colonialism and the fall of the Berlin Wall led to many such instances in the period after World War II.

At first, we take the perspective of a constitutional convention behind the veil of ignorance, where vested interests are kept outside the picture. Here, the case for cohesive institutions becomes quite compelling, and we provide a formal statement of this point. Next, we consider real-time strategic political reform, studying the choice of political institutions made by a period-1 incumbent in our core model. This simulates the experience of older and more established polities such as Sweden or the United Kingdom, where political reform has been an evolutionary process. However, the analysis is relevant to any polity where the incumbent can propose a change in the constitution. We explore the forces that shape the choice of θ in this setting and point out how incumbency bias creates forces that move the state away from cohesiveness.

This chapter affords an opportunity to make contact, albeit superficially, with large literatures in the fields of political economics and comparative politics that look at the detailed workings of political institutions, theoretically and empirically. Representing political institutions through reduced-form parameters such as θ and γ is crude at best and remote from the detailed modeling of alternative rules for elections, legislative processes, and forms of government. We start the second part of the chapter by sketching out micropolitical foundations for parameters θ and γ.

Up to that point in the chapter, we simply assume that any changes in the rules for rulemaking can be enforced. In practice, constitutions are typically enforced by rules that impose costs of change, such as requiring decisions by supermajorities and/or popular referenda. We next explore how such rules create institutional inertia, which can either help or inhibit the creation of cohesive institutions. A more ambitious step is to revisit the implications of political violence in this new setting. The threat of political violence enters the analysis in two ways. Since incumbents can use violence to reduce the chances of political turnover, they become more likely to opt for noncohesive institutions. But the costs of realized violence under noncohesive institutions tend to pull in the opposite direction.

It is relatively straightforward to measure de jure cohesiveness of political institutions. However, informal institutions and norms may be important determinants of de facto political cohesiveness. Some countries appear to have robust democratic cultures based on a generalized trust in the system. We also discuss such issues in the context of our framework to motivate how history may be an important force behind cohesive political institutions.

Some Basic Facts The Polity IV data suggest that reform toward more cohesive political institutions is a general feature of the data. This can be seen quite clearly in Figure 7.1, based on a sample of all of the 51 countries that appear continuously in this data set since the year 1900. For each of the 100 years from 1900 to 2000, the figure plots the proportion of these countries that is classified as having the highest score for executive constraints, namely a score of 7, a variable we used earlier as a measure of cohesiveness.

Based on this definition, a little less than 30% of the sample is classified as having cohesive institutions in 1900. Prevalence rises at first as more countries adopt the principles of parliamentary democracy. But it falls back in the 1930s

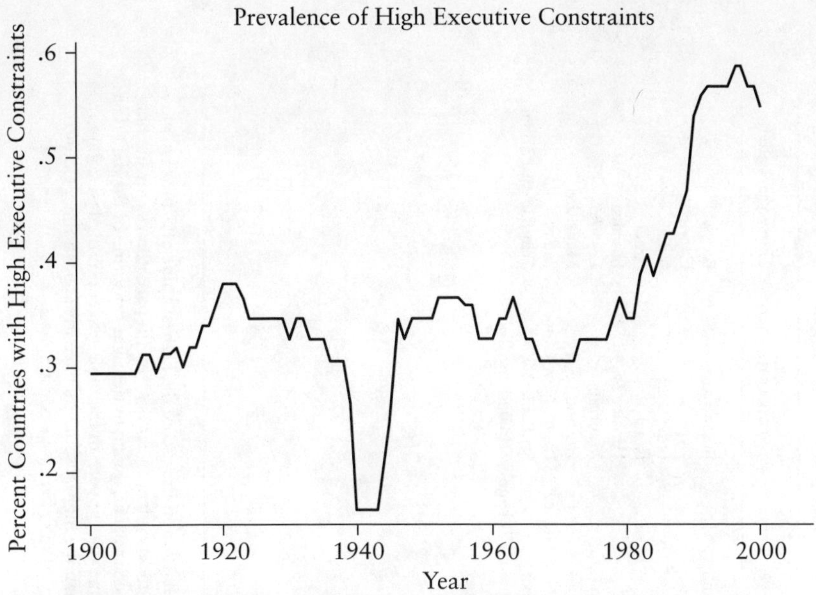

Figure 7.1 Prevalence of high executive constraints among 51 countries.

and 1940s with a pronounced descent into authoritarianism, which, to some extent, is maintained in the early days of the Cold War. However, the period from 1980 on sees a significant move toward strong executive constraint, as a number of countries in Latin America and Asia turn from military autocracy toward political democracy. This is cemented by the fall of the Berlin Wall, such that the prevalence of cohesive institutions has almost doubled by the end of the century. The figure reinforces the point that the twentieth century has seen a great deal of political change. To the extent that high executive constraint is a good measure of θ in our model, we should expect that these political dynamics led to significant changes in the motives for investing in state capacity and political violence.

However, Figure 7.1 is only relevant to older established nations. It is interesting to look at the picture for nations that were created more recently. We thus look at all of the 113 countries that were created in the 50 years between 1945 and 1995, mostly former colonies in Africa and Asia and previous members of the Soviet Bloc. For each of these countries, we take note whether its first year of independence is associated with the highest score for executive constraints. If so, we list it in the leftmost column of Table 7.1. Only 22 countries, thus about one-fifth of the new countries, appear in that column.

Table 7.1 Persistence of high executive constraints

At independence	Five years after	Ten years after	Fifteen years after	Twenty years after	Thirty years after
Belarus (1991)*	Botswana (1966)	Botswana	Botswana	Botswana	Botswana
Cyprus (1960)	Czech Republic ǀ	Fiji	*Cyprus*	Cyprus	Cyprus
Czech Republic (1993)	Estonia ǀ	India	Fiji*	India	India
Estonia (1991)	Fiji	Israel	India	Israel	**Israel**
Fiji (1970)	India (1947)	Jamaica	Israel	Jamaica	**Jamaica**
Guyana (1966)*	Israel	Myanmar*	Jamaica	Mauritius	*Lesotho*
Israel (1948)	Jamaica	Mauritius	Mauritius	*Nigeria*	**Mauritius**
Jamaica (1962)	Latvia ǀ	Malaysia*	Papua New Guinea	Papua New Guinea*	*Sudan*
Latvia (1991)	Lithuania ǀ	Pakistan (1947)*	Sri Lanka	Sri Lanka*	**Trinidad and Tobago**
Lesotho (1966)	Moldova (1991) ǀ	Papua New Guinea	Trinidad and Tobago	Trinidad and Tobago	
Lithuania (1991)	Myanmar	Sri Lanka			
Myanmar (1948)	Mauritius	*Sudan*			
Mauritius (1968)	Malaysia	Syria			
Malaysia (1957)	Nigeria	Trinidad and Tobago			
Nigeria (1960)	Papua New Guinea				
Papua New Guinea (1975)	Somalia*				
Sudan (1956)	Slovak Republic (1993) ǀ				
Somalia (1960)	Slovenia ǀ				
Slovenia (1991)	Sri Lanka				
Sri Lanka (1948)	Trinidad and Tobago				
Trinidad and Tobago (1962)					
Uganda (1962)*					

Notes: The table lists all countries coming into existence as independent states after 1945, if they score the highest value of 7 for the Polity score on executive constraints at one of the time horizons listed in the table. The independence year is given (in parentheses) for the first entry in the table. Countries are marked with "ǀ" in the last column in which they can appear, owing to the right censoring of the data (last entries in the Polity IV data for 2000). Countries are marked with "*" the last time they appear in the table (except in the last column). Countries are printed in italics if they re-enter the table after a period with less than the highest score on executive constraints. Countries are printed in bold in the last column of the table if they have a full 30-year history of high executive constraints.

The following five columns of the table list the states that have cohesive political institutions after 5, 10, 15, 20, and 30 years of independence.[1] We see that there is a gradual movement away from cohesive political institutions. Six African countries—Lesotho, Mauritius, Nigeria, Somalia, Sudan, and Uganda—start out with cohesive institutions in the sense of high executive constraints. But these are generally lost over time, although some countries such as Nigeria and Sudan enter and exit the table. The same pattern applies to Belarus, Fiji, Guyana, Malaysia, Myanmar, Papua New Guinea, and Sri Lanka.

In fact, only four countries—Israel, Jamaica, Mauritius, and Trinidad and Tobago—have continuous histories of cohesive political institutions from their inception up to 30 years after independence. Naturally, it is too early to tell if some of the initial adopters in Eastern Europe after 1990 that have maintained cohesive institutions in the first 10 years of their existence will maintain them for 30 years.

The table also shows that some countries undertook reform toward cohesive institutions at a later point in time than independence. However, after some time with high executive constraints most of those late adopters or readopters tend to bounce back. Interestingly, among the late adopters only Botswana and India—which both had cohesive institutions after 5 years of independence—have maintained their cohesive institutions continuously 30 years after independence.

All in all, Table 7.1 illustrates that by this measure of θ, only a small minority of newly independent states, 27 out of 112, ever acquired cohesive political institutions. Among those that did, the predominant tendency is for θ to decline. This table and Figure 7.1 underscore how important it is to analyze what drives reform of political institutions in theory and practice. We explore this question through the lens of our modeling approach.

Plan of the Chapter The next section of the chapter discusses incentives to reform θ in our core model from earlier chapters, assuming at first that political transitions are peaceful. In the benchmark approach, we allow θ to be chosen costlessly. This choice is made either once and for all under a veil of ignorance about who will hold power or strategically by the period-1 incumbent.

Section 7.2 turns from macro to micro, laying some micropolitical foundations for parameters θ and γ. This allows us to discuss the mapping from

1. We take the Polity IV assessments of this at face value.

common institutional arrangements to abstract notions of political cohesiveness and political stability. In two extensions of the core model, we consider costs of constitutional change owing to supermajority rules for rule changes or to endogenous political violence. We also consider the role of trust in maintaining political cohesion. Finally, we pick up a theme from Chapter 3 and consider what set of governance institutions might emerge in the wake of a small elite that is strongly motivated to seek rents through predation.

In Section 7.3, we briefly discuss how one might analyze real-world political reform in view of the preceding theoretical discussion. This section makes some methodological points that can be used to interpret existing econometric and case study evidence. We provide three examples and discuss how the ideas can be tested. Section 7.4 concludes the chapter, before we turn to notes on the literature.

7.1 *The Core Model and Political Reform*

We now expand the choices in our baseline model to include the parameter θ, the degree to which institutions are cohesive. To fix ideas, we begin as simply as possible. Specifically, we assume that θ can be chosen from its permissible interval $\theta \in [0, 1/2]$ and that (peaceful) political turnover, γ, is given exogenously and independently of θ. Thus for the moment, we are ignoring the implications for political violence. Further on in Section 7.2 we explore the micropolitical foundations for the decision on θ, as well as the possibility of endogenous interactions with γ when there is political violence.

In each period, there can be a choice of political institutions. We suppose that these are chosen one period ahead, as were the state capacity and violence investments in earlier chapters. For the moment, we also suppose that such investments are costless. In practice, of course, there are time and effort costs when rules are changed. More interesting still, there may be efforts by citizens to preserve their political rights, which can make for endogenous costs of change. The discussion of these issues is also postponed to Section 7.2.

Preliminaries We contrast two main cases of institutional choice: constitutional choice and strategic choice. Therefore, we allow choices to be made at two points in time; one point is prior to any economic or policy decisions and the other decision point coincides with the time when period-1 state-capacity investments are made.

To be precise, the new timing of decisions is as follows:

1. We begin with initial stocks of state capacities $\{\tau_1, \pi_1\}$.
2. Period–1 political institutions, θ_1, are chosen.
3. Nature determines the incumbent group I_1, α_1, and R.
4. I_1 chooses a set of period-1 policies $\{t_1, r_1^I, r_1^O, p_1^I, p_1^O, g_1\}$ and determines (through investments) the period-2 stocks of fiscal and legal capacity $\{\tau_2, \pi_2\}$. (If political violence is modeled, I_1 and O_1 simultaneously invest in violence levels L^I and L^O.) If permitted, I_1 also chooses period-2 political institutions, θ_2.
5. I_1 remains in power with probability $1-\gamma$ (or $1-\Gamma(Z, \nu, \xi)$ if political violence is modeled), and nature determines α_2.
6. I_2 chooses period-2 policies $\{t_2, r_2^I, r_2^O, p_2^I, p_2^O, g_2\}$.

One feature of this approach is that state-capacity investments and policy decisions are always left in the hands of incumbents given the choice of θ. We consider two possibilities. First, we consider the design of a binding constitution at stage 2 when there is no option to alter that choice at stage 4. Second, we study the decision about θ_2 when the incumbent can change the constitution at stage 4.

As in earlier chapters, we look for a subgame perfect equilibrium in policy and state-capacity investments. To find the value of changing θ_2, we have to solve the model backward.

7.1.1 Political Reform under a Veil of Ignorance

Let us begin with a one-off decision over political institutions, θ_1, at stage 2 that is binding for the entire two-period setting. Hence, we set $\theta_1 = \theta_2$ at stage 4. In particular, we have in mind the outcome of a constitutional convention in which (representatives of) all citizens get together to choose political institutions. They do so behind a veil of ignorance without knowing which group they belong to (or equivalently which group will be the incumbent in period 1). We assume that all citizens are equally likely to belong to either group (or that both groups are equally likely to hold power) and hence that the criterion is Utilitarian.

As we noted earlier, policy and state-capacity choices are made by subsequent incumbents, with the latter summarized by the functions

$$\tau_2 = T\left(\tau_1, \pi_1; \theta, \alpha_1\right) \quad \text{and} \quad \pi_2 = P\left(\tau_1, \pi_1; \theta, \alpha_1\right).$$

These are the outcomes determined in Section 3.1, where γ is exogenous.

Indirect Payoffs Let $U_s^J\left(\tau_s, \pi_s; \theta\right)$ for $J \in \{I, O\}$ be the value of entering period s with state-capacity vector $\left\{\tau_s, \pi_s\right\}$ and institutions θ. Now observe that for fixed $\left\{\tau_2, \pi_2\right\}$,

$$\frac{U^I\left(\tau_2, \pi_2; \theta\right) + U^O\left(\tau_2, \pi_2; \theta\right)}{2} = \left(1 + \tau_2\left[E(\lambda_2; \theta) - 1\right]\right) y\left(\pi_2\right) + E(\lambda_2; \theta) R,$$

where

$$E\left(\lambda_2; \theta\right) = \begin{cases} \phi\alpha_H + (1-\phi)\,\alpha_L & \text{if } \alpha_L \geq 2\,(1-\theta) \\ \phi\alpha_H + (1-\phi) & \text{otherwise} \end{cases}$$

is the expected value of future public funds. Since we have linear utility and the groups have equal weights, expected redistribution nets out of the planner's payoff. Hence, the payoff function is the same as the one adopted by a Utilitarian planner:

$$\begin{aligned} \hat{U}\left(\alpha_1, \theta; \tau_2, \pi_2\right) = {} & \left(1 + \tau_1\left[\lambda_1 - 1\right]\right) y\left(\pi_1\right) - \lambda_1 m_1 + \lambda_1 R \\ & + \left(1 + \tau_2\left[E(\lambda_2; \theta) - 1\right]\right) y\left(\pi_2\right) + E(\lambda_2; \theta) R, \end{aligned} \tag{7.1}$$

where $\lambda_1 = \max\left\{\alpha_1, 2\,(1-\theta)\right\}$ and $m_1 = \mathcal{F}(\tau_2 - \tau_1) + \mathcal{L}(\pi_2 - \pi_1)$.

Optimal Constitutional Choice Now, the optimal institution, θ, maximizes

$$\begin{aligned} & \phi\hat{U}\left(\alpha_H, \theta; T\left(\tau_1, \pi_1; \theta, \alpha_H\right), P\left(\tau_1, \pi_1; \theta, \alpha_H\right)\right) \\ & + (1-\phi)\,\hat{U}\left(\alpha_L, \theta; T\left(\tau_1, \pi_1; \theta, \alpha_L\right), P\left(\tau_1, \pi_1; \theta, \alpha_L\right)\right). \end{aligned}$$

We now have the following:

Proposition 7.1: *Under a veil of ignorance, citizens choose cohesive institutions with* $\alpha_L \geq 2\,(1-\theta)$.

To see this, observe that (by the results in Sections 2.1 and 3.1) if $\alpha_L \geq 2\,(1-\theta)$, state-capacity investments $\left\{\tau_2, \pi_2\right\}$ will be exactly the same as those that would be chosen by a Utilitarian planner. Since the unknowing citizens share the planner's objective, cohesive institutional rules implement their preferred choice.[2] One way to think of this result is that cohesive institutions provide a form of commitment, guaranteeing that all spending will be on public goods. Thus the constitutional choice of high θ creates that credible commitment by assumption.

Proposition 7.1 describes the sense in which a common-interest state is a natural situation in our framework. This sense rhymes well with the many benefits we have identified for such states throughout this book. However, the result supposes that political institutions are chosen to maximize welfare and that they are credibly binding on all incumbents at all times—two strong and unrealistic assumptions. The fragility of these assumptions can be explored by studying stage 4 of the model and allowing the period-1 incumbent to change θ_2 by implementing a constitutional change. This will allow us to assess how robust the demand for a cohesive constitution might be in practice under the maintained assumption that the necessary institutions can be credibly put in place.

Before looking at strategic institutional choice, it is worth noting that constitution designers in our model would be indifferent about the way that institutions affected γ. This is because the choice of cohesive institutions creates common interests, making all the rules that regulate turnover irrelevant. Clearly, this is a stark view and in richer models—e.g., models that include private risk aversion—full cohesiveness may not be feasible. In such cases, a Pigouvian planner with a preference for equality may wish to choose institutional arrangements that prevent too much entrenchment in power to even out any distributional gains from incumbency.

7.1.2 Strategic Political Reform

Consider now the decision at stage 4 when, along with decisions on state capacity, the incumbent can also choose θ_2. Our explicit assumption (which is common in the literature on endogenous institutions) is that the incumbent government can bind its successor one period ahead. This is weaker than in the previous subsection, where institutions were chosen once-and-for-all. But it could still be regarded as too strong an assumption and we revisit it later.

2. How can we rule out an optimum where $\alpha_L < 2(1-\theta)$ and θ is chosen so that $2[(1-\gamma)(1-\theta)+\gamma\theta] = 1$? This condition can hold for all $\gamma \in [0, 1]$ only if $\theta = 1/2$, which is a contradiction (except in the nongeneric case of $\gamma = 1/2$, where θ is irrelevant).

Payoff and Equilibrium The forward-looking period-2 payoff of the period-1 incumbent is

$$W^I = (1-\gamma)\, U^I\left(\tau_2, \pi_2; \theta\right) + \gamma U^O\left(\tau_2, \pi_2; \theta\right) \tag{7.2}$$

$$= \left(1 + \tau_2\left[E(\lambda_2) - 1\right]\right) y\left(\pi_2\right) + E(\lambda_2)R, \tag{7.3}$$

where, as in Section 3.1,

$$E(\lambda_2) = \phi\alpha_H + (1-\phi)\lambda_2^L \tag{7.4}$$

is the *expected* value of period-2 public funds with

$$\lambda_2^L = \begin{cases} \alpha_L & \text{if } \alpha_L \geq 2(1-\theta) \\ 2[(1-\theta)(1-\gamma) + \gamma\theta] & \text{otherwise.} \end{cases} \tag{7.5}$$

We are interested in understanding the choice of $\theta \in [0, 1/2]$ that maximizes (7.2).

To study this problem, we observe that the effect of a change in θ on this payoff is

$$\frac{\partial W^I}{\partial \theta} = \begin{cases} (1-\phi)\, 2(2\gamma - 1)[\tau_2 y\left(\pi_2\right) + R] & \text{if } 2\,(1-\theta) > \alpha_L \\ 0 & \text{otherwise.} \end{cases} \tag{7.6}$$

Clearly, if $\gamma < 1/2$, this expression is everywhere decreasing in θ and if $\gamma > 1/2$, it is everywhere increasing. This proves the following proposition:

Proposition 7.2: *A period-1 incumbent chooses cohesive institutions with* $\alpha_L \geq 2\,(1-\theta)$ *when the prospect of replacement is high* ($\gamma \geq 1/2$) *and noncohesive institutions with* $\theta = 0$ *when the prospect of replacement is low* ($\gamma < 1/2$).

This result makes sense, even if it is somewhat stark in our framework. When $\gamma \geq 1/2$, the incumbent does not want to gamble on being out of office in the next period so she chooses cohesive political institutions to protect herself from being in opposition. The opposite is true when $\gamma < 1/2$.[3]

3. Since everyone is risk-neutral, there is no risk-reduction benefit associated with cohesive institutions. If we added risk aversion to the framework, we would expect such benefits to pull down the critical replacement rate at which it would be worthwhile for the incumbent to choose cohesive institutions.

Discussion Proposition 7.2 implies that an entrenched incumbent does not invest in cohesive institutions, whereas an incumbent that faces a serious threat of replacement may well choose to do so. Thus, if a constitutional convention initially endows a country with cohesive institutions, an incumbent will try to reform the constitution away from cohesive institutions if she does not expect to be replaced. So far, we are taking γ as exogenous, but this result will become particularly interesting once γ is endogenous, as we discuss later.

Although the setting is very different, the argument is somewhat related to the work by Lagunoff (2001), which shows how constitutionally guaranteed rights of civil liberties can become part of a self-enforcing equilibrium in a dynamic game with underlying social conflict. The reason is essentially that members of an incumbent's group may find themselves in opposition at a later point, so that more entrenched incumbents tend to choose less tolerant constitutionally granted rights. A similar intuition underlies the result in de Figueiredo (2002) that electorally weak groups may be more likely than electorally strong groups to put institutional structures that limit future bureaucratic discretion in place.

One feature of Proposition 7.2 that gives pause for thought is that we will never observe a weak state being strategically chosen for period 2. This is because the condition for $\theta = 0$ to be chosen is that $\gamma < 1/2$, which implies that the state is redistributive rather than weak. Hence, to explain the persistence of weak states, we have to look elsewhere. We return to this issue in Section 7.2, as well.

It is interesting to compare the incumbent's choice with a Pigouvian planner's preference. As observed in Subsection 7.1.1., if the Pigouvian planner is Utilitarian, he will maximize

$$\frac{U^I\left(\tau_2, \pi_2; \theta\right) + U^O\left(\tau_2, \pi_2; \theta\right)}{2}.$$

Changing θ has no effect on average utility since it has a purely redistributive effect. As utility is linear in money, the planner does not care about distribution. Note, however, that any preference for equality would generate a preference for consensual institutions, even without curvature in the utility function.

To see this, take the case where the Pigouvian planner is Rawlsian. Then, θ is chosen to maximize

$$\min\left\{U^I\left(\tau_2, \pi_2; \theta\right), U^O\left(\tau_2, \pi_2; \theta\right)\right\}.$$

It is straightforward to see that this objective is maximized when $\alpha_L \geq 2\left(1-\theta\right)$.

Endogenous Entrenchment We now consider the possibility that, as well as choosing θ_2, an incumbent could also affect her prospects of remaining in power, i.e., the extent of her *entrenchment* in office. What would happen at stage 4 of the model if the incumbent could also choose γ_2, which denotes the institutional choices determining the probability of an incumbent's survival? In Section 7.2 we discuss how to derive this parameter from specific institutional choices.

The following observation is immediate:

Proposition 7.3: *The period-1 incumbent's preferred combination of period-2 institutions is* $\theta_2 = \gamma_2 = 0$.

Thus, a period-1 incumbent would like maximal entrenchment with the weakest possible constraints on her power. This result follows by observing that (7.2) is decreasing in γ whenever $U^I(\tau_2, \pi_2; \theta) > U^O(\tau_2, \pi_2; \theta)$, i.e., when there is any kind of incumbency advantage. This advantage is reinforced by having a low θ_2.

The result is not particularly surprising in the context of our setup. But a similar result would hold in any model in which incumbents enjoy holding power, directly or indirectly. This is the essential reason why almost every system of government takes the decision over the rules for governing political institutions as far from the hands of incumbents as possible. Note that if θ_2 is specified in a binding constitution, as in the prior subsection, there is no incentive to lower γ_2. Hence, a binding constitution mitigates the entrenchment incentives.

Taking Stock This section has introduced some building blocks needed for understanding endogenous institutional choice in the core model of this book. There is a strong ex ante case for a constitutional convention to pick cohesive institutions. However, this prescription is vulnerable to manipulation without any safeguards against incumbents reducing institutional cohesiveness and increasing entrenchment. Based on the analysis in this section, we would thus expect countries to gravitate toward redistributive states without appropriate safeguards to prevent constitutional manipulation. Our brief review of the evidence at the beginning of this chapter, to which we return in Section 7.3, certainly suggests that this expectation has some resonance with practical experience.

Our analysis so far has been somewhat optimistic when describing the forces that may motivate countries to engineer their checks and balances. If these forces were the complete story, it would be quite difficult to explain why weak states of the kind that we have described would persist. There would always be strong pressures toward reforms that increase the cohesiveness of institutions. In the next section, we show how an extended analysis may suggest a story that is less rosy.

7.2 *Developing the Model*

Arguably, the last section may have exaggerated the likelihood of institutional change by making it very easy to change the rules of the political game. In some countries, it is striking how difficult it is to change these rules, even for very determined incumbents. To understand these hurdles to change, we have to consider how the microstructure of institutional choice might work and what might be the costs of trying to manipulate and change institutions for strategic, self-interested reasons.

7.2.1 Micropolitical Foundations for θ

We have assumed that institutional designers are capable of choosing θ directly. But this parameter imposes a direct restriction on policy. More realistically, institutional choice involves a design of the rules under which political decisions are made. Thus, it is most natural to think of $\theta(i, \ell)$ and $\gamma(\ell)$, where $\ell \in \mathcal{L}$ are constitutional rules, and where i is defined below. The core variables $\theta(i, \ell)$ and $\gamma(\ell)$ now become endogenous outcomes that describe how the rules of the game affect who holds office and her equilibrium policy choices.

To illustrate this way of thinking and to tie it to modern political economics, we consider two examples. This subsection concerns the forces that shape $\theta(i, \ell)$ and the next looks at the forces that shape $\gamma(\ell)$.

Bargaining over Transfers Suppose that policymaking is delegated to a subset of citizens, the *policymaking set*. In a democracy, this set most naturally corresponds to a legislature whose members are chosen in an election. However, in other contexts, the policymaking set could be an elite with a particular ethnic composition, a group of generals who form a military junta, the politburo in a communist dictatorship, or members of a clan. We assume that policy proposal power is in the hands of the majority group within the set of decision-makers. Let $i \geq 1/2$ be the size of the incumbent group's representation among the decisionmakers.[4] We assume a two-stage decision making procedure, where:

1. The (majority) incumbent group in the policymaking set unilaterally chooses $\{p_s^J, p_s^O, g_s, t_s\}$ in period s and $\{\tau_2, \pi_2\}$ in period 1.
2. The incumbent group and the opposition in the policymaking set bargain over the allocation of $\{r_s^I, r_s^O\}$.

The second stage corresponds to a classic "divide-the-dollar" transfer game where the size of the redistributive cake per capita is

$$(R + t_s y(\pi_s) - m_s - g_s) = z_s.$$

Any transfer allocation must satisfy $r_s^O + r_s^I \leq 2z_s$.

Clearly, this is a very partial perspective on bargaining, since the opposition has no decisionmaking rights at all with respect to policies other than transfers. This is perhaps less of an issue here, since there will tend to be agreement in the choices over other policies. However, a more complete treatment of the bargaining structure would also have to include at least t_s and state-capacity choices as part of the bargaining process. This would be somewhat more complex.

Bargaining Protocol We specify a very simple bargaining rule, which is *one-round* and *closed-rule* in the jargon of the legislative-bargaining literature rooted in Baron and Ferejohn (1989). Thus, the incumbent group in the policymaking set offers a level of transfers $r_s^O \leq 2z_s$ and the comparable opposition group chooses whether or not to accept this offer. If the opposition members accept, the transfers are implemented.

If they reject the offer, then there will be one of two outcomes. With probability $\Omega(i, \ell)$, the opposition group receives a default transfer of $\underline{r}_s^O = \Psi(\ell)\, 2z_s$, where parameter $\Psi(\ell) \leq 1/2$ can be interpreted as the share of revenues that accrues to the opposition in the default case. But with probability $1 - \Omega(i, \ell)$, the opposition group gets nothing, i.e., $r_s^O = 0$. As a higher i denotes a larger share of the incumbent group in the policymaking set, it is natural to assume that $\Omega(i, \ell)$ is decreasing in i.

4. In the knife-edge case where $i = 1/2$, we assume that the proposer is chosen at random.

The rules of the decisionmaking process are embedded in the institutional rules ℓ, which influence $\Omega(i, \ell)$ and $\Psi(\ell)$. An extensive literature on legislative bargaining procedures emphasizes how the rules for recognizing proposal and counterproposal power can influence bargaining power. For example, some rules such as the filibuster or amendment rules are created to enhance minority rights. Moreover, some legislatures have supermajority provisions for some legislative choices.

Bargaining Outcomes at Stage 2 Working backward, it is easy to see that the opposition group in the policymaking set can always guarantee itself an expected transfer of $\Omega(i, \ell)\Psi(\ell)2z_s$ by saying no to an offer made by the incumbent group. Consequently, the opposition will accept an offer of r_s^O at stage 2 only as long as

$$r_s^O \geq \Omega(i, \ell)\Psi(\ell)2z_s.$$

Under the given bargaining protocol, it is always optimal for the incumbent group to offer the opposition the minimum needed to get the offer accepted. (If the incumbent is offered $r_s^O = 0$, the opposition can still guarantee itself $\Omega(i, \ell)\Psi(\ell)2z_s$ by saying no.)

It follows that this very simple microfoundation has

$$r_s^O = 2\Omega(i, \ell)\Psi(\ell)z_s = 2\theta(i, \ell)z_s,$$

where $\theta(i, \ell) = \Omega(i, \ell)\Psi(\ell)$ becomes the key parameter that we have used throughout the book. In our simple model, this is the product of the bargaining power of the opposition, as represented by $\Omega(i; \ell)$, and the opposition's status quo outcome, as represented by $\Psi(\ell)$. Fully cohesive institutions would correspond to the case where $\Omega(i, \ell) = 1$ and $\Psi(\ell) = 1/2$. Noncohesive institutions would arise where either $\Omega(i, \ell) = 0$ or $\Psi(\ell) = 0$, i.e., the opposition group has no outside option owing to neglible bargaining power or a complete lack of protection in the status quo.

Policy Outcomes at Stage 1 Turning now to stage 1, other policies will be determined exactly as we have specified in earlier chapters, as they reflect the forward-looking payoffs of the incumbent, where he gains $2(1 - \theta(i, \ell))$ of any residual tax revenues as transfers. In other words, this specification is indeed a microfoundation for the model that we have been studying throughout the book.

It is clear that things can and should be complicated in many ways. For example, it would be interesting to take seriously the idea of $\Psi(\ell)$ as a status quo allocation of transfers. Then, $\Psi(\ell)$ would reflect the transfer policies inherited from the past, analogously to the setup in Baron (1996). This would introduce strategic aspects into today's transfer policy because of the way it would influence tomorrow's choice. It would be interesting to understand whether a cohesive status quo where $\Psi(\ell)$ is likely to be self-enforcing given the ability of future opposition groups to invoke it.

Checks and Balances and Forms of Government We can now think about changing $\theta(i, \ell)$ by changing the bargaining rules to influence policy outcomes. Cohesive institutions are now defined by $\mathcal{L}^C$ such that $\alpha_L \geq 2(1 - \theta(i, \ell))$ for all $\ell \in \mathcal{L}^C$. Recall that we defined the opposition's equilibrium share of transfers by $\theta(i, \ell) = \Omega(i, \ell)\Psi(\ell)$. Higher bargaining power $\Omega(i, \ell)$ or more "minority protection" $\Psi(\ell)$ for the opposition thus increases its equilibrium share of transfers. Hence, it is reasonable to interpret $\Omega(i, \ell)$ as greater checks and balances on the executive.

This is also what we have done in the empirical sections of the previous chapters, where we have used the Polity IV measure of executive constraints as a measure of θ. In practice, this measure gives a high weight to parliamentary democracy, since an operating parliamentary form of government keeps the executive constantly accountable to the legislative assembly through a confidence requirement. Diermeier and Feddersen (1998), Huber (1996), and Persson, Roland, and Tabellini (2000) discuss how the bargaining outcomes in legislatures depend on the confidence requirement. One of the results in the last paper is that governments in parliamentary regimes internalize the preferences for a larger share of the population than do governments in presidential regimes, which comes close to a higher value of θ and has similar effects on the incentives to provide public goods rather than redistribution.

Centralization The interpretation of the default allocation $\Psi(\ell)$ to the opposition is harder to interpret in a straightforward way, but perhaps we could think about it as reflecting the vertical, rather than the horizontal, separation of powers in a setting where the groups are geographically concentrated. Concretely, this would mean that federal states would have a higher θ, all else being equal, than unitary states. But such a claim would need further theoretical work to be substantiated, in particular since we would expect the vertical allocation of policy responsibility to spill over onto the incentives for policymaking both at the central and regional level [see, e.g., Besley and Coate (2003) and Persson and Tabellini (1996a,b)].

Electoral Systems Another aspect of political arrangements is the selection of the policymaking set. To the extent that this occurs through elections, the electoral system also comes into play, indirectly, in the preceding political bargaining model because of the presence of parameter i in the function $\Omega(i, \ell)$. Recall that i represents the majority of the incumbent group in the policymaking set. Clearly, then, i ought to reflect the electoral rule. Indeed, the political-science literature deals with the electoral rule precisely as the mapping from vote shares to seat shares, with a much steeper seat-vote curve for plurality systems than for proportional representation (PR) systems [see Taagepera and Shugart (1989)].

Based on this insight and the fact that $\Omega(i, \ell)$ is declining in i, we would expect the higher representation for the opposition under PR to imply a higher value of $\theta(i, \ell)$ than plurality rule, all else being equal. Of course, this is but one of many possibilities of how electoral rules help shape the political game.

Taking Stock As the preceding discussion implies, there may not be a unique set of institutional arrangements that implement cohesive outcomes. This is an interesting observation in view of the diverse political arrangements that are associated with high executive constraints, according to the Polity IV data discussed in the introduction to this chapter. Our macro approach would say that these details may not matter, as long as there is sufficient cohesiveness for the state to be run along common-interest lines. Moreover, as we discuss at a later point in this section, traditions and history may help achieve political cohesiveness. But the mapping between micro and macro is clearly interesting in its own right. Furthermore, such knowledge is, of course, vital if one is interested in the design of real-world country-specific reform.

7.2.2 Micropolitical Foundations for γ

In this subsection, we provide alternative interpretations of γ, our second crucial macropolitical parameter, in terms of underlying institutional arrangements. We do so in a simple model for determining the composition of the policymaking set. This allows us to analyze how γ is determined with peaceful political transitions and how this depends on institutional choice. The simple model allows us to think about the way institutions can shape political stability, even if the groups are of equal size.

Constituencies Suppose that representation in the policymaking set is organized by *constituencies*. In a democracy, it is natural to treat these constituencies as electoral districts. But they could also represent ethnic groups, units in the army, or regional communist-party organizations. Parameter i in the last subsection, the size of the majority in the policymaking set, is now the outcome of a representation process across a large number of such constituencies. In particular, there is a continuum of constituencies indexed by $d \in [0, 1]$, where the fraction of individuals from group J in constituency d is $\beta^J(d; \ell)$, where selection rules ℓ may affect, for instance, who is able to express an opinion.

We order the constituencies from the most to least favorable for group J. Thus $\beta^J(d; \ell)$ is decreasing in d. To "win" a constituency, we suppose that there is a threshold of numerical dominance, denoted by $\frac{1}{2} + n(\ell)$. In an electoral democracy that threshold is at $n^J(\ell) = 0$, whereas $n^J(\ell) < 0$ represents an institution favorable to group J, i.e., this group needs fewer than half of the supporters to represent a particular constituency.

In the electoral interpretation, we are implicitly assuming that the electoral system operates by plurality rule. To address explicitly how $\theta(i, \ell)$ depends on electoral rule—as discussed at the end of the previous subsection—it would then be interesting to contrast the outcomes under plurality rule and proportional representation, along the lines of Lizzeri and Persico (2001), Milesi-Ferretti, Perotti, and Rostagno (2002), or Persson and Tabellini (1999). We leave such an analysis for further research. Given the analysis to follow in this subsection, however, a reasonable conjecture is that the choice of electoral rule would not only affect equilibrium cohesiveness, $\theta(i, \ell)$, but also equilibrium turnover, $\gamma(\ell)$.

Popularity Shocks We also allow for an aggregate random shock $\tilde{u}_s^J$ toward group J in period s, which reflects its "popularity."[5] This could be due to bias in media reporting in favor of group J or perhaps that group J is genuinely more popular on noneconomic issues. This setup will ring a bell among readers who are familiar with probabilistic voting models, which are widely used in political economics [see, e.g., Persson and Tabellini (2000) for an overview].

5. The shock for the other group is clearly $-\tilde{u}_s^J$.

Specifically, we start period 1 with some initial value of the shock, $\tilde{u}_1^J$. We then suppose that the period-2 value is

$$\tilde{u}_2^J = \varphi(\ell)\,\tilde{u}_1^J + (1 - \varphi(\ell))\,\eta,$$

where η is symmetrically distributed with mean zero on $\left[-\frac{1}{2\varrho}, \frac{1}{2\varrho}\right]$. Parameter $\varphi(\ell)$ allows for serial correlation in the realization of shocks, which could depend on institutional rules in a wide sense, to represent such things as incumbent control of the media.

Preliminaries In this setting, group J will win constituency d if

$$\beta^J(d;\ell) - \left(1 - \beta^J(d;\ell)\right) + \tilde{u}_s^J \geq n^J(\ell).$$

Now, define the pivotal constituency for group J, $\widetilde{d}_s^J$ implicitly from

$$\beta^J\left(\widetilde{d}_s^J;\ell\right) = \frac{1 + \left(n^J(\ell) - \tilde{u}_s^J\right)}{2}.$$

This variable gives us the fraction of the policymaking set that supports group J, given a shock of $\tilde{u}_s^J$. Then, group J becomes the incumbent group if

$$i_s^J = (\beta^J)^{-1}\left(\frac{1 + \left(n^J(\ell) - \tilde{u}_s^J\right)}{2};\ell\right) \geq 1/2.$$

It follows that group J is more likely to be the incumbent when, all else being equal: (1) it has a large popularity shock $\tilde{u}_s^J$; (2) it faces a weaker selection threshold, i.e., $n^J(\ell)$ is lower; and (3) the distribution of support, represented by d, across constituencies favors group J.

Endogenous Political Stability Group J, which makes up half of the population, will receive support commensurate with its population size only if $n(\ell) = \tilde{u}_s^J = 0$ and $\beta^J\left(\frac{1}{2};\ell\right) = 1/2$. In this case, $i^J = 1/2$. We refer to this as the unbiased case, in which the incumbent is replaced with probability 1/2.

Our simple framework can now be used to determine the probability that incumbent group I_1 loses political control in period 2. With the assumptions regarding the distribution of the popularity shock, this probability is given by

$$\gamma(\ell) = \text{Prob}\left\{(\beta^I)^{-1}\left(\frac{1+\left(n^I(\ell) - \varphi(\ell)\,\tilde{u}_1^J - (1-\varphi(\ell))\,\eta\right)}{2};\ell\right) < 1/2\right\},$$

where the randomness is due to the uncertainty about η, conditional on $\tilde{u}_1^I$. Persistence in shocks, a higher value of $\varphi(\ell)$, generates stability as a proincumbent bias, i.e., $\gamma(\ell) < 1/2$, even in the unbiased case because an incumbent group carries its current popularity shock into the next period.

To illustrate this for a simple case, suppose that $\beta^I(d;\ell) = 1 - d$ and that η is uniformly distributed. Then

$$\gamma(\ell) = \begin{cases} 0 & \text{if } \varrho\left[\dfrac{n^I(\ell) - \varphi(\ell)\,\tilde{u}_1^I}{1-\varphi(\ell)}\right] \le -\frac{1}{2} \\ \frac{1}{2} + \varrho\left[\dfrac{\frac{1}{2} - n^I(\ell) - \varphi(\ell)\,\tilde{u}_1^I}{1-\varphi(\ell)}\right] & \\ 1 & \text{if } \varrho\left[\dfrac{n^I(\ell) - \varphi(\ell)\,\tilde{u}_1^I}{1-\varphi(\ell)}\right] \ge \frac{1}{2}. \end{cases}$$

Thus persistence of power comes through $\varphi(\ell) > 0$, assuming that $\tilde{u}_1^I > 0$, i.e., the initial condition favors the incumbent and/or $n^I(\ell) > 0$.

This way, our simple model gives a micropolitical foundation for $\gamma(\ell)$. As simple as the model is, it provides a basis for discussing how political institutions matter for peaceful political transitions. But, of course, to exploit theoretical predictions in practice would require further work in terms of empirical measurement

Structure of Representation One of the key issues in any system of representative government is who is chosen to be a policymaker. This depends on the structure of representation, which is captured by function $\beta^J(d;\ell)$ in our model. This function describes how supporters for each group are distributed among the citizens who are allowed to participate in the selection of the policymaking set. The possibility that $\beta^J\left(\frac{1}{2};\ell\right) \neq 1/2$ can reflect a number of institutional restrictions that would keep incumbent groups in power.

For example, a large literature in political science discusses how institutional arrangements can be manipulated to favor one group by the strategic drawing up of district boundaries, other forms of gerrymandering such as overrepresentation of certain geographical areas with many prospective supporters, or electoral thresholds for representation. Such restrictions serve to keep down $\gamma(\ell)$, i.e., to give incumbents a more secure hold on power [see, e.g., Erikson (1972), Grofman (1985), and Grofman, Koetzle, and Brunell (1997)].

Franchise Restrictions A second issue concerns which citizens are allowed to express an opinion about who should be in the policymaking set—i.e., who among the citizenry are enfranchised. Even with two groups of equal size in the population, voting restrictions could maintain an electoral advantage for one group. It could even be that the function $\beta^J(d;\ell)$ is such that $\beta^J(d;\ell) > 1/2$ for all $d \in [0,1]$, i.e., one group is totally dominant. This might correspond to selection methods, where members of a certain income, racial, or ethnic group are seriously disadvantaged by facing much higher costs of participating in politics, or—in the worst case—by being entirely disenfranchised. History is full of examples of such restrictions. To take just a few, many European countries in the nineteenth century had weighted voting schemes, where high-income earners or high-wealth holders had more votes than others and/or there were outright income restrictions on the franchise. Blacks were effectively disenfranchised in the U.S. South by the selective use of poll taxes, reading and writing tests, and a host of other means from the 1880s to the passage of the Voting Right's Act in the mid-1960s [see Alt (1994) for a discussion].

Regulation of the franchise is thus another important aspect of political institutions that can be used by incumbents to decrease $\gamma(\ell)$, the probability of opposition takeover. This is a rationale for using the Polity IV measure of *competitiveness* in executive recruitment as one part of our empirical measure of γ.

Bias in Representation Another burning issue in the politics of many countries is that every group does not have the same chance of being represented in the policymaking process. In the preceding model, this would correspond to a group-specific bias in the threshold of representation for the policymaking set, such that $n^I(\ell) > 0$. In the limiting case, the incumbent group can set $n^I(\ell) = -1/2$ to ensure that only its own candidates can be selected. For example, in the U.S. race example, the number of blacks elected to hold political office in the southern states went quickly to zero after the restrictions imposed in the 1880s and did not start rising again until after the political reforms 80 years later.

Such restrictions constitute another route for incumbents strategically to keep down the threat of replacement $\gamma(\ell)$. This is a rationale for using the Polity IV measures of *openness* in executive recruitment as the other part of our empirical measure of γ.

Media and Openness Yet another dimension of institutional choice, which affects the peaceful rate of political turnover, concerns the extent to which one group can isolate itself from public scrutiny in office. In the preceding model, a crude way of capturing such institutions of nonaccountability and entrenchment is to think about the incumbent group making itself immune to popularity shocks $\tilde{u}_s^I$. The most important interpretation is that a group may maintain a persistent positive $\tilde{u}_s^I$ owing to an inflation of positive news or repression of bad news by the media, as in the media-capture model of Besley and Prat (2006). In reality, most autocratic regimes maintain more or less strict controls on the media for political purposes [see, e.g., the overview by Prat and Strömberg (2010)].

Taking Stock In this subsection and the previous one we have suggested ways in which our second macropolitical parametrization of political institutions $\{\theta, \gamma\}$ can be mapped into features of the rules that affect policy choice and political selection. Obviously, we have done so in a very simple and stylized way. However, we hope that it illustrates where a bridge could potentially be built between the earlier material in the book and the burgeoning political-economics literature on pre-election and postelection politics as surveyed, e.g., by Persson and Tabellini (2000). As with the microeconomic foundations before, there is a trade-off between specifying the detailed workings of micro models and the broad patterns coming out of a macro approach. But pinpointing where the join can be made is important, especially since the literature tends to bifurcate into one strand of studies that focuses on details of rules and another that looks at broad patterns. These two agendas should be viewed as complements rather than substitutes.

7.2.3 Constitutional Rules

We now study the possibility that changing the constitution is not a unilateral decision by the incumbent. In some countries, constitutional provision is deliberately established to increase the cost of political change, especially when it comes to rules for rulemaking. Such changes often require citizen approval and may even require a supermajority. For example, the Indian constitution requires a supermajority of two-thirds of members present and voting in both houses of the Indian Parliament to amend the constitution. The U.S. constitution requires a supermajority of two-thirds in both houses of Congress to propose a constitutional amendment, and—on top of that—three-quarters of the state legislatures have to approve the proposed amendment. In these and other cases, it is clear that the strict rules are intended to raise the cost of political reform.

However, the United States and, to some extent, India rely on a tradition of strong checks and balances. In other countries, similar supermajority provisions may have less bite. For example, Uganda's 1995 constitution stated that any amendment to the constitution would require a two-thirds majority in Parliament and a referendum. But this did not prevent President Yoweri Museveni from changing the rules, permitting him to run beyond the term limits laid down in the constitution.

At the end of the day, the existence of rules for institutional change begs the question of how such rules are enforced. To be binding, the rules require an overarching legal framework to ensure that the incumbent acts in accordance with them. Why people respect such authority is an interesting question. In the end, it may come down to social norms or some kind of dynamic punishment to enforce compliance that cannot easily be captured in our simple two-period setting.

Supermajority Requirement If constitutional rules can be not only created but also enforced, it may crucially impact on the behavior of the period-1 incumbent. To illustrate this, let us assume that there is a supermajority requirement for any change in θ, which is adhered to by the incumbent. In our two-group model, this amounts to a Wicksellian arrangement, requiring unanimous support for any change in θ.

Quite simply, this implies that any proposed change in θ_1 will only be accepted if it makes the opposition better off. The period-2 payoff of the opposition is $\gamma U^I\left(\tau_2, \pi_2; \theta\right) + (1-\gamma)\, U^O\left(\tau_2, \pi_2; \theta\right)$. Differentiating this expression with respect to θ yields

$$\frac{\partial\left[\gamma U^I\left(\tau_2, \pi_2; \theta\right) + (1-\gamma)\, U^O\left(\tau_2, \pi_2; \theta\right)\right]}{\partial\theta}$$
$$= \begin{cases} (1-\phi)\, 2(1-2\gamma)[\tau_2 y\left(\pi_2\right) + R] & \text{if } 2\,(1-\theta) > \alpha_L \\ 0 & \text{otherwise.} \end{cases}$$

Comparing this expression to (7.6) in Section 7.1, we see immediately that the opposition group has a diametrically opposite preference to the incumbent group. Hence, the opposition prefers $\theta_2 = 0$ if $\gamma \geq 1/2$ and $\alpha_L \geq 2(1-\theta_2)$ if $\gamma < 1/2$. This implies that when $\alpha_L < 2\left(1-\theta_1\right)$, there will be no change in the constitution, and if $\alpha_L \geq 2\left(1-\theta_1\right)$, there can be no move away from cohesive institutions.

Thus, we have the following:

Proposition 7.4: *If changing θ requires a supermajority, then $\theta_2 = \theta_1$.*

A supermajority requirement only guarantees that cohesive institutions prevail if they are the starting point, i.e., when $\theta_1 = 1/2$. If a polity begins with $\theta_1 = 0$, then an entrenched group will effectively acquire veto power, which prevents any improvement in institutions. Thus creating costs of change through supermajorities does not guarantee cohesive political institutions. It merely guarantees a status quo bias.

This simple argument illustrates that a commitment to a constitution, which limits the ability to change institutions, can become a powerful means of preserving institutions. Normatively speaking, one would only want to move to such a constitutional arrangement once cohesive institutions have been established. Indeed, it would be dangerous to create such provisions when institutions are not cohesive.

This creates a first insight into why a weak state may persist. Suppose that a state is created where an entrenched ruler (i.e., a ruler with a low value of γ) manages to set $\theta = 0$ and offers some constitutional protection that makes changing institutions costly or difficult. Then, even in the wake of weaker political control, so that γ increases, it may be impossible to galvanize political support to change the political institutions toward something more cohesive. This way, the weak state persists.

7.2.4 Political Violence

We now reintroduce political violence into the model, following the approach that we developed in Chapter 4. The effect of constitutional change is now to affect $\gamma\left(L^I, L^O; \xi\right)$, the equilibrium rate of turnover, by changing L^I and L^O. To home in on the effect of the choice of θ_2, we hold state capacities $\left\{\tau_2, \pi_2\right\}$ fixed, as we did in Chapter 4.

The period-1 incumbent optimizes by choosing $\{L^I, \theta\}$ to maximize

$$\left(1-\gamma\left(L^I, L^O; \xi\right)\right) U^I\left(\tau_2, \pi_2; \theta\right)+\gamma\left(L^I, L^O; \xi\right) U^O\left(\tau_2, \pi_2; \theta\right) \\ -\omega\left(\pi_1\right) \lambda_1 L^I .$$

As in Section 4.1, the opposition chooses L^O to maximize

$$\gamma\left(L^I, L^O; \xi\right) U^I\left(\tau_2, \pi_2; \theta\right)+\left[1-\gamma\left(L^I, L^O; \xi\right)\right] U^O\left(\tau_2, \pi_2; \theta\right) \\ -\omega\left(\pi_1\right) \nu L^O .$$

We are interested in decisions that form a Nash equilibrium. The conditions for political violence are essentially unchanged from those that we derived in Chapter 4.

Choice of Cohesiveness—Preliminaries The new condition that we have to study is for the choice of θ. As we saw earlier in the model with an exogenous turnover rate, whether an increase in θ is desirable from the incumbent's point of view depends critically on $\gamma \gtreqless 1/2$. However, now the expected rate of turnover depends on the investments in violence $\left(L^I, L^O\right)$ at the Nash equilibrium.

Studying the choice of θ is somewhat complicated by the fact that the payoff function is not concave and is discontinuous at $\theta=1-\frac{\alpha_L}{2}$. As in Proposition 7.2, we find that the optimal θ is at a corner solution, either with fully cohesive institutions or fully noncohesive institutions. The cost of noncohesive institutions is that the incumbent has to spend resources on violence. If these costs are large enough, it will help cement the creation of cohesive institutions.

Cohesiveness under the Threat of Violence We now study formally the choice of θ. Let $\{\hat{L}_0^I, \hat{L}_0^O\}$ denote the equilibrium investments in violence by the incumbent and the opposition under maximally noncohesive institutions, i.e., when $\theta=0$, and let

$$\gamma_0=\gamma\left(\hat{L}_0^I, \hat{L}_0^O; \xi\right)$$

be the corresponding turnover probability at this Nash equilibrium.

We now have the following:

Proposition 7.5: *Suppose that $\phi<1$. Then, if $\gamma_0 \geq 1/2$, the period-1 incumbent chooses cohesive institutions. If $\gamma_0<1/2$, the period-1 incumbent chooses cohesive institutions if and only if*

$$\left[R+\tau_2 y\left(\pi_2\right)\right](1-\phi)\left[2\left(1-\gamma_0\right)-\alpha_L\right]-\omega\left(\pi_1\right) \lambda_1 \hat{L}_0^I \leq 0 .$$

Proof: It is useful to define

$$\hat{U}(\theta) = \left[\left(1-\gamma\left(L^I, L^O; \xi\right)\right) U^I(\tau_2, \pi_2; \theta) + \gamma\left(L^I, L^O; \xi\right) U^O(\tau_2, \pi_2; \theta)\right].$$

Observe that from Proposition 5.1, $d\gamma\left(\hat{L}^I, \hat{L}^O; \xi\right)/d\theta > 0$. This implies that if $\gamma_0 \geq 1/2$, then $\gamma\left(\hat{L}_0^I, \hat{L}_0^O; \xi\right) > 1/2$ for all $\theta \in \left[0, 1-\frac{\alpha_L}{2}\right)$. It follows that

$$\hat{U}_\theta(\theta) = (1-\phi)\, 2\left[2\gamma\left(\hat{L}_0^I, \hat{L}_0^O; \xi\right) - 1\right]\left[R + \tau_2 y(\pi_2)\right] > 0$$

for all $\theta \in \left[0, 1-\frac{\alpha_L}{2}\right)$ when evaluated at the Nash equilibrium for violence. Since this derivative is everywhere increasing, cohesive institutions will be chosen. The payoff is discontinuous, but increasing, at $\theta = 1-\frac{\alpha_L}{2}$ since

$$\left[R + \tau_2 y(\pi_2)\right]\ (1-\phi)\left[\alpha_L - 2(1-\gamma)\right] > 0$$

when $\gamma \geq 1/2$.

Now suppose that $\gamma_0 < 1/2$. If $\gamma(0, 0; \xi) < 1/2$ then

$$\hat{U}_\theta(\theta) = (1-\phi)\, 2\left[2\gamma\left(\hat{L}_0^I, \hat{L}_0^O; \xi\right) - 1\right]\left[R + \tau_2 y(\pi_2)\right] < 0$$

for all $\theta \in \left[0, 1-\frac{\alpha_L}{2}\right)$. Since the payoff of the incumbent is discontinuous, either $\theta = 0$ will be chosen or $\theta \geq 1-\frac{\alpha_L}{2}$. Comparing the payoffs with $\theta = 0$ and $\theta \geq 1-\frac{\alpha_L}{2}$ yields the condition stated in the proposition.

Finally, consider the case where $\gamma(0, 0; \xi) \geq 1/2 \geq \gamma_0$. Observe that by Proposition 5.3, $\lim_{\theta \to 1-\frac{\alpha_L}{2}} \gamma\left(\hat{L}^I, \hat{L}^O; \xi\right) \to \gamma(0, 0; \xi)$. Define $\hat{\theta}$ as the value of θ such that

$$\gamma\left(\hat{L}_0^I, \hat{L}_0^O; \xi\right) = 1/2.$$

Now observe that $\hat{U}(\theta)$ is strictly convex on $\left[0, 1-\frac{\alpha_L}{2}\right)$ since

$$\hat{U}_{\theta\theta}(\theta) = (1-\phi)\, 4 \frac{d\gamma\left(\hat{L}_0^I, \hat{L}_0^O; \xi\right)}{d\theta}\left[R + \tau_2 y(\pi_2)\right] > 0.$$

Thus, $\hat{U}(\theta)$ is decreasing in θ as $\theta \in \left[0, \hat{\theta}\right)$ and increasing as $\theta \in \left(\hat{\theta}, 1-\frac{\alpha_L}{2}\right)$. Maximizing a strictly convex function yields a corner solution with either

$\theta = 0$ or $\theta \geq 1 - \frac{\alpha_L}{2}$. To see that the latter is indeed the solution, note that the incumbent's payoff is discontinuous, but increasing, at $\theta = 1 - \frac{\alpha_L}{2}$ since

$$\left[R + \tau_2 y\left(\pi_2\right)\right](1-\phi)\left[\alpha_L - 2\left(1 - \gamma\left(0, 0; \xi\right)\right)\right] > 0$$

when $\gamma\left(0, 0; \xi\right) \geq 1/2$. Comparing the payoffs at $\theta = 0$ and $\theta \geq 1 - \frac{\alpha_L}{2}$ gives the condition stated in the proposition. ■

The first part of Proposition 7.5 says that an incumbent unable to reduce turnover sufficiently when $\theta = 0$ will find it optimal to go for cohesive institutions. The second part says that if the incumbent can indeed create low turnover by making institutions noncohesive, it will be worthwhile if the benefits of securing access to redistribution outweigh the costs of violence.

Interpretation Comparing the result in this proposition with Proposition 7.2, we see that latent violence has two distinct effects on the choice of cohesive institutions. One goes against choosing cohesive institutions and the other in favor. For institutions to be cohesive with certainty, the incumbent has to feel enough of a threat of replacement, i.e., a high enough rate of turnover, when $\theta = 0$. Since $\gamma_0 < \gamma\left(0, 0; \xi\right)$, this condition is more demanding than the condition in the absence of violence. Absent violence, the incumbent cares only about the peaceful turnover rate, which is higher than the turnover rate in the presence of violence. This effect makes cohesive institutions less likely.

But there is also a cost associated with maintaining noncohesive institutions. Noncohesive institutions lead to political violence, which constitutes a drain on public resources. The incumbent has to trade off this resource cost against the benefits of higher expected transfers. The costs of using political violence may make it more likely that an incumbent will pick cohesive institutions. In effect, the prospect of violence acts as a check on the incumbent. In other words, any factor that reduces the cost of having the opposition invest in political violence may actually make it more likely that the government will decide to choose cohesive institutions. The discussion here further reinforces the point made in Chapter 5 that it would be important to extend the analysis so as to endogenize parameters such as ν and ξ into endogenous variables, e.g., by explicitly studying investments in military technology.

The argument in this subsection is related to the work by Acemoglu and Robinson (2000) on the extension of the franchise. They argue that an elite may want to extend the franchise to the rest of society, even though this implies a redistributive cost in the future. The reason is that an extended franchise avoids the potential cost to the elite of a mass revolution. Such franchise extension is similar to an increase in θ, in terms of the interpretation in Subsection 7.2.2, where we argued that $\theta(i, \ell)$ could be a reflection of the representation or bargaining power of the opposition. The cost of a revolution in Acemoglu and Robinson's argument is similar to the latent cost of political violence discussed in this subsection.

Our argument is also related to recent work by Fearon (2010), who shows that the threat of a rebellion against a ruling government if it tries to rig elections may serve to make democratic rule a self-enforcing equilibrium.

Development Assistance and Resource Rents Revisited The model with political violence allows us to extend our earlier analyses in Chapters 4 and 6. In particular, we can now predict the effect of aid or natural resource rents on the choice of political institutions. This effect depends upon whether there is repression or civil war at $\theta = 0$.

Proposition 7.6: *An increase in aid or natural resources, R, increases the likelihood that the period-1 incumbent chooses noncohesive institutions in repression but has an ambiguous effect on this choice in civil war.*

To see this, first observe that γ_0 is decreasing in R from Proposition 5.1. This means that a higher value of R makes the second case of Proposition 7.5 more likely.

Now suppose that $\gamma_0 < 1/2$ and ask how the incumbent's objective $U^I = [R + \tau_2 y(\pi_2)](1 - \phi)[2(1 - \gamma_0) - \alpha_L] - \omega(\pi_1)\lambda_1 \hat{L}_0^I$ depends on R. Under repression, we have

$$\frac{dU^I}{dR} = [2(1 - \gamma_0) - \alpha_L] > 0,$$

using the envelope condition for $\hat{L}^I$. This makes it less likely that cohesive institutions will be chosen. Intuitively, higher R makes being in a redistributive regime more attractive given that the survival probability is higher.

However, with civil war,

$$\frac{dU^I}{dR} = [2(1 - \gamma_0) - \alpha_L] - \omega(\pi_1)\nu\frac{d\hat{L}^O}{dZ},$$

using the first-order condition for the choice of $\hat{L}^O$. The sign of the derivative is now ambiguous, since an increase in R increases the intensity of fighting by the opposition. This additional effect lowers the incumbent's prospect of political survival and encourages the incumbent to choose cohesive institutions.

Based on their evidence Djankov, Montalvo, and Reynal-Querol (2008) have argued that aid reduces the probability that a regime will become democratic. This is certainly consistent with Proposition 7.6 and in line with arguments frequently made by opponents of aid. Proposition 7.6 provides yet another example—beyond those in Chapter 6—of the need carefully to consider the details of a recipient country's political equilibrium before assessing the impact of aid. It also highlights the need to unpack regime heterogeneity to understand the effect of aid on political institutions.

7.2.5 Trust

Next, we explore the implications of informal mechanisms for sustaining cohesive institutions, which we place under the broad heading of "trust." Our discussion of micropolitical foundations in Section 7.2.1 described a world where institutional rules map uniquely into policy outcomes. This is also the traditional view of institutions as shaping the rules of the game. But this traditional view leaves no room for trust or social norms. At the other extreme, we have a world entirely without formal institutions, where the norms of cooperation evolve to determine resource allocation. Many primitive societies can evolve complex social and political orders, which are built on few formal rules but seem to operate on a fairly cooperative basis. Moreover, societies with many formal rules may see these rules ignored in practice. Even though the world of trust is often viewed as somewhat murky by economists, our understanding of how political reform works and how cohesiveness becomes established has to encompass these ideas.

Our discussion of these issues is deliberately superficial. We still wish to flag a very important area for further exploration, given our observations throughout this book that building cohesive institutions is essential for effective and peaceful states. The material in this subsection should be seen as a signpost to indicate where such modeling might go.

Trust as Behavior There are two broad approaches to studying trust in economics. The first sees trust as established through some form of repeated play, where private or collective punishments are invoked to increase trustworthy behavior.[6] In our context, such an approach would seek a foundation for θ from repeated interaction of the two groups in office when the members of the group are strategic and forward-looking. A world where the incumbent does not take all of the residual public revenues as transfers $\theta = 0$ would then be part of a long-term strategy, given some alternation in power. A nice feature of such reputational models is their potential to explain something we have simply assumed, namely that the choice of θ_2 is binding. We have also taken for granted that the period-1 incumbent can choose period-2 institutions, even though the short-term interests of the period-2 incumbent may very well call for a reversion to $\theta_2 = 0$. In a setting with repeated interactions, such behavior could be punished, thus creating the possibility of sustaining cohesiveness.

Models along these lines have been developed in Alesina (1988) and Dixit, Grossman, and Gul (2000). Such models are good news and bad news in the search for micropolitical foundations of cohesive institutions. The good news is that even weak formal institutions can sustain strong norms of cooperation. The bad news is that there are typically multiple equilibria, such that a polity could end up in a bad outcome (corresponding to $\theta = 0$) owing to pessimistic, self-fulfilling beliefs. History can condition these beliefs and make it difficult to change the cohesiveness of institutions. This is the view, for instance, that underpins the interpretation by Nunn (2008) of the persistent effects of slavery on economic performance. It may be possible to change expectations through the reform of rules, but the weight of history may strongly condition beliefs. In terms of our model framework, this could mean that establishing cohesive institutions might be hard or impossible regardless of γ. Thus, the absence of trust could explain why some countries are locked into weak states, even if political instability is high.

Trust as a Trait The class of work discussed so far models trust as behavior. Individuals are actually not trustworthy in any well-defined sense. They are really self-interested, but they cooperate because their self-interest dictates that cooperation is a sensible strategy. If intertemporal links are broken for some reason, the trust may break down suddenly and forcefully. An alternative approach is to see trust as a product of individual "types." Some people keep their word, find cheating distasteful, and are willing to share what they have

6. The standard model is described in Fudenberg and Maskin (1986) and the model with community enforcement is due to Kandori (1989).

with complete strangers—even with those they will never interact with again. Experimental evidence on so-called "divide-the-dollar" games overwhelmingly supports the idea that some people are naturally cooperative. Moreover, such traits are more prevalent in some societies than in others. Cohesive societies are often described as having cooperative norms of behavior, but these norms do not have any strategic underpinnings. Social capital as popularized by Putnam (1993) is often described in these terms.

When it comes to politics, the parameter θ could reflect such societal traits. The traits may also reflect political selection, if some polities are better able to promote individuals with cooperative traits to public office. This second view of the origins of cohesive institutions also brings good and bad news. The good news is that we expect societal traits to be slow moving. As a result, cohesiveness might stick because it is really embedded in people's preferences. Thus, we may not see θ changing much in response to changes in γ. A cohesive set of political institutions will tend to be maintained. The bad news is that the same argument applies to societies whose ethics entrench low θ. Changing institutions may then have only a limited impact on increased cohesiveness. Improving political selection by trying to find trustworthy politicians may help. But if there are few moral people around, this may be difficult.

For this second interpretation of trust and cohesiveness, the way to change cohesiveness is to change society. This opens up an interesting line of work, following recent contributions, such as the one by Tabellini (2008). Suppose that parents can choose to endow their children with preferences for political cohesiveness so they behave as if $\theta = 1/2$ when selected for political office or with low cohesiveness so they behave as if $\theta = 0$. Moreover, suppose that the equilibrium policy outcome depends on the composition of the legislature. Now, the setup involves a game between parents who try to anticipate what other parents will be doing. If the children are happier when society adopts their own preferred norm, there will be a tendency for the equilibrium to have conformity, but this could be conformity with either $\theta = 1/2$ or $\theta = 0$. On this basis alone, whether a society ends up with a common-interest state could also be an issue of coordinating on the cohesive norm. Here, we would expect a complementarity with state capacity since the part of utility that is affected by preferences over θ is the public domain. Larger collective consumption makes the payoff to the bequeathed norm more important.

Taking Stock Two interesting and related themes emerge from the brief discussion in this subsection.

If trust is indeed important in building cohesiveness, history matters. The choice of institutions and/or the working of institutions can depend on slow-moving factors. This is consistent with the recent empirical findings of Persson and Tabellini (2009) that a long history of being democratic (or many democracies in the geographic neighborhood) endows a country with "democratic capital," which lowers the probability of transitions out of democracy.

Following from this, societies may have natural costs in adopting more or less cohesive institutions. For any country, we could write a reduced-form cost function $C(\theta; X)$, where X is a vector of relevant country characteristics, including its political history. Exactly who pays this cost of regime change is not clear—it could be paid privately or through interactions in the public budget. An explicit model with micropolitical foundations would be needed to open this black box. But the idea captures the possibility that raising θ could be very costly in some societies. In such societies, the real choice might be between a weak state and a redistributive state. If so, greater security of political power might become a (second-best) device for improving the working of the state. But the international community might also have a role in raising the cost of $\theta = 0$ and reducing the cost of $\theta = 1/2$ by whatever means it has at its disposal.

7.2.6 Governance

Thus far, our discussion in this chapter has highlighted the role of political institutions in allocating the public budget fairly between groups. Intergroup resource allocation is indeed important and lies at the heart of the way that many political institutions work in practice. But there are also important issues associated with intragroup resource allocation. We now turn to these issues and their dependence on political institutions. As we discussed in Section 3.2.4, a predatory ruler who is able to extract resources through private expropriation will not wish to invest in legal capacity since this would limit his power. As a result, the economy may end up in a legal-capacity trap. In Chapter 3, we introduced the governance parameter $\varsigma \in [0, 1]$ to denote the transaction costs an incumbent incurs when trying to extract resources via expropriation and predation. We now analyze a reform aimed at increasing ς and the incentive that a period-1 incumbent might have to undertake such a reform.

What Transaction Costs? In a search for micropolitical foundations, the governance parameter ς can be thought of primarily as representing inducing transparency and individual accountability. To what extent will a public official be able to make a private gain from public office that goes unmonitored and unpunished? In practice, we expect the answer to this question to be strongly correlated with constraints on the executive, our core empirical measure of θ. However, governance is wider than these constraints and might reflect such things as government openness and freedom of the press. To home in on incentives to reform, we follow the same approach as in our discussion about θ and assume that raising ζ carries no direct cost. Obviously, then, any costs of reform would just serve to further diminish the incentive to pursue good governance.

A Simple Binary Case We focus on a binary case where $\zeta \in \{0, 1\}$ such that governance is either bad $\zeta = 0$ or good $\zeta = 1$. The task is to understand the incentive of a period-1 incumbent to implement good governance. As in Chapter 3, we look at the case when an elite e^I controls power within the group and earns all the returns from predation, if any. An increase in p_s^J will increase the cost of predation and, hence, reduce the likelihood that the state will be predatory. We focus on the case when, under bad governance, it is optimal not to extend formal legal protection to either group, $p_s^I = p_s^O = 0$. Let $y(0)$ be the income per capita in each group in the bad-governance case.

To home in on governance, suppose as well that $\theta = 1/2$, i.e., the institutions used to allocate resources through the public budget are fully cohesive. This assumption is clearly unrealistic in situations where governance can be bad, but it will serve cleanly to isolate this separate dimension of political reform. With good governance, we have $p_s^I = p_s^O = \pi_s$, full extension of legal protection within the confines of available legal capacity.

In terms of Proposition 3.9, we are thus dealing with parameters such that $\zeta_H < 1$ and $\zeta_L > 0$. Adopting the same notation as in Section 3.2.4, we let

$$\hat{\Pi}_0 = \frac{\sum_{J \in \{I,O\}} \left[\mu\left(\hat{\chi}_0, 0\right) \tilde{y}(0) - C\left(\hat{\chi}_0\right)\right]}{e^I} \tag{7.7}$$

be the level of rents for each member of the elite when there is bad governance. Recall that $\hat{\chi}_0$ is the associated predation level defined in equation (3.28). Now let

$$\begin{aligned} U^I\left(\tau_2, \pi_2; \zeta\right) &= (1-\zeta)\,\hat{\Pi}_0 + \\ &\quad \left[1 + \tau_2\left(\left[\phi\alpha_H + (1-\phi)\,\alpha_L\right] - 1\right)\right]\left[\zeta y\left(\pi_2\right) + (1-\zeta)\, y(0)\right] \end{aligned}$$

and

$$U^O\left(\tau_2, \pi_2; \zeta\right) = \left[1 + \tau_2\left(\left[\phi\alpha_H + (1-\phi)\,\alpha_L\right] - 1\right)\right]\left[\zeta y\left(\pi_2\right) + (1-\zeta)\, y(0)\right]$$

be the payoff to the period-1 incumbent elite if their group is the incumbent or the opposition in period 2. With good governance, $\zeta = 1$, $U^I = U^O$, i.e., there is no incumbency advantage in period 2 because we have assumed that $\theta = 1/2$.

Equilibrium Governance The optimal choice of governance by the period-1 incumbent maximizes

$$(1-\gamma)\, U^I\left(\tau_2, \pi_2; \zeta\right) + \gamma U^O\left(\tau_2, \pi_2; \zeta\right).$$

There will also be investments in state capacities, where the usual investment costs, $\lambda_1\left[\mathcal{F}\left(\tau_2 - \tau_1\right) + \mathcal{L}\left(\pi_2 - \pi_1\right)\right]$, are taken into account.

Our core result on governance reform is as follows:

Proposition 7.7: *The period-1 incumbent prefers good governance ($\zeta_2 = 1$) in period 2 if and only if*

$$(1-\gamma)\,\hat{\Pi}_0 - \left[1 + \tau_2\left(\left[\phi\alpha_H + (1-\phi)\,\alpha_L\right] - 1\right)\right]\left(y\left(\pi_2\right) - y\left(0\right)\right) \leq 0.$$

A good governance reform is less likely the smaller the elite and the lower the state capacity.

The condition in the proposition just says that the expected value of the rents to the incumbent elite is smaller than the income gains (direct and through the public budget) of eliminating them.

As in our discussion of cohesiveness in Section 7.2.2, good governance is most likely to be chosen when expected political turnover is high. However, there is no guarantee that $\gamma \geq 1/2$ suffices to improve governance. In particular, the higher the gains from predation, $\hat{\Pi}_0$, the weaker the motives for reform. As shown clearly by (7.7), the smaller the elite the higher the per-member predation gains.

Taking Stock Proposition 7.7 reveals another complementarity between state capacity and governance reforms. If π_2 is high, the prospective income gains from improving governance and hence better exploiting the legal system are greater. If τ_2 is high, this additional income has a higher value because of the public goods that can be provided. These complementarities suggest a further source of clustering in that weak state capacities and poor governance tend to reinforce each other. This suggests the possibility of a governance trap, where owing to the absence of fiscal and legal capacity the elite have weak incentives to create good governance institutions. As indicated by the proposition, the risk of such a governance trap is particularly acute when politics is dominated by small powerful elites.

The condition in Proposition 7.7 can fail to hold even if political instability is high. This fact suggests that states that are weak owing to high predation may be especially resistant to political reform. To the extent that it is hard to raise θ without raising ζ—since both may involve increased accountability on the part of the executive—this may have a knock-on effect on the resistance to reform toward cohesive institutions. If this is correct, we should rarely find cohesive institutions together with bad governance.

We can combine the insights from this subsection with those from Subsection 7.2.4 regarding political reform and political violence. As violence brings about a lower value of γ, it will further retard governance reform. Moreover, as argued in Chapter 4, weak governance encourages political violence. Thus, a further vicious circle of violence and bad governance may be unleashed with additional implications for clustered misery. On a more positive note, our analysis underlines the dynamic gains from conquering poor governance and creating incentives for stronger and more peaceful states. The only question is how far small and unwilling political elites can be expected to swallow that bitter pill. Sadly, the experience of postwar development does not give us much ground for optimism.

7.3 *Political Reform in Practice*

The analysis in this chapter has touched upon a number of issues regarding endogenous political reform, relying on models of macropolitics as well as models with micropolitical foundations. As the analysis has been preliminary and exploratory, it is not so easy to come down with a clear bottom line in terms of empirical predictions. In this section, we nevertheless try to use specific insights from the theory to sketch a few examples of how one can think systematically about how to approach the data. Thus we emphasize methodology more than substance.

Political Stability and Political Reform A common theme in Sections 7.1 and 7.2.4 on strategic reforms, with and without the threat of violence, is that reform toward more cohesive political institutions is more likely, when incumbents perceive a higher probability that they will be replaced in the future. This theme is reflected in Proposition 7.2 as well as Proposition 7.5. How can we test this prediction in the data?

By way of illustration consider the simpler case in Proposition 7.2. This proposition implies a simple condition for reform toward cohesive political institutions, i.e., $\theta \geq \frac{1-\alpha_L}{2}$, to be undertaken, namely

$$\tfrac{1}{2} - \gamma \leq 0. \tag{7.8}$$

Suppose we have measures of the θ and γ, such as the proxies we have used from the Polity IV data. The problem with using these in an empirical study is clearly illustrated by the analyses in Sections 7.2.2 and 7.2.3. Summary measures of θ and γ, like our empirical proxies in earlier chapters, are most likely correlated with each other, e.g., because the political rules of the game—called ℓ in the chapter—reflect some common underlying socioeconomic variables. Thus, putting $\theta(i, \ell)$ on the right-hand side and $\gamma(\ell)$ on the left-hand side may give us a correlation, but it says little about the causal relation from political stability to cohesiveness because of an omitted-variable problem.

The Likelihood of Reform To drive home that point and see possible ways out of the conundrum, consider an empirical approach similar to the one we outlined in Section 4.3. Specifically, suppose that we can write peaceful expected political turnover by the incumbent in country c at date s as the following sum:

$$\gamma_{c,s} = \gamma(\ell_{c,s}) + \widetilde{\gamma}_{c,s}. \tag{7.9}$$

In this expression, $\gamma(\ell_{c,s})$ is an observable empirical proxy of the "endogenous" part of stability, whereas $\widetilde{\gamma}_{c,s}$ is an observable measure of an "exogenous" stability component, where endogenous and exogenous refer to being correlated and uncorrelated with $\theta(i_{c,s}, \ell_{c,s})$.

Suppose now that there is a stochastic net cost of cohesive political reform in country c at date s, which is additive (with a minus sign) to $\gamma_{c,s}$ and is denoted by $\eta_{c,s}$. Let $\eta_{c,s}$ have a country-specific distribution function $Q^c(\eta)$. Using (7.9), we can then rewrite the condition for reform toward cohesive institutions in (7.8) as

$$\eta_{c,s} \leq \gamma(\ell_{c,s}) + \widetilde{\gamma}_{c,s} - \tfrac{1}{2}.$$

Given the model in Section 7.1 and the result in Proposition 7.2, the conditional likelihood of observing reform can now be expressed as

$$\text{Prob}[\theta(i_{c,s+1}, \ell_{c,s+1}) \geq 1 - \frac{\alpha_L}{2} \mid \theta(i_{c,s}, \ell_{c,s}) = 0] = Q^c(\gamma(\ell_{c,s}) + \widetilde{\gamma}_{c,s} - \tfrac{1}{2}). \tag{7.10}$$

The expression in (7.10) gives us a stepping stone for discussing alternative approaches to confronting the theory with data.

We now suggest three examples of how the theory can be applied. First, we consider an existing econometric study. We then discuss two possible cases studies built around specific instances of institutional change. In each instance, we discuss a prospective source of exogenous variation in $\gamma_{c,s}$ to be exploited. The point of the ensuing discussion is to illustrate the value of interpreting the data armed with an explicit theory, which links prospective political turnover and political reform together.

Example 1: Political Assassinations and Institutional Change The expression in (7.10) suggests a way of looking at the link between political turnover and the move toward cohesive institutions. To make this operational requires a measurable exogenous stability component $\widetilde{\gamma}_{c,s}$. A recent paper by Jones and Olken (2009) offers a potential way out via an ingenious identification strategy. Specifically, they use successful and unsuccessful assassination attempts against political leaders, over a period of 130 years, to predict within-country political regime changes. The identifying assumption is that the difference between success and failure creates comparable treatment and control groups, since the success of an assassination attempt can be considered as good as random. Jones and Olken (2009) find that successful assassinations result in a higher probability of democratic transitions compared to unsuccessful ones. For this purpose, democracy is coded as a binary variable based on an overall democracy score in the Polity IV data. They show, moreover, that these regime changes are durable 10 years after the event.

This empirical strategy fits neatly into the framework that we have sketched in this subsection and Section 7.1, if we assume that: (1) democracy is a more cohesive political system compared to autocracy, i.e., θ is higher, and (2) successful assassinations (exogenously) induce more political instability $\widetilde{\gamma}$ compared to unsuccessful ones. Assumption (1) is certainly plausible a priori. Assumption (2) is not only plausible a priori, but also receives support from

Jones and Olken's auxiliary results, which show that successful assassinations raise the intensity of civil conflicts.

Thus, the theoretical framework that we have developed in this section offers an interpretation of the results from Jones and Olken's (2009) empirical study. A similar approach could be used to analyze reforms for alternative measures of cohesive political institutions and alternative measures of within-country time variation in political instability. The aim should be to look for credibly exogenous time-series variation in γ within countries alongside changes in the adoption or abandonment of strong executive constraints.

Example 2: The Switch toward Proportional Representation in Western Europe
When the data required for a panel-data econometric study is not available, there is still the possibility of using case studies. Even though this is not the typical description adopted by authors, interpreting such studies in terms of a theory requires clarity about the source of exogenous variation that is being appealed to.

In this vein, we look at a second example based on a famous hypothesis, formulated in Rokkan (1970) and further extended (and tested) by others, including Boix (1999). The hypothesis concerns causes of the switch from plurality to PR elections in many countries, such as Denmark, Sweden, Belgium, and the Netherlands. These switches occurred under incumbent governments dominated by right-of-center parties around the turn of the twentieth century, in connection with the introduction of universal suffrage, and was then followed by several other countries in the wake of World War I.

Rokkan's hypothesis is that the switch to PR was made to limit the electoral losses of left-wing parties, which had grown stronger owing to industrialization and the rise of the labor movement. But a similar switch did not occur in several other countries such as the United Kingdom and Canada. According to the hypothesis, this depended on cross-cutting cleavages in other dimensions, which made the established rural and urban elites based on land and capital more or less united in their interests. It was only where established elites and parties were politically divided that the rising labor movement imposed a more formidable threat and the switch to PR occurred.

These ideas can be placed in our framework as follows. Suppose we consider—as Section 7.2 argued we might—a move from plurality rule to PR as an increase in cohesiveness, i.e., a higher θ. The political threat to the incumbent governments of the rising labor movements is then interpreted as an upward shift in γ. At first sight then, the Rokkan hypothesis appears to fit neatly into the framework of this chapter. The discussion around equation (7.10) should give us some cause for concern, however. Was the threat to the incumbent right-center parties really an *exogenous* change in political stability, i.e., a change in $\tilde{\gamma}$? It may plausibly be argued that the rise of organized labor was tied to structural change, which was, in turn, driven by technological innovation. But can we really claim that the different coalitions between urban and rural elites, which were assumed to distinguish the cases of, say, Sweden and the United Kingdom, were exogenous to other forces that may have pushed more or less in the direction of PR, such as the ethnic composition of the population or the geographical preconditions for agriculture and industry? Perhaps. It would seem that this is best not judged a priori, though, but rather through a careful comparative historical case study, with the aim of verifying or rejecting the exogeneity requirement. However, putting things in terms of our framework certainly sharpens the nature of this debate.

Example 3: Institutional Deterioration in Africa Finally, we return to the empirical observations in Table 7.1, which showed that many of the independent countries founded in the last 50 or so years have never adopted cohesive institutions as measured by the highest score on the Polity IV executive constraints variable. Further, among the few countries that started out with cohesive institutions, very few retained them. The African case is particularly noteworthy. Mauritius and Botswana maintained their initial (or early adopted) cohesive institutions, whereas Lesotho, Nigeria, Somalia, Sudan and Uganda lost their initially cohesive institutions—sooner rather than later. Moreover, other African states have never introduced cohesive institutions.

It is possible to look at these failures to implement cohesiveness reforms through the lens of the theory in Sections 7.1, 7.2.4, and 7.2.6. The theory suggests that the reversions away from cohesiveness would likely reflect the desire of long-lived rulers to take advantage of a relatively secure hold on power, i.e., a low value of γ, to destroy (or never create) any existing checks and balances. By doing so, they would be able to extend favors to broad groups of supporters and/or enrich themselves or the members of a small elite. Moreover, such motives are strengthened by having significant natural-resource rents or aid (recall Proposition 7.6). In addition, leaders may also have been supported by military aid from abroad, especially as a concomitant of strategic alignments during the Cold War (recall parameter ξ and its effect on violent turnover in Chapters 4 and 5).

As in the case study of the Rokkan hypothesis, a few detailed comparative case studies would be a rewarding way to check out whether these hypotheses hold water empirically. Once again, the challenge would be to explain not only cases of reform away from cohesive institutions but also those in the direction of cohesiveness. This may not be completely straightforward. On the surface there appear to be some anomalies. Botswana has considerable natural resources and has had more-or-less uninterrupted rule by the same incumbent party, while retaining cohesive institutions. Mauritius is ethnically and culturally diverse, but has also retained cohesive political institutions since independence. But the principle is clear. A successful case study in terms of the theory would involve a credible argument about differences across time and countries in the exogenous component of political stability $\tilde{\gamma}$.

7.4 *Final Remarks*

In this chapter, we have taken some steps toward integrating endogenous political reform into the core model. A general finding is that forces that lead to political stability generally reduce the motives of ruling groups to undertake political reforms toward greater cohesiveness.

We have also sketched some micropolitical foundations for the main macropolitical parameters in the core model, political cohesiveness, and (peaceful) political turnover, and tried to relate them to real-world tangible political institutional rules and regulations. As in the case of tax compliance in Chapter 2, we have noted that cohesiveness in political life may reflect not only formal institutions, but also informal rules of behavior, trust, and social norms. This is in line with studies that focus on the role of social capital. Consonant with one of our recurrent themes, we have also considered political reform in a predatory state and given reasons for resistance toward reforms that promote common-interest politics. This discussion reinforces the observation that reform may be particularly problematic in such states.

We have tried to develop the theory in a manner that is mindful of the need to match theoretical progress with empirical explanation. Toward this end, we sketched a theoretical interpretation of Jones and Olken's (2009) empirical study of democratic reform following successful assassinations of political leaders. We have also argued that historical case studies could usefully be informed by the theory. The central idea is that comparative case studies have to begin from a proper discussion of exogenous variation across time and/or across countries. There are already some case studies based explicitly on theory in the development literature. A notable example is Lucas (1993), who uses the neoclassical growth model to look at why South Korea, but not the Philippines, "made a miracle." Similarly, the four country cases considered in Acemoglu and Robinson (2005) are clearly related to an explicit theoretical structure.[7]

The discussion around the Anna Karenina matrix at the end of Chapter 5 gave pride of place to cohesive institutions in promoting peace and prosperity. There, we argued that to understand development clusters, theoretical and empirical knowledge about the interactions among economic, social, cultural, and political variables that might create cohesiveness is of first importance. This chapter has merely scratched the surface of this question in the context of our framework, and much more work remains to be done.

7.5 *Notes on the Literature*

There is a large literature in political science on the choice of constitutional arrangements, such as electoral systems and forms of government and their consequences within the political system. Classics in this literature include Powell (1989, 2000), who poses the choice between plurality and PR elections as a trade-off between accountability and representation; Shugart and Carey (1992), who study the choice between presidential and parliamentary systems; and Diermeier and Feddersen (1998), who lay the micropolitical foundations for these alternative forms of government based on the presence or absence of the confidence procedure. Cox (1997) and Taagepera and Shugart (1989) discuss different features of electoral systems and Myerson (1999) summarizes the theoretical literature on the consequences of different electoral rules. Lijphart (1977, 1984, 1999) discusses democratic institutions in terms of their cohesive features—his notion of consociational democracy being similar to our concept of cohesiveness.

The study of policy choice in multiple dimensions as political equilibrium was impeded for a long time by negative results in the field of social choice, emanating from the nonexistence results in Arrow (1951). Various ways around the

7. This is in the spirit of the analytic narratives approach of Bates, Greif, Levi, Rosenthal, and Weingast (1998).

Arrow paradox have since been followed in the literature. One is to specify the agenda-setting procedure with a view to real-world political arrangements as in the agenda-setting approach in Romer and Rosenthal (1979) and the legislative-bargaining approach in Baron and Ferejohn (1989). Another way to convexify voter preferences is the probabilistic-voting model with roots in Hinich, Ledyard, and Ordeshook (1972) and adapted to redistributive policymaking by Lindbeck and Weibull (1987). More recently, the citizen-candidate models of Besley and Coate (1997) and Osborne and Slivinsky (1996) solve the problem by restricting attention to ex post optimal choices. Overviews of the resulting literatures can be found in Austen-Smith and Banks (2005) and Persson and Tabellini (2000).

A more recent literature in political economics has discussed the economic consequences of alternative constitutional arrangements. An accessible overview of this work can be found in Persson and Tabellini (2004). Persson and Tabellini (2003) provide a broad empirical investigation of the economic consequences of constitutional arrangements for spending and other policies using cross-country data. Besley and Case (2003) survey the empirical literature on the consequences of different political institutions at the U.S. subnational level, with an emphasis on institutional differences across states.

Another body of work has examined incentives to change political institutions. Brennan and Buchanan (1985) and Buchanan (1987) emphasize the role of constitutional rules to constrain incumbent discretion. Frey (1983) offers a parallel approach. Aghion and Bolton (2003) study the design of constitutions as the choice of an incomplete social contract, where society chooses political decisionmaking procedures behind a veil of ignorance. This analysis is extended by Aghion, Alesina, and Trebbi (2004), who analyze the costs and benefits of insulating political leaders from changes in voters preferences or from aggregate shocks. Ticchi and Vindigni (2010) study the endogenous choice of a constitution.

There is now a literature in political economics on the reasons behind extension of the franchise, beginning with the theoretical paper by Acemoglu and Robinson (2000) with supportive evidence. More systematic evidence on the hypothesis from Western Europe is provided in Aidt and Jensen (2010). A classic paper on the consequences of the franchise extension on the amount of redistributive policies in various U.S. states is Husted and Kenny (1997). Aidt and Jensen (2009b) study how the extensions of the franchise in Western Europe from the middle of the nineteenth century and onward affected levels of taxation and the size of government.

Acemoglu and Robinson (2006) study the dynamics between autocracies and democracies in theory. Persson and Tabellini (2009) propose a theoretical and empirical model based on the idea of democratic capital. Boettke, Coyne, and Leeson (2008) offer a general discussion of institutional stickiness based on cultural factors, motivated especially by the heterogeneous experiences of the former Eastern Bloc countries. Political culture and its importance is also a theme in Hillman and Ursprung (2000). Moore (1966) is a classic reference emphasizing the economic and social structures that support democracies, putting weight on the rise of the middle class. Boix (2003) and Przeworski, Alvarez, Cheibub, and Limongi (2000) study the effects of democracy and discuss its sustainability more generally.

How political institutions lead to less corrupt behavior in government has been a central theme in models of elections and political institutions. In general, such models must deal with the agency problem that arises between the government and the governed. Barro (1973) and Ferejohn (1986) are early contributions, whereas Persson, Roland, and Tabellini (1997) extend the model to include separation of powers among various policymakers. Besley (2006) offers an overview of political-agency models and emphasizes that a blend of incentive and selection effects has to be studied in order to appreciate how accountability effects play out. Accountability models lead naturally to thinking about the role of the media in promoting good governance. This topic is examined by Besley and Prat (2006). Coyne and Leeson (2009) and Prat and Strömberg (2010) survey the emerging literature on media, politics, and economic development.

CHAPTER 8

Lessons Learned

> By *development* I mean the *movement upward of the entire social system,* and I believe this is the only logically tenable definition. This social system encloses, besides the so-called economic factors . . . the distribution of power in society; and more generally economic, social, and political stratification; broadly speaking, institutions and attitudes. . . . The dynamics of the system are determined by the fact that among all the endogenous conditions there is *circular causation,* implying that if one changes, others will change in response, and those secondary changes in their turn cause new changes all around, and so forth.
>
> Gunnar Myrdal, "What Is Development?," *Journal of Economic Issues,* 1974 pp. 729–730

We started out in Chapter 1 by noting that development clusters. Thus, income per capita, strong state institutions, and peaceful resolution of differences tend to go hand in hand. Understanding the causes and consequences of this clustering is an important end for a curious social scientist trying to explain the process of development. But a better understanding is also an important means for a concerned policymaker trying to design bilateral or multilateral development assistance.

We have taken a few steps toward a better understanding of why development clusters. This effort has involved gradually building a core theoretical model, adding more and more dimensions to obtain a richer story. The core model helps us think about the forces behind purposeful investments by governments in the extractive and productive capabilities of the state. These investments enable taxes on broad bases to be used for public-goods provision or income redistribution; they also enable support for private markets by removing frictions that are due to imperfectly enforced contracts or poorly protected property rights. The core model also helps us understand the forces behind purposeful investments in political violence by governments and prospective insurgents, in order to raise their probabilities to maintain or seize political authority.

Against the background of these theoretical predictions, we have explored empirically the worldwide patterns of different state capacities, different forms of violence, and their prospective determinants. Most of our empirical work has involved computing an array of partial correlations suggested by the theory. In Chapter 4, however, we have shown how our theory can be used to design a more structural empirical strategy to address the data.

Plan of the Chapter In this final chapter, we sum up and take stock of our findings. The first section discusses the lessons we have learned. Returning to the three main questions formulated in Chapter 1, we summarize the answers suggested in the various chapters. We also relate our approach to various strands of thinking about economic development.

In Section 8.2, we attempt to crystallize the main thrust of our argument in simple empirical fashion. Specifically, we define and compute a *Pillars of Prosperity Index,* based on empirical counterparts to the central outcomes emphasized by our theory. We also use the theory—as summarized in the Anna Karenina matrix of Chapter 5—to predict the values of this index, based on empirical counterparts of the central determinants uncovered by our theory. Comparing the actual and predicted values of the Pillars of Prosperity Index for 150 countries, we learn about successes as well as failures of the theory.

This book marks much more of a start than an end of a research program. In line with that fact, Section 8.3 highlights the provisional character of our findings by enumerating some important omissions and suggesting theoretical and empirical issues for further research,

8.1 What We Have Learned

8.1.1 Answers to the Three Main Questions

Having demonstrated the dramatic clustering of different development outcomes in Chapter 1, we posed three central questions as main themes of the book. These are closely related to the sufficient conditions for prosperity set forth by Adam Smith in the mid-1700s, namely "peace, easy taxes and a tolerable administration of justice."

Specifically, our three questions were:

1. What forces shape the building of different state capacities and why do these capacities vary together?
2. What factors drive political violence in its different forms?
3. What explains the clustering of state institutions, violence, and income?

1. State Capacities According to our analysis, one important answer to the first question is that investments in different parts of the state are often complements to one another. We derived such a complementary relationship for fiscal and legal capacity in the core model of Chapter 3. The specialized microeconomic models described later in the same chapter suggest additional reasons for complementarities to arise. Another side of state-capacity complementarity is that many determinants of fiscal and legal capacity will be common. Therefore, countries and times in which incumbents have strong motives to invest—e.g., owing to strong common interests or cohesive political institutions—will see a joint expansion of the two dimensions of the state, whereas those where incumbents have feeble investment motives will see stagnant state institutions. These possibilities come out clearly in our typology of common-interest, redistributive, and weak states.

Extending the analysis to include predation and elite control, we also identified how poor governance results in a predatory state. Such states do not invest in legal capacity. Since poor-governance institutions and low-cohesiveness institutions are likely to go together, we would expect predatory states to cluster among redistributive and weak states.

2. Political Violence An important answer to the second question is that one-sided political violence—repression by incumbent governments against oppositional elements—and two-sided political violence—outright civil war between the government and insurgent forces—have common roots. What are these roots? Our analysis in Chapter 4 revealed that some of them are exactly the same as the roots underlying the weak motives for investing in the state. The theoretical and empirical analyses in that chapter also emphasized how nontax government revenues, provided by large resource rents or flows of cash aid, can trigger violence. But these results came with an important proviso:

getting the predicted effect on violence requires weak common interests and/or noncohesive political institutions. These predictions come out clearly in our typology of peace, repression, and civil war.

Revisiting the recurring theme of predatory states in this context, we found that the elites in such states generally have stronger motives to invest in violence than incumbents in nonpredatory states.

3. Development Clusters As for the forces behind clustering of high (low) state capacity and peaceful (nonpeaceful) outcomes, the common roots are one important answer. But the analysis in Chapter 5 identified another possibility. Factors that facilitate the organization and conduct of an insurgency—such as geography or foreign intervention—will increase the risk of civil war, and this can feed back to weaker collective motives for building the state.

The negative relation between income and (risk of) violence goes two ways, which helps us understand the clustering of income and violence. We saw in Chapter 4 how higher (wage) incomes decrease the likelihood of repression and civil war by raising the opportunity cost of investing in violence. In Chapter 5, we illustrated an effect in the other direction: a higher risk of civil war and the ensuing destruction of capital or land decrease the expected returns to private investments and therefore the growth of income.

Analogous two-way forces between income and state-capacity investments were discussed in Chapter 3 as a possible cause behind the clustering of income and state capacity. Exogenous growth of market incomes strengthens the motives for incumbents to invest in fiscal as well as legal capacity, provided that institutions are not too noncohesive and political instability is not too much of a problem. But the growth of state capacity also feeds back to income as endogenous growth. Higher legal capacity reduces frictions and raises incomes by making markets work better. Also, higher fiscal capacity can raise incomes by reducing the motives for incumbents to earn rents by inefficient regulation of markets or by distorting predation on producers.

It is now easy to see how income, institutions, and violence may cluster. First, they have some determinants in common. Second, there exists a set of positive feedback loops among the central variables that raise the possibility of virtuous and vicious circles that make all outcomes move together. This possibility of mutually reinforcing dynamic feedbacks is a close analog to Gunnar Myrdal's conception of development as a process of cumulative effects and circular causation in the quote at the beginning of this chapter. Our approach to analyzing development is also reminiscent of the one taken by Myrdal in its emphasis on institutions and the interplay between economic and political forces [see e.g., Myrdal (1968)].

Development Assistance Our framework has allowed us to discuss problems and pitfalls in the allocation of development assistance. The main thrust of our analysis in Chapter 6 was that a one-size-fits-all approach to aid is bound to be misguided. Although this insight is certainly not new to the aid community, our approach suggests a consistent way of thinking about different forms of development assistance in different types of recipient countries.

One hallmark of that analysis is that various important decisions in recipient countries will be responsive to the nature of aid flows, including policies such as public-goods provision, investments in the state, investments in violence, and perhaps—as discussed in Chapter 7—the design of political institutions. Our results show that these responses may be crucially different, depending on the strength of the recipient country's state institutions, as well as its propensity for violence—in short, its location in the Anna Karenina matrix of Chapter 5.

Another hallmark of the analysis is that alternative forms of aid are likely to generate quite different responses even in a country with given state institutions and propensity for violence. One example comes from our recurring theme of resource dependence, which suggests different propensities across countries for resorting to political violence.

Common Interests A few specific determinants of state capacity stand out. In particular, the theory pinpoints common interests in society, as manifested in fiscal capacity being used to provide public goods to the broad population rather than to redistribute in favor of incumbent groups. This can come about because of circumstances, such as an external threat against the nation (parameter ϕ in the modeling). It can also come about because cross-cutting cleavages in society are weak enough not to result in polarization (parameter ι in the modeling). But common interests can also emanate because existing political institutions constrain the policies of incumbent governments, either by checks and balances on executives or by representation of opposition groups in the policymaking process (parameter θ in the modeling).

Strong common interests for either of these reasons promote a common-interest state (recall Chapters 2 and 3) and a peaceful resolution of conflicts (recall Chapter 4), bringing the overall outcome into the blissful upper-right corner of the Anna Karenina matrix (recall Chapter 5). Out of that corner, the picture is more complex, and outcomes for state building and violence are determined by the interaction of specific circumstances and institutions. According to our Anna Karenina principle of development: "all nonprosperous countries are nonprosperous in their own way."

Persistence of Weak States This raises the question of why not all countries choose to be prosperous by reforming political institutions toward those promoting common interests. Clearly, the simple core model paints too rosy a picture of prospects for institutional reform. For example, Section 3.4 shows how entrenched elites from either group may have strong incentives to abuse their temporary hold on power for their own enrichment.

Further, our provisional analysis of endogenous reform in Chapter 7 suggests that strong forces—in particular, perceived security in power for incumbent groups—may, in fact, bring about reform in the other direction, toward noncohesive institutions. Moreover, such institutions may be kept in place once they have been created, with political opponents in redistributive or weak states being kept in check by government repression.

Persistence of Predatory States Adding the possibility of predation and elite control, another of the recurring subthemes of the book, we can also ask why predatory states survive. Based on the analyses in Chapters 3 and 4, Chapter 7 shows that low expectations of political turnover and a small elite are possible answers. A small elite group with a strong hold on power will not wish to undertake reforms that reduce the scope for them to maintain power and exploit it for their private gain. There is a clear connection between this argument and the general thrust of the analysis in Acemoglu and Robinson (2010).

Predatory states are weak from the perspective of legal capacity and tend to have low incomes. Since institutions that improve governance also bring about greater cohesiveness, this gives a further reason to expect predatory states to be either redistributive or weak in terms of our basic definitions.

8.1.2 Our Analysis and Traditional Development Research

Our analysis relates to a number of currents in development research.

The 1960s and 1970s—Developmental States Rule Traditional research in development economics, such as Chenery and Elkington (1979) or Chenery and Strout (1966), placed little emphasis on the issues studied in our book. In particular, the role of institutional change took a back seat relative to traditional themes such as capital accumulation and technological change. The developmental state stood at the heart of this approach. However, the view of the government tended to be technocratic, with little or no attention paid to the incentives or ability of government to put the economic institutions that would make policy effective in place. There was a strong focus on planning. Cost-benefit analysis was supposed of be an essential tool for identifying public interventions. But how such policies would be implemented, or whether governments would even follow the prescribed interventions, was not really a part of that analysis.

In some places, this vision materialized as emphasized by Amsden (1992) and Wade (1990) in their commentaries on the East Asian experience. But the experience of state-led development was much less successful elsewhere. Many countries failed to grow and some even regressed. Further, as we discussed in Chapter 7, the quality of political institutions deteriorated with poor executive constraints and high levels of corruption.

The 1980s: Policy Recommendations Rule As these aspects of poor government became apparent, the 1980s were dominated by the so-called Washington Consensus. This was a program of reform advocated by the IMF and the World Bank, which aimed at improving macroeconomic stability, increasing openness, and reducing public intervention, in the hope that growth would follow. However, little attention was paid to fixing the institutional and political failures that fostered the resource misallocation to which these very policy recommendations were a response.

The 1990s: Institutions Rule During the following decade, debates about institutional reform and issues of governance became increasingly central in mainstream economics as well as in the policy sphere. These debates gained a boost from the fall of the Berlin Wall and the economic transitions that followed. The idea that development is about "getting the institutions right" is now a widely accepted dictum. There is nothing particularly new in the idea that development and institutional change are closely linked. This insight was central in Myrdal's work that we cited earlier in this chapter. It was also very much at the heart of Douglass North's work, based on a diagnosis of the factors behind the industrial revolution.

The preoccupation with good institutions in contemporary development thinking builds on North's insights. The institutional approach shifts the development debate away from the specific policies making up the Washington Consensus onto the incentives to pursue good policy in practice. Our approach is very much in the spirit of this institutional approach. Although it provides a guide for identifying good institutions—those promoting cohesiveness in public decisions and making rent extraction by incumbents costly—we would also argue that any precise prescriptions should be sensitive to the history and culture of a particular country, in line with the discussions of development assistance in Chapter 6 and political reform in Chapter 7.

Research on institutions has uncovered strong correlations between contemporary income levels and historical factors such as slavery, inequality, and settler mortality [see Nunn (2009) for a broad review of this work]. Much of the recent interest stems from Acemoglu, Johnson, and Robinson's (2001) seminal paper on colonial institutions. Although most of this work looks at the broad macro picture, an earlier literature in development emphasizes the richness of long-lived and highly persistent institutions [see Besley and Jayaraman (2010)]. This theme resurfaces in our approach when we stress that the cost of creating cohesive institutions can be higher in some societies than others.

The 2000s: Experiments Rule Microeconomic research on the effectiveness of specific policy interventions, using randomized-controlled trials (or natural experiments), currently dominates the research frontier at the expense of theoretical and macroeconomic research on development. At first sight, such microeconomic research might seem to be quite remote from the big-picture concerns in this book. However, our approach does in fact connect with this important and innovative line of research.

The connections are twofold. Increasing common interests is a key message throughout our analysis. Thus with a critical mass of microeconomically effective interventions, we could expect a macroeconomic effect. At best, this might put in motion a virtuous circle of reduced violence and investment in state capacities. This possibility was mentioned in Chapter 6.

Moreover, the experimental approach is being developed to look for some forms of interventions to improve governance or enhance cohesiveness. Such micropolitical insights can contribute to the process of political reform that we discussed in Chapter 7. As we have stressed, this could lead to fundamental shifts in fortune.

8.2 *The Pillars of Prosperity Index*

Thus far, the summary of our argument has been theoretical and abstract. A more concrete way of summarizing our main message is via an empirical measurement of development clusters. In this section, we define and compute our own Pillars of Prosperity Index, which is based on the principal outcome variables in the theory. We also show how well one can predict the values of this index by the main determinants that appear in our theory.

This exercise can be seen as an alternative to the various existing indexes of fragile and weak states that were discussed in Chapters 1 and 6, as we make a clear—and theory-based—distinction between outcomes and determinants of fragility. Comparing the actual and predicted values of the index also teaches us something about the strengths and weaknesses of our framework and the validity of our measurements. We caution the reader, however, that the index defined in this section and the predictions of it should be taken for what they are, namely simple empirical illustrations of the development clusters we observe in the data and some political and economic variables that correlate systematically with these clusters.

8.2.1 Defining the Index

Our theory has highlighted the extractive and productive capabilities of the state—labeled fiscal and legal capacity—as critical outcome variables. Thus, it is natural to include empirical counterparts to these variables in our index. The theory has also focused on political violence—in the form of government repression and civil war—as a central outcome. We therefore use empirical counterparts of these variables as well—or rather the absence of them—in our index. Finally, income has also been a central outcome variable in our modeling. Even though it appears more like a by-product of government and private investment, we still include income per capita as an additional component of our index.

How State Capacity Is Measured We have mainly modeled fiscal capacity as a constraint on the government's ability to levy an income tax. The closest empirical measure in the IMF data we used in Chapters 1–3 is probably the share of the income tax in total government revenue. In the theory, fiscal capacity is a stock variable, which is the cumulative result of previous investments. Thus, it makes sense to measure the income-tax share as late as possible. Given that we also want to include as many countries as possible, we use the wide-ranging IMF data from Baunsgaard and Keen (2005) and extract the revenue share of the income tax in the year 1999 (the data set goes one year further, but the last year has quite a bit of attrition). This measure of the income tax share is available for 129 countries. We scale it between 0 and 1 by first subtracting from each country's income tax share the minimum in the sample and then dividing by the sample range. Following the model notation, we refer to the resulting variable for country i as τ_i.

When it comes to legal capacity, we have mainly modeled it as a constraint on the government's ability to enforce contracts in financial markets. The closest empirical measure in the World Bank data we used in Chapter 3 is probably the index of contract enforcement in the Doing Business survey. This measure is from 2006, so it gauges the stock of legal capacity quite close to the present. As in Chapter 3, we use the rank of this index, with high values corresponding to high legal capacity. As for fiscal capacity, we scale the measure to lie between 0 and 1 by dividing each country's rank (minus 1) with the number of countries (minus 1) for which the index is available, namely 173. We refer to the resulting variable as π_i.

How Political Violence Is Measured For peaceful outcomes, we want to gauge the absence of repression and civil war. In this case, it is hard to think of a current measure with the dimension of a stock. In the theory, the violence outcome depends on the investments made by incumbent and opposition groups in each given period. Thus, it makes sense to measure these investments by the violence outcomes over some time up to the present.

For civil war, we use the Armed Conflict Dataset discussed in Chapter 4. Specifically, we look at the last 30 years of available data, i.e., from 1976 to 2006, computing the share of years between 1976 (or since independence if that is later) and 2006 that a country has been involved in civil war. The underlying civil-war variable is available for 170 countries. When it comes to repression, we use the purges data from Banks (2005), which was also introduced in Chapter 4. Here, too, we look at data from 1976 to the last year available (2005). We gauge the share of these years each country has nonzero purges, given that it does not have a civil war in the same year. The data for purges is available for 195 countries. By definition, the civil-war and repression measures are scaled between 0 and 1. We refer to their values for country i as c_i and r_i.

How Income Is Measured As the other outcome variables, we measure income as late as possible for as many countries as possible. As in earlier chapters, we use the logarithm of GDP per capita (in 2005 constant international prices) in the last year of the 6.3 Penn World Tables, namely 2006. This gives us income per capita for 186 countries. As for our other measures, we scale income between 0 and 1 by deducting the minimum in the sample from each country's income level and then dividing by the full sample range. We refer to income per capita as y_i.

Weighting The next practical question is how to aggregate the five variables we have just defined. Since they span very different outcomes, any weighting scheme has a certain degree of arbitrariness. For lack of a better principle, we assign equal weights to the three central concepts of state capacity, peaceful outcomes, and income.

To define the index, we first construct a combined state-capacity index, s_i, by adding our fiscal- and legal-capacity variables together. If both of them are available for country i, we give them equal weight, i.e., we set $s_i = \frac{\tau_i + \pi_i}{2}$. But we also allow one of them to be missing, in which case we just use the one available variable, i.e., we set $s_i = \tau_i$ or $s_i = \pi_i$. By construction, this state-capacity index lies between 0 and 1.

We then construct an index of peaceful outcomes, p_i. To reflect the fact that civil war is a more serious form of violence, we give it twice the weight compared to repression. Thus, we define the peacefulness index for country i as $p_i = 1 - \frac{r_i}{2} - c_i$. As $r_i + c_i \leq 1$ because we have defined civil war and repression as mutually exclusive events, the peacefulness index lies between 0 and 1 by construction.

Finally, we define the Pillars of Prosperity Index for country i as

$$pop_i = \frac{s_i + p_i + y_i}{3},$$

assuming that all three subindexes are available. We allow one of the components to be absent, however, in which case we add the two available subindexes together with equal weights, although this is the case only for 10 out of the 150 countries. By construction, the final index lies between 0 and 1 (as all its components are scaled between 0 and 1). Naturally, several judgmental assumptions go into the construction of the index. But experiments with different weighting schemes and alternative measures of the central variables do not yield very different results.

The Resulting Index With these preliminaries in hand, we are ready to go. Given the definitions and the availability of the underlying variables, we can compute the Pillars of Prosperity Index for a total of 184 countries. Table 8.1 shows the value of the index and its three components for 150 countries. This is the entire set, where, given the determinants discussed in the next subsection, we can also predict the index. Most of the 34 excluded countries are small island states in the Caribbean or the Pacific that do not meet the criterion of at least one-half million inhabitants used in the Polity IV data set.

Table 8.1 orders the 150 countries from low to high values. The index assigns the two lowest values to Zaire and Afghanistan. Other countries among the bottom ten include Myanmar, Somalia, and Sudan. Generally, these countries score uniformly low on all three dimensions of the index. The most surprising entry among the bottom ten is India. Although its recent growth has brought income per capita above the very lowest in 2006, India still has an underdeveloped tax system and many remaining market frictions, as well as a history of internal political violence. We get back to the case of India in the next subsection. In the next ten from the bottom, we find countries such as Chad and Iraq, with quite bad outcomes on all three subindexes. We also find Colombia, however, a richer country with a history of permanent civil war in the last three decades, and hence a 0 score on the peacefulness index.

At the other end of the table, the top two performers are Sweden and Switzerland, with scores near the top on all three subindexes. Others in the top ten include United States, Japan, Canada, and the remaining two Scandinavian countries. Among the top twenty, we find another set of European nations, but also Singapore and South Korea (Iceland, Luxembourg, and Hong Kong are not included in the table, as they do not enter the Polity IV data, but would otherwise rank in the top ten or twenty).

Evidently, the Pillars of Prosperity Index captures some intuitive aspects of development clusters. Figure 8.1 presents the information in Table 8.1 in a graphic format, which is somewhat cruder, but also more digestible. This Pillars of Prosperity Atlas indicates the scores of all countries among the 150, as these are partitioned into deciles. The bottom decile of the index—i.e., the bottom 15 countries—is indicated by black, the top decile by white, and the deciles in between marked on a gradual gray scale.

Figure 8.1 has clear similarities with the maps showing the Brookings and Polity IV indexes of weak and fragile states at the beginning of Chapter 1. That is, we see a concentration of bad outcomes in Africa and South Asia, owing to a combination of low income, low state capacity, and frequent internal conflicts.

Table 8.1 Pillars of Prosperity Index and components

Country	Index value	Peacefulness	State capacity	Income
Zaire	0.011	n/a	0.017	0.004
Afghanistan	0.084	0.081	0.052	0.118
Sudan	0.204	0.194	0.092	0.326
India	0.236	0.065	0.216	0.426
Myanmar	0.240	0.032	0.447	n/a
Uganda	0.261	0.145	0.422	0.216
Somalia	0.263	0.484	n/a	0.042
Ethiopia	0.267	0.129	0.479	0.194
Angola	0.275	0.129	0.237	0.460
Burundi	0.298	0.516	0.278	0.100
Chad	0.303	0.323	0.232	0.354
Colombia	0.304	0	0.350	0.563
Mozambique	0.308	0.484	0.114	0.326
Liberia	0.315	0.629	n/a	0
Iraq	0.320	0.226	0.249	0.485
Cambodia	0.340	0.323	0.324	0.372
Guatemala	0.341	0.339	0.164	0.520
Philippines	0.356	0	0.603	0.464
Guinea-Bissau	0.375	0.919	0.116	0.089
Sri Lanka	0.386	0.290	0.351	0.516
Sierra Leone	0.386	0.677	0.189	0.293
Indonesia	0.403	0.226	0.495	0.490
Lebanon	0.412	0.516	0.150	0.569
Nepal	0.427	0.645	0.327	0.308
Peru	0.428	0.371	0.389	0.525
Central African Republic	0.440	0.982	0.182	0.155
Rwanda	0.441	0.645	0.470	0.208
Vietnam	0.441	0	0.462	0.420
Morocco	0.450	0.548	0.299	0.504
Mali	0.465	0.968	0.192	0.234
Turkey	0.469	0.242	0.601	0.564
Bangladesh	0.472	0.984	0.094	0.339
El Salvador	0.476	0.565	0.361	0.504
Benin	0.480	1	0.192	0.248
Madagascar	0.485	1	0.295	0.159
Laos	0.487	0.968	0.162	0.331
Niger	0.495	1	0.325	0.159
Algeria	0.496	0.484	0.473	0.532
Togo	0.496	1	0.327	0.162
Cameroon	0.501	1	0.137	0.367

Table 8.1 *(continued)*

Country	Index value	Peacefulness	State capacity	Income
Burkina Faso	0.502	1	0.263	0.242
Pakistan	0.508	0.903	0.205	0.416
Haiti	0.510	0.952	0.314	0.266
Congo	0.511	0.903	0.205	0.425
Senegal	0.516	1	0.243	0.304
Lesotho	0.530	0.989	0.269	0.337
Djibouti	0.537	1	0.146	0.465
Malawi	0.541	0.984	0.408	0.230
Syria	0.543	0.871	0.369	0.389
Guinea	0.555	1	0.236	0.428
Paraguay	0.556	0.984	0.209	0.474
Tanzania	0.557	1	0.504	0.166
Honduras	0.562	0.984	0.279	0.423
Eritrea	0.563	0.929	0.671	0.090
Nicaragua	0.566	0.645	0.723	0.329
Macedonia	0.566	n/a	0.590	0.543
Iran	0.566	0.532	0.549	0.617
Zimbabwe	0.582	0.855	0.574	0.318
Ivory Coast	0.584	1	0.416	0.337
Gambia	0.587	1	0.516	0.246
Tajikistan	0.590	0.625	0.780	0.366
Bolivia	0.592	1	0.345	0.432
Guyana	0.595	1	0.408	0.377
Ghana	0.595	0.968	0.550	0.269
Mauritania	0.600	1	0.457	0.344
Egypt	0.603	1	0.308	0.503
China	0.607	0.823	0.435	0.563
Kenya	0.612	0.984	0.531	0.321
Albania	0.623	0.968	0.434	0.467
Swaziland	0.623	1	0.309	0.560
Zambia	0.626	0.984	0.587	0.307
Jordan	0.628	1	0.396	0.486
Panama	0.628	1	0.296	0.589
Ecuador	0.629	0.952	0.417	0.519
Uruguay	0.635	0.984	0.266	0.654
Dominican Republic	0.638	1	0.315	0.598
Brazil	0.639	1	0.312	0.605
Nigeria	0.640	0.968	0.620	0.333
South Africa	0.646	0.581	0.738	0.618
Venezuela	0.650	1	0.304	0.646

Table 8.1 *(continued)*

Country	Index value	Peacefulness	State capacity	Income
Papua New Guinea	0.657	1	0.642	0.330
Fiji	0.663	1	0.461	0.527
Costa Rica	0.665	1	0.353	0.643
Poland	0.667	0.968	0.358	0.675
Bahrain	0.667	1	0.201	0.800
Mauritius	0.672	1	0.276	0.739
Russia	0.673	0.498	0.861	0.659
Argentina	0.682	0.935	0.422	0.688
Namibia	0.691	1	0.541	0.530
Gabon	0.691	1	0.502	0.571
Chile	0.700	0.952	0.424	0.725
Azerbaijan	0.702	0.717	0.809	0.581
Moldova	0.703	1	0.688	0.421
Mongolia	0.704	0.984	0.769	0.359
Mexico	0.713	1	0.503	0.636
Uzbekistan	0.715	1	0.832	0.311
Israel	0.715	1	0.370	0.776
Bhutan	0.715	1	0.682	0.464
Trinidad and Tobago	0.721	1	0.378	0.784
Thailand	0.724	0.984	0.588	0.600
Jamaica	0.728	0.984	0.616	0.584
Georgia	0.729	0.813	0.821	0.554
Saudi Arabia	0.732	1	0.445	0.752
Kyrgyzstan	0.736	1	0.786	0.423
Kuwait	0.738	1	0.327	0.888
Tunisia	0.755	1	0.654	0.611
Bulgaria	0.758	0.968	0.705	0.602
Italy	0.762	1	0.472	0.815
Romania	0.764	0.952	0.746	0.595
Slovenia	0.769	1	0.520	0.785
Malaysia	0.777	1	0.612	0.720
Botswana	0.785	1	0.759	0.595
Slovak Republic	0.790	1	0.665	0.706
Oman	0.803	1	0.631	0.777
Cuba	0.804	0.984	n/a	0.624
Czech Republic	0.810	1	0.676	0.755
Taiwan	0.814	1	0.647	0.795
Ukraine	0.819	1	0.855	0.603
Portugal	0.831	1	0.747	0.746
Armenia	0.832	1	0.902	0.593

Table 8.1 *(continued)*

Country	Index value	Peacefulness	State capacity	Income
Croatia	0.838	1	0.844	0.670
Germany	0.844	n/a	0.859	0.828
Kazakhstan	0.845	1	0.850	0.684
Greece	0.845	1	0.732	0.803
Belarus	0.849	1	0.798	0.750
Libya	0.859	0.984	n/a	0.734
Spain	0.870	1	0.782	0.827
Estonia	0.870	1	0.890	0.721
Latvia	0.873	1	0.942	0.675
South Korea	0.873	0.935	0.908	0.775
New Zealand	0.873	1	0.829	0.789
Hungary	0.874	0.968	0.936	0.717
Singapore	0.874	1	0.738	0.884
United Kingdom	0.877	1	0.798	0.832
Austria	0.878	n/a	0.904	0.852
Lithuania	0.886	1	0.983	0.674
France	0.889	1	0.844	0.820
Ireland	0.889	1	0.787	0.881
Netherlands	0.891	1	0.829	0.845
Cyprus	0.892	1	n/a	0.784
United States	0.893	0.839	0.950	0.891
Belgium	0.905	0.984	0.890	0.842
Finland	0.907	1	0.888	0.831
Canada	0.908	1	0.869	0.856
Denmark	0.917	1	0.906	0.846
Japan	0.918	1	0.926	0.828
Australia	0.918	1	0.901	0.854
Norway	0.929	1	0.878	0.908
Switzerland	0.932	1	0.934	0.862
Sweden	0.936	1	0.972	0.837

We also find a few malperforming states in Latin America, mostly due to a long history of internal conflicts. By contrast, most of Europe and the other OECD democracies enter into the top decile, with high scores on all three components of the index.

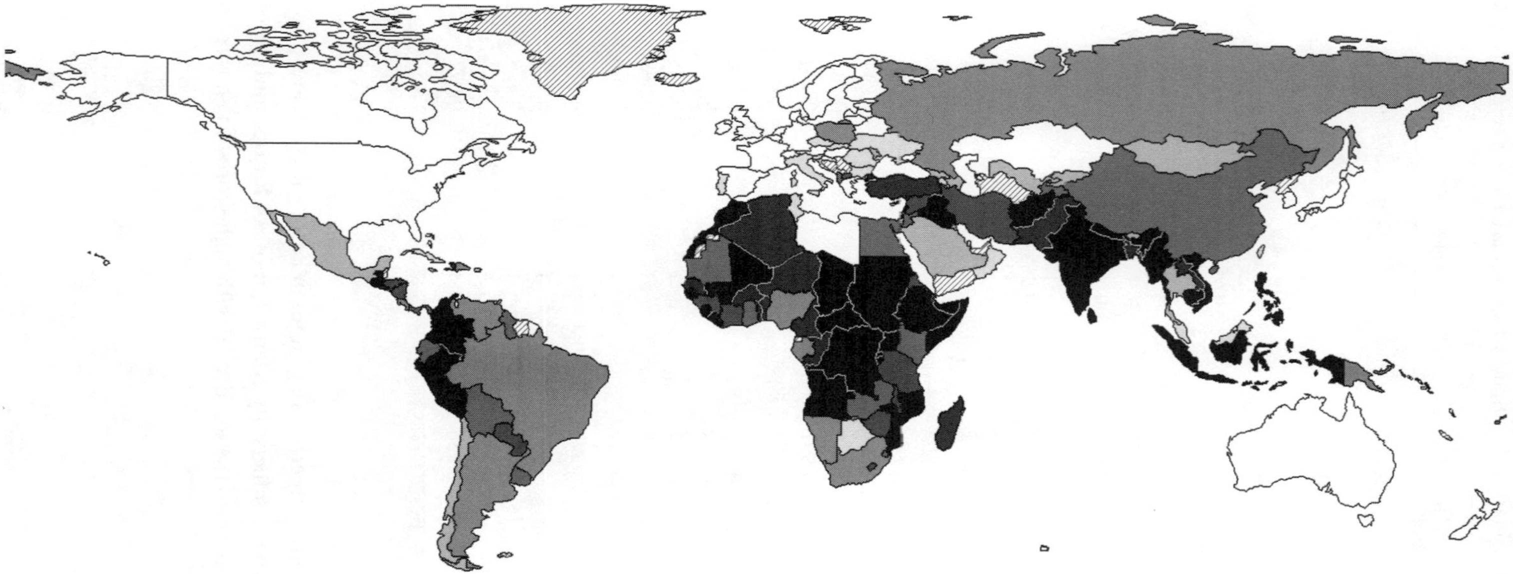

Figure 8.1 The Pillars of Prosperity Atlas.

8.2.2 Predicting the Index

Our theory in the preceding chapters suggested a number of variables that determine state capacity (and thus, indirectly, income) as well as political violence. We now ask how well the Pillars of Prosperity Index can be predicted by the variables that our theory has pinpointed. Make no mistake, however; the econometric exercise we are about to undertake should be seen just as an exercise in prediction. That is, we make no claims whatsoever about isolating a causal relation.

The Determinants Included in the Prediction At the end of Chapters 2 and 3, we saw that a number of variables proxying for some of the main determinants of state-capacity investments were systematically correlated with alternative measures of fiscal as well as legal capacity in the data. Specifically, we used the historical prevalence of wars from the Correlates of War data set and a measure of ethnic homogeneity from Fearon (2003) as proxies for common interests (parameters ϕ and ι in the theory). We constructed two variables from the scores in the Polity IV data set: the historical prevalence of constraints on the executive as a proxy for cohesive institutions (parameter θ in the theory) and the historical prevalence of nonopen and noncompetitive executive recruitment as a proxy for political stability (parameter γ in the theory). Finally, we used four legal-origin indicators from La Porta, Lopez de Silanes, Shleifer, and Vishny (1998) as a proxy for different costs of legal-capacity investments (function $\mathcal{L}$ in the theory). In Chapter 4, we argued that the same variables in the theory (except γ, which was then endogenous) would also help predict investment in political violence although with the opposite sign.

As we would like a very parsimonious specification when predicting the index, we stay with this small set of variables. As the Pillars of Prosperity Index is in the nature of a stock variable dated 2006, we would like to capture the conditions for investment—captured by the preceding parameter proxies—in earlier periods. Therefore, we measure any historical average up to the year 2000, as we did in Chapters 2 and 3. In the interest of transparency, we do not rely on any of the nonlinearities suggested by the theory. In particular, we carry out the prediction by a simple linear regression of the Pillars of Prosperity Index on the eight variables we just enumerated.

The Predicted Index Estimation results from this linear specification are displayed in the first column of Table 8.2. All of the eight variables enter with

Table 8.2 Predicting the Pillars of Prosperity Index

	(1) Index value	(2) State-capacity subindex	(3) Income per capita	(4) Peacefulness subindex
Prevalence of external war before 2000	0.249*	0.714***	0.390**	−0.223
	(0.136)	(0.237)	(0.155)	(0.272)
Average executive constraints before 2000	0.288***	0.304***	0.402***	0.113
	(0.064)	(0.086)	(0.064)	(0.101)
Average nonopen executive recruitment before 2000	0.150*	0.159*	0.239***	0.024
	(0.078)	(0.086)	(0.089)	(0.129)
Ethnic homogeneity	0.230***	0.091	0.312***	0.202**
	(0.058)	(0.073)	(0.062)	(0.099)
English legal origin	0.042	0.085**	−0.171	0.055
	(0.032)	(0.041)	(0,037)	(0.058)
Scandinavian legal origin	0.166***	0.377***	0.094**	0.077
	(0.040)	(0.058)	(0.042)	(0.061)
German legal origin	0.173***	0.362***	0.133**	0.100*
	(0.039)	(0.052)	(0.052)	(0.054)
Socialist legal origin	0.087**	0.026***	0.006	0.048
	(0.036)	(0.047)	(0.033)	(0.058)
Observations	150	145	150	147
R-squared	0.470	0.540	0.539	0.076

Notes: Robust standard errors in parentheses: * significant at 10%; ** significant at 5%; *** significant at 1%. French legal origin is the omitted category.

the expected positive sign (from the theory or earlier empirical specifications). Almost all of the predictors are statistically significant, although a couple of them only marginally so. The parsimonious linear specification accounts for about half of the variance in the index across countries. The next three columns inspect the sources of the prediction by running an identical specification for the three components that make up the Pillars of Prosperity Index. It is easy to see that the included variables do quite well in predicting the state-capacity index and income per capita. But the prediction is considerably worse for peacefulness, where only ethnic homogeneity and German legal origin are statistically significant predictors of the index.

The Predicted Pillars of Prosperity Index Atlas in Figure 8.2 shows the predicted values graphically, i.e., the coloring of each individual country on the map reflects its predicted index. The coloring scheme is completely analogous with that in our atlas for the actual index. That is, countries predicted to be in the lowermost decile are black, countries predicted to be in the uppermost decile are white, and countries in the other deciles are marked on a gradually changing gray scale.

Comparing Actual and Predicted Indexes The general picture is quite similar to Figure 8.1, with Africa clearly overrepresented in the dark part of the spectrum and Europe clearly overrepresented in the light part. Interestingly, countries in South Asia are generally predicted to have a higher prosperity score than their actual one, whereas the opposite is true for countries in Latin America.

Clearly, our prediction of the Pillars of the Prosperity Index captures the major variation in the data. Interestingly, the prediction not only picks up the variation across major regions, but also some variation within these regions. For example, two of the success cases in Sub-Saharan Africa—Botswana and Mauritius—are doing well both in terms of actual and predicted outcomes. Botswana has an actual rank of 112 (from the bottom, out of 150) and a predicted rank of 123, and Mauritius has an actual rank of 86 and a predicted rank of 90.

But some countries have quite different colors in the maps of Figures 8.1 and 8.2. These represent cases where the main thrust of our theory does not fit very well. It is of particular interest to take a closer look at these instances, in order to figure out what we may be missing. To home in on the failures, Table 8.3 lists the largest deviations between predicted and actual index values. Specifically, the table includes all those countries where the predicted index is off the actual index by at least 50 steps in the ranking. For each country, the table displays the ranks of each country on the actual and predicted index, as well as the difference between its actual and predicted values of the index.

Underperformers Panel A of Table 8.3 shows the largest underperformers, a total of ten countries according to our 50-step definition. India is the country with the largest difference in both rank and index value. As already noted, India suffers from a low value of state capacity as well as a great deal of political violence. In terms of the predictors, however, India has quite cohesive political institutions, being one of the oldest democracies in the developing world (recall

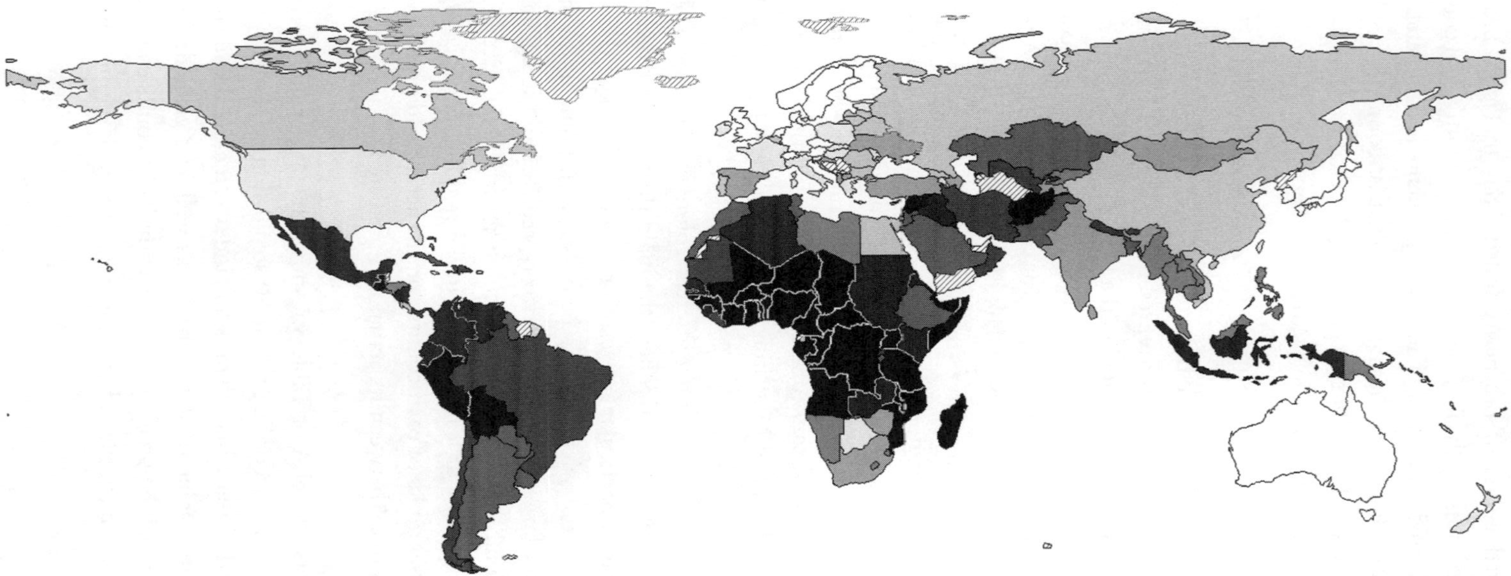

Figure 8.2 The predicted Pillars of Prosperity Index Atlas.

Table 8.3 Prediction errors on the Pillars of Prosperity Index

Country	Actual rank	Predicted rank	Actual minus predicted index value
Panel A: Largest underperformers (more than 50 steps off in ranking)			
India	4	93	−0.35
Myanmar	5	81	−0.31
Ethiopia	8	62	−0.32
Burundi	10	64	−0.28
Cambodia	16	88	−0.31
Philippines	18	87	−0.29
Sri Lanka	20	105	−0.31
Vietnam	28	115	−0.28
Turkey	31	96	−0.21
China	67	120	−0.13
Panel B: Largest overperformers (more than 50 steps off in ranking)			
Ivory Coast	59	6	0.17
Ghana	64	13	0.15
Nigeria	78	18	0.17
Gabon	90	4	0.29
Mexico	95	37	0.19
Kuwait	105	45	0.20
Oman	114	56	0.26
Kazakhstan	123	65	0.26
Singapore	133	74	0.27

Table 7.1). It is ethnically fragmented, which works against common interests in the state, but it has a history with threats of external conflict, which works in favor of common interests. For these reasons, India is predicted to be quite prosperous in terms of our index. One interpretation of the country's recent growth spurt and reforms to improve the way its markets work is that India is now catching up with its "institutional possibility frontier," to borrow a phrase from Djankov et al. (2003).

Interestingly, China is also among the ten countries with an index farthest away from its predicted value. In terms of the variables highlighted by the theory, China's relative ethnic homogeneity does promote common interests in the state. Chinese political institutions are not very cohesive, however, which draws down its predicted index. On the other hand, it has a great deal of political stability according to our measure. Thus, China fits the conception of a strongly redistributive and repressive state (low θ and low γ) relatively well. We could view its growth miracle as another instance of a country catching up with its own potential. The smaller distance between China's actual and predicted index for 2006, compared to India, can then be seen as reflecting the fact that China has had 15 more years of rapid growth than India.

Several other countries in Panel A, notably Sri Lanka, the Philippines, and Turkey, have endured civil war and/or repression during most or all of the last 30 years. In these cases, the large difference between the actual and the predicted indexes is largely explained by the fact that we are unable to predict (the absence of) political violence very precisely with the parsimonious sets of variables used here—recall the estimates in column (4) of Table 8.2.

Overperformers Panel B of Table 8.3 shows the opposite type of failure—the nine countries that overperform their predicted indexes by at least 50 steps in the ranking. Four of these are located in Sub-Saharan Africa—Ivory Coast, Ghana, Nigeria, and Gabon. These African countries have on the whole avoided large-scale political violence, despite quite bad institutions (at least until recently, in the case of the Ivory Coast). In analogy with the Philippines, Sri Lanka, and Turkey among the underperformers, the difference between the actual and the predicted indexes in these countries mostly reflects our lack of success in predicting political violence or its absence.

Three other overperformers in Panel B, with higher actual and predicted indexes, are Singapore, Kuwait, and Mexico. These countries score better on most of the three subindexes than their parameters suggest. Singapore and Kuwait are not democracies, and stable democracy is relatively recent in Mexico. One interpretation is that those autocracies have had the benefit of relatively benign and growth-oriented leaders. It has to be acknowledged that we have not allowed the personal quality of leaders to play any role in our theory and measurement, even though common sense and research by authors such has Jones and Olken (2005, 2009) and O'Donnell and Schmitter (1986) suggest otherwise when it comes to both political reform and income.

Taking Stock By and large, the Pillars of Prosperity Index that we have defined and computed captures important aspects of the development clusters that motivate the present book. We selected a parsimonious set of variables, to represent main determinants of state capacity and political violence in our theory, and showed how these help predict quite a bit of the variation in the index. The largest differences between actual and predicted values of the index can partly be attributed to some countries approaching their institutional potential. But the differences also reflect the fact that our simple theory and measurement do a lackluster job of predicting the cross-country variation in violence and do not assign any significant role to the quality of leaders in countries with weak political institutions.

These deficiencies certainly suggest roads for improvement of the theory. But they also suggest an important role for case studies of the countries where predictions fail, namely to find new mechanisms that go beyond our existing theory. This is not the usual role for case studies, which rather tend to be selected in order to provide illustration and support for some particular theory.

8.3 *Where Next?*

Our analysis in this book has been preliminary in many important respects. This section serves as a reminder of the many things that are missing. At the same time, the omissions suggest a number of topics where future research efforts might be directed. Such efforts would involve a deepening as well as a broadening of the research in this book.

Model More Carefully The core model we have put forward is very simple and relies on many special assumptions. Simplicity has the advantage of keeping the theoretical analyses managable and transparent, allowing us to come up with some clean insights. But it is important to go further and test the theoretical robustness of our findings, asking whether our insights hold under more realistic conditions. We have taken some steps in that direction in the Developing the Model section in previous chapters.

An important task in this endeavor is to link our analysis in a better way to traditional models of growth and development. One specific question is how well the results that we have derived in simple two-period models survive in truly dynamic multiperiod models of economic growth. Our analysis in Section 2.2.8 took some steps in that direction, but it is very much a first attempt. The analysis there could be extended further, e.g., by studying non-Markov-perfect equilibria. This would be an important extension because it would allow for reputational forces, which could potentially alleviate the underlying commitment problem that drives many of our results, namely that groups cannot credibly promise—beyond parameter θ—not to use their political power to redistribute in favor of their own members.

As another example, the microfounded model in Section 3.2.1 is a close cousin of the traditional/advanced-sector model of Lewis (1954). The links with that earlier literature, in particular the role of different institutions, could be much more thoroughly investigated.

Consider Human Capital Another point where we have failed to make contact with other research on development is the importance of human capital. There is an ongoing debate in the literature about the relative importance of institutions and human capital in driving development [see Acemoglu, Johnson, Robinson, and Yared (2005) and Glaeser, La Porta, Lopez de Silanes, and Shleifer (2004)]. Although we do not take a firm stand in this debate, it is clear that human capital could be introduced into our framework in at least two ways.

One way would highlight the standard role of human capital as an engine of growth in parallel with other forms of accumulation. This would be relatively easy to do, along lines similar to the way we added private capital accumulation in Chapters 3 and 5. Most probably this would lead to conclusions similar to those for physical capital, namely a magnification of the effects on income via government investments in state capacity and collective investments in violence.

Another interesting possibility would be to explore the suggestion made by Glaeser, Ponzetto, and Shleifer (2007) regarding a more nonstandard role for human capital, namely as a driver of democratic institutions by fostering nonviolent conflict resolution, an idea that goes back to Lipset (1959). This is an interesting notion, but it is not completely clear how it could be integrated with the models of violent conflict and political reform in Chapters 4 and 7. Perhaps human capital is one of the channels whereby countries with long-term democratic experience become more resistant to relapses into noncohesive institutions, as in the theory and evidence on democratic capital in Persson and Tabellini (2009). Building human capital may also foster common interests, which would effectively work like a higher value of parameter ϕ.

Disaggregate More The core model framework carried through the book is an aggregate reduced-form model of the interaction between economic and political forces. To reach a better understanding of structures and institutions, it is necessary to further disaggregate these models. On the economic side, we provided some examples in Chapters 2 and 3 of how one can formulate economic microfoundations to better understand the nuts and bolts of legal and fiscal capacity. More such work is needed, e.g., to better understand the interaction between corruption and state building.

On the political side, we provided some examples in Chapter 7 of how one can formulate political microfoundations to better understand the details of what might drive reform toward or away from cohesive institutions in the context of development. More structural work on the political side is needed to understand the role of other political institutions, such as federalism.

But microfoundations are also needed on the violence side, where we have black-boxed many issues by working with an aggregate conflict technology (contest function). As stressed by Blattman and Miguel (2009) in their survey of civil war, we know almost nothing about what drives individual participation in violence. Building such empirical knowledge would be facilitated by microfounded models of violence [see Yanagizawa (2010) for an interesting attempt]. This would be an input in modeling the links noted earlier between human capital and peaceful conflict resolution. But microfoundations for violence may also be vital for understanding such phenomena as coups, which are essentially transitions of power within the same general group or elite. To make progress here, we have to unpack the group and carefully consider the incentives for its individual members, perhaps along the lines of our modeling of predatory states in Chapters 3, 4, and 7.

Bridge Micro and Macro The approach in the book is inherently macroeconomic and macropolitical, in that we try to understand the big picture in the data. Yet, as we have just stressed, microeconomic and micropolitical studies are vital if we are to reach further in this understanding. How does our approach come together with the recent wave in development research, with its stress on randomized-controlled trials and natural experiments at a very disaggregated level? As noted in Chapter 6, we can think about this research as providing information about socially profitable projects and thus raising the prospective return to public-goods provision. Similar work on the micropolitics of village decisionmaking, which is just getting off the ground, can inform us about useful mechanisms for peacefully resolving conflicts of interest.

But to ultimately become useful in assisting development and not only help alleviate poverty or disease in a small and well-controlled testing ground, the empirical small-scale insights have to face up to the hurdles of large-scale implementation. This means confronting the kind of macroeconomic and macropolitical issues that form the subject matter of this book. This way, micro- and macro-oriented approaches to development are complements, not substitutes.

Understand State Legitimacy Our models of state-capacity formation have focused on top-down administrative reforms, and the incentives for incumbent governments to undertake such reforms depending on circumstances and institutions. Although this is a significan piece, it is by no means the entire puzzle. An important reason why some states function so well is that their citizens have come to expect them to. Consider Sweden and Argentina. Most Swedes pay their taxes because they expect other citizens to do the same and they expect the government not to squander the money. These expectations, in turn, work as a bottom-up accountability mechanism that keeps alternative governments and bureaucrats reasonably careful and honest when handling the public purse. In Argentina, by contrast, individuals do not expect other citizens to pay their taxes and might expect that a good part of the budget will be squandered in various corrupt activities. Thus, the accountability mechanism on public officials from the trust and legitimacy of the state is gone and the citizens' pessimistic expectations tend to become self-fulfilling.

How are such norms of tax compliance and similar norms of obedience to the law built and maintained? Above all, how do they interact with the building of administrative capacities such as those we have stressed in the book? These are important issues for further research. We hinted at a preliminary answer in our short discussion of the microfoundations of fiscal capacity in Section 2.4.1, and the potential interaction between deterrence and social norms. In Section 7.2.6, we also gave some hints regarding the role of trust in fostering political cohesion. But the reality is certainly much more complicated and probably involves the formation of social and behavioral norms at the individual as well as the social levels [see, e.g., Benabou and Tirole (2010) for a recent formal analysis of the interactions between laws and norms].

There are other closely related issues about the legitimacy of the state. An important research strand in political science and political sociology stresses that legitimate political institutions, which give citizens a true say on how the money is spent, might be a necessary quid pro quo for them to go along with increased collection of taxes. It is argued that such "fiscal contracts" may explain the historical joint building of tax capacity and representative political institutions in many developed countries [see, e.g., Levi (1988)] and that a similar mechanism might be operating in developing countries today [see, e.g., the contributions in Bräutigam, Fjeldstad, and Moore (2008)]. In the language of this book, this argument suggests a complementarity between the building of state capacity and cohesive political institutions.

Bring in Social Capital and Identity Our analysis has focused exclusively on formal state institutions and investments to improve these. We have not paid attention to private governance and institutional arrangements that support and sustain markets. In effect, we have assumed throughout that no private enforcement technology or institutions are available in the absence of legal capacity created by government. Private governance has been studied extensively in its own right [see, e.g., Dixit (2004), Greif (2006), Ostrom (1990), and Platteau (2000)]. But the links between private governance and the formation of effective states has not been resolved in either theory or practice. There are two broadly contrasting views.

Some authors, mostly in the Hayekian tradition, emphasize the value of spontaneous order as a substitute for state action [see, e.g., Hayek (1979)]. In this spirit, Benson (1989) and Leeson (2006) have argued that private law and institutional enforcement can function in some contexts without the need for coercive authorities. Leeson (2007) even argues that Somalia functions better without a state.

Others, especially authors in the literature on social capital, have stressed the complementarity between state institutions and private networks. This line is taken, for instance, in the classic study of social capital by Putnam (1993), which argues that government works more effectively in parts of Italy where social capital is strong.

A related issue concerns how a sense of identity and belonging to a polity is created, leading people to set aside sectional interests and support the common interest. Recent work on identity and the way that it matters in economic settings by Akerlof and Kranton (2010) is relevant here. Shayo (2009) is an interesting exploration of how (endogenous) national and group identities interact in fostering redistribution. A key issue is how far a sense of national identity that creates common interests can be actively fostered. In Chapter 1, we mentioned the work on nationalism by authors such as Gellner (1983) and Posen (1993), which is also a natural starting point.

Viewed from the perspective of the themes in this book, the preceding comments suggest the need to study how identity, social capital, and state capacities evolve together in a dynamic process with feedbacks in both directions.

Deal with Multiple Countries Our approach has focused on a single-country context. A host of new issues arises in a multicountry world. We have appealed to the role of external warfare in shaping common interests. Threats of war have to come from other societies, however, and this creates interesting sources of interdependence across countries with the possibility of geographic institutional clusters.

We have also taken the countries in our analysis as given. However, it would be interesting to study a broader process of state formation in our framework, as one country tries to seize the territory of another and extend its institutions. One could also explore the incentives for colonialism using the tools we have constructed and potentially look for underlying structural determinants of the so-called "democratic peace" [see Maoz and Russett (1993)].

Interesting issues also arise when we allow for open markets for goods and factors. The first of these would be particularly relevant if we were to consider the decision of a country to open up to trade when, owing to low fiscal capacity, it is dependent on trade taxes. Mobile people and capital may exercise discipline on governments that perform poorly.

Distinguish between Centralized and Decentralized States In our core and extended models, we have focused exclusively on the incentives faced by a unitary state with all taxing and spending decisions being made centrally. But many countries operate on a decentralized basis and have some important state capacities at the local level. Political violence may also play a part in specific territories.

One frequent role of decentralization is to improve government performance. This could be because political cohesiveness and good governance are easier to achieve when government is decentralized. But if performance means heterogeneous performance, there may be winners and losers compared to having a central state. Either way, it would be interesting to extend the models developed here to consider such issues. Furthermore, from an empirical point of view, studying heterogeneous performance of governments exploiting within-country variation opens up new possibilities.

Bridge Theory and Empirical Work While working on the book, we were strongly motivated by the broad patterns in the data. We have also kept revisiting the data throughout the preceding chapters. But most of our empirical analyses have revolved around simple partial correlations in a large cross section of countries. Although these correlations were informed by our theory, they were not properly derived from that theory. Moreover, the well-known pitfalls in cross-sectional empirical analysis cast serious doubts on any causal interpretation of the results.

The one exception to this rule is our analysis in Chapter 4, where we show how our simple model of political violence can be used to guide an empirical strategy, seeking out the more rewarding results on the basis of within-country variation. We believe that future empirical work in the field should follow this example. In particular, one might conduct more convincing tests of theoretical predictions on state-capacity formation relying on historical data. For example, one could use a theory-based empirical strategy to analyze whether important reforms of fiscal capacity over time are indeed systematically related to events such as wars and reform of political institutions. This kind of research would require collecting new panel data, say, about the introduction of the income tax [as in Aidt and Jensen (2009a)] or the VAT or important reforms of these tax systems, say, about the introduction of income-tax withholding.

Use Theory and Data to Design Case Studies Although econometric studies are valuable, much can also be said for careful case studies. In the latter part of the book, we presented two somewhat unconventional arguments regarding how such case studies might be selected and conducted. One appeared in Section 7.3 on political reform in practice, where we argued that one should use a well-specified theoretical model to search for exogenous variables in comparative case studies. In Section 8.2.2 we discussed how theoretical anomalies identified by a systematic statistical approach can serve as a stepping stone for case studies that search for new mechanisms to enrich the theory.

Understand the Persistence of Weak States One of the major problems is to acquire an understanding of the mechanisms behind the persistence of poor, weak, and violence-stricken states. Our theory has provided some clues as to what circumstances and institutions might enmesh a country in such a combination of unhappy outcomes. But we have only been able to give a few hints on pathways out of the unhappy downward left part of our Anna Karenina matrix. Under what circumstances can we expect countries to commit themselves to economic and political reforms that allow them to break out of a weak-fiscal-state trap or a predatory-legal-state trap? Can foreign assistance in any form assist countries in this difficult task? In light of the development clusters that motivate this book, these may be the most important questions of all.

8.4 Concluding Remarks

Nearly 250 years ago, Adam Smith identified peace, easy taxes, and a tolerable administration of justice as key drivers of the wealth of nations. Our pillars of prosperity are closely related to those identified by Smith all those years ago. That said, we have reached this conclusion by a rather different route, using the tools of modern economics and benefiting from an additional quarter of a millennium of experience. Unlike Smith, who wrote before the advent of democracy and the industrial revolution, we can learn from the diversity of subsequent country experiences. Our conception of easy taxes has more to do with the ease of extracting taxes than with the level of taxes. Peace refers to domestic peace, whereas we have seen that a hostile external neighborhood can be a key force behind state building. We have also put far more weight than Smith did on the role of political institutions in constructing the pillars of prosperity.

Our entire project is theory-driven with a core model at the heart of the approach. It ties together three different, but related, facets of development: breaking out of poverty, building a state strong enough to support markets and provide public goods, and putting an end to violent political conflicts. Although the modeling is deliberately simple, we have been able to explore many different dimensions of the key ideas.

We have used this theoretical approach to argue that it is essential to understand the pillars of prosperity in terms of their common roots. Long-run progress requires tackling the underlying problems, such that stronger institutional cohesiveness and better governance can set in motion a process of positive feedbacks between the central outcomes.

We make no claim to have delivered any definitive insights and much of our analysis is synthetic, building on the contributions of prior research. In this area, there is more unexplored territory than settled ground. Our hope is that this book will help open up a whole new research program, and we invite development researchers and graduate students to join us in pursuing these issues. Whether or not this happens is the metric of success on which we would like to be judged.

References

Abadie, Alberto, and Javier Gardeazabal (2003), "The Economic Costs of Conflict: A Case Study of the Basque Country," *American Economic Review,* vol. 93, 113–132.

Acemoglu, Daron (2003), "Why Not a Political Coase Theorem: Social Conflict, Commitment, and Politics," *Journal of Comparative Economics,* vol. 31, 620–652.

——— (2005), "Politics and Economics in Weak and Strong States," *Journal of Monetary Economics,* vol. 52, 1199–1226.

——— (2006), "Modeling Inefficient Institutions," in Blundell, Richard, Whitney Newey, and Torsten Persson (eds.), *Advances in Economic Theory and Econometrics: Proceedings of the Ninth World Congress of the Econometric Society,* Cambridge, U.K.: Cambridge University Press.

Acemoglu, Daron, Mikhail Golosov, and Aleh Tsyvinski (2008), "Political Economy of Mechanisms," *Econometrica,* vol. 76, 619–641.

——— (2009), "Power Fluctuations and Political Economy," NBER Working Paper 15400.

Acemoglu, Daron, and Simon Johnson (2005), "Unbundling Institutions," *Journal of Political Economy,* vol. 113, 949–995.

Acemoglu, Daron, Simon Johnson, and James A. Robinson (2001), "The Colonial Origins of Comparative Development: An Empirical Investigation," *American Economic Review,* vol. 91, 1369–1401.

Acemoglu, Daron, Simon Johnson, James A. Robinson, and Pierre Yared (2005), "From Education to Democracy," *American Economic Review, Papers and Proceedings,* vol. 95, 44–49.

Acemoglu, Daron, and James A. Robinson (2000), "Why Did the West Extend the Franchise? Democracy, Inequality, and Growth in Historical Perspective," *Quarterly Journal of Economics,* vol. 115, 1167–1199.

——— (2006),*Economic Origins of Dictatorship and Democracy,* Cambridge: Cambridge University Press.

——— (2010), *Why Nations Fail,* book manuscript.

Acemoglu, Daron, Davide Ticchi, and Andrea Vindigni (2011), "Emergence and Persistence of Inefficient States," *Journal of the European Economic Association,* vol. 9, 177–208.

Addison, Tony (2003), "Africa's Recovery from Conflict: Making Peace Work for the Poor—A Policy Brief," WIDER, Helsinki.

Aghion, Philippe, Alberto Alesina, and Francesco Trebbi (2004), "Endogenous Political Institutions," *Quarterly Journal of Economics,* vol. 119, 565–612.

Aghion, Philippe, and Patrick Bolton (1990), "Government Debt and the Risk of Default: A Politico-Economic Model of the Strategic Role of Debt," in Dornbusch, Rüdiger, and Mario Draghi (eds.), *Public Debt Management: Theory and History,* Cambridge: Cambridge University Press.

——— (2003), "Incomplete Social Contracts," *Journal of the European Economic Association,* vol. 1, 38–67.

Aghion, Philippe, and Peter Howitt (1998), *Endogenous Growth Theory,* Cambridge, MA: MIT Press.

Aghion, Philippe, Peter Howitt, and David Mayer-Foulkes (2005), "The Effect of Financial Development on Convergence: Theory and Evidence," *Quarterly Journal of Economics,* vol. 120, 173–222.

Aidt, Toke S., and Peter S. Jensen (2009a), "The Taxman Tools Up: An Event History Study of the Introduction of the Personal Income Tax," *Journal of Public Economics,* vol. 93, 160–175.

——— (2009b), "Tax Structure, Size of Government, and the Extension of the Voting Franchise in Western Europe, 1860–1938," *International Tax Public Finance,* vol. 16, 362–394.

——— (2010), "Workers of the World, Unite! Franchise Extensions and the Threat of Revolution in Europe, 1820–1938," mimeo, Cambridge University.

Aizenman, Joshua, and Yothin Jinjarak (2008), "The Collection Efficiency of the Value Added Tax: Theory and International Evidence," *Journal of International Trade and Economic Development,* vol. 17, 391–410.

Akerlof, George, and Rachel Kranton (2010), *Identity Economics: How Our Identities Shape Our Work, Wages, and Well-Being,* Princeton: Princeton University Press.

Alesina, Alberto (1988), "Credibility and Political Convergence in a Two-party System with Rational Voters," *American Economic Review,* vol. 78, 796–805.

Alesina, Alberto, Reza Baqir, and William Easterly (1999), "Public Goods and Ethnic Divisions," *Quarterly Journal of Economics,* vol. 114, 1243–1284.

Alesina, Alberto, and David Dollar (2000), "Who Gives Foreign Aid to Whom and Why?," *Journal of Economic Growth,* vol. 5, 33–63.

Alesina, Alberto, and Roberto Perotti (1996), "Income Distribution, Political Instability and Investment," *European Economic Review,* vol. 40, 1203–1228.

Alesina, Alberto, and Dani Rodrik (1994), "Distributive Politics and Economic Growth," *Quarterly Journal of Economics,* vol. 109, 465–490.

Alesina, Alberto, and Guido Tabellini (1990), "A Positive Theory of Fiscal Deficits and Government Debt," *Review of Economic Studies,* vol. 57, 403–414.

Allingham, Michael G., and Agnar Sandmo (1972), "Income Tax Evasion: A Theoretical Analysis," *Journal of Public Economics,* vol. 1, 323–338.

Alt, James E. (1994), "The Impact of the Voting Rights Act on Black and White Voter Registration in the South," in Davidson, Chandler and Bernard Grofman (eds), *Quiet Revolution in the South: The Impact of the Voting Rights Act, 1965–1990,* Princeton: Princeton University Press.

Amsden, Alice H. (1992), *Asia's Next Giant: South Korea and Late Industrialization,* New York: Oxford University Press.

Arrow, Kenneth J. (1951), *Social Choice and Individual Values,* New Haven: Cowles Comission.

Aslaksen, Silje, and Ragnar Torvik (2006), "A Theory of Civil Conflict and Democracy in Rentier States," *Scandinavian Journal of Economics,* vol. 108, 571–585.

Atkinson, Anthony, and Joseph Stiglitz (1980), *Lectures on Public Economics,* London: McGraw-Hill.

Austen-Smith, David, and Jeffrey S. Banks (2005), *Positive Political Theory II Strategy & Structure,* Ann Arbor: University of Michigan Press.

Azam, Jean-Paul (2002), "Looting and Conflict between Ethno-regional Groups: Lessons for State Formation in Africa," *Journal of Conflict Resolution,* vol. 46, 131–153.

——— (2005), "The Paradox of Power Reconsidered: A Theory of Political Regimes in Africa," *Journal of African Economies,* vol. 15, 26–58.

Azam, Jean-Paul, Robert H. Bates, and Biais Bruno (2009), "Political Predation and Economic Development," *Economics and Politics,* vol. 21, 255–277.

Azam, Jean-Paul, and Anke Hoeffler (2002), "Violence against Civilians in Civil Wars: Looting or Terror?," *Journal of Peace Research,* vol. 39, 461–485.

Azam, Jean-Paul, and Jean-Jacques Laffont (2003), "Contracting for Aid," *Journal of Development Economics,* vol. 70, 25–58.

Azam, Jean-Paul, and Tahsin Saadi-Sedik (2003), "Aid v. Sanctions for Taming Oppressors: Theory and Application to the Iraqi Kurds," *Defence and Peace Economics,* vol. 15, 311–334.

Azzimonti, Marina (2009), "Barriers to Investment in Polarized Societies," mimeo, forthcoming in *American Economic Review.*

Bai, Jinhui B., and Roger Lagunoff (2011), "On the 'Faustian' Dynamics of Policy and Political Power," *Review of Economic Studies,* vol. 78, 17–48.

Banerjee, Abhijit (2003), "Contracting Constraints, Credit Markets and Economic Development," in Dewatripont, Mathias, Lars Peter Hansen, and Stephen Turnovsky (eds.), *Advances in Economics and Econometrics: Theory and Applications: Eighth World Conference of the Econometric Society,* Vol. III, Cambridge: Cambridge University Press.

Banerjee, Abhijit, and Esther Duflo (2005), "Growth Theory Through the Lens of Development Economics," in Aghion, Philippe, and Stephen Durlauf (eds.), *Handbook of Economic Growth,* Vol. 1a, Amsterdam: Elsevier.

——— (2009), "The Experimental Approach to Development Economics," NBER Working Paper No. 14467.

——— (2010), "Giving Credit Where Credit is Due," MIT Department of Economics Working Paper No. 10-3, available at SSRN: http://ssrn.com/abstract=1572913.

Banerjee, Abhijit V., Paul J. Gertler, and Maitreesh Ghatak [2002), "Empowerment and Efficiency: Tenancy Reform in West Bengal," *Journal of Political Economy,* vol. 110, 239–280.

Banerjee, Abhijit, and Ruimin He (2008), "Making Aid Work," in Easterly, William (ed.), *Reinventing Foreign Aid,* Cambridge, MA: MIT Press.

Banks, Arthur (2005), *Cross-National Time-Series Data Archive,* Databanks International.

Baron, David (1996), "A Dynamic Theory of Collective Goods Programs," *American Political Science Review,* vol. 90, 316–330.

Baron, David, and John Ferejohn (1989), "Bargaining in Legislatures," *American Political Science Review,* vol. 83, 1181–1206.

Barro, Robert J. (1973), "The Control of Politicians: An Economic Model," *Public Choice,* vol. 14, 19–42.

Barro, Robert J., and Xavier Sala-i-Martin (1992), "Public Finance in Models of Economic Growth," *Review of Economic Studies,* vol. 59, 645–661.

Bates, Robert H. (1981), *Markets and States in Tropical Africa: The Political Basis of Agricultural Policies,* Berkeley: University of California Press.

——— (2001), *Prosperity and Violence: The Political Economy of Development.* New York: Cambridge University Press.

——— (2008), "The Logic of State Failure: Learning from Late-Century Africa," *Conflict Management and Peace Science,* vol. 25, 297–314.

——— (2009), *The Logic of State Failure: Learning from Late-Century Africa. Dealing with Failed States,* London: Routledge.

Bates, Robert H., Avner Greif, Margaret Levi, Jean-Laurent Rosenthal, and Barry Weingast, (1998), *Analytic Narratives,* Princeton: Princeton University Press.

Battaglini, Marco, and Stephen Coate (2007), "Inefficiency in Legislative Policy-Making: A Dynamic Analysis," *American Economic Review,* vol. 97, 118–149.

——— (2008), "A Dynamic Theory of Public Spending, Taxation, and Debt," *American Economic Review,* vol. 98, 201–236.

Bauer, Peter (1972), *Dissent on Development,* Cambridge: Harvard University Press.

——— (1975), "N.H. Stern on Substance and Method in Development Economics," *Journal of Development Economics,* vol. 2, 387–405.

Baumol, William, J. (1967), "Macroeconomics of Unbalanced Growth: The Anatomy of Urban Crisis," *American Economic Review,* vol. 57, 415–426.

Baunsgaard, Thomas, and Michael Keen (2005), "Tax Revenue and (or?) Trade Liberalization," mimeo, IMF.

Beck, Thorsten (2010), "Legal Institutions and Economic Development," forthcoming in the *Oxford Handbook of Capitalism.*

Benabou, Roland (1997), "Inequality and Growth," *NBER Macroeconomics Annual 1996,* Cambridge, MA: MIT Press.

Benabou, Roland, and Jean Tirole (2010), "Laws and Norms," mimeo, Princeton University.

Benson, Bruce (1989), "The Spontaneous Evolution of Commercial Law," *Southern Economic Journal,* vol. 55, 644–661.

Berg, Elliot (1993), *Rethinking Technical Cooperation: Reforms for Capacity Building in Africa,* New York: United Nations Development Program.

Berry, Francis Stokes, and William D. Berry (1992), "Tax Innovation in the States: Capitalizing on Political Opportunity," *American Journal of Political Science,* vol. 36, 715–742.

Besley, Timothy (1995), "Property Rights and Investment Incentives: Theory and Evidence from Ghana," *Journal of Political Economy,* vol. 103, 903–937.

——— (2006), *Principled Agents? The Political Economy of Good Government,* Oxford: Oxford University Press.

Besley, Timothy, and Anne Case (2003), "Political Institutions and Policy Choices: Evidence from the United States," *Journal of Economic Literature,* vol. 41, 7–73.

Besley, Timothy, and Stephen Coate (1997), "An Economic Model of Representative Democracy," *Quarterly Journal of Economics,* vol. 112, 85–114.

——— (1998), "Sources of Inefficiency in a Representative Democracy: A Dynamic Analysis," *American Economic Review,* vol. 88, 139–156.

——— (2003), "Centralized versus Decentralized Provision of Local Public Goods: A Political Economy Approach," *Journal of Public Economics,* vol. 87, 2611–2637.

Besley, Timothy, and Maitreesh Ghatak (2009), "Property Rights and Economic Development," in Rodrik, Dani and Mark Rosenzweig (eds.), *Handbook of Development Economics,* vol. V, Amsterdam: Elsevier.

Besley, Timothy, and Rajshri Jayaraman (eds.) (2010), *Institutional Microeconomics of Development,* Cambridge, MA: MIT Press.

Besley, Timothy, Ethan Ilzetzki, and Torsten Persson (2010), "Weak States, Strong States and Steady States: The Dynamics of Fiscal Capacity," mimeo, London School of Economics.

Besley, Timothy, and Hannes Mueller (2010), "Estimating the Peace Dividend: Evidence from House Prices in Northern Ireland," forthcoming in the *American Economic Review.*

Besley, Timothy, and Torsten Persson (2008), "Wars and State Capacity," *Journal of the European Economic Association,* vol. 6, 522–530.

——— (2009a), "Repression or Civil War?," *American Economic Review, Papers and Proceedings,* vol. 99, 292–297.

——— (2009b), "The Origins of State Capacity: Property Rights, Taxation and Politics," *American Economic Review,* vol. 99, 1218–1244.

——— (2010a), "State Capacity, Conflict and Development," *Econometrica,* vol. 78, 1–34.

——— (2010b), "The Logic of Political Violence," forthcoming in the *Quarterly Journal of Economics.*

——— (2010c), "From Trade Taxes to Income Taxes: Theory and Evidence on Economic Development and State Capacity," mimeo, London School of Economics.

——— (2011), "Fragile States and Development Policy," paper underlying the 2010 EEA Presidential Address, forthcoming in the *Journal of the European Economic Association.*

Besley, Timothy, and Andrea Prat (2006), "Handcuffs for the Grabbing Hand? Media Capture and Government Accountability," *American Economic Review,* vol. 96, 720–736.

Bird, Richard, and Oliver Oldman (eds.) (1980), *Readings on Taxation in Developing Countries,* 3rd Edition, Baltimore: Johns Hopkins University Press.

Blackstone, William (1765–1766), *Commentaries on the Law of England,* Oxford: Clarendon Press.

Blattman, Christopher, and Edward Miguel (2009), "Civil War," *Journal of Economic Literature,* vol. 48, 3–57.

Blomberg, S. Brock, and Gregory D. Hess (2002), "The Temporal Links between Conflict and Economic Activity," *Journal of Conflict Resolution,* vol. 46, 74–90.

Bloom, David E., and Jeffrey D. Sachs (1998), "Geography, Demography and Economic Growth in Africa," *Brookings Papers on Economic Activity,* no 2, 207–272.

Bockstette, Valerie, Areendam Chanda, and Louis Putterman (2002), "States and Markets: The Advantage of an Early Start," *Journal of Economic Growth,* vol. 7, 347–369.

Boettke, Peter, Christopher Coyne, and Peter Leeson (2008), "Institutional Stickiness and the New Development Economics," *American Journal of Economics and Sociology,* vol. 67, 331–358.

Bohlken, Anjali Thomas, and Ernest Sergenti (2010), "Ethnic Violence and Economic Growth: An Empirical Investigation of Hindu-Muslim Riots in India," *Journal of Peace Research,* vol. 47, 589–600.

Boix, Carles (1999), "Setting the Rules of the Game: The Choice of Electoral Systems in Advanced Democracies," *American Political Science Review,* vol. 93, 609–624.

——— (2003), *Democracy and Redistribution,* Cambridge: Cambridge University Press.

Bonney, Richard (ed.) (1999), *The Rise of the Fiscal State in Europe c1200–1815,* Oxford: Oxford University Press.

Boone, Peter (1996), "Politics and the Effectiveness of Foreign Aid," *European Economic Review,* vol. 40, 289–329.

Bräutigam, Deborah, Odd-Helge Fjeldstad, and Mick Moore [2008), *Taxation and State-Building in Developing Countries,* Cambridge: Cambridge University Press.

Brennan, Geoffrey, and James M. Buchanan (1985), *The Reason of Rules: Constitutional Political Economy,* Cambridge: Cambridge University Press.

Brewer, John (1989), *The Sinews of Power: War, Money and the English State, 1688–1783,* New York: Knopf.

Bruckner, Markus, and Antonio Ciccone (2008), "Growth, Democracy, and Civil War," CEPR Discussion Paper No. 6568.

Buchanan, James M. (1967), *Public Finance in Democratic Process: Fiscal Institutions and Individual Choice,* Chapel Hill: University of North Carolina Press.

——— (1987), "The Constitution of Economic Policy," Nobel Prize Lecture, *American Economic Review,* vol. 77, 243–250.

Buchanan, James M., and Gordon Tullock (1962), *The Calculus of Consent,* Ann Arbor: University of Michigan Press.

Bueno de Mesquita, Bruce, Alastair Smith, Randolph Siverson, and James Morrow (2003),*The Logic of Political Survival,* Cambridge, MA: MIT Press.

Burgess, Robin, and Nicholas Stern (1993), "Taxation and Development," *Journal of Economic Literature,* vol. 31, 762–830.

Burnside, Craig, and David Dollar (2000), "Aid, Policies and Growth," *American Economic Review,* vol. 90, 847–868.

Cantoni, Davide, and Noam Yuchtman (2009), "Medieval Universities, Legal Institutions and the Commercial Revolution," mimeo, Harvard University.

Cárdenas, Mauricio (2010), "State Capacity in Latin America," *Economía,* vol. 10, 1–45.

Cárdenas, Mauricio, and Didem Tuzemen (2010), "Under-Investment in State Capacity: The Role of Inequality and Political Instability," mimeo, The Brookings Institution.

Caselli, Francesco (2006), "Power Struggles and the Natural Resource Curse," mimeo, London School of Economics.

Caselli, Francesco, and Nicola Gennaioli (2008), "Economics and Politics of Alternative Institutional Reforms," *Quarterly Journal of Economics,* vol. 123, 1197–1250

Centeno, Miguel A (1997), "Blood and Debt: War and Taxation in Latin America," *American Journal of Sociology,* vol. 102, 1565–1605.

Chamberlain, Gary (1980), "Analysis of Covariance with Qualitative Data," *Review of Economic Studies,* vol. 47, 225–238.

Chanda, Areendam, and Louis Putterman (2004), "The Quest for Growth: What Role Does History Play?," *World Economics,* vol. 5, 1–28.

Chassang, Sylvain, and Gerard Padró i Miquel (2009), "Economic Shocks and Civil War," *Quarterly Journal of Political Science*, vol. 4, 211–228.

Chauvet, Lisa, and Paul Collier (2006), "Helping Hand? Aid to Failing States," DIAL - Document de Travail DT/2006-14.

Chenery, Hollis B. (1975), "The Structuralist Approach to Development Policy," *American Economic Review, Papers and Proceedings*, vol. 65, 310–316.

Chenery, Hollis B., and Hazel Elkington (1979), *Structural Change and Development Policy*, New York: Oxford University Press.

Chenery, Hollis B., and Alan M. Strout (1966), "Foreign Assistance and Economic Development," *American Economic Review*, vol. 56, 679–733.

Chong, Alberto, and Mark Gradstein (2007), "Inequality and Institutions," *Review of Economics and Statistics*, vol. 89, 454–465.

Clark, Gregory (2008), *A Farewell to Alms: A Brief Economic History of the World*, Princeton: Princeton University Press.

Coase, Ronald H. (1960), "The Problem of Social Cost," *Journal of Law and Economics*, vol. 3, 1–44.

Collier, Paul (1999), "On the Economic Consequences of Civil War," *Oxford Economic Papers*, vol. 51, 168–183.

——— (2007), *The Bottom Billion*, Oxford: Oxford University Press.

——— (2008), *Wars, Guns and Votes: Democracy in Dangerous Places*, London: Bodley Head.

Collier, Paul, and David Dollar (2004), "Development Effectiveness: What Have We Learnt?," *Economic Journal*, vol. 114, F244–F271.

Collier, Paul, V. L. Elliott, Håvard Hegre, Anke Hoeffler, Marta Reynol-Querol, and Nicolas Sambanis (2003), *Breaking the Conflict Trap: Civil War and Development Policy*, New York: Oxford University Press, for the World Bank.

Collier, Paul, and Jan Willem Gunning (1999), "Explaining African Economic Performance," *Journal of Economic Literature*, vol. 37, 64–111.

Collier, Paul, and Anke Hoeffler (2004), "Greed and Grievance in Civil War," *Oxford Economic Papers*, vol. 56, 563–595.

Collier, Paul, and Dominic Rohner (2008), "Democracy, Development and Conflict," *Journal of the European Economic Association*, vol. 6, 531–540.

Cowell, Frank (1990), *Cheating the Government*, Cambridge, MA: MIT Press.

Coyne, Christopher J. (2008a), *After War: The Political Economy of Exporting Democracy*, Palo Alto, CA: Stanford University Press.

——— (2008b), "The Politics of Bureaucracy and the Failure of Post-War Reconstruction," *Public Choice*, vol. 135, 11–22.

Coyne, Christopher J., and Peter J. Boettke (2009), "The Problem of Credible Commitment in Reconstruction," *Journal of Institutional Economics*, vol. 5, 1–23.

Coyne, Christopher J., Gregory M. Dempster, and Justin P. Isaacs [2010), "Asset Values and the Sustainability of Peace Prospects," *The Quarterly Review of Economics and Finance*, vol. 50, 146–156.

Coyne, Christopher J., and Peter Leeson (2009), *Media, Development, and Institutional Change,* Cheltenham: Edward Elgar.

Coyne, Christopher J., and Adam Pellillo (2011), "Economic Reconstruction Amidst Conflict: Insights from Afghanistan and Iraq," forthcoming in *Defence and Peace Economics.*

Cox, Gary (1997), *Making Votes Count,* Cambridge, U.K.: Cambridge University Press.

Cukierman, Alex, Sebastian Edwards, and Guido Tabellini (1992), "Seignorage and Political Instability," *American Economic Review,* vol. 82, 537–555.

Dal Bó, Ernesto, and Pedro Dal Bó (2006), "Workers, Warriors and Criminals: Social Conflict in General Equilibrium," forthcoming in the *Journal of the European Economic Association.*

Davenport, Christian (2007), "State Repression and Political Order," *Annual Review of Political Science,* vol. 10, 1–23.

Deininger, Klaus (2003), "Causes and Consequences of Civil Strife: Micro-Level Evidence from Uganda," *Oxford Economic Papers,* vol. 55, 579–606.

Deininger, Klaus, and Lyn Squire (1996), "A New Data Set Measuring Income Inequality," *The World Bank Economic Review,* vol. 10, 565–591.

de Figueiredo, Rui J. P. Jr. (2002), "Electoral Competition, Political Uncertainty, and Policy Insulation," *American Political Science Review,* vol. 96, 321–333

De Long, J. Bradford (2000), "Overstrong Against Thyself: War, the State, and Growth in Europe on the Eve of the Industrial Revolution," in Olson, Mancur, and Satu Kahkohnen (eds.), *A Not-So-Dismal Science: A Broader View of Economies and Societies,* Oxford: Oxford University Press.

De Long, J. Bradford, and Andrei Shleifer (1993), "Princes and Merchants: European City Growth Before the Industrial Revolution," *Journal of Law and Economics,* vol. 36, 671–702.

de Ree, Joppe, and Eleonora Nillesen (2009), "Aiding Violence or Peace? The Impact of Foreign Aid on the Risk of Civil Conflict in Sub-Saharan Africa," *Journal of Development Economics,* vol. 88, 301–313.

Diamond, Jared (1997), *Guns, Germs, and Steel: The Fates of Human Societies,* W.W. Norton & Company.

Diamond, Peter, and James Mirrlees (1971), "Optimal Taxation and Public Production: I. Production Efficiency," *American Economic Review,* vol. 61, 8–27.

Diermeier, Daniel, and Tim Feddersen (1998), "Cohesion in Legislatures and the Vote of Confidence Procedure," *American Political Science Review,* vol. 92, 611–621.

Dincecco, Mark (2011), *Political Transformations and Public Finances: Europe, 1650–1913,* Cambridge: Cambridge University Press forthcoming.

Dincecco, Mark, and José Mauricio Prado Jr. (2010), "Warfare, Fiscal Capacity, and Performance," mimeo, IMT Lucca Institute for Advanced Studies.

Dixit, Avinash (1987), "Strategic Behavior in Contests," *American Economic Review,* vol. 77, 891–898.

——— (2004), *Lawlessness and Economics: Alternative Modes of Governance* (Gorman Lectures in Economics, University College London), Princeton: Princeton University Press.

——— (2009), "Governance Institutions and Economic Activity," *American Economic Review,* vol. 99, 5–24.

Dixit, Avinash, Gene M. Grossman, and Faruk Gul (2000), "The Dynamics of Political Compromise," *Journal of Political Economy,* vol. 108, 531–568.

Djankov, Simeon, Edward Glaeser, Rafael La Porta, Florencio Lopez de Silanes, and Andrei Shleifer (2003), "The New Comparative Economics," *Journal of Comparative Economics,* vol. 31, 595–619.

Djankov, Simeon, Rafael La Porta, Florencio Lopez de Silanes, and Andrei Shleifer (2002), "The Regulation of Entry," *Quarterly Journal of Economics,* vol. 117, 1–37.

Djankov, Simeon, Caralee McLiesh, and Andrei Shleifer (2007), "Private Credit in 129 Countries," *Journal of Financial Economics,* vol. 84, 299–329.

Djankov, Simeon, Jose G. Montalvo, and Marta Reynal-Querol (2008), "The Curse of Aid," *Journal of Economic Growth,* vol. 13, 1835–1865.

Doucouliagos, Hristos, and Martin Paldam (2008), "Aid Effectiveness on Growth: A Meta Study," *European Journal of Political Economy,* vol. 24, 1–24.

Drury, Cooper, and Richard Olson (1998), "Disasters and Political Unrest: An Empirical Investigation," *Journal of Contingencies and Crisis Management,* vol. 6, 153–161.

Dube, Oeindrila, and Juan Vargas (2008), "Commodity Price Shocks and Civil Conflict: Evidence from Colombia," mimeo, Harvard University.

Duflo, Esther, Rachel Glennerster, and Michael Kremer (2007), "Using Randomization in Development Economics Research: A Toolkit," CEPR Discussion Paper No 6059.

Dunning Thad, (2010), "Endogenous Oil Rents," *Comparative Political Studies,* vol. 43, no. 3, 379–410.

Easterly, William (2003), "Can Foreign Aid Buy Growth?," *Journal of Economic Perspectives,* vol. 17, 23–48.

——— (2006), *The White Man's Burden: Why the West's Efforts to Aid the Rest Have Done So Much Ill and So Little Good,* New York: Penguin Books.

Elbadawi, Ibrahim, and Nicholas Sambanis (2002), "How Much Civil War Will We See? Explaining the Prevalence of Civil War," *Journal of Conflict Resolution,* vol. 46, 307–334.

Engerman, Stanley L., and Kenneth L. Sokoloff (2002), "Factor Endowments, Inequality, and Paths of Development among New World Economies," *Economia,* vol. 3, 41–88

ERD (2009), *Overcoming Fragility in Africa. Forging a New European Approach, European Report on Development,* San Domenico de Fiesole: EUI.

Erikson, Robert S. (1972), "Malapportionment, Gerrymandering, and Party Fortunes in Congressional Elections," *American Political Science Review,* vol. 66, 1234–1245.

Esteban, Joan, and Debraj Ray (1994), "On the Measurement of Polarization," *Econometrica,* vol. 62, 819–851.

——— (1999), "Conflict and Distribution," *Journal of Economic Theory,* vol. 87, 379–415.

——— (2008a), "On the Salience of Ethnic Conflict," *American Economic Review,* vol. 98, 2185–2202.

——— (2008b), "Polarization, Fractionalization and Conflict," *Journal of Peace Research,* vol. 45, 163–182.

Esteban, Juan, Debraj Ray, and Jean-Yves Duclos (2004), "Polarization: Concepts, Measurement, Estimation," *Econometrica,* vol. 72, 1737–1772.

Fearon, James (2003), "Ethnic and Cultural Diversity by Country," *Journal of Economic Growth,* vol. 8, 195–222.

——— (2004), "Why Do Some Civil Wars Last so Much Longer than Others?," *Journal of Peace Research,* vol. 41, 275–301.

——— (2008), "Economic Development, Insurgency and Civil War," in Helpman, Elhanan (ed.), *Institutions and Economic Performance,* Cambridge, MA: Harvard University Press.

——— (2010), "Coordinating on Democracy," forthcoming in the *Quarterly Journal of Economics.*

Fearon, James, and David Laitin (2003), "Ethnicity, Insurgency and Civil War," *American Political Science Review,* vol. 97, 75–90.

Fei, John, and Gustav Ranis (1964), *Development of the Labor Surplus Economy,* Homewood, IL.

Feld, Lars P., and Stefan Voigt (2003), "Economic Growth and Judicial Independence: Cross-country Evidence Using a New Set of Indicators," *European Journal of Political Economy,* vol. 19, 497–527.

Ferejohn, John (1986), "Incumbent Performance and Electoral Control," *Public Choice,* vol. 50, 5–25.

Ferrer-i-Carbonell, Ada, and Paul Frijters (2004), "How Important is Methodology for the Estimates of the Determinants of Happiness?," *Economic Journal,* vol. 114, 641–659.

Field, Erica (2007), "Entitled to Work: Urban Property Rights and Labor Supply in Peru," *Quarterly Journal of Economics,* vol. 122, 1561–1602.

Frey, Bruno S. (1983), *Democratic Economic Policy: A Theoretical Introduction,* Oxford: Blackwell.

Frey, Bruno S., and Friedrich Schneider (1986), "Competing Models of International Lending Activity," *Journal of Development Economics,* vol. 20, 225–245.

Fudenberg, D., and Eric Maskin (1986), "The Folk Theorem in Repeated Games with Discounting or with Incomplete Information," *Econometrica,* vol. 54, 533–554.

Gallup, John Luke, Jeffrey D. Sachs, and Andrew Mellinger (1999), "Geography and Economic Development," *International Regional Science Review,* vol. 22, 179–232.

Garfinkel, Michelle R., and Stergios Skaperdas (2007), "Economics of Conflict: An Overview," in Sandler, Todd, and Keith Hartley (eds.), *Handbook of Defense Economics,* Vol. II, Amsterdam: Elsevier.

Gellner, Ernest, (1983), *Nations and Nationalism,* Ithaca: Cornell University Press.

Gerschenkron, Alexander (1962), "Agricultural Backwardness in Historical Perspective," chapter 1 in Gerschenkron, Alexander, *Agricultural Backwardness in Historical Perspective,* Cambridge, MA: Harvard University Press.

Gibney, Mark, Linda Cornett, and Reed Wood (2007), *Political Terror Scale 1976 to 2006,* available at www.politicalterrorscale.org.

Glaeser, Edward, Rafael La Porta, Florencio Lopez de Silanes, and Andrei Shleifer (2004), "Do Institutions Cause Growth?," *Journal of Economic Growth,* vol. 9, 271–303.

Glaeser, Edward, L., Giacomo A. Ponzetto, and Andrei Shleifer [2007), "Why Democracy Needs Education," *Journal of Economic Growth,* vol. 12, 77–99.

Goldin, Claudia D., and Frank D. Lewis (1975), "The Economic Cost of the American Civil War: Estimates and Implications," *Journal of Economic History,* vol. 35, 299–326.

Golosov, Mikhail, Aleh Tsyvinski, and Ivan Werning (2006), "New Dynamic Public Finance: A User's Guide," *NBER Macroeconomics Annual,* Cambridge, MA: MIT Press.

Gordon, Roger (ed.) (2010), *Taxation in Developing Countries: Six Case Studies and Policy Implications,* New York: Columbia University Press.

Gordon, Roger, and Wei Li (2009), "Tax Structures in Developing Countries: Many Puzzles and a Possible Explanation," *Journal of Public Economics,* vol. 93, 855–866

Gradstein, Mark (2008), "Institutional Traps and Economic Growth," *International Economic Review,* vol. 49, 1043–1066.

Greif, Avner (2005), "Commitment, Coercion and Markets: The Nature and Dynamics of Institutions Supporting Exchange," in Ménard, Claude and Mary M. Shirley (eds.), *Handbook of New Institutional Economics,* Dordrecht: Springer.

——— (2006), *Institutions and the Path to the Modern Economy: Lessons from Medieval Trade,* Cambridge: Cambridge University Press.

Grofman, Bernard N. (1985), "Criteria for Districting: A Social Science Perspective," *UCLA Law Review,* vol. 33, 77–184.

Grofman, Bernard N., William Koetzle, and Thomas Brunell (1997), "An Integrated Perspective on the Three Potential Sources of Partisan Bias: Malapportionment, Turnout Differences, and the Geographic Distribution of Party Vote Shares," *Electoral Studies,* vol. 16, 457–470.

Grossman, Herschel (1991), "A General Equilibrium Model of Insurrection," *American Economic Review,* vol. 81, 912–921.

——— (1992), "Foreign Aid and Insurrection," *Defence and Peace Economics,* vol. 3, 275–288.

Grossman, Herschel I., and Minseong Kim (1995), "Swords or Plowshares? A Theory of the Security of Claims to Property," *Journal of Political Economy,* vol. 103, 1275–1288.

Grossman, Herschel I., and Suk Jae Noh (1994), "Proprietary Public Finance and Economic Welfare," *Journal of Public Economics,* vol. 53, 187–204.

Gstoettner, Markus, and Anders Jensen (2010), "Aid and Public Finance: A Missing Link?," *Atlantic Economic Journal,* vol. 38, 217–235.

Gupta, Sanjeev, Catherine Pattillo, and Smita Wagh (2006), "Are Donor Countries Giving More or Less Aid?," *Review of Development Economics,* vol. 10, 535–552.

Hall, Robert, and Chad Jones (1999), "Why Do Some Countries Produce So Much More Output per Worker than Others?," *Quarterly Journal of Economics,* vol. 114, 83–116.

Hamilton, Alexander, John Jay, and James Madison (1788), *The Federalist: A Collection,* New York: J. and A. McLean.

Hansen, Henrik, and Finn Tarp (2001), "Aid and Growth Regressions," *Journal of Development Economics,* vol. 64, 547–570.

Hayek, Friedrich (1979), *Law, Legislation and Liberty,* Vol. 3: *The Political Order of a Free People,* Chicago, University of Chicago Press.

Herbst, Jefferey I. (1990), "War and the State in Africa," *International Security,* vol. 14, 117–139.

——— (2000), *States and Power in Africa: Comparative Lessons in Authority and Control,* Princeton: Princeton University Press.

Hettich, Walter, and Stanley Winer (1999), *Democratic Choice and Taxation: A Theoretical and Empirical Analysis,* Cambridge: Cambridge University Press.

Hillman, Arye L. (2011), "Rent Seeking," in Reksulak, Michael, Laura Razzolini, and William F. Shughart II (eds.), *The Elgar Companion to Public Choice,* 2nd edition, Cheltenham, U.K: Edward Elgar.

Hillman, Arye L., and Heinrich W. Ursprung (2000), "Political Culture and Economic Decline," *European Journal of Political Economy,* vol. 16, 189–213.

Hinich, Melvin, A., John O. Ledyard, and Peter Ordeshook (1972), "Nonvoting and the Existence of Equilibrium under Majority Rule," *Journal of Economic Theory,* vol. 4, 144–153.

Hinrichs, Harley H. (1966), *A General Theory of Tax Structure Change During Economic Development,* Cambridge, MA: The Law School of Harvard University.

Hintze, Otto (1906), "Military Organization and the Organization of the State," reprinted in Gilbert, Felix (ed.) (1970), *The Historical Essays of Otto Hintze,* New York: Oxford University Press.

Hirshleifer, Jack (1989), "Conflict and Rent-Seeking Success Functions: Ratio vs. Difference Models of Relative Success," *Public Choice,* vol. 63, 101–112.

Hodgson, Geoffrey M. (2006), "Institutions, Recessions and Recovery in the Transitional Economies," *Journal of Economic Issues,* vol. 40, 875–894.

Hodgson, Geoffrey M., and Shuxia Jiang (2007), "The Economics of Corruption and the Corruption of Economics: An Institutionalist Perspective," *Journal of Economic Issues,* vol. 41, 1043–1061.

Hoffman, Philip, and Jean-Laurent Rosenthal (1997), "Political Economy of Warfare and Taxation in Early Modern Europe: Historical Lessons for Economic Development," in Drobak, John, and John Nye (eds.), *The Frontiers of the New Institutional Economics,* San Diego: Academic Press.

Hseih Chang-Tai, and Peter Klenow (2009), "Misallocation and Manufacturing TFP in China and India," *Quarterly Journal of Economics,* vol. 124, 1403–1448.

——— (2010), "Development Accounting," *American Economic Journal: Macroeconomics,* vol. 2, 207–223.

Huber, John D. (1996), "The 'Vote of Confidence in Parliamentary Democracies," *American Political Science Review,* vol. 90, 269–282.

Humphreys, Macartan (2005), "Natural Resources, Conflict, and Conflict Resolution: Uncovering the Mechanisms," *Journal of Conflict Resolution,* vol. 49, 508–537.

Humphreys, Macartan, Jeffrey D. Sachs, and Joseph E. Stiglitz (eds.) (2007), *Escaping the Resource Curse,* New York: Columbia University Press.

Husted, Thomas, and Lawrence Kenny (1997), "The Effect of the Expansion of the Voting Franchise on the Size of Government," *Journal of Political Economy,* vol. 105, 54–82.

Jellema, Jan, and Gérard Roland (2010), "Institutional Clusters and Economic Performance," forthcoming in the *Journal of Economic Behavior and Organization.*

Jensen, Anders (2010), "Natural Resources and Ability to Tax," mimeo, London School of Economics.

Johnson, Simon, John McMillan, and Christopher Woodruff (2002), "Property Rights and Finance," *American Economic Review,* vol. 92, 1335–1356.

Jones, Bejamin F., and Benjamin A. Olken (2005), "Do Leaders Matter? National Leadership and Growth Since World War II," *Quarterly Journal of Economics,* vol. 120, 835–864.

——— (2009), "Hit or Miss? The Effect of Assassinations on Institutions and War," *American Economic Journal Macroeconomics,* vol. 1, 55–87.

Kaldor, Nicholas (1963), "Taxation for Economic Development," *Journal of Modern African Studies,* vol. 1, 7–23.

Kandori, Michhiro (1989), "Social Norms and Community Enforcement," *Review of Economic Studies,* vol. 59, 63-80.

Karaman, K. Kivanc, Sevket Pamuk (2011), "Different Paths to the Modern State in Europe: The Interaction between Domestic Political Economy and Interstate Competition," mimeo, London School of Economics.

Keen, Michael (2010), "Taxation and Development Again," mimeo, IMF.

Keen, Michael, and Ben Lockwood (2010), "The Value Added Tax: Its Causes and Consequences," *Journal of Development Economics,* vol. 92, 138–151.

Kenny, Lawrence, and Stanley Winer (2006), "Tax Systems in the World: An Empirical Investigation into the Importance of Tax Bases, Administrative Costs, Scale and Political Regime," *International Tax and Public Finance,* vol. 13, 181–215.

King, Robert G., and Ross Levine (1993), "Finance and Growth: Schumpeter Might Be Right," *Quarterly Journal of Economics,* vol. 108, 717–737.

Klerman, Daniel M., and Paul G. Mahoney (2005), "The Value of Judicial Independence: Evidence from 18th Century England," *American Law and Economic Review,* vol. 7, 1–27.

Kletzer, Kenneth (2005), "Aid and Sanctions," mimeo, EC Santa Cruz.

Kleven, Henrik, Claus Thustrup Kreiner, and Emmanuel Saez (2009), "Why Can Modern Governments Tax So Much? An Agency Model of Firms as Fiscal Intermediaries," NBER Working Paper 15218.

Knack, Stephen (2001), "Aid Dependence and the Quality of Governance: A Cross Country Empirical Test," *Southern Economic Journal,* vol. 68, 310–329.

Krueger, Anne (1974), "The Political Economy of the Rent-Seeking Society," *American Economic Review,* vol. 64, 291–303.

Krusell, Per, and José-Víctor Ríos-Rull (1996), "Vested Interests in a Positive Theory of Stagnation and Growth," *Review of Economic Studies,* vol. 63, 301–329.

Kuziemko, Ilyana, and Eric Werker (2006), "How Much Is a Seat on the Security Council Worth? Foreign Aid and Bribery at the United Nations," *Journal of Political Economy,* vol. 114, 905–930.

Kydland, Finn E., and Edward C. Prescott (1977), "Rules Rather than Discretion: The Inconsistency of Optimal Plans," *Journal of Political Economy,* vol. 85, 473–492.

La Porta, Rafael, Florencio Lopez de Silanes, Andrei Shleifer, and Robert Vishny (1998), "Law and Finance," *Journal of Political Economy,* vol. 106, 1113–1155.

——— (1999), "The Quality of Government," *Journal of Law Economics and Organization,* vol. 15, 222–279.

La Porta, Rafael, Florencio Lopez de Silanes, and Andrei Shleifer [2008), "The Economics Consequences of Legal Origins," *Journal of Economic Literature,* vol. 46, 285–332.

Lacina, Bethany Ann, and Nils Petter Gleditsch (2005), "Monitoring Trends in Global Combat: A New Dataset of Battle Deaths," *European Journal of Population,* vol. 21, 145–165.

Lagunoff, Roger (2001), "A Theory of Constitutional Standards and Civil Liberty," *Review of Economic Studies,* vol. 68, 109–132.

Landes, David (1998), *The Wealth and Poverty of Nations: Why Some Are So Rich and Some So Poor,* New York: W. W. Norton.

Leeson, Peter (2006), "Efficient Anarchy," *Public Choice,* vol. 130, 41–53.

——— (2007), "Better Off Stateless: Somalia Before and After Government Collapse," *Journal of Comparative Economics*, vol. 35, 689–710.

——— (2008), "Escaping Poverty: Foreign Aid, Private Property, and Economic Development," *Journal of Private Enterprise*, vol. 23, 39–64.

Levi, Margaret (1988), *Of Rule and Revenue*, Berkeley: University of California Press.

——— (1998), "A State of Trust," in Braithwaite, Valerie, and Margaret Levi (eds.), *Trust & Governance*, New York: Russell Sage Foundation.

Levine, Ross (2005), "Finance and Growth: Theory, Evidence," in Aghion, Philippe, and Steven Durlauf (eds), *Handbook of Economic Growth*, Amsterdam: Elsevier.

Lewis, W. Arthur (1954), "Economic Development with Unlimited Supplies of Labour," *The Manchester School*, vol. 22, 129–191.

Lijphart, Arend (1977), *Democracy in Plural Societies: A Comparative Exploration*, New Haven: Yale University Press.

——— (1984), *Democracies*, New Haven: Yale University Press.

——— (1999), *Patterns of Democracy: Government Forms and Performance in Thirty-Six Countries*, Oxford: Oxford University Press.

Lindbeck, Assar (1976), "Stabilization Policy in Open Economies with Endogenous Politicians," Richard T. Ely Lecture, *American Economic Review, Papers and Proceedings*, vol. 66, 1–19.

Lindbeck, Assar, and Jörgen Weibull (1987), "Balanced-budget Redistribution as the Outcome of Political Competition," *Public Choice*, vol. 52, 273–297.

Lipset, Seymour Martin (1959), "Some Social Requisites for Democracy: Economic Development and Political Legitimacy," *American Political Science Review*, vol. 53, 69–105.

Lizzeri, Alessandro, and Nicola Persico (2001), "The Provision of Public Goods under Alternative Electoral Incentives," *American Economic Review*, vol. 91, 225–239.

Lucas, Robert (1993), "Making a Miracle," *Econometrica*, vol. 61, 251–272.

Ma, Debin (2010), "Rock, Scissors, Paper: The Problem of Incentives and Information in the Traditional Chinese State and the Origin of the Great Divergence," mimeo, London School of Economics.

Mahdavy, Hossein (1970), "The Patterns and Problems of Economic Development in Rentier States: The Case of Iran," in Cook M. A. (ed.), *Studies in the Economic History of the Middle East*, Oxford University Press.

Mann, Michael (1986), *The Sources of Social Power*, Vol. I, New York: Cambridge University Press.

——— (1993), *The Sources of Social Power*, Vol. II, New York: Cambridge University Press.

Maoz, Zeev, and Bruce Russett (1993), "Normative and Structural Causes of Democratic Peace, 1946–1986," *American Political Science Review*, vol. 87, 624–638.

Mathias, Peter, and Patrick O'Brien (1976), "Taxation in Britain and France 1715–1810: A Comparison of the Social and Economic Consequences of Taxes Collected for the Central Governments," *Journal of European Economic History,* vol. 5, 601–650.

Mauro, Paolo (1995), "Corruption and Growth," *Quarterly Journal of Economics,* vol. 110, 681–712.

McGillivray, Mark (2006), "Aid Allocation and Fragile States," WIDER Discussion Paper 2006/01, Helsinki.

McGuire, Martin C., and Mancur Olson (1996), "The Economics of Autocracy and Majority Rule: The Invisible Hand and the Use of Force," *Journal of Economic Literature,* vol. 34, 72–96.

Mehlum, Halvor, Karl O. Moene, and Ragnar Torvik (2006), "Institutions and the Resource Curse," *Economic Journal,* vol. 116, 1–20.

Meltzer, Alan, and Scott Richards (1981), "A Rational Theory of the Size of Government," *Journal of Political Economy,* vol. 89, 914–927.

Migdal, Joel S. (1988), *Strong Societies and Weak States: State-Society Relations and State Capabilities in the Third World,* Princeton: Princeton University Press.

Miguel, Edward, Shanker Satyanath, and Ernest Sergenti (2004), "Economic Shocks and Civil Conflict: An Instrumental Variables Approach," *Journal of Political Economy,* vol. 112, 725–753.

Milesi-Ferretti, Gian-Maria, Roberto Perotti, and Marco Rostagno [2002), "Electoral Systems and the Composition of Public Spending," *Quarterly Journal of Economics,* vol. 117, 609–657.

Milgrom, Paul, and Chris Shannon (1994), "Monotone Comparative Statics," *Econometrica,* vol. 62, 157–180.

Mokyr, Joel (1990), *The Lever of Riches: Technological Creativity and Economic Progress,* Oxford: Oxford University Press.

Montalvo, José G., and Marta Reynal-Querol (2005), "Ethnic Polarization, Potential Conflict, and Civil Wars," *American Economic Review,* vol. 95, 796–816.

Moore, Barrington (1966), *Social Origins of Dictatorship and Democracy,* Boston: Beacon Press.

Moore, Mick (2004), "Revenues, State Formation and the Quality of Governance in Developing Countries," *International Political Science Review,* vol. 25, 297–319.

Moselle, Boaz, and Benjamin Polak (2001), "A Model of a Predatory State," *Journal of Law, Economics, and Organization,* vol. 17, 1–33.

Myerson, Roger (1999), "Theoretical Comparison of Electoral Systems: 1998 Schumpeter Lecture," *European Economic Review,* vol. 43, 671–697.

Myrdal, Gunnar (1968), *Asian Drama. An Inquiry into the Poverty of Nations,* New York: Pantheon.

——— (1974), "What Is Development?" *Journal of Economic Issues,* vol. 8, 729–736.

Nel, Philip, and Marjolein Righarts (2008), "Natural Disasters and the Risk of Violent Civil Conflict," *International Studies Quarterly*, vol. 52, 159–185.

Newbery, David, and Nicholas Stern (eds) (1987), *The Theory of Taxation for Developing Countries*, Oxford: Oxford University Press for the World Bank.

North, Douglass C. (1990), *Institutions, Institutional Change and Economic Performance*, Cambridge: Cambridge University Press.

North, Douglass C., and Robert Paul Thomas (1973), *The Rise of the Western World: A New Economic History*, New York: Cambridge University Press.

North, Douglass C., and Barry R. Weingast (1989), "Constitutions and Commitment: The Evolution of Institutional Governing Public Choice in Seventeenth-Century England," *Journal of Economic History*, vol. 44, 803–832.

North, Douglass C., Barry Weingast, and John Wallis (2009), *Violence and Social Orders: A Conceptual Framework for Interpreting Recorded Human History*, Cambridge: Cambridge University Press.

Nunn, Nathan (2008), "The Long-term Effects of Africa's Slave Trades," *Quarterly Journal of Economics*, vol. 123, 139–176.

——— (2009), "The Importance of History for Economic Development," *Annual Review of Economics*, vol. 1, 1–28.

Nunn, Nathan, and Nancy Qian (2010), "Aiding Conflict: The Unintended Consequences of U.S. Food Aid on Civil War, 1976–2004," mimeo, Harvard University.

O'Brien, Patrick (2001), "Fiscal Exceptionalism: Great Britain and its European Rivals from Civil War to Triumph at Trafalgar and Waterloo," mimeo, available at http://www2.lse.ac.uk/economicHistory/pdf/WP6501.pdf.

——— (2005), "Fiscal and Financial Preconditions for the Rise of British Naval Hegemony: 1485–1815," mimeo, London School of Economics.

O'Donnell, Guillermo A., and Philippe C. Schmitter (1986), *Transitions from Authoritarian Rule: Tentative Conclusions about Uncertain Democracies*, Baltimore: Johns Hopkins University Press.

OECD (2010a), *Do No Harm: International Support for State Building*, Paris: OECD publications.

——— (2010b), *Development Cooperation Report*, Statistical Annex, OECD, Paris.

Olson, Mancur (1993), "Dictatorship, Democracy, and Development," *American Political Science Review*, vol. 87, 567–576.

Olsson, Ola, and Heather Congdon Fors (2004), "Congo: The Prize of Predation," *Journal of Peace Research*, vol. 41, 321–336.

Osborne, Martin J., and Al Slivinsky (1996), "A Model of Political Competition with Citizen-candidates," *Quarterly Journal of Economics*, vol. 111, 65–96.

Ostrom, Elinor (1990), *Governing the Commons: The Evolution of Institutions for Collective Action*, Cambridge: Cambridge University Press.

Pagano, Marco, and Paolo Volpin (2001), "The Political Economy of Finance," *Oxford Review of Economic Policy*, vol. 17, 502–519.

——— (2005), "The Political Economy of Corporate Governance," *American Economic Review*, vol. 95, 1005–1030.

——— (2006), "Shareholder Protection, Stock Market Development, and Politics," *Journal of the European Economic Association,* vol. 4, 315–341.

Parente, Stephen L., and Edward C. Prescott (2000), *Barriers to Riches,* Cambridge, MA: MIT Press.

Parker, Geoffrey, (1988), *The Military Revolution: Military Innovation and the Rise of the West 1500–1800*. Cambridge: Cambridge University Press.

Perotti, Enrico, and Ernst-Ludwig von Thadden (2006), "The Political Economy of Corporate Control and Labor Rents," *Journal of Political Economy,* vol. 114, 145–174.

Perroni, Carlo, and Kimberly Scharf (2007), "Taxation and Property Rights," mimeo, University of Warwick.

Persson, Torsten, Gérard Roland, and Guido Tabellini (1997), "Separation of Powers and Political Accountability," *Quarterly Journal of Economics,* vol. 112, 1163–1202.

——— (2000), "Comparative Politics and Public Finance," *Journal of Political Economy,* vol. 108, 1121–1161.

Persson, Torsten, and Lars E.O. Svensson (1989), "Why a Stubborn Conservative Would Run a Deficit: Policy with Time-Inconsistent Preferences," *Quarterly Journal of Economics,* vol. 104, 325–345.

Persson, Torsten, and Guido Tabellini (1994), "Is Inequality Harmful for Growth?," *American Economic Review,* vol. 84, 600–621.

——— (1996a), "Federal Fiscal Constitutions: Risk Sharing and Moral Hazard," *Econometrica,* vol. 64, 623–646.

——— (1996b), "Federal Fiscal Constitutions: Risk Sharing and Redistribution," *Journal of Political Economy,* vol. 104, 979–1009.

——— (1999), "The Size and Scope of Government: Comparative Politics with Rational Politicians," 1998 Marshall Lecture, *European Economic Review,* vol. 43, 699–735.

——— (2000), *Political Economics: Explaining Economic Policy,* Cambridge, MA: MIT Press.

——— (2002), "Political Economics and Public Finance," Chapter 24 in Auerbach, Alan, and Martin Feldstein (eds), *Handbook of Public Economics,* Vol. 3, Amsterdam: Elsevier.

——— (2003), *The Economic Effects of Constitutions,* Cambridge MA: MIT Press.

——— (2004), "Constitutions and Economic Policy," *Journal of Economic Perspectives,* vol. 18, 75–98.

Persson, Torsten, and Guido Tabellini (2009), "Democratic Capital: The Nexus of Economic and Political Change," *American Economic Journal: Macroeconomics,* vol. 1, 88–126.

Platteau, Jean-Philippe (2000), *Institutions, Social Norms, and Economic Development,* Amsterdam: Harwood Academic Publishers.

Posen, Barry R. (1993), "Nationalism, the Mass Army, and Military Power," *International Security,* vol. 18, 80–124.

Powell Jr., G. Bingham (1989), "Constitutional Design and Citizen Electoral Control," *Journal of Theoretical Politics*, vol. 1, 107–130.

——— (2000), *Elections as Instruments of Democracy*, New Haven and London: Yale University Press.

Prat, Andrea, and David Strömberg (2010), "The Political Economy of Mass Media," paper presented at the 10th World Congress of the Econometric Society.

Przeworski, Adam, Michael Alvarez, Jose Cheibub, and Fernando Limongi (2000), *Democracy and Development: Political Institutions and Well-Being in the World 1950–1900*, Cambridge: Cambridge University Press.

Putnam, Robert (1993), *Making Democracy Work: Civic Traditions in Modern Italy*, Princeton: Princeton University Press.

Putterman, Louis (2008), "The Role of the State and Markets in Development," in Dutt, Amitava, and Jaime Ros (eds.), *International Handbook of Development Economics*, Vol. 2, Amsterdam: Edward Elgar.

Qian, Nancy, and David Yanagizawa (2009), "Watchdog or Lapdog? Media and the U.S. Government," mimeo, Institute for International Economic Studies.

Rajan, Raghuram, and Arvind Subramanian (2008), "Aid and Growth: What Does the Cross Country Evidence Really Show?," *Review of Economics and Statistics*, vol. 90, 643–665.

Rajan, Raghuram, and Luigi Zingales (2003), "The Great Reversal: The Politics of Financial Development in the Twentieth Century," *Journal of Financial Economics*, vol. 69, 5–50.

Restuccia, Diego, and Richard Rogerson (2008), "Policy Distortions and Aggregate Productivity with Heterogeneous Plants," *Review of Economic Dynamics*, vol. 11, 707–720.

Reynal-Querol, Marta (2002), "Ethnicity, Political Systems, and Civil Wars," *Journal of Conflict Resolution*, vol. 46, 29–54.

Rice, Susan, and Stewart Patrick (2008), *Index of State Weakness in the Developing World*, Washington, DC: The Brookings Institution.

Riddell, Roger (2007), *Does Foreign Aid Really Work?*, Oxford: Oxford University Press.

Robinson, James A., Ragnar Torvik, and Thierry Verdier (2006), "Political Foundations of the Resource Curse," *Journal of Development Economics*, vol. 79, 447–468.

Rodrik, Dani, Arvind Subramanian, and Francesco Trebbi (2004), "Institutions Rule: The Primacy of Institutions Over Geography and Integration in Economic Development," *Journal of Economic Growth*, vol. 9, 131–165.

Rogoff, Kenneth (1985), "The Optimal Degree of Commitment to an Intermediate Monetary Target," *Quarterly Journal of Economics*, vol. 100, 1169–1189.

Rokkan, Stein (1970), *Citizens, Elections, Politics. Approaches to the Comparative Study of the Processes of Development*, New York: MaKay.

Romer, Thomas, and Howard Rosenthal (1979), "Bureaucrats versus Voters: On the Political Economy of Resource Allocation by Direct Democracy," *Quarterly Journal of Economics*, vol. 93, 563–587.

Rosenberg, Nathan, and L.E. Birdzell (1986), *How the West Grew Rich: The Economic Transformation of the Industrial World,* New York: Basic Books.
Ross, Michael (2004), "What Do We Know about Natural Resources and Civil War?," *Journal of Peace Research,* vol. 41, 337–356.
Rothstein, Bo (2000), "Trust, Social Dilemmas and Collective Memories," *Journal of Theoretical Politics,* vol. 12, 477–501.
Sachs, Jeffrey (2005), *The End of Poverty: Economic Possibilities for Our Time,* New York: Penguin Books.
Sachs, Jeffrey, John. W. McArthur, Guido Schmidt-Traub, Margaret Kruk, Chandrika Bahadur, Michael Faye, and Gordon McCord (2004), "Ending Africa's Poverty Trap," *Brookings Papers on Economic Activity,* no 1, 117–240.
Sachs, Jeffrey D., and Andrew Warner (1995), "Natural Resource Abundance and Economic Growth," NBER Working Paper No. 5398.
——— (2001), "The Curse of Natural Resources," *European Economic Review,* vol. 45, 827–838.
Sambanis, Nicholas (2004), "What is Civil War: Conceptual and Empirical Complexities of an Operational Definition," *Journal of Conflict Resolution,* vol. 48, 814–858.
Scheve, Ken, and David Stasavage (2010), "Democracy, War, and Wealth: Evidence of Two Centuries of Inheritance Taxation," mimeo, New York University.
Schumpeter, Joseph A. (1918), "The Crisis of the Tax State," *International Economic Papers,* vol. 4, 5–38.
——— (1934), *The Theory of Economic Development,* (1968 edition translated by R. Opie, with an introduction by J. E. Elliott) New Brunswick and London: Transactions Books.
Shayo, Moses (2009), "A Model of Social Identity with an Application to Political Economy: Nation, Class, and Redistribution," *American Political Science Review,* vol. 103, 147–174.
Shleifer, Andrei (2009), "Peter Bauer and the Failure of Foreign Aid," *Cato Journal,* vol. 29, 355–371.
Shugart, Matthew, and John Carey (1992), *Presidents and Assemblies: Constitutional Design and Electoral Dynamics,* Cambridge: Cambridge University Press.
Skaperdas, Stergios (1992), "Cooperation, Conflict, and Power in the Absence of Property Rights," *American Economic Review,* vol. 82, 720–739.
——— (1996), "Contest Success Functions," *Economic Theory,* vol. 7, 283–290.
——— (2010), "The Costs of Organized Violence: A Review of the Evidence," forthcoming in *Economic Governance.*
Slemrod, Joel, and Shlomo Yitzhaki (2002), "Tax Avoidance, Evasion, and Administration," in Auerbach, Alan, and Martin Feldstein (eds.), *Handbook of Public Economics,* Vol. 3, Amsterdam: Elsevier.
Smith, Alastair (2006), "Pernicious Foreign Aid?: A Political Economy of Political Institutions and the Effect of Foreign Aid," mimeo, New York University.
Smith, Benjamin (2004), "Oil Wealth and Regime Survival in the Developing World, 1960–1999," *American Journal of Political Science,* vol. 48, 232–246.

Solow, Robert (1956), "A Contribution to the Theory of Economic Growth," *Quarterly Journal of Economics,* vol. 70, 65–94.

Song, Zheng, Kjetil Storesletten, and Fabrizio Zillibotti (2011), "Growing Like China," *American Economic Review,* vol. 101, 202–241.

Stasavage, David (2003), *Public Debt and the Birth of the Democratic State: France and Great Britain, 1688–1789,* Cambridge: Cambridge University Press.

——— (2007), "Partisan Politics and Public Debt: The Importance of the 'Whig Supremacy' for Britain's Financial Revolution," *European Review of Economic History,* vol. 11, 123–153.

Stern, Nicholas, Jean-Jacques Dethier, and F. Halsey Rogers [2005), *Growth and Empowerment: Making Development Happen,* Cambridge, MA: MIT Press.

Strayer, Joseph R. (1970), *On the Medieval Origins of the Modern State,* Princeton: Princeton University Press.

Svensson, Jakob (1998), "Investment, Property Rights and Political Instability: Theory and Evidence," *European Economic Review,* vol. 42, 1317–1341.

——— (2000a), "Foreign Aid and Rent-seeking," *Journal of International Economics,* vol. 51, 437–461.

——— (2000b), "When is Foreign Aid Policy Credible? Aid Dependence and Conditionality," *Journal of Development Economics,* vol. 61, 61–84.

——— (2003), "Why Conditional Aid Doesn't Work and What Can Be Done About It?," *Journal of Development Economics,* vol. 70, 381–402.

——— (2005), "Eight Questions about Corruption," *Journal of Economic Perspectives,* vol. 19, 19–42.

Taagepera, Rein, and Matthew S. Shugart (1989), *Seats and Votes: The Effects and Determinants of Electoral Systems,* New Haven: Yale University Press.

Tabellini, Guido (2008), "The Scope of Cooperation: Values and Incentives," *Quarterly Journal of Economics,* vol. 123, 905–950.

Tanzi, Vito (1987), "Quantitative Characteristics of the Tax Systems of Developing Countries," in Newbery, David, and Nicholas Stern (eds), *The Theory of Taxation for Developing Countries,* Oxford: Oxford University Press for the World Bank.

——— (1992), "Structural Factors and Tax Revenue in Developing Countries: A Decade of Evidence," in Goldin, Ian, and L. Alan Winters (eds.), *Open Economies: Structural Adjustment and Agriculture,* Cambridge: Cambridge University Press.

Temple, Jonathan (2010), "Aid and Conditionality," in Rodrik, Dani, and Mark Rosenzweig (eds.), *Handbook of Development Economics,* Vol. 5, Amsterdam, Elsevier.

Ticchi, Davide, and Andrea Vindigni (2010), "Endogenous Constitutions," *Economic Journal,* vol. 120, 1–39.

Tilly, Charles (ed.) (1975), *The Formation of National States in Western Europe,* Princeton: Princeton University Press.

——— (1985), "Warmaking and State Making as Organized Crime," in Evans, Peter, Dietrich Rueschemeyer, and Theda Skocpol (eds.), *Bringing the State Back In,* Cambridge: Cambridge University Press.

——— (1990), *Coercion, Capital and European States, AD 990–1992,* Oxford: Blackwell.

Torgler, Benno (2007), *Tax Morale and Tax Compliance: A Theoretical and Empirical Analysis,* Cheltenham U.K.: Edward Elgar.

Torvik, Ragnar (2002), "Natural Resources, Rent Seeking and Welfare," *Journal of Development Economics,* vol. 67, 455–470.

——— (2009), "Why Do Some Resource-abundant Countries Succeed while Others Do Not?," *Oxford Review of Economic Policy,* vol. 25, 241–256.

Treisman, Daniel (2000), "The Causes of Corruption: A Cross-National Study," *Journal of Public Economics,* vol. 76, 399–457.

Tullock, Gordon (1967), "The Welfare Costs of Tariffs, Monopolies, and Theft," *Western Economic Journal,* vol. 5, 224–232.

——— (1980), "Efficient Rent Seeking," in Buchanan, James, Richard Tollison and Gordon Tullock (eds.), *Toward a Theory of the Rent-Seeking Society,* College Station: Texas A & M University Press.

UNDP (2002), *Development Policy Journal* 2, Special Issue: Technical Cooperation.

Urdal, Henrik (2008), "Population, Resources and Violent Conflict: A Sub-National Study of India 1956–2002," *Journal of Conflict Resolution,* vol. 52, 590–617.

U.S. Agency for International Development (USAID) (2005), *Fragile States Strategy,* available at http://www.usaid.gov/policy/2005_fragile_states_strategy.pdf.

Vallings, Claire, and Magüi Moreno-Torres (2005), "Drivers of Fragility: What Makes States Fragile?," PRDE Working Paper No. 7. London, U.K.: DFID.

van der Ploeg, Frederick, (2011), "Natural Resources: Curse or Blessing?" forthcoming in the *Journal of Economic Literature.*

Wade, Robert (1990), *Governing the Market: Economic Theory and the Role of Government in East Asian Industrialization,* Princeton: Princeton University Press.

Weingast, Barry R. (1997), "The Political Foundations of Democracy and the Rule of Law," *American Political Science Review,* vol. 91, 245–263.

——— (2005), "The Constitutional Dilemma of Economic Liberty," *Journal of Economic Perspectives,* vol. 19, 89–108.

Yanagizawa, David (2010), "Propaganda and Conflict: Theory and Evidence from the Rwandan Genocide," mimeo, Institute for International Economic Studies.

Zolt, Eric M., and Richard M. Bird (2005), "Redistribution via Taxation: The Limited Role of the Personal Income Tax in Developing Countries," *UCLA Law Review,* vol. 52, 1627–1695.

Zussman, Asaf, Noam Zussman, and Morten Orregaard Nielsen (2008), "Asset Market Perspectives on the Israeli-Palestinian Conflict," *Economica,* vol. 75, 84–115.

Name Index

Page numbers for entries occurring in notes are suffixed by an *n*.

Subject Index

Page numbers for entries occurring in figures are suffixed by an *f;* those for entries in notes, by an *n;* and those for entries in tables, by a *t.*